The Revelation Worldview

The Revelation Worldview
Apocalyptic Thinking in a Postmodern World

JON K. NEWTON

WIPF & STOCK · Eugene, Oregon

THE REVELATION WORLDVIEW
Apocalyptic Thinking in a Postmodern World

Copyright © 2015 Jon K. Newton. All rights reserved. Except for brief quotations in critical publications or reviews, no part of this book may be reproduced in any manner without prior written permission from the publisher. Write: Permissions. Wipf and Stock Publishers, 199 W. 8th Ave., Suite 3, Eugene, OR 97401.

Wipf and Stock
An Imprint of Wipf and Stock Publishers
199 W. 8th Ave., Suite 3
Eugene, OR 97401

www.wipfandstock.com

ISBN 13: 978-1-62564-769-6

Manufactured in the U.S.A.   02/04/2015

*To my wife Judy
and my first PhD supervisor, Dr Ian Weeks,
both of whom had faith that this project was worth pursuing*

Contents

Preface | ix

Introduction | 1

CHAPTER 1
Times Are Changing: Christianity in a Postmodern World | 16

CHAPTER 2
Revelation in Context | 62

CHAPTER 3
The Reality of the Spirit World | 119

CHAPTER 4
The Validity of Revelation | 151

CHAPTER 5
The Significance of Personhood | 197

CHAPTER 6
The Centrality of the Biblical Story: Postmodernism and History | 236

CHAPTER 7
Rival Narratives | 279

CONCLUSION
Towards a Christian Worldview for the Twenty-First Century: Recapitulating the Study | 310

Bibliography | 315
Index of Subjects | 337
Index of Modern Authors | 351
Index of Ancient Documents | 355

Preface

THIS BOOK IS A heavily revised version of my original PhD thesis, entitled "Postmodernism, Christianity and the Book of Revelation," submitted in 2006 to Deakin University, Australia.

In this book I am attempting to construct a biblical Christian worldview, and define its main elements, in a way that is relevant to the twenty-first-century "postmodern" world. My strategy has been to construct a conversation between postmodernism (as a way of thinking or worldview), Christian theology, and the Book of Revelation. In the introduction, I explain the rationale and methodology involved in more detail.

For many years, I have been fascinated and challenged by the Book of Revelation. I have had many conversations about its meaning and have read both highly outrageous and highly scholarly efforts to explain it to a contemporary readership. However, this book is not a commentary on Revelation or even an attempt to explain its meaning; before long, I hope to attempt that task, and have made a beginning with several journal articles and my shorter book *Revelation Reclaimed*. Rather, in this book I am attempting something that has never before been done at such length (as far as I am aware): I am asking rather different questions of Revelation, questions that arise in part from the advent of the way of thinking commonly known as "postmodernism."

The concept of "worldview" is also central to this project. During my years of involvement in the modern Christian schools movement (approximately 1976–2004), I was influenced by many who saw the establishment of Christian schools as a way of defining and promoting a Christian worldview that would help our students "think Christianly" and avoid the influence of "secular humanism." Looking back over this period, I would say that this attempt was not always clear sighted or successful, partly because of confusion about what a Christian worldview was (a set of doctrines? political opinions? values? a Christian philosophy? a denominational position?) and partly because of a failure to fully understand and grapple with alternative worldviews of our generation. I hope this book goes some way to remedying these deficiencies by clarifying what a worldview is, what worldview changes are happening right now, and what a biblically informed response might be to the issues this raises for Christians. This challenge meant that I needed to grapple with postmodernism. This term is not as widely used as it was when I began my doctoral studies in 2000. However, it is clear that the way of thinking of people in the Western world (at least) has been changing in important ways over the past half-century or so. The modernist way of thinking, centered on reason and science, with strong faith in progress and liberal democracy, is still with us and very much alive. However, greater awareness of alternative worldviews, especially those associated with Eastern religions, and the influence of the massive technological developments, often called the "communications revolution," have affected the worldview of contemporary people in ways that are profound but still not fully clear. Philosophical currents associated with movements such as poststructuralism, neo-pragmatism, and postmodernism have helped explain and influence these intellectual changes.

Christians have often struggled to respond to massive changes in worldview. Responses to modernism have lain behind the liberal-fundamentalist divide in the twentieth century. Modernism has influenced even Christians who reject its ideas about theology or the Bible, such as the Pentecostal movement, which I have been part of for over forty years. Christian responses to postmodernism have frequently been confused, contradictory, and ill-informed. I hope this book will bring some clarity and focus to these discussions.

****

The development of the ideas in this book, especially as a doctoral thesis, owed a lot to my supervisors and other advisors in 2000–2006. I want to acknowledge the enormous help and faith in me on the part of my original doctoral supervisor at Deakin, Dr. Ian Weeks. He took the risk of supporting a very ambitious and wide-ranging proposal, helped me find good conversation partners, and pushed me to present papers where I could work out some of my early ideas. My subsequent supervisor, now Associate Professor Lyn McCredden, helped keep me on track and ensured I couldn't get away with any unfair criticism of postmodernism. Doctor Matthew Sharpe helped with the philosophical aspects of the project. Doctor Keith Dyer of Whitley College (University of Divinity) helped me interpret and use the text of Revelation responsibly and supported me in having this book published. Doctor Geoff Jenkins gave me invaluable help with my research on ancient worldviews of the first century. Of course, any faulty thinking in this book is my own responsibility. I also want to acknowledge the help and support of Dr Barry Chant as I labored to make a PhD thesis into a book.

I also want to thank my colleagues at Harvest Bible College, Melbourne, Australia, for their encouragement in seeing this book take shape. It was the sudden call to teach a Harvest masters cohort in Denmark in 2010 that forced me to reconsider my earlier judgment that my thesis could never become a book.

I want to thank my patient wife, Judy Newton, without whose support this project would never have materialized, and my daughter-in-law, Deanne Newton, who helped me with the final layout of the manuscript.

Finally, I want to acknowledge the staff at Wipf and Stock for accepting this book for publication and working with me to make it a reality.

Jon Newton
Melbourne, 2014

Introduction

How should people think? Or at least, how should Christians think? There has been quite a bit said and written about this in recent decades. It is also the issue behind many discussions among Christians and dialogues between Christians and other people today.

Consider, for example, debates over "creationism" and evolution, or science and faith more broadly. Evolutionists privilege empirical thought—that is, observation and reasoning from empirical evidence—over thought that starts, say, with faith or religious experience. Hence they expect believers in God to adjust their thinking about creation to fit in with the generally accepted scientific views. And many believers are only too happy to make this adjustment, sometimes without much consideration of the implications or consequences for their faith. So-called "creationists,"[1] on the other hand, insist that Christian positions must start with what the Bible says and scientific study must fit in with the clear teaching of Scripture, though they sometimes fail to consider some of the complexities involved in interpreting the text of Scripture. But what both are assuming is a particular view about how people, and Christians in particular, should think.

Christians have trouble being taken seriously in today's Western world. Either they are dismissed as out of date, a curious relic of the Middle Ages who can be safely ignored because they will surely fade away in time, or they are ferociously attacked because they argue for positions completely at odds with modern or postmodern values.

A few years ago I took part in the "March for the Babies," a protest against ultra-liberal abortion legislation passed by the parliament of the state of Victoria, Australia.[2] One or two thousand Christians marched to our parliament house, outside of which they were confronted by about fifty

---

[1] I use quotation marks here because all Christians are creationist in the basic sense of believing God created the universe.

[2] Organized, it should be said, by a Catholic member of parliament.

determined pro-abortion protesters. The pro-abortionists shouted punchy slogans through loud hailers. The anti-abortionists largely tried to ignore them as they made their speeches. It struck me that there was no room for dialogue here. Both sides were largely shouting at each other. And it's true that over some issues in today's society there is no space for negotiation, dialogue, or compromise, because both sides are beginning from different presuppositions. Abortion is mostly wrong if the Bible is right and mostly permissible if "human rights" (especially the rights of women over their own bodies) determine the outcome. No wonder the pro-abortionists carried banners saying, "Keep religion out of politics."

The real issue behind this impasse, it seems to me, is one of conflicting worldviews. Christians struggle to be heard in the public square because they seem either quaintly irrelevant or illogically, even dangerously, fundamentalist. The general public, perhaps especially the more educated Westerner, cannot understand Christianity because its worldview assumptions are so foreign. And debates among believers are also often at heart debates about worldview; in particular, debates about how much our thinking should be dominated by the prevailing worldview of the surrounding culture.

Worldviews are basically plausibility structures. A person's worldview, or the worldview of a culture, determines what ideas and claims can be considered plausible, or possible, and what ideas can just be rejected out of hand. Or, to put it another way, "people argue *from* but not *to* presuppositions."[3]

Consider questions related to healing. We all want to live in good physical health. Most Westerners try to achieve this goal by a combination of more or less healthy lifestyle choices (diet, exercise, moderation, etc.) and reliance on "doctors and drugs" when problems occur. All these strategies are promoted and defended on the basis of scientific evidence. More recently we have seen the growth of "natural" and "alternative" health therapies and a burgeoning industry of alternative therapists and medications alongside conventional medicine. Some of these even have a spiritual basis, usually in "Eastern" religion. Many people, wedded to modern medicine, dismiss these alternatives; they do not seem plausible since they lack a solid scientific base. But plausibility structures are changing, so many Westerners are happy to try new therapies and judge them on results—do they work? Testimony of others often provides the motivation to take this leap of faith. Such testimony creates an alternative plausibility structure that sits more or less uneasily alongside a science-based worldview.

But how does this all relate to the Bible's stories of healing miracles? Many people, including many professing Christians, simply cannot take

---

3. Naugle, *Worldview*, 307. Naugle discusses the thinking of R. G. Collingwood.

them seriously; they have to be explained (away) due to their inconsistency with the presumptions behind scientific progress. A whole project has arisen to explain such stories on the basis of ancient superstition, allegorical or spiritual intention, or perhaps psychological factors. Somehow the stories must be subordinated to a modern Western worldview. Other Christians insist on taking such stories literally as historical fact because of their strong faith in the Bible as God's Word, but only so long as they are safely relegated to the past. Modern claims to healings are rejected by such "Bible-believing" churches with the same vehemence as others reject biblical claims. Such Christians, mainly conservative Protestants, are trapped between two competing worldviews or plausibility structures.

But a lot of other Christians, particularly Catholics and Pentecostals, are just as open to the possibility of miracles of healing today as in the biblical past.[4] Their theological approaches may be quite different, but they share at least elements of a common plausibility structure. Such differences represent a clash of worldviews, a conflict between a modernist mindset and the more premodern thinking of the Bible and of some Christians today.

Many Christian writers have employed the term "worldview" to help define Christianity as a belief system, as against rivals such as humanism or Islam, or to make an apologetic case for a comprehensive paradigm based in Scripture and influencing Christians' views on economics, science, politics, history, and other discourses. Often the meaning of the term "worldview" was not well thought through, however; relevant anthropological and psychological research on this topic was ignored and the variations in worldview among strong Christians were glossed over. Consequently the concept of worldview has been eclipsed to some degree in the most recent Christian dialogues.[5] But the effort to define a Christian worldview was not in itself misguided. If Christians are going to represent the Bible and the teaching and work of Jesus to our twenty-first-century fellow citizens, especially in the West, we may need to readdress this issue. Certainly part of the goal of this book is to make a Christian worldview plausible to twenty-first-century readers.

---

4. For a recent discussion of miracles, backed by multitudes of recent claims to miraculous experiences, see Keener, *Miracles*.

5. For a thorough discussion of the history of the concept of "worldview" among Christians, see Naugle, *Worldview*, chs. 1–2.

EXPLAINING WORLDVIEW

So what does "worldview" mean? The term has been used in different contexts with a range of meanings. In cultural anthropology, it refers to the deepest level beliefs[6] of a culture about reality. As Charles Kraft explains,

> The worldview is the central systematization of conceptions of reality to which the members of the culture assent (largely unconsciously) and from which stems their value system. The worldview lies at the very heart of culture, touching, interacting with, and strongly influencing every other aspect of the culture.[7]

Such worldviews are both expressed in and shaped by language,[8] and inculcated from the early stages of a person's life as part of their culture.[9]

I remember as a young schoolteacher in Papua New Guinea (in the 1970s) coming face to face with the difference in worldviews between my Western mindset and my students' world. To these young people, ages fifteen to twenty-three, spirits were very much part of reality, affecting people's health and well-being in a range of ways, and capable of being manipulated by sorcery. This made no sense to me, due to the plausibility structures in my mind, but they could provide evidence to confirm their belief; they had each had experiences that could only be explained that way. No argument could persuade either them or me that we were wrong about this.

Christian missionaries and anthropologists are very aware of the complex issues and conflicts that arise when a modern Western worldview comes into contact with a non-Western one. Christian missionaries actually find themselves in a three-way dilemma here: their Christian presuppositions lie somewhere in between a Western and a more "animistic" worldview, and they have to make difficult decisions about which way to lean when they face a conflict between the two, for instance, when sickness is diagnosed in two radically different ways and two very different treatments are put forward. Likewise, national Christians are torn between the demands of two radically different worldviews here: do I take my sick mother to the clinic or to the "witchdoctor," or maybe both?

On the other hand, in philosophical discourse, "worldview" can roughly translate the German *Weltanschauung*, and refers to the way such fundamental ideas are articulated to provide coherent answers to basic

---

6. Cf. Walsh and Middleton, *Transforming Vision*, 35.

7. Kraft, *Christianity in Culture*, 53. Comp. Johns, "Pentecostalism and Postmodern Worldview," 75–77.

8. Walsh and Middleton, *Transforming Vision*, 34.

9. Burnett, *Clash of Worlds*, 20.

questions about reality and our relationship to it,[10] or to the presuppositions vital to a plausible philosophical or religious position, in the form of "an intertwined, interrelated, interconnected *system* of beliefs."[11]

The concept of worldview can be clarified also by comparison with other related but different concepts. For instance, *ideology* refers to the beliefs and ideas held by a particular social class or group, especially as developed by those who claim to represent that group,[12] whereas, as Eagleton (for example) acknowledges, "worldviews are usually preoccupied with fundamental matters such as the meaning of death or humanity's place in the universe . . ."[13] Examples of ideology in the modern era include Marxism, which claims to represent the working class in modern industrial society; nationalism, which seeks to express the surpassing value of a specific nation or ethnic group; and liberalism, which is the common belief of the middle classes and expresses their aspirations for freedom and prosperity.

Religion frequently involves the expression of worldviews in a formal organized system of belief, ethic, and ritual.[14] Some writers use "worldview" as a term to cover both religions and secular faiths.[15] However, the same worldview may underlie a range of possible religions; for example, Hindus and Buddhists frequently share a common worldview,[16] though their specific doctrines and practices are different. And the same religion may vary from place to place according to the basic worldviews of its adherents; for instance, Christians in Africa tend to think very differently about spirits than those in Europe, and African Christians perhaps share more worldview assumptions with their non-Christian neighbors than with their European coreligionists.

Philosophy may include the attempt to systematize, analyze, and justify answers to worldview issues and thus explicitly express the connections between such ideas, and their rational foundations, in a logical way.[17] The

---

10. Cf. ibid., 12–14; and Plantinga, *Where the Conflict Really Lies*, ix–x, 76. For a comprehensive history of the concept, see Naugle, *Worldview*, chs. 3–8.

11. Dewitt, *Worldviews*, 3 (italics original). However, in practice Dewitt uses "worldview" as roughly equivalent to "cosmology."

12. Eagleton, *Ideology*, 29.

13. Ibid., comp. 43, 48, 101, 106–10. Comp. Johns, "Pentecostalism and Postmodern Worldview," 75.

14. Newbigin, *Pluralist Society*, 172.

15. For an example see Smart, *Worldviews*, xi, 1–5.

16. Cf. Newbigin, *Pluralist Society*, 96. Similarly, "The traditional Japanese worldview was formed by three ancient religious traditions: Shintoism, Confucianism and Buddhism" (Walsh and Middleton, *Transforming Vision*, 19).

17. Cf. Smart, *Worldviews*, 32–33.

two words are thus frequently used interchangeably,[18] but worldviews are more deep-seated and usually less systematic than either philosophical or theological systems;[19] as Pentecostal philosopher James Smith puts it, worldviews are "pretheoretical" as opposed to "beliefs that we consciously, rationally reflect upon."[20] Moreover, as a formal study, "Philosophy is restricted to the intellectuals, but everyone has a worldview."[21] Some modern philosophical systems or ideas that addressed worldview questions include logical positivism, which asserted that only statements capable of being empirically verified were meaningful, and materialism, which in a similar way asserts that all reality is fundamentally material and no non-material things exist. Both of these views are to some degree self-refuting, because they themselves do not pass the test they impose on others.

Cosmology is used to describe the most important feature of a worldview: its beliefs about the fundamental nature of the universe.[22] But cosmology doesn't include such other aspects of worldview as epistemology and anthropology. Moreover, the term is also used more restrictively to describe the study of the physical universe, such as the nature of stars, galaxies, black holes, and similar entities. So a worldview is much more comprehensive than a cosmology.[23]

Myths are the fundamental stories of a culture that express or communicate worldviews at an imaginative and emotional level.[24] For example, Australian Aboriginals have their "dreamtime stories," which not only retell deeply held beliefs about origins but also express a very different idea of time than that held by other Australians. The literature produced within a culture tends to express (or sometimes challenge) the worldview of that culture.[25] Hence modernist art, music, and literature was also often called avant-garde: it expressed the ways modern Western culture was changing and helped direct those changes. For example, modern art, from expressionism to cubism and other abstract painting, reflected the fact that people were becoming less sure about the nature of reality and the best way of portraying it. It also began to challenge one of the strongest myths

---

18. Cf. Eagleton, *Ideology*, 118; Naugle, *Worldview*, 134.
19. Walsh and Middleton, *Transforming Vision*, 35; Smith, *Thinking in Tongues*, 4–5.
20. Smith, *Thinking in Tongues*, 28.
21. Burnett, *Clash of Worlds*, 14.
22. Cf. Adams, *Constructing the World*, 41.
23. Cf. Smith, *Thinking in Tongues*, 28.
24. Cf. Kraft, *Christianity in Culture*, 54–55; Naugle, *Worldview*, 297–303; Friesen, "Myth and Symbolic Resistance in Revelation," 13, 282, 285–86.
25. Cf. Newbigin, *Pluralist Society*, 56.

that came out of the Enlightenment—the myth of progress, which asserted the essential goodness of humankind and the inevitability of progress to a more democratic, tolerant, and prosperous world through the operation of human reason, science, and technology.

Conflicts at the level of myth, philosophy, religion, ideology, and even politics often reflect more basic, frequently unarticulated, conflicts between rival worldviews. For example, as I suggested earlier, controversy among Christians about the possibility of miracles today is usually conducted as a theological or exegetical debate, but underlying that is a worldview issue influenced particularly by the thinking of modernity: is the idea of a supernatural realm or power coherent and credible in the light of modern science?[26]

A worldview has certain elements in it that make it a literal *world*-view, as opposed to more peripheral elements. First of all, a worldview provides answers to basic questions faced by human beings: What is real? What happens to people when they die? How do we know anything? What drives history? How can we decide how to live? What are human beings?[27] It does not necessarily address less fundamental (though very significant) issues, such as property ownership, war, or abortion, though it may provide tools for analyzing such issues and will tend to determine the values of its holders.[28]

Second, worldviews create "plausibility structures" that constrain what one may or may not believe (or even understand) in a given culture[29] and filter out non-conforming ideas.[30] For example, Walter Wink points out that modern Westerners are unable to take seriously any talk of angels, demons, or Satan:

> The dominant materialistic worldview has absolutely no place for them . . . no categories, no vocabulary, no presuppositions by which to discern what it was in the actual experiences of people that brought these words to speech. And it has massive resistance even to thinking about these phenomena.[31]

Third, worldviews tend to define the groups that hold them and set them apart from other groups of people at a much more fundamental level

26. Cf. ibid., 11. Comp. ibid., 36, 69, 217.

27. Cf. Walsh and Middleton, *Transforming Vision*, 35; Burnett, *Clashing Worlds*, 34.

28. Walsh and Middleton, *Transforming Vision*, 32.

29. Cf. Newbigin, *Pluralist Society*, 8–10, 232.

30. Kraft, *Christianity in Culture*, 56. Comp. Burnett, *Clash of Worlds*, 16–20; Juergensmeyer, *Terror*, 13.

31. Wink, *Unmasking the Powers*, 1.

8   THE REVELATION WORLDVIEW

than (say) ideology.³² They help people gain meaning in the flux of experienced reality by explaining how reality works.³³ They also predict what will happen to some degree, since a vision of the future is part of most worldviews.³⁴

Hence worldviews provide emotional security and support for a culture or group, enabling them to cope with reality and providing a sense of hope even in crisis.³⁵ In fact, it is often in times of crisis (such as sickness, death, or disaster) that a person's real worldview (as opposed to their professed religion, ideology, or philosophy) comes to the fore.³⁶

What makes the contemporary world different to the recent past is the intense interaction and tension among different worldviews. While worldviews have changed in the past, currently much more rapid change than previously existed is putting pressure on all worldviews.³⁷ For instance, Mark Juergensmeyer's study of religious violence in the contemporary world concludes that it can frequently be attributed to extreme worldviews.³⁸ The difference between such extremists and "normal" Westerners is not just one of opinion or theology: it goes to the very structure of thinking about what is real or important.³⁹ Moreover the tensions caused by rapid change and the forced interaction of differing worldviews, caused by large-scale population movements and international communication media, are pushing some people to extreme ideologies expressing, and changing, their deeply held worldviews. Thus, for example, Al-Qaeda is arguably an extreme but postmodern phenomenon, the product of interaction between traditional Arabic Islam and the modern Western world. Osama Bin Laden and his followers were trying to recreate the (partly mythical) past of the Islamic caliphate, but their methods were modern, and even postmodern (for example, the use of the Internet to recruit followers and present their ideology) and their attitudes to other cultures and religions were probably much more hostile and extreme than those of the original Muslims, who were more tolerant of Jews and Christians. To put this another way, the young people following Osama bin Laden and his successors think very differently

---

32. Cf. Kraft, *Christianity in Culture*, 55; Burnett, *Clash of Worlds*, 21–22.

33. Kraft, *Christianity in Culture*, 54.

34. Walsh and Middleton, *Transforming Vision*, 32.

35. Kraft, *Christianity in Culture*, 55.

36. Burnett, *Clash of Worlds*, 27.

37. Cf. Kraft, *Christianity in Culture*, 56–57; Burnett, *Clash of Worlds*, 23–24, 121–204.

38. Juergensmeyer, *Terror*, 8, 206, 222–24, 228.

39. Cf. ibid., 7–10, 149, 206, 216–17.

to their Muslim parents but share enough in common with them to neutralize opposition to their more postmodern Islam.

As Kraft argues, differences between worldviews are not resolvable by reason; while all peoples use reason in a similar way, they do not start from the same presuppositions or assumptions.[40] Hence, for example, trying to persuade a radical Islamist not to engage in suicide bombing is probably impossible unless the persuasion comes from another conservative Muslim with similar worldview assumptions, or, less likely, the radical in question is somehow forced to change his or her worldview.[41] This is one reason why worldviews do not easily or quickly change. My Papuan students in the 1970s were receiving a Western education on top of Christian teaching derived from missionaries, but retained aspects of a worldview that they had inherited from their ancestors and traditional culture and imbibed from their parents.

Moreover I will argue below that *postmodernism* indicates a shift in the worldview of modern Western culture, modifying or even replacing the dominant worldview of modernity, in the light of this time of change. Christians need to respond to this shift by discussing the possibilities of a contemporary Christian worldview.

A CHRISTIAN WORLDVIEW?

Can there be such a thing as a *Christian* worldview? Surely it is more accurate to speak of Christian worldviews, or of cultural worldviews to which Christianity more or less adapts in different places. Certainly there is no uniform Christian worldview across all places and in all eras of time. But in this book I hope to demonstrate, by interacting with modern and postmodern thought and with an ancient Christian text, that there are features of a Christian worldview that stand out as distinct from, though in dialogue with, the worldviews of the particular cultures Christians live among. For example, I will try to define a Christian approach to truth and knowledge that is not just dependent on premodern, modern, or postmodern views.

Inevitably and deliberately, however, the issues raised today are those that the postmodern shift brings to the center of attention. Thus the Christian worldview I will try to articulate will be a postmodern Christian worldview in the sense that it responds to these issues and seeks to be coherent and credible to people living in postmodern times. It will be different in some ways to the worldview that earlier Christian thinkers have articulated.

40. Kraft, *Christianity in Culture*, 57–60.
41. A recent case in point is related by Mosab Hassan Yousef in *Son of Hamas*.

It will also inevitably be different in some respects to the Christian worldview that might emerge from a study conducted by, say, a Japanese Christian scholar or one whose theological perspective is different to mine. A Christian worldview can be expressed in different ways. But a Christian worldview will also have features that are distinct from a purely postmodernist way of thinking (if such a thing as a "purely postmodernist way of thinking" exists); it will give different answers to the basic worldview questions than either postmodernists or people steeped in any other past or present worldview. So the process of defining a Christian worldview is not, I believe, a hopeless task, though it will be an ongoing process.

How might this work in practice? It will take a whole book to answer that, but to begin, let's revisit one of the issues raised at the outset of this chapter: the question of healing. This is a good issue to use because our attitudes to sickness and healing are a litmus test of our worldview. For example, animists tend to see all sickness as the work of evil spirits and sorcery; they may tend to blame significant people for such sickness[42] and look for treatment largely from "witchdoctors" who demonstrate some kind of power over spirits. Modernist Westerners pour scorn on any such idea; we tend to look always for natural, scientific causes—germs, viruses, genetic defects and the like—and rely largely on modern medicine and surgery for healing, even though medical science has a long way to go to defeat all diseases, and new ones keep breaking out—"swine flu" was infecting thousands of people all over the world as I began to write this book, for example. But recently there have been significant changes among Westerners in thinking about healing: a revival of traditional folk remedies, a more open attitude to therapies based on non-Western worldviews, such as acupuncture and reiki, a more holistic approach to medicine that views the person not as a mind or spirit inhabiting a body (the modernist view born with Descartes) but as a single unitary individual or even as a member of the wider "body" of society. Our worldview is changing.

Christians (especially in the West) have often struggled with these changes. It has been argued that Western missionaries were the greatest promoters of modern medicine and the modern worldview in the world. On the other hand, they were often fending off challenges to their faith and scriptures from the same worldview, because it was obvious that the Bible took both evil spirits and the possibility of miraculous healing very seriously indeed. One of the great areas of debate between serious Christians and modern skeptics was (and is) over the miracles in the Bible. But, as

---

42. Sometimes with violent consequences in countries like Papua New Guinea, where such thinking is particularly entrenched.

I observed earlier, many evangelical Christians who eagerly defended the miracles in Scripture were just as strongly opposed to the thought that miracles might happen today.

However, in the "two-thirds world" people have no such inhibitions. The form of Christianity that is growing rapidly in Africa, parts of Asia, and Latin America is substantially Pentecostal[43] in flavor. This is due in no small part to the openness of Pentecostals to the possibility of miracles and healing today and to the reality of the spirit world. These Christians do not necessarily reject doctors and drugs, but they are more skeptical of them and more inclined to resort to prayer and laying on of hands when they encounter sickness, partly because they have not embraced the modern Western "scientific" worldview in its totality.

Pentecostal Christians worldwide thus share some beliefs that go back to a premodern worldview, one held by the original writers and readers of the Christian Scriptures and their contemporaries, and indeed by most people to some degree until the Enlightenment and the birth of modern science in the West. But such Christians do not live in a premodern world, even in today's "majority world" countries. Hence they must somehow balance seemingly contradictory beliefs derived from two (or more) different worldviews. Alternatively, they can ditch one or other of such contradictions, but that will mean either giving up their Pentecostal faith in favor of a Christianity more attuned to modern/postmodern thought (as liberal Christians tried to do) or isolating themselves from the modern/postmodern world completely like some fundamentalists. Both these alternatives have been tried; in my opinion, neither works and neither is necessary. But to accept (or at least understand) such a claim, you will need to read this whole book.

Before going on to the strategy of this book, let me briefly summarize the options I see as available for Christian thinking in the twenty-first century. Simplifying to the extreme, I regard the "live" options as follows:

1. *Surrender* to prevailing ideas in the wider culture. For Western believers, this means *adopting* a modern or postmodern worldview and fitting their Christian beliefs into it. Liberal-modernist theology attempted something like this as it tried to communicate Christian faith and make it credible in a modern world. Some forms of postmodernist theology are on a similar track, as I will argue later, and perhaps the "emerging church" phenomenon represents a similar shift. But it can be difficult to retain key Christian beliefs within this strategy, as modern debates about the resurrection of Jesus have demonstrated.

---

43. Using this term in its broadest sense to include all Christians who are open to the supernatural work of the Holy Spirit among them today, including healing.

2. *Separation* from prevailing ideas in the wider culture. In the Western context, this means *resisting* a modern or postmodern worldview and trying to express their Christian beliefs by means of a more or less premodern worldview instead. Some forms of fundamentalism and Pentecostalism have gone down this road. I will argue that this alternative is literally impossible. The context inevitably creeps in, as the history of Pentecostal healing ministry probably demonstrates, for example.

3. *Something in between.* This will involve either *negotiation* with prevailing ideas in the wider culture or *selective adoption* of some prevailing ideas in the wider culture alongside retention of key Christian beliefs.

4. *Something else altogether.* This is what I will try to articulate in this book.

THE STRATEGY OF THIS BOOK

I am trying to define and describe a Christian worldview that is in some way plausible in a postmodern world. How can this be done? It seems to me that at least two steps must be included, not necessarily in order of importance:

1. A *Christian* worldview must be defined in relation to the documents that authoritatively define the Christian faith, that is, primarily, the Bible. Whatever view you hold about the Bible's origins or reliability, I take it as axiomatic that a Christian mindset must in some way be grounded in the Bible, as opposed to (say) the Koran or the teachings or traditions of any specific church or theologian.

2. A Christian *worldview for today* must interact with the questions being asked and the answers being given in today's world, that is, primarily, what we call "postmodernism."

Now, even to describe either the Bible's worldview or position (positions?) on worldview questions is a huge job and so is defining postmodernism. So to make the task manageable, I am going to opt for a slightly simpler strategy. I will begin with a very sketchy overview of postmodernism and analyze how Christianity and postmodernism have interacted to date. Then I will use the last book of the Bible, the Book of Revelation, to help identify a Christian worldview that can be brought into conversation with postmodernism. I want to identify essential aspects of a Christian worldview that seem to be implied by (or are latent in) the text of Revelation and then test such proposals critically in the light of contemporary experience and scholarship.

On the face of it, this appears problematic. After all, Revelation was written in the first century and its worldview reflects the thinking of that time; what possible relevance could it have to people living in the twenty-first century? I chose to use Revelation as the basis for a Christian response to postmodernism, and as a guide towards a Christian worldview, for a number of reasons in addition to my personal fascination with this text.

First, Revelation seems to be at the same time the most open book in the Bible to a postmodern interpretation and the most hostile book in the Bible to at least some postmodern ideas, as will become clear through this study.

Second, I chose Revelation because it is seen by some scholars as summing up much of the story of the Bible as a whole, and giving us a particularly succinct window onto the worldview of many of the biblical writers. This is a controversial claim but will become more plausible as a result of the arguments in this book, I hope.

Finally, Revelation is one of the most "foreign" books in the New Testament to contemporary Western readers, in spite of books that attempt to "make Revelation plain." This foreignness is partly because of the mysterious symbols and apocalyptic generic features in the text. But it is also because of its foreign worldview. Many modern and postmodern criticisms of Revelation show this to be true, and it is something that all Christians need to reckon with in order to interpret the text responsibly. This also means that Revelation is a place for competing worldviews to be revealed and to justify themselves, which makes this book an ideal choice for my topic.

THE REVELATION WORLDVIEW

Several recent studies of Revelation have begun to wrestle with its worldview in relation to the worldview(s) of its own historical setting and in terms of implications for contemporary thinking. Some of these studies have approached Revelation from a postmodernist perspective, and these will be analyzed in chapter 1. Others have sought to bring the worldview of Revelation itself into focus and explore the implications this might have for contemporary thinking, following the lead of some earlier writers such as Mathias Rissi, who studied the concept of time and the nature of history in Revelation.[44]

---

44. Rissi, *Time and History*. Also worthy of mention are Paul S. Minear's two articles, "Ontology and Ecclesiology in the Apocalypse" and "The Cosmology of the Apocalypse."

For example, Steven Friesen's 2005 monograph[45] largely draws on archaeological evidence to explore Revelation's critique of the Roman imperial cult. But in his lengthy introduction, he analyzes modern and postmodern concepts of religion and myth and shows how problematic they can be when applied to an ancient or foreign setting. For instance, "the very notion that politics can be severed from the sacred is a misconstrual that would . . . allow one to dismiss imperial cults as 'bad' religion or politics."[46] In other words, the frequent modern reaction to the Roman imperial cults reflects a modern Western concept of religion that would be literally incomprehensible to anybody living before the European Enlightenment.

Friesen identifies four categories of "mythic consciousness" from Lawrence Sullivan's study of indigenous South American religions[47] and uses these to make sense of the relation between Revelation and imperial cults. All of these categories are relevant to the worldview areas discussed in this book, so I want to take time to explore them briefly:

1. Cosmogony: the story of origins and a "primordial age" that may end with "cataclysm, disaster and destruction," thus giving rise to the contemporary world.[48] This has some similarity with the exploration of a Christian view of history later in this book.

2. Cosmology: "a mythic cosmology must both maintain and arrange multiple perspectives on reality," including spatial and temporal relationships, for example, which kinds of beings dwell where and how festivals express a sense of time and space.[49] Some of this will be explored in several chapters of this book because it relates to the ontology of a worldview—its view of what is real—and its concept of human history.

3. Human maturation: the worldview's concept of the nature of the human person and human origins and growth.[50] A chapter in this book is devoted to the nature of the human person.

4. Eschatology: defined as "the destiny of the human race and its individual members" and "speculations about the terminal conditions of existence" as revealed in a culture's rituals about death and "hope for

---

45. Friesen, *Imperial Cults*.
46. Ibid., 9.
47. Sullivan, *Icanthu's Drum*.
48. Friesen, *Imperial Cults*, 12.
49. Ibid., 13.
50. Ibid.

a new emergent order."⁵¹ Clearly Revelation speaks loudly about this aspect of worldview and it will be addressed later in this book.

Friesen also seeks to relate John's message to current issues in late modern society. According to him, Revelation challenges the modern view of true human life centered on individual freedom, the almost universal (ancient and modern) acceptance of force, and the epistemology of "Western rationality" undergirding them.⁵² In other words, Revelation has something radical to say to our changing Western worldview.

Another scholar, Michael Gilbertson, specifically discusses the implications of Revelation for a Christian view of history in the light of trends in philosophy of history over the past century.⁵³

Such studies are helping us identify and analyze the worldview of Revelation itself. But in this book I want to go a step farther. There is a deliberate double meaning in the title of this book. The "Revelation worldview" is *both* the worldview expressed in the *Book* of Revelation *and* a biblical worldview for today grounded in the *concept* of revelation. Applying ideas about worldview questions to a contemporary context is a task fraught with difficulties and readers of this book will find their own assumptions challenged. I can only ask the reader to read the whole argument before passing judgment on whether or not I have successfully articulated a Christian worldview that makes sense in a postmodern world.

However, to begin with, it is necessary for me to clarify what postmodernism is and survey the current state of the interaction of postmodernism and Christian thinking, with particular attention to postmodernist views of biblical interpretation and Revelation itself. This will be the task of chapter 1.

---

51. Ibid., 13–14.
52. Ibid., 215–16.
53. Gilbertson, *God and History*. See chapter 6 below for more details.

CHAPTER 1

Times Are Changing

Christianity in a Postmodern World

WE ARE LIVING IN tumultuous times. I'm a "baby boomer" born not long after the end of World War II. That means I missed out on World War I, the Great Depression, the Russian revolution, Hitler, the Holocaust, and Hiroshima. But I've lived through the Cold War, the H-bomb, Vietnam, the Berlin Wall, the assassinations of John F. Kennedy and Martin Luther King Jr., Mao and the "cultural revolution," the Six-Day War in 1967, the Yom Kippur War of 1973, the first Gulf War, 9/11, and the rise and fall of apartheid. I've seen the coming of TV (1956 in Australia), CDs, PCs, DVDs, KFC, McDonalds, Subway, ATMs, satellite communication, cell phones, the Internet, Google, email, Facebook, YouTube, and Twitter. Recently we've been facing the GFC (or its effects on Europe and the USA in particular), debates over climate change and radical terrorism, and the problems with the Eurozone, the rise of China and India, the Arab Spring, civil war in Syria, and other continued tensions in the Middle East. Our lives have been changed by globalization and the Internet, and politically, economically, and culturally everything is different to when I was growing up. Homosexuality used to be illegal, but now it's legal and "proud"; abortion used to be illegal, but now it's regarded as a woman's right; divorce was frowned on, but now it's a daily occurrence; the environment has taken center stage in modern politics; and the level of choices in people's lives is at unheard of levels, but the level of common thinking on morals is much lower. And, at least in Australia, you can no longer assume that nearly everyone is at least a nominal Christian.

What is more significant is the changing way we think.

MODERNISM: THE FIRST REVOLUTION IN WESTERN THOUGHT

There have been two massive shifts in European thinking over the last five hundred years. The first shift took us from the Middle Ages to the modern era. The basic worldview of European people had been unchanged in many respects for over a thousand years, but the rise of modern humanism, the split in Western Christianity brought about by the Reformation, the discovery by Europeans of "new worlds" in America and elsewhere, the European Enlightenment, and the rise of modern science and technology caused a revolution in thinking that literally makes it impossible for us to think like a person of 1500.[1]

Consider that the average Western European in 1500 not only believed in Christianity but held firmly to such beliefs as:

- The supremacy of the pope in the church and among the Christian kingdoms
- The power of witches and the need to put them to death
- The need to pray to dead saints in order for them to approach Jesus for you
- The centrality and fixity of the earth in God's universe
- The authority of Aristotle and other ancients in science
- Tradition as the most important feature determining our beliefs
- The need to follow the same occupation as your father, unless perhaps you were called to be a monk
- The right of kings and nobles to rule
- The authority of the Bible, and the church as its interpreter, to tell us what to think and how to live

---

1. McGowan (*Postmodernism*, 4) identifies several factors in the rise of modernity, including the rise of Protestantism, the discovery of "radically different societies in other parts of the globe," new scientific discoveries, new economic practices, the growth of towns and cities, and the challenge to oligarchy/monarchy.

Ideas such as democracy, tolerance, individualism, human rights, rationalism, empirical science, technological growth, capitalism, socialism, and progress would have been meaningless to them.

It took a series of revolutionary changes to change the Western worldview.

- The Renaissance put the focus on humanity, human learning, and human possibilities with its revival of Greco-Roman culture.

- The Reformation championed the right of individual believers to read the Bible (in their own language) and make up their own minds about what it meant. It also, inadvertently, undermined the authority of Christianity in people's thinking by splitting the (institutional) church from the Bible.[2]

- The Enlightenment looked for a new basis for knowledge in human reasoning and "criticism." As Kant famously wrote, "To criticism everything must submit."[3]

- Modern science looked for answers about the natural realm through empirical research (that is, going out and looking and doing experiments) instead of traditional speculative reasoning.

- The Industrial Revolution unleashed the power of technology and the free market to give everyone a hope of progress and prosperity (albeit at incredible cost in upheaval of people's lives, as documented by writers like Charles Dickens).[4]

- The American and French Revolutions championed the ideas of individual rights, the secular state, and democracy.

The result was the new world order known broadly as modernity. Reason and science, rather than church and Bible, now became the authoritative basis of all thinking, at least in the public sphere. Increasingly, people in the West expected unlimited progress towards freedom, democracy, peace, and prosperity—or put their faith in other models of progress such as nationalism or Marxism. Even the twentieth-century disasters of two world

---

2. As Bruce ("Cathedrals to Cults," 23–24) observes, "Modernization makes the church form of religion [one in which an institution claims exclusive access to God] impossible. The church requires either cultural homogeneity or an elite sufficiently powerful to enforce conformity," both of which were destroyed by the kinds of changes that transformed Europe in the sixteenth to eighteenth centuries.

3. As quoted by McGowan, *Postmodernism*, 32.

4. Cf. Blanning, *Pursuit of Glory*, chs. 3–4 on the industrial and agricultural revolutions in Europe.

wars, the Great Depression, and the threat of nuclear obliteration barely dented this new worldview.

Let's look a bit more deeply into this revolutionary change.

The Enlightenment

We often think of the shift to modernity as being a result of science, but that is misleading. The key shift in thought came about more as a result of the Enlightenment. The European Enlightenment was a broad movement in thinking that, while rooted in the Renaissance of the fourteenth to sixteenth centuries,[5] began to emerge in the seventeenth and eighteenth centuries and reached its peak of influence in the twentieth. The leaders of the Enlightenment were strong critics, indeed opponents, of accepted thinking up to their time, such as the whole medieval Christian worldview—a worldview that had been seriously threatened by the division of the Reformation and the subsequent Thirty Years' War of the seventeenth century. To the Enlightenment thinkers, this period seemed like a "dark age" now being superseded by the age of reason, a literal "enlightenment."[6] Immanuel Kant, for instance, contended that *"Enlightenment is man's emergence from his self-incurred immaturity."*[7] The Enlightenment was therefore anti-traditional, anti-authoritarian (since "'authority' was regarded as virtually synonymous with the political oppression of the *ancien regime*" to Enlightenment thinkers[8]), anti-clerical, and often anti-Christian.[9]

Positively, the Enlightenment stood for a new set of values. It contended, first, for the power of human reason to investigate truth, establish ethics, solve human problems, and create a better world unfettered by tradition, prejudice, superstition, passions, or authority (especially religious authority.) As Lyotard explains, "All peoples have a right to science. If the social subject is not already the subject of scientific knowledge, it is because that has been forbidden by priests and tyrants."[10] Similarly, Kant wrote,

---

5. It is, of course, possible to trace the roots of Enlightenment modernism farther back, for instance to the rise of the nominalists in the later Middle Ages, or to the ancient Greco-Roman world.

6. Cf. Barth, *Protestant Theology*, 33.

7. Kant, "What Is Enlightenment?," 51.

8. McGrath, *Passion for Truth*, 39.

9. Cf. Juergensmeyer, *Terror*, 224. Enlightenment thinkers tended to be deistic in religion, as they sought to construct a religion based on "universally valid and accessible norms or resources, such as 'reason,' 'experience' or 'culture'" (McGrath, *Passion for Truth*, 25).

10. Lyotard, *Postmodern Condition*, 31. Cf. Miller, "Emerging Postmodern World," 3.

"The motto of enlightenment is . . . *Sapere aude!* Have courage to use your *own* understanding!"[11] Hence, modernity can be defined as "the condition in which society must legitimate itself by its own self-generated principles, without appeal to *external* verities, deities, authorities, or traditions."[12] The Enlightenment was fundamentally humanistic: its starting point was not revelation from God (through the church or the Bible); rather, individual human beings discovering truth for themselves, in the manner of Descartes, who took as his starting point, "*Cogito ergo sum*" ("I think, therefore I am").

Second, the Enlightenment stood for progress towards a just and egalitarian society, where slavery and other abuses of human rights would be abolished.[13] As John Dewey eloquently put it, "The future rather than the past dominates the imagination. The Golden Age lies ahead of us not behind us."[14] Modernists were thus criticizing the medieval Christian view, which pictured mankind as declining from the past perfection of the Garden of Eden, but the classical ancient view also looked back to a past golden age, as I will explore in chapter 2. This was perhaps the first time in history that human thinkers had expressed such hopes of a humanly created paradise.

Third, the Enlightenment looked increasingly to science to explain how the world/universe really works, hence other disciplines were increasingly measured by comparison with the natural sciences "as embodying the paradigm of true knowledge."[15] The corollary of this was that the natural world was increasingly seen as "given" rather than created or dependent on God, and able to be understood in its own terms rather than in reference to the Creator. Or to put it another way, "The Enlightenment was eager to deny religious transcendence and to affirm that everything was to be found within a single, orderly System of Nature."[16]

Finally, Enlightenment thinkers and their successors had a strong faith in technology and social organization as the means to unshackle human

---

11. Kant, "What Is Enlightenment?" 51.

12. McGowan, *Postmodernism*, 3 (italics added).

13. Cf. Grenz, *Primer on Postmodernism*, 4. This contrasted with the actual progress that made modernism dominant, which was strongly associated with European expansion and imperialism, the slave trade, and the exploitation of landless peasants in the new factories of the Industrial Revolution (cf. Barth, *Protestant Theology*, 38).

14. As quoted in Middleton and Walsh, *Truth Is Stranger*, 14.

15. Hekman, *Gender and Knowledge*, 4. Similarly, Lyotard (*Postmodern Condition*, 27) observes that scientists tended to see "narrative" forms of knowledge as primitive and undeveloped because they are not subject to scientific standards of proof, a form of cultural imperialism.

16. Gellner, *Postmodernism, Reason and Religion*, 82. Cf. Cunningham, "Wittgenstein After Theology," 81–83 for a tracing of the roots of this in the late Middle Ages.

potentiality[17] and bring the world of nature and humanity under beneficial control.[18] As one of the forerunners of modern science, Francis Bacon stated, "I am come in very truth to lead you to nature with all her children, to bind her to your service and make her your slave."[19]

The "Enlightenment Project" was thus a very ambitious attempt to understand reality and bring it under human control (intellectually and technologically). As Edmund Husserl wrote,

> In a bold, even extravagant, elevation of the meaning of universality, begun by Descartes, this new philosophy seeks nothing less than to encompass, in the unity of a theoretical system, all meaningful questions in a rigorous scientific manner. . . . Growing from generation to generation and forever, this one edifice of definitive, theoretically interrelated truths was to solve all conceivable problems . . .[20]

Similarly, David Harvey writes,

> Generally perceived as positivistic, technocentric, and rationalistic, universal modernism has been identified with the belief in linear progress, absolute truths, the rational planning of ideal social orders, and the standardization of knowledge and production.[21]

This way of thinking spawned the modern era and helped unleash a whole new world of political, economic, technological, scientific, medical, and philosophical change.[22] By the early twentieth century, the Enlightenment worldview seemed to have the world at its feet until the first world war shook the prevailing Western confidence that modern humanity could, and would, create a just, peaceful, prosperous new age. The era of modernity was thus bookended by huge European wars: the Thirty Years' War and the Revolutionary/Napoleonic Wars at one end, and the two world wars of the twentieth century at the other.

---

17. Cf. Cahoone, ed., *Modernism to Postmodernism*, 12 on the key features of the self-image of modernity.

18. As Hekman (*Gender and Knowledge*, 106) observes, in some premodern thought nature was seen as "a mysterious but nurturing mother," but in the modernist view it became "a wild force that must be subordinated to a dominant mankind."

19. Ibid., 115.

20. Husserl, "Crisis of European Sciences," 228.

21. Harvey, *Condition of Postmodernity*, 9.

22. For an admiring summary of the achievements of modernism or "natural science," see Gellner, *Postmodernism, Reason and Religion*, 58–60.

Modernism and Christianity

The church was slow to catch on to the shift to modernity and struggled with how to respond. Its authority, and the authority of its Bible, were undermined, first by the split in European Christianity: now ordinary people could not be sure whose interpretation of Scripture was authoritative and wars were fought, ostensibly at least, over such issues.[23] It was in the midst of such fighting that René Descartes, searching for a new ground for certainty, embarked on his project of radical doubt that led to his famous dictum, "I think, therefore I am," a process that perhaps marks the start of the European Enlightenment, with its faith in individual human enquiry.[24]

Second, the authority of church and Bible were compromised by the uneasy relationship that developed between faith and the emerging modern empirical science. The early modern scientists were all Christian believers and espoused an epistemology similar to Francis Bacon's view: science studies God's works just as theology studies his words, and there is no inherent conflict between the two.[25] But in practice, beginning with Copernicus' revolution in cosmology, the potential for tensions between the teachings of the Bible, as traditionally understood, and the conclusions of science grew, and this reached its climax with the Darwinian theory of evolution. Christians often found themselves "on the back foot" as they attempted to respond to such developments.

Third, the authority of the Bible was undermined "from within" when Enlightenment criticism entered the theological academy and investigated

---

23. Cf. Barth, *Protestant Theology*, 92–93 for a description of the effects of the religious wars on the thinking of eighteenth-century Europeans. Cavanaugh argues that the "religious wars" of the seventeenth century are a myth in that they were not uniformly Catholic versus Protestant; rather Roman Catholic countries fought each other as well and the main contest was between the Catholic houses of Bourbon and Habsburg (Cavanaugh, "City," 190–91). This is true as far it goes; however, it ignores certain facts: first, the wars were precipitated by religious factors; second, they were part of a continent-wide struggle for dominance or toleration; third, the issues and results were perceived by many in the late seventeenth century and eighteenth century as invalidating the religious positions involved and requiring a new approach to issues of truth. To postmodernists, moreover, Cavanaugh's observations reinforce their idea that religious ideas are adopted for political purposes, an idea with roots in Marxism, as we will see.

24. The religious wars of the seventeenth century resulted in an uneasy peace between Catholics and Protestants that included a limited toleration of the other side's view but effectively ceased discussion between them until the mid-twentieth century. It also had the effect of "localizing" truth: where you lived determined what kind of Christianity you adhered to. However, this began to break down late in the seventeenth century, as in the Toleration Acts of 1689 in Britain.

25. Cf. Lessl, *Rhetorical Darwinism*, ch. 2.

the Bible without the presumption that it was God's holy words, but rather on the basis that it was an ancient text (or collection of texts) like any other. Historical-critical study of Christianity's core text made it the object of human knowledge, rather than its primary source and sure foundation, and led to substantial doubt about the origins of, and historical claims in, biblical books from Genesis to the Gospels.

Finally, the Bible and the church seemed to be fighting a rear guard action against the values of emerging modernity and the aspirations of modern people. In the twentieth century this was particularly evident in debates over gender and sexuality. The quest for equality between men and women and for freedom of sexual expression became almost a holy grail for Western people, especially in the wake of the "sexual revolution" of the 1960s, and the response of churches seemed hopelessly confused and out of touch, even authoritarian, if not hypocritical when sexual abuse by priests was uncovered.

What response could Christians make to all these developments? Mainly they split into two camps, which may fairly be labeled liberal and fundamentalist. Liberal theology tried to make peace with modernity by jettisoning any Christian belief or moral standard that seemed out of step with modern ideas and trying to ground the "new look" modern faith in feelings and experiences rather than revelation and Scripture. Fundamentalism[26] went the other way, trying to tighten definitions of the Bible and its teachings and to defend these against all comers, especially liberal theologians and biblical critics, but also modernists of all stripes, such as evolutionists. Both reactions were fatal to the credibility of the Christian faith as modern thinking increasingly took over in society. To modern people, liberals seemed to have nothing distinctive to say, while fundamentalists seemed to be talking nonsense; both appeared hopelessly out of date. And the modern worldview was strongly secular anyway: the separation of church and state, increasingly defined as the exclusion of faith from public discussion, was one of its fundamental beliefs.

The Enlightenment had offered to solve the problem of truth in the aftermath of the religious wars. Reason and science would fill the void left by the shattered Christian consensus and provide absolute truth to a liberal society. Hence, as Gellner puts it, "Rationalism was the continuation of exclusive monotheism by other means."[27] Faith would be tolerated, but

---

26. I hesitate to use this word because of its misleading associations but it still expresses the idea I am describing best.

27. Gellner, *Postmodernism, Reason and Religion*, 58.

sidelined or perhaps "humanized."[28] In the distinction between fact and value—one able to be proved, the other more a matter of private perspective—religious belief was increasingly placed in the camp of value and thus divorced from the sphere of public truth able to claim the allegiance of all people by reason of its objective, accessible, absolute nature.[29] Religious truth (and in many cases moral truth also) was relativized and privatized. Humanity, not God, was now the measure of all things.[30] As Karl Barth once wrote, "the amazing scientific spirit of that time ... was unquestionably one of the manifestations of *all-conquering, absolute man.*"[31] God (if he existed at all) was allowed only into the home and the individual heart.[32]

But meanwhile the times moved on.

THE ADVENT OF POSTMODERNISM

The Unraveling of Modernist Thought

The new modern worldview had hardly emerged when its own foundations started to be undermined. First, the Romantic movement showed that human reason, science, and progress towards liberal democracy were only one possible set of humanist values. With its stress on feelings, nature, folk traditions, and group identity, the Romantic movement provided an

---

28. As Barth (*Protestant Theology*, 84–135) argues was the trend of the eighteenth century.

29. "Liberalism invariably offers some version of the public/private split, where the public designates the grounds for communal life and the private indicates the grounds for individuality" (McGowan, *Postmodernism*, 40). As McGowan (ibid.) explains, the role of Kant in defining and justifying this kind of split was fundamental (cf. Hampshire, "Fallacies in Moral Philosophy," 51). Similarly, Miller ("Emerging Postmodern World," 5) writes that "This comprehensive dualism [between the "phenomenal" and the "noumenal," "pure and practical reason," "knowledge and faith," "the scientific and the religious"] has been the central mark of modern culture."

30. Eighteenth-century people were the first to feel the full effects of the Copernican revolution, which showed that humans and their earth were not the literal center of the universe. Nonetheless, for Enlightenment thinkers "man is all the greater for this, man is in the center of all things ... for he was able to discover this revolutionary truth by his own resources ..." (Barth, *Protestant Theology*, 37).

31. Ibid., 41 (italics added).

32. Eighteenth- and nineteenth-century Europeans believed in God but distanced themselves increasingly from Christian dogma and the organized church in favor of either some kind of pietism or a more or less deistic religion that shaped God into "reasonable" form and substituted virtue for discipleship (cf. Barth, *Protestant Theology*, 66, 73–76 on the eighteenth century). Secular education increasingly took the place of church in training the young (ibid., 60–62).

alternative Enlightenment that attracted many for whom stark reason was unable to meet every need.[33] The Romantic movement was just as "humanistic" as the rationalist Enlightenment and could be said to take many of the Enlightenment positions even farther,[34] but it provided an alternative metanarrative that exalted the original goodness and equality of primitive humans over than the cultivated civilization celebrated by the mainstream Enlightenment. Individual human experience and enquiry must therefore give space for emotions, traditions, and cooperation; as a result, socialism and nationalism emerged as serious competitors to individualistic liberalism as the great ideology of human progress in a post-Christian world.

Simultaneously, some of the more skeptical thinkers in the Enlightenment exposed the limitations of human reason and even empirical evidence. For example, Scottish philosopher David Hume questioned the innate assumptions of causality underlying science. Immanuel Kant, an Enlightenment man with a profound faith in reason,[35] but as such unwilling just to follow the slogans of the Enlightenment, determined to respond to the skeptical writing of Hume,[36] by investigating the claims of reason to ensure that rational knowledge is possible. Hence he also became the first philosopher to question the correspondence view of truth,[37] building his view of knowledge on coherence between our beliefs and our experiences of reality ("phenomena") rather than between our ideas and the external world as it is in itself ("noumena").[38] He delimited reason's sphere, calling for tolerance of difference and freedom in those areas where reason cannot decide things (such as religion),[39] but he also elevated the thinking subject with his view of "transcendental" philosophy, celebrating the ability of the mind to transcend the limitations of normal experience and culture. As McGowan

---

33. Cf. McGowan, *Postmodernism*, 5–6.

34. Barth points out that Rousseau still held firmly to reason and many of the ideals of the Enlightenment and wrote a powerful critique of revealed religion from a basically rationalist standpoint, wishing to substitute for it a "natural" religion, including a strong conviction of the innate goodness of humankind. He was, like others of the Enlightenment, optimistic, but differed mainly in his stress on feelings and nature. Cf. Barth, *Protestant Theology*, ch. 5.

35. Cf. McGowan, *Postmodernism*, 32.

36. Cf. Grenz, *Primer on Postmodernism*, 75–77.

37. McGowan, *Postmodernism*, 31–32.

38. Ibid. Cf. Grenz, *Primer on Postmodernism*, 77; Miller, "Emerging Postmodern World," 4.

39. Cf. McGowan, *Postmodernism*, 34. Or, as Miller ("Emerging Postmodern World," 5) explains, "though *knowledge* of the world as a whole, of the self, and of God were denied by Kant, *faith* in them, he argued, was absolutely necessary for practical reasons."

puts it, "His profoundly ahistorical view means that the investigation of reason as experienced now will yield a transcendental knowledge applicable to all places and at all times."[40]

The nineteenth century was a century of great technological, social, and liberal progress as the foundations of traditional Christian faith were seriously weakened. But the new ideas that obviously challenged Christianity more surreptitiously dug away at their own foundations as well. The most clear-cut example is Darwinian evolution. Darwin's theories were seen, perhaps rightly, as a threat to Christian traditions and the authority of the Bible: fundamental doctrines of the faith, such as Creation and the Fall of mankind, were called into serious question and had to be abandoned or reinterpreted—a process still going on to this day. Conventional arguments for belief in God were destroyed or weakened, most notably the argument from design, propagated especially by William Paley, a specific target of Darwin's writings, but most other natural theology arguments as well. For example, if evolution could explain reality in the natural world, what use were the old arguments towards a Creator?[41]

But evolution also threatened to cut the ground from under the feet of its very advocates and promoters. For if the nature of human beings—not just their physical shape but the workings of their brains as well—could be explained completely by processes like natural selection, then what was the status of human beliefs and thoughts, including the theory of evolution itself? The modernist project was predicated on human independence: the ability of individual human enquirers to stand at a distance from the real outside world and study it using reason and scientific method. But if human enquirers were themselves merely part of the world of nature, how could they study it objectively? What standing did their conclusions have? To put it more crassly, if the scientist is a descendant of ape-like ancestors, are his or her thoughts any more likely to be valid (in the sense of corresponding to reality) than those of such distant ancestors or their other descendants found in a modern zoo?

Karl Marx's theories of dialectical materialism had similar implications, but in a different way. Marx saw everything as controlled by economic forces and class warfare.[42] This included religion, culture, philosophy,[43] and

---

40. Ibid., 32. Cf. also Grenz, *Primer on Postmodernism*, 78–81.

41. Cf. McGrath, *Darwinism and the Divine*, chs. 3–6.

42. Eagleton asserts that Marxism has two or three specific basic tenets: material production as the determining factor of social existence, the class struggle as "the central dynamic of historical development," and (at least in its Leninist version) a call to political insurrection (Eagleton, *Against the Grain*, 81–82).

43. Cf. for example George Thomson's thesis that philosophy arose out of such

even science. Marx was as much a son of the Enlightenment as Darwin. In fact, according to Susan Hekman, "It might even be possible to argue that Marxists are the quintessential modernists because Marx's project is an attempt to complete the Enlightenment project of liberation that liberalism failed to achieve."[44] Moreover Marx attempted to set this socialist project of liberation on a firmly "scientific" basis that could make his predictions of socialist revolution a matter of historical necessity, combining the "scientific" evolution of Darwin with Hegelian teleology, since, as Laclau and Mouffe observe,

> Darwinism alone does not offer 'guarantees for the future,' since natural selection does not operate in a direction predetermined from the beginning. Only if a Hegelian type of teleology is added to Darwinism—which is totally incompatible with it—can an evolutionary process be presented as a guarantee of future transitions.[45]

Both Marx and Darwin, then, constructed alternative versions of the Enlightenment metanarrative; but unlike Darwin, Marx consciously relativized truth and knowledge as tools in the class war,[46] anticipating the insights of Michel Foucault about knowledge and power, though he failed to apply those insights to his own metanarrative. Thus Marxists have been troubled by "Mannheim's paradox"—"if all ideas are motivated by economic interest or if all ideas carry the stamp of the ruling class's views, then how can Marx explain his own privileged access to real causes?"[47] Nevertheless, "deeply inherent" in Marxist theory is "its monist aspiration to capture with its categories the essence or underlying meaning of History."[48]

Sigmund Freud carried this process a step further. The Enlightenment had attempted to make humanity, and human reason particularly, the measure of all things. So long as rational minds were studying the world of nature outside themselves, this picture of knowledge had a chance of being convincing. But once the social sciences began to emerge, there were two

---

events as the invention of coinage in ancient Greece (Eagleton, *Against the Grain*, 123).

44. Hekman, *Gender and Knowledge*, 40.

45. Laclau and Mouffe, *Hegemony and Socialist Strategy*, 20.

46. Thus bringing to prominence the notion of ideology as "the conscious . . . legitimation of the prevailing social arrangements" (McGowan, *Postmodernism*, 64–65). Vanhoozer (Vanhoozer, *Is There a Meaning?*, 67) labels Freud, Marx, and Nietzsche the "masters of suspicion" in that they showed that human subjects are not "immune from the effects of history and culture" but are "subject to unconscious psychological, social, and historical forces."

47. McGowan, *Postmodernism*, 66.

48. Laclau and Mouffe, *Hegemony and Socialist Strategy*, 4.

unavoidable consequences: first, the fact/value distinction started to break down. This distinction was predicated on science staying out of the realm of value, which basically was the realm of the individual. But Darwinian evolution redefined the individual human as merely an advanced animal, then Marx claimed that individual (and societal) belief systems—supposedly rational (at least potentially)—were in fact just a rationalization of class interests. In a further step, Freudian psychology suggested that both the facts and the values held by the individual could be explained by such factors as the individual's sexual development and childhood experiences. Values could thus not only be explained factually, but could decide factuality in the individual consciousness. Thus absolute truth (at least absolute knowledge based on reason) was again under threat. If, say, Darwin's theory of evolution or Marx's "dialectical materialism" could potentially be put down to the results of his relationship with his mother,[49] reason would be dethroned in the name of reason! Hence, Robert Bellah has called Freud "the gravedigger of the Enlightenment" because he disclosed the "enormous nonrational forces of the unconscious" not susceptible to rational analysis[50] and "emphasized the relative weakness and fragility of rational processes."[51] Freud was also a forerunner of postmodernism in his focus on "the other": aspects of experience (dreams, popular culture[52]) neglected or de-emphasized by rationalist thought that revealed hidden realities.

Other social sciences took this another step farther. Sociology and anthropology studied the social role played by value systems, religion, customs, economic systems, and the like. This led to a more comparative approach to the beliefs, practices, and values of different societies and cultures. As often happened, the first casualty of this was religion. The idea that any religious belief could be absolutely true was undermined by the ability of social scientists to explain the role of religion in terms of social and cultural needs and developments[53] and by the comparative nature of scientific study

---

49. I know of no actual attempt to do that, but it is hypothetically possible for a Freudian to come up with such an explanation.

50. Bellah, *Beyond Belief*, 239; Vanhoozer, *Is There a Meaning?*, 67.

51. Bellah, *Beyond Belief*, 252.

52. Cf. Collective, *Postmodern Bible*, 158.

53. For example, Bellah (*Beyond Belief*, chs. 1–13) outlines how religious truth has been relativized by the social sciences, sketches the evolution of religion, describes the emergence of a civil religion in the U.S. that fulfills the social functions of religion while placing less emphasis on Christian doctrine, and portrays the use of religious symbols as "fictions" about reality. He specifically attacks the "objectivist fallacy" that confuses religious experience with cognitive truths. In other words, religion is to be understood in terms of its social functions in a given culture, with the actual belief system seen as secondary and relative to that culture.

of this realm. But once again, ultimately it was not just religion but all human knowledge that was relativized by the procedures and findings of the social sciences.[54]

Other important developments grew out of the emerging "social sciences." First, there was the debate between "humanism" and "positivism" over the nature of truth in the social or human sciences: were these studies to be modeled on the natural sciences and seen as "objective truth"[55] (or perhaps a "second-class" science if this proved impossible), or were they to seek a more "humanist" model, a different way of knowing based on language, since social/human studies depended on texts (that is, on oral and written communications of human beings) to a much greater degree than natural science, which studied "actual reality"?

Second, there was a growing problem in the subject-object dichotomy, basic for Enlightenment epistemology, when the "object" of study was human[56]—perhaps even the "subject" himself (even more so when the "himself" became a "herself": this undermined the whole modernist model of knowledge in which women were often not seen as subjects).[57]

The effect of all such developments was that the Enlightenment project was digging its own grave. The rational modern subject, standing "outside" of time and nature so as to study it objectively, had come to be seen as influenced by feelings (Romanticism), situated in a particular historical moment (Hegel), part of the evolutionary process (Darwin), representing a particular socioeconomic class's interests (Marx), influenced by subconscious forces from early childhood (Freud), and playing a definite sociocultural role in a (geographically and historically) particular society. How could he (or especially she) ever be "free" to be objective? How could his conclusions ever have the status of absolute truth?

Moreover, by the end of the twentieth century, the achievements of modernity, while monumental, were starting to look more than a little tarnished. Technological and scientific developments had solved many

---

54. In ch. 15 of *Beyond Belief*, Bellah sharply criticizes secularization and the Enlightenment approach to religion and explains how the emerging social sciences in the late nineteenth and early twentieth centuries began to rediscover non-rational elements of human life, such as the unconscious, linked to religion: "Convinced of the invalidity of traditional religion, each rediscovered the power of the religious consciousness" (ibid., 240). The implications of this went beyond religion: Parsons concluded that "part of the reality that man needs to make sense of is nonempirical" (ibid., 242) and other social scientists spoke of multiple realities not reducible to each other.

55. Cf. Hekman's description of Weber's dilemma in this regard, in Hekman, *Gender and Knowledge*, 98.

56. Cf. Bellah, *Beyond Belief*, 252.

57. Cf. Hekman, *Gender and Knowledge*, 94–96.

problems, opened up many new achievements, improved the life expectancy and prosperity of millions, and even eliminated some diseases. However, they had also led to devastating wars and development of weapons of mass destruction, destruction of the environment that perhaps threatened the future of life and the planet, and a world where the gap between rich and poor was widening rather than narrowing.

And some of the other foundations of the modern edifice were starting to look a little shaky: Einstein's theory of relativity seriously modified the Newtonian order of things in physics;[58] the modernist project seemed to have been privileging some kinds of people (specifically white middle-class males) over others; and many of the rational conclusions of the Enlightenment seemed to be somewhat partial and culture-bound when the Western world was forced by new technology (air travel, television, satellites, the Internet) to seriously confront other cultures and ways of looking at reality. Now some critics were seeing modernity "as a movement of ethnic and class domination, European imperialism, anthropocentrism, the destruction of nature, the dissolution of community and tradition, the rise of alienation, the death of individuality in bureaucracy."[59]

With these shifts the second revolution in Western thinking was underway. The provisional name for it is postmodernism.[60]

The Postmodernist Critique of Modernism

A new school of thinkers emerged in the twentieth century who saw the flaws in modernism. They were not inclined to overturn modernist thinking completely or go back to a premodern, medieval worldview. However, they questioned the paradigms of Enlightenment modernity and modified its assumptions. For example, they questioned the ability of individual rational human beings to look objectively at the world around them and come

---

58. Postmodern science has moved far from the order and predictability of the Newtonian model. Thus, according to Lyotard (*Postmodern Condition*, 60), "It is changing the meaning of the word *knowledge*, while expressing how such a change can take place. It is producing not the known but the unknown." And McKnight (*Post-Modern Use*, 202) argues, "With Einstein, the sense of the clear scientific separation of subject and object began to come to an end. No longer was it possible to separate the observer from the observed; the observer is also the observed." Cf. Miller, "Emerging Postmodern World," 9–10 on other relevant developments in science.

59. Cahoone, *Modernism to Postmodernism*, 12; comp. Griffin, *Spirituality and Society*, xi. Cf. Middleton and Walsh, *Truth Is Stranger*, 22–27 for a graphic description of the growing anxiety of the postmodern Western world.

60. The origins of the term "postmodernism" are discussed below.

to a sure place of knowledge uninfluenced by their own prejudices, cultural blind spots, and personal ambitions.

Secondly, such postmodernists (as they came to be known, for reasons I will explore below) questioned the modernist faith in progress,[61] either because humankind is often too limited to bring it off or because no one can know the future or because the very view of progress triumphant in the Enlightenment is culturally narrow, controlling, and exclusive of minorities. Thus the worldview of modernity came to be viewed as inherently oppressive. This challenge to modernism was especially revealed in the attempts to rewrite history from a perspective that showed the oppression of, say, women, homosexuals, or aboriginal peoples by triumphant modern Western civilization.[62]

Postmodernists also questioned the privileging of natural science over other forms of knowledge and investigation. Science had had a lot of success in studying the world "out there" and bringing it under human control. However, scientific "laws" were often now seen as a representation of reality rather than exactly how reality works; thus Husserl (a predecessor of postmodernism) spoke of "the surreptitious substitution of the mathematically substructured world of idealities for the only real world, the one that is actually given through perception" in the growth of science from Galileo.[63] Kuhn showed that scientific revolutions depended on changes of paradigms, which, though driven in part by new evidence, could not be fully resolved by "the evaluative procedures characteristic of normal science" but only by "the assent of the relevant [scientific] community."[64] Moreover science had arguably not been a successful model for studying human beings and societies.[65] Thus Lyotard suggested that "the game of science is . . . put on a par with the others"[66] and must legitimate itself by recourse to narrative knowledge.[67]

Finally, postmodernists questioned the blind faith modernists had in technology. Technological progress had helped solve many problems, but it

61. Cf. Grenz, *Primer on Postmodernism*, 13.

62. Cf. Middleton and Walsh, *Truth Is Stranger*, 9–13.

63. Husserl, "Crisis of European Sciences," 233–36.

64. Kuhn, "Scientific Revolutions," 311.

65. For instance, the philosopher Gadamer explored experiences of truth outside the realm of natural science (such as in art), concluded that the model of the natural sciences was not the only valid model of knowledge, and finally argued that all understanding, including that of science, is "hermeneutic," that is, language related (Hekman, *Gender and Knowledge*, 13).

66. Lyotard, *Postmodern Condition*, 40.

67. Ibid., 27–29.

had not been an unalloyed good, especially in the uses for which it had been deployed. Postmodernists were suspicious of "technology's ever-increasing hegemony in the West, especially when that hegemony is inexorably and, perhaps, inevitably, linked to an ideology of mastery and hence to practices of violence."[68] Moreover they came to see that technology could even distort the search for truth, especially in science, which requires increasingly sophisticated and expensive technology for research and thus becomes subject to those providing the money (whether corporations or the state).[69]

I commented previously on the humanism that is central to Enlightenment modernity. Postmodernists, while generally still humanistic in the sense of deriving all meaning, truth, and values from human experience and ideas rather than a transcendental source such as God, tended to have a more jaundiced, ironical, or limiting view of what human beings are worth or can achieve.

Frequently, too, they tended to reject what Laclau and Mouffe call "the abstract Enlightenment universalism of an undifferentiated human nature,"[70] especially under the influence of Michel Foucault, who remarked, "As the archaeology of our thought easily shows, man is an invention of recent date. And one perhaps nearing its end."[71] Postmodernists were more inclined to stress the *differences* among human beings in different cultures and different ages, not to mention within common cultures.

Postmodernists, then, were looking around for better explanations than those provided by the Enlightenment project to the questions and problems faced by humanity. They did not want to go back to the premodern thinking of the ancient and medieval world, so they were searching for new ways forward. As David Ray Griffin writes, "modernity can be successfully overcome only by going *beyond* it, not by attempting to *return* to a premodern form of existence."[72]

---

68. Collective, *Postmodern Bible*, 10.

69. Cf. Lyotard, *Postmodern Condition*, 44–47.

70. As quoted by Bertens, *Idea of the Postmodern*, 190.

71. Foucault, *Order of Things*, as quoted in Grenz, *Primer on Postmodernism*, 129. Cf. Hekman, *Gender and Knowledge*, 19–20.

72. Griffin, ed., *Spirituality and Society*, ix (italics added).

Defining Postmodernism

"Postmodernism is an exasperating term," said Hans Bertens,[73] which has never been defined to everyone's satisfaction.[74] Others have called it a "fashionably ambiguous term,"[75] though it is less fashionable than it was. Some kind of definition must be attempted, while allowing for the fact that there have been many "postmodernisms." The term seems to have been used in three main senses: as a series of trends or changes in world economic, cultural, and political life (for which I prefer to use the word "postmodernity"[76]); as the changes in thinking among the general populace arising from these broader changes; or more narrowly, as a set of allied trends in intellectual discourse that have influenced popular thinking, which is the sense I will mainly focus on.

A. Post-modern-ism

First, postmodern-*ism*, as the suffix implies, may be seen as a specific trend (or trends) in thinking, what Lawrence Cahoone described as "a contemporary intellectual movement, or rather, a not very happy family of intellectual movements."[77] These trends in thinking took shape during the twentieth century, though the term "postmodernism" was coined more recently to describe them.[78] The core figures recognized as the leaders in this trend were the French poststructuralists[79] (such as Jacques Derrida, Michel Foucault, and Jean-François Lyotard) and American neopragmatists (such as Richard

---

73. Bertens, *Idea of the Postmodern*, 3–5.

74. Ibid., 12.

75. Collective, *Postmodern Bible*, 9.

76. On the interrelationship between postmodernism and postmodernity, see for example Bertens, *Idea of Postmodern* (e.g., p. 10) and Harvey, *Condition of Postmodernity*.

77. Cahoone, *Modernism to Postmodernism*, 1.

78. The origins of the term "postmodernism" are still debated. It may have been used first by Rudolf Pannowitz in 1917, describing the "nihilism" of twentieth-century Western culture (Cahoone, *Modernism to Postmodernism*, 3), though it may go back as far as the 1870s (Bertens, *Idea of the Postmodern*, 20). And Tarnas (*Passion*, 26–30) identifies trends of thinking in the ancient Greek Sophists that resemble many ideas of postmodernism.

79. The relationship between postmodernism and poststructuralism has been debated. Bertens (*Idea of the Postmodern*, 16–17), for example, wants to keep them very much apart, but has to admit that poststructuralism has contributed strongly to postmodernism and that at least one leading poststructuralist (Lyotard) "has played a major role in theorizing the postmodern."

Rorty and Stanley Fish), even though many of them never used, or even rejected, the label "postmodernist."

Second, *post*-modernism, as the prefix implies, functions as a critique of, and movement beyond, the "discourses of modernity,"[80] the thought-world that arose largely out of the Enlightenment and dominated Western culture in the nineteenth and twentieth centuries (though Lyotard traces it as far back as Augustine).[81] For example, Cahoone referred to postmodernism as "the latest wave in the critique of the Enlightenment,"[82] though according to Bertens, this needs qualifying: "postmodernism challenges . . . not modernism *per se*, but its essentialist, rationalistic and humanistic underpinnings."[83] This development has been traced earlier in this chapter.

Finally, postmodernism may also imply a critique of postmodernity or contemporary society, as in Lyotard's *Postmodern Condition*, where, among other things, he thoroughly analyzed the commercialization of knowledge that flowed from computerization and the sheer cost of scientific research today.[84] Similarly, Jameson and others, especially Marxists, portrayed the postmodern world as the latest development in capitalism.[85]

B. Postmodernist Positions

One way of understanding postmodernism is to identify what postmodernists have criticized. For example, postmodernists have been opposed to, or critical of:

- *Foundationalism*, the idea that humans can attain to certain knowledge by using rational methods on the basis of solid or indubitable foundations

---

80. Harvey (*Condition of Postmodernity*, 7) argues that the one agreed feature of postmodernism is that it "represents some kind of reaction to, or departure from, 'modernism.'" Cf. Lyotard, "Narratives," 30; Lyotard, "Legitimacy," 62; Lyotard, "Svelte Appendix," 26.

81. Lyotard, "Universal History and Cultural Differences," 314–15.

82. Cahoone, *Modernism to Postmodernism*, 2.

83. Bertens, *Idea of the Postmodern*, 190, paraphrasing Chantal Mouffe. Of course, as Cahoone (*Modernism to Postmodernism*, 13) writes, "The term 'modernism' is used in a famously ambiguous way. It can refer to the philosophy or culture of the modern period as a whole . . . [or] . . . to a much more historically circumscribed movement in the arts during the period 1850 to 1950 . . . a form of art characteristic of high or actualized or late modernity . . ."

84. Lyotard, *Postmodern Condition*, 4–6, 44–47.

85. Jameson, *Cultural Logic*, xviii, 5, 35–36.

- *Metanarratives*, stories or explanations that attempt to explain the overarching structures of human history[86]
- *Closure*, the idea that there can be a final answer to a question or a comprehensive interpretation of a text
- *Totalizing*, a viewpoint or thesis that pretends to provide the final answer to a specific question or field of inquiry and thus excludes alternative possibilities

This first bracket of postmodern targets reflect the fact that postmodernism has been skeptical of the idea of absolute or universal truth or of any authority (human or otherwise) to which humans are accountable in their thinking or behavior.[87]

Postmodernism has also been critical of binary thinking.[88] Modernist thought is often dichotomous, working in opposites such as objective/subjective, true/false, logical/illogical, scientific/unscientific, rational/intuitive, subject/object, text/interpretation, white/black, masculine/feminine—with the first element being privileged, and the second either rejected or at least seen as inferior, dependent, or derivative.[89] To postmodernism, such opposites are arbitrary or cultural; they are either oppressive (such as the male/female[90] or black/white dichotomies have arguably been) or at least rule out the potentiality for valuable insight buried in the opposite that is rejected or downgraded.[91] Hence, "A characteristic feature of postmodern debates in a variety of cultural arenas is the insistence on the hearing of alternative voices."[92]

So what ideas has postmodernism advocated? In discussion of truth and knowledge, postmodernists have tended to think in ways that are:

1. PERSPECTIVAL

One of the common ideas in postmodernism is the contention that humans cannot know or see what is true in any final sense, because we all

---

86. Lyotard, *Postmodern Condition*, xxiv.
87. Cf. Derrida, "Faith and Knowledge," 8.
88. Hekman (*Gender and Knowledge*, 22) contends that "one of the central tenets of [Derrida's] work is his rejection of binary oppositions."
89. Cf. Collective, *Postmodern Bible*, 122.
90. Some feminists would argue that all the dichotomies of Enlightenment thinking are founded on gender, e.g., Hekman, *Gender and Knowledge*, 8.
91. Cf. the insightful discussion in McGowan, *Postmodernism*, 19.
92. Middleton and Walsh, *Truth Is Stranger*, 13.

inevitably view everything from our own cultural, historical, and individual perspectives, which are particularly constructed by language. According to Cahoone, postmodernism "denies that anything is 'immediately present,' hence *independent of* signs, language, interpretation, disagreement, etc."[93]

Does this stress on perspectives leave postmodernism open to relativism, as Ernest Gellner, for example, claims?[94] In reply to such claims, postmodernists have argued "that all knowledge is contextual and historical, thus rendering the opposition between absolute and relative obsolete."[95] Fairlamb contended that "the ultimate issue for rationalism is what makes one community *more* rational than another";[96] postmodernists asserted that such an assertion is meaningless since we have no outside perspective from which to make final judgments between cultures.

2. Particularist

Postmodernist thought privileges the particular over the general, the local over the universal. It tends to see truth as local, community created, and contextual[97]—"rooted in tradition and prejudice"[98]—which amounts to rejecting the possibility of absolute, universally true or timeless propositions. For example, Rorty quoted his pragmatist as saying, "'All that can be done to explicate "truth," "knowledge," "morality," "virtue" is to refer us back to the concrete details of the culture in which these terms grew up and developed,'" though he rejected the objection that this means, "'Truth and virtue are simply what a community agrees that they are.'"[99] Ironically, all these Rorty statements are themselves seen as generally true.

---

93. Cahoone, *Modernism to Postmodernism*, 14 (italics added).

94. Gellner, *Postmodernism, Reason and Religion*, 24. Cf. Rorty's defense of himself against this charge in Rorty, *Consequences of Pragmatism*, 166–69.

95. Hekman, *Gender and Knowledge*, 153. For a different defense, cf. Collective, *Postmodern Bible*, 3.

96. Fairlamb, *Critical Conditions*, 58. Cf. ibid., 175, and Gellner, *Postmodernism, Reason and Religion*, 49–50.

97. Cf. Hekman, *Gender and Knowledge*, 108.

98. Ibid., 14. She refers particularly to Gadamer. Cf. ibid., 64; Grenz, *Primer on Postmodernism*, 12.

99. Rorty, *Consequences of Pragmatism*, 173.

3. Pluralist

Postmodernism tends to stress multiple interpretations and even contradictory perspectives: there is more than one valid way of describing any particular situation or reality or of understanding a particular text. The postmodernist view of truth thus tends towards pluralism: "there are 'truths,' not 'Truth.'"[100] And postmodern culture is similarly eclectic. As Lyotard comments,

> Eclecticism is the degree zero of contemporary general culture: you listen to reggae, you watch a western, you eat McDonald's at midday and local cuisine at night, you wear Paris perfume in Tokyo and dress retro in Hong Kong, knowledge is the stuff of TV game shows.[101]

4. Political

Rather than seeing knowledge or truth in terms of the individual confronting outside reality, postmodernism tends to see it in terms of "language games." In this view, knowledge claims are validated within the rules of a particular form of discourse[102] (a game) that is developed for a particular set of human purposes.[103] Thus, according to Lyotard, "every utterance should be thought of as a 'move' in a game" and "to speak is to fight, in the sense of playing."[104] So rather than the individual scientist in his laboratory (the paradigm of modernity), we are looking at players in a game of chess; the question is, who will win,[105] that is, whose truth claims will be most validated within the rules of the game? Because of this, postmodernism has

---

100. Hekman, *Gender and Knowledge*, 63. Though Derrida has apparently denied being a pluralist (Hart, *Trespass of the Sign*, 144).

101. Lyotard, "What Is the Postmodern?," 17.

102. As Hekman (*Gender and Knowledge*, 63) puts it, "knowledge, along with subjects and objects, is constituted collectively through forms of discourse." Lyotard attempts to identify the rules of the science language game in *The Postmodern Condition*, 23–24. Cf. ibid., 42–43.

103. Miller, "Emerging Postmodern World," 11.

104. Lyotard, *Postmodern Condition*, 10. Cf. Rorty, *Consequences of Pragmatism*, 127; MacIntyre, *Whose Justice*, 5.

105. Lyotard (*Postmodern Condition*, 10) insists that people do not necessarily play to win but often for the sheer pleasure of it, but he concedes that "even this pleasure depends on a feeling of success won at the expense of an adversary" such as "the accepted language, or connotation."

tended to see truth in political terms, both in theory and practice.[106] Such insights owe a lot to Michel Foucault's studies on the relationship between power and knowledge, not only on the macro level (the state) but also in "micro-politics" in local situations (schools, hospitals, and so on).[107]

Postmodernists also pointed out that traditional forms of hermeneutics have tended to obscure the extent that they are political, in the sense of serving the interests of a particular class, race, gender, or other group.[108] Hence, "postmodern readings function as political and ethical responses to other readings which claim that their own foundations exist outside a field of power" and "are part of the broader political activity to call reigning structures of power and meaning into question."[109]

This illustrates the way postmodernists approached the interpretation of texts. The meaning of a text was seen as not *in* the text or the intention of the original author but *between* the text and the reader—that is, in the interaction of thought between text and reader.[110] The original author has no final authority to say what the text means;[111] rather the "death of the author" gave rise to "the birth of the reader."[112] There can be no one true interpretation or literal meaning of a text,[113] and to attempt to formulate one is to be guilty of closure or totalizing thought. The meaning of a text is dynamic and plural.[114] As Jack puts it, "Once the text is delivered from the false control of the author, it is free to become a playful affirmation of indeterminacy,"[115] and this "makes problematic all methods of interpreting texts which bolster a text's unity over its multiple or dissenting voices."[116]

In practice, then, for postmodernist critics, what makes one reading of a text better than another is not so much its accuracy in unpacking the

---

106. Bertens, *Idea of the Postmodern*, 7. Cf. ibid., 13–14, 103.

107. Cf. Harvey, *Condition of Postmodernity*, 45–46; Lyotard, *Postmodern Condition*, 46.

108. Jack, *Texts Reading Texts*, 26.

109. Collective, *Postmodern Bible*, 3. Comp. Eagleton, *Literary Theory*, 169.

110. Cf. Fowler, "Postmodern Biblical Criticism," 11.

111. Cahoone, *Modernism to Postmodernism*, 15. Cf. Eagleton, *Literary Theory*, 120; Collective, *Postmodern Bible*, 130; McKnight, *Post-Modern Use*, 248–49.

112. Hekman, *Gender and Knowledge*, 67. The slogans quoted here are now generic to postmodern literary criticisms. Cf. Vanhoozer, *Is There a Meaning?*, 69–73; McKnight, *Post-Modern Use*, 161; Sutcliffe, *Is There an Author?*, 97–110.

113. Taylor, *Erring*, 174.

114. Eagleton, *Literary Theory*, 120. Cf. Hatina, "Intertextuality and Historical Criticism," 30–31.

115. Jack, *Texts Reading Texts*, 19.

116. Ibid., 14.

grammar and vocabulary of the language, for instance, as its ideological progressiveness. As one group of postmodernists affirmed, "Better ideological readings are those that support and encourage positive social change that affirms difference and inclusion."[117]

This political perspective has raised a number of issues. For example, on what basis can "progressive" views be privileged in an epistemological context of pluralism? Strictly speaking, deconstruction and other postmodern insights necessitate that all interpretations are, if not equal, at least permissible. It is thus difficult to find a firm foundation for concepts such as justice or love[118] or for rejecting unjust viewpoints such as fascism. Also the politicization of truth can lead to the sort of pressure sometimes labeled "political correctness."[119] For example, when Stanley Fish wrote, "it is interpretive communities, rather than either the text or the reader, that produce meanings,"[120] since such communities dictate to readers what they should look for in a text, was he suggesting that meaning is produced by a form of peer pressure? If so, is this inevitable or justifiable? In my experience, postmodernism has frequently seemed in practice to amount to PC/progressive peer pressure.

Postmodernism and Worldview Shifts

Significant and basic issues are being thrown up, or addressed in new ways, by postmodernist thought. These include questions of ontology (what is real?), cosmology (what does the universe consist of?), epistemology (how can we know what is real?), truth (what is truth and who decides?), hermeneutics (how can meaning be determined?), teleology (is history meaningful, and where is it going?), psychology (what is the nature of human persons and what drives them?), and anthropology (what is the nature and place of human beings in the scheme of things?). The confident answers given to such questions by at least some followers of the Enlightenment have been questioned by postmodernists. But these are the basic questions that shape the worldview of a culture.

"We are living at the juncture of two ages, when a senescent worldview is contending with its upstart successor and the boundaries of what seems

---

117. Collective, *Postmodern Bible*, 302.

118. Cf. McGowan, *Postmodernism*, 28. Cf. Charlesworth, *Philosophy and Religion*, 172.

119. Lyotard (*Postmodern Condition*, 63) himself alludes to scientists whose work was "ignored or repressed" because "it too abruptly destabilized the accepted positions."

120. Fish, *Is There a Text?*, 14.

possible liquefy," claimed Walter Wink.[121] What seems to be happening in the ferment of postmodernism is that, just as the premodern thinking of the medieval world gave way to the Enlightenment worldview of the modern era, so the worldview of modernity is itself being superseded, or at least altered.[122]

There is a fundamental shift taking place, not just in *what* people think, but in *how* they think, as postmodernism increasingly influences the broader world. Postmodernism, or something like it, is becoming the new "common sense" of Western culture.[123] There can be no return to the pure Enlightenment model or its predecessor. This has powerful implications for Christianity and calls for a response from Christians.

POSTMODERNISM AND CHRISTIANITY

Religious Effects of the Shift to Postmodernism

As I noted earlier, in the new order of Enlightenment rationality, religious truth was relativized and privatized,[124] divorced from the sphere of "public" truth able to claim the allegiance of all people, because Enlightenment thinking demanded that all valid knowledge must be "universally accessible" in all times and places.[125] Christianity suffered from "the scandal of particularity" since it arose within a particular culture and did not appear to be understandable or credible in other settings.[126] Secular education increasingly took the place of church in training the young,[127] leading to the substantial exclusion of religion from public life.[128] Enlightenment modernity "proclaimed the death of religion" as part of "the collapse of an old world view."[129]

Christianity also had to endure withering criticism from followers of Darwin, Marx, Nietzsche, and Freud. Freud, for example, saw religion as "essentially a mass neurosis, its rituals as obsessional, its adherents as

---

121. Wink, *Unmasking the Powers*, 172.
122. Johns, "Pentecostalism and the Postmodern Worldview," 83.
123. Cf. Grenz, *Primer on Postmodernism*, 12.
124. Cf. Miller, "Emerging Postmodern World," 5. Miller relates this to the fact/value dualism that Kant bequeathed to modernity.
125. McGrath, *Passion for Truth*, 88. Cf. Newbigin, *Pluralist Society*, 2.
126. Newbigin, *Pluralist Society*, 72.
127. Barth, *Protestant Theology*, 60–62.
128. Cf. Juergensmeyer, *Terror*, 224.
129. Ibid., 225.

infantile."¹³⁰ Like most late modernist thinkers, he could explain religion (away) in terms of human needs, just as Marx had called it "the opium of the people." On the other hand, Nietzsche, while attacking Christian morality, was conscious of the consequences of the "death of God" implicit in the Enlightenment worldview, calling attention to the problems involved in the whole effort "to supply a *rational foundation* for morality." He saw this as simply an attempt to justify the existing moralities of the day without taking note either of the existence of alternative moralities in other places and times or of the real motivation of people ("will to power").¹³¹

But one of the side effects of the postmodern questioning of Enlightenment rationality is that the possibility of religion (or at least spirituality) has been gaining in credibility. Postmodernists are not always sympathetic to Christian claims. Lyotard, for example, while happy to draw on the conceptual world of the Bible, seemed to see Christianity as outmoded, having "stopped shaping the social, political, economic, and cultural institutions of Western communities long ago."¹³² He explicitly rejected the idea that religion could fill the gap caused by the decline of modernity's metanarratives.¹³³ On the other hand, Derrida seemed sympathetic at times to some place for religion, albeit not orthodox Christianity.¹³⁴

Christian thinkers in the Kuyperian stream may fairly be claimed to have anticipated many postmodern critics of the modernist worldview as well as some key postmodern Christian thinkers. For example, Kuyper¹³⁵ and his followers "showed that human reason is not neutral in its operation, but functions under the influence of a set of antecedent assumptions that condition all thinking and acting," which lead them to "a powerful critique of the modern ideal of scientific neutrality and objectivity."¹³⁶

However, today's Christian thinkers are often ambivalent about the shift to postmodernism. For example, Kevin Vanhoozer, writing about Derrida, argues,

---

130. Collective, *Postmodern Bible*, 189.

131. Nietzsche, "Natural History of Morals," 104. Cf. ibid., 105; cf. Williams, *Shadow of the Antichrist*, 209–16.

132. Lyotard, "Wall," 114.

133. Lyotard, "Universal History and Cultural Differences," 318.

134. Cf. Caputo, *Prayers and Tears*; Caputo, ed., *Deconstruction*, 20–25; Charlesworth, *Philosophy and Religion*, 157.

135. A Dutch theologian, journalist, educator, and politician (1837–1920); Dutch prime minister 1901–1905.

136. Naugle, *Worldview*, 23–24.

Like Kant, he correctly perceives, as a philosopher, the implications for knowledge and interpretation of the death of God; henceforth, we have "only human" (e.g. fallible) knowledge, "only human" (e.g. relative) truth. Yet he sees further than Kant in perceiving that the loss of God leads to the loss of the knowing subject (the hero of modernity) as well. Derrida has correctly analyzed the modern situation, or at least an aspect of it, *but he has done so by bracketing out orthodox Christian beliefs.*[137]

Vanhoozer wants to recruit Derrida for his argument that knowledge rests on shaky foundations without God, but he realizes that Derrida's position is radically different to that of orthodox Christianity.

John Thornhill, on the other hand, affirms modernity in its revolt against a medievalism "gone to seed," though he finds fault with the Enlightenment thinkers for their narrow use of reason as a purely methodological instrument, their abandonment of the sense of meaning and purpose in human life, morality, and society by an exclusive concentration on "quantitative" measurement in the scientific methodology,[138] their failure to preserve what was good in medieval (and ancient) thought,[139] and their displacement of God from the center of the universe (in favor of humanity) so that religion was banished to the sidelines of private opinion.[140] He argues that, for all its faults, the project of modernity is compatible with Christianity and that "their concerns converge in a way which is important for the future of humanity."[141]

The relationship of postmodernism and Christianity is thus in a state of ferment and Christians have struggled to produce a coherent response to the issues raised by postmodernism, just as they did with the Enlightenment.

Postmodernist Influence on Christian Theology

Some contemporary theologians and Christian philosophers have responded to the postmodernist shift by reinterpreting Christian theology in the light of insights and themes derived from postmodernist thinking. As might be expected, such reinterpretations have taken a variety of forms. The

---

137. Vanhoozer, *Is There a Meaning?*, 52 (italics original).
138. Thornhill, *Modernity*, 24.
139. Ibid., 18–20.
140. Ibid., 139.
141. Ibid.,, 179.

following four categories of postmodern theologies were derived from Terrence Tilley's classification of ten alternative approaches.[142]

A. "Postmodern Dissolutions"

Perhaps the most radically deconstructive postmodern theologian has been Mark C. Taylor. His thought is well expressed, if not exactly explained, in his book *Erring*.[143] After attacking theologians who try in vain to go back to past thinking to find answers to difficult problems,[144] Taylor spent much of *Erring* "deconstructing" four key concepts of traditional (Christian) theology: God, self, history, and book—all of which are overturned in some way by the "death of God," Taylor's Nietzschean starting point.[145] His deconstructive criticism sought to unravel "the very fabric of most Western theology and philosophy" by attacking from within so that it "subverts the hierarchical system of theological concepts" and thus "creates a new opening for the religious imagination."[146] Taylor disavowed a systematic rationalist approach to theology in favor of one that wanders around the boundaries of thought and "is neither *properly* theological nor nontheological, theistic nor atheistic, religious nor secular, believing nor nonbelieving."[147]

Taylor traced how "the humanistic atheist denies God in the name of self by transferring the attributes of the divine Creator to the human creature,"[148] but showed how this leads ironically to "the disappearance of the self," the end of history (as a "unified totality"), and the defeat of the attempt to "master" reality by "overcoming absence and repressing difference."[149] Modernity's critique of religion turned back on itself, so to speak. But in Taylor's "deconstructive a/theology," "the death of God" leads us to radically interpret the notion of God, the doctrine of Christ, and other

---

142. Tilley, *Postmodern Theologies*.

143. Taylor, *Erring*.

144. Ibid., 6.

145. According to Johnson ("Rethinking Theology," 7), however, this is a misconceived starting point. The "God" who is dead is not the living God of Scripture, the Abba of Jesus, but the philosophical "God of classic theism."

146. Taylor, *Erring*, 10–11; what he call elsewhere a "thought experiment" (ibid., 17).

147. Ibid., 12.

148. Ibid., 13.

149. Ibid., 13–15.

concepts of theology.[150] Traditional themes in Christian theology are abandoned, called into question, or radically reinterpreted.

Don Cupitt too accepted the thinking of postmodernism as a starting point: "the age of Authority, of grand institutions, of legitimating myths and capital-T Truth is over,"[151] and Westerners should "reverse our received worldview and assumptions" based on "the metaphysics of presence"[152] in favor of language-based philosophy (that is, one in which language is the starting point and ultimate reality) like his "Energetic Spinozism."[153] This was allied with, or expressed through, what Cupitt called "Poetical Theology," which is a view of Christian doctrine as "epic narrative poetry"[154] that functions (in sociological fashion) as the law defining Christians as against other believers and that is "wide open to endlessly-varied reinterpretation and re-enactment."[155] I have found both writers stimulating but confusing; like Derrida, their postmodern form of expression trades in ambiguity, tension, and density of language.

B. "Constructive Postmodernisms"

David Ray Griffin has attempted to provide a very different kind of postmodern Christian critique of modernity that specifically rejects deconstruction and poststructuralism in favor of a "revisionary" approach that nonetheless challenges many of the ideas of modernity.[156]

The main problem of modernity, from Griffin's perspective, was its individualism and anthropocentric dualism that saw nature as a resource for human use rather than seeing humans as part of nature. Hence the crisis of ecology:

> What is the biggest of all stories? It is that one of the millions of species of life on our planet has now, in our century, developed the power to threaten not only its own existence but also that of most of the other species of life on our planet. This has never happened before.[157]

---

150. Ibid., 15.
151. Cupitt, "Post-Christianity," 218.
152. Ibid., 220.
153. Ibid., 221–25.
154. Ibid., 226.
155. Ibid., 227.
156. Griffin, *Archetypal Process*, 6–7, as quoted in Tilley, *Postmodern Theologies*, 17. Cf. Griffin, ed., *Spirituality and Society*, x.
157. Griffin, *Postmodern Politics*, 70, as quoted in Tilley, *Postmodern Theologies*, 26.

Where Griffin differed from some ecological thinkers, however, was in his attempt to find a theological basis for addressing the planetary crisis in the panentheism of process theology,[158] rooted in the thought of Alfred North Whitehead.[159] This arose from his diagnosis of the movement in modernism from a "disenchanted" nature (the first—theistic—stage of modernism) to a "desouled" world, a destructive form of materialism, in modernism's second stage.[160]

Griffin called for a postmodern spirituality that restores some elements of the premodern but retains the good features of the modern era.[161] Specifically, he advocated a turn from individualism to a relational view of human identity, a turn from modernist dualism and materialism to "organicism," embracing ecological concern alongside emphasis on human welfare, a turn from a modernist obsession with the present to a respect for tradition and concern for the long-term future of the planet,[162] and a rejection of *both* modernist materialism *and* traditional supernaturalist views of God[163] in favor of an emphasis on the immanence of the divine accessible through "a nonsensory level of perception."[164] His new worldview thus has a postmodernist ecological center.[165] Griffin's thinking is relatively easy to follow but his spirituality seems to be so broad as to be almost vacuous.

C. Postliberalism

A different quasi-postmodernist theology has been expressed by the theologians known as "postliberals."[166] Postliberals sought to examine how reality looks from within a biblical framework,[167] but without making any universal

---

158. Tilley, *Postmodern Theologies*, 20. Cf. Griffin, ed., *Spirituality and Society*, 17, where he calls this *"naturalistic panentheism."*

159. Cf. Griffin, "Liberation Theology," 135–43.

160. Tilley et al., *Postmodern Theologies*, 19. Cf. Griffin, "Peace and the Postmodern Paradigm," 144–45.

161. Griffin, "Postmodern Spirituality," 2.

162. Ibid., 14–17.

163. Ibid., 4–6, 14–16; idem, "Peace and Paradigm," 145–46; idem, *Varieties of Postmodern Theology*, 1–3.

164. Ibid., 17. This concept is derived from Whitehead (Griffin, "Liberation Theology," 140–41).

165. Tilley, *Postmodern Theologies*, 25.

166. Sometimes known as the "New Yale" school (ibid., 89).

167. Or what are the rules, or grammar, of the Christian "language game," using the categories of Wittgenstein (Tilley, *Postmodern Theologies*, 91–92)?

claims that this is how the world really is. As George Lindbeck, one of the founders of the postliberal move, put it,

> Intratextual theology redescribes reality within the scriptural framework rather than translating Scripture into extra-scriptural categories. It is the text, so to speak, which absorbs the world rather than the world the text.[168]

This approach resembles postmodernism in its emphasis on particular and local truth as opposed to universal truth discernible by human reason. Thus Christian doctrines are understood as the rules that govern and constitute the Christian community (the regulative or rule theory of doctrine)[169] rather than universal or absolute truths, a concept similar to the idea of "language games."

Lindbeck thus rejected the "cognitivist" or "propositionalist" view of doctrine, which insists that doctrinal truths must be true always and everywhere (partly because it is unhelpful for ecumenical dialogue[170]) in favor of a "cultural-linguistic" approach.[171] However, his view does not preclude Christians making truth claims and he was equally opposed to the traditional liberal "experiential expressivist" view of doctrine.[172] Many aspects of postliberalism are attractive but, like most postmodernism, it doesn't seem to be able to articulate a solid reason to believe in Christianity as opposed to a different faith; in fact, it eschews such an effort.

D. Theologies of Communal Praxis

This group of postmodern theologies has been distinguished particularly by an emphasis on the political nature of truth. Liberation theology, for example, sees that "Classic European theology has been not only the dominant theology, but the theology of the dominant."[173]

Liberation theologians emphasized the social location of the theologian. "Theology grows out of the theologian's experience, out of the theologian's authenticity, and out of the theologian's social location," whether it

---

168. Lindbeck, *Nature of Doctrine*, 118. Cf. comment in Grenz and Franke, *Beyond Foundationalism*, 6.

169. Lindbeck, *Nature of Doctrine*, 18. Cf. Tilley, *Postmodern Theologies*, 94–95.

170. Tilley, *Postmodern Theologies*, 99.

171. Lindbeck, *Nature of Doctrine*, 18.

172. Tilley, *Postmodern Theologies*, 97–100.

173. Ibid., 123.

be a comfortable seminary or a slum.¹⁷⁴ More importantly, they consciously took the side of the "other."¹⁷⁵ They sought to read the Bible and history from the perspective of the poor, the "underside,"¹⁷⁶ but without dividing history into secular and sacred; rather "the history of salvation is the very heart of human history"¹⁷⁷ viewed as a "Christo-finalized" history.¹⁷⁸

Postmodernist feminist theology also challenged traditional modern and premodern attitudes, perspectives, and truths, redescribing history, society, theology, etc. from a "postpatriarchal" perspective. For example, one early postmodernist feminist theologian, Sharon Welch, posited "a relativist limitation of truth claims and a qualified nihilism, an acceptance of the fact that might does shape reality . . ."¹⁷⁹ Her position flowed from her conviction that "The ideal of universal or absolute truth is intrinsically correlated with oppression."¹⁸⁰ Specifically, she criticized Western theology; for example, linking what she calls "the erotics of domination" with belief in an omnipotent God.¹⁸¹ Her god is totally immanent, defined as our "relational power," and she celebrates "a presence that is both healing and fragile, constitutive of life and unambiguously present in the human condition . . . [but] absent in the atrocities of history and in humankind's despoliation of the earth."¹⁸² Such a concept resembles the panentheism of Griffin.

Alternate Christian Responses

Moving beyond Tilley's four categories of postmodern theology, we find many Christian writers who felt that the demise of modernity opened new

---

174. Ibid., 121.

175. Gutierrez, *Truth Shall Make You Free*, 7, as quoted in Tilley, *Postmodern Theologies*, 124.

176. Tilley, *Postmodern Theologies*, 125–26.

177. Gutierrez, *Truth Shall Make You Free*, 124, as quoted in Tilley, *Postmodern Theologies*, 126.

178. Gutierrez, *Truth Shall Make You Free*, 126, as quoted in Tilley, *Postmodern Theologies*, 126.

179. Welch, *Communities of Resistance*, 84, as quoted in Tilley, *Postmodern Theologies*, 132.

180. Welch, *Communities of Resistance*, 72, as quoted in Tilley, *Postmodern Theologies*, 132. Cf. ibid., 135–36.

181. Tilley, *Postmodern Theologies*, 133–34. Welch sees the idea of a transcendent God as infected with human power and domination (cf. ibid., 140).

182. Welch, *Feminist Ethic of Risk*, 177, as quoted in Tilley, *Postmodern Theologies*, 140.

apologetic windows for Christianity. Diogenes Allen,[183] for example, saw the breakdown of four key modernist assumptions (a self-contained universe, a secular basis for ethics, progress, and the inherent goodness of knowledge) as making room for Christianity to be taken seriously by postmoderns.[184] For example, Christianity could be shown to have explanatory power for some of our commonly held ideas, such as that of human value.[185]

Similarly, Alister McGrath rejoiced that Christian apologetics "no longer labors under the tedious limitations of the intensely restrictive Enlightenment worldview, fettered by the illusions and pretensions of pure reason,"[186] though the postmodernist attack on objective truth was just as problematic.[187]

For many Christian thinkers, however, this apologetic opportunity required a change in some of the concepts used to explain and communicate Christianity to a postmodern world.[188] In particular, Grenz suggests that "The postmodern situation requires that we embody the gospel in a manner that is *post-individualistic, post-rationalistic, post-dualistic,* and *post-noeticentric*."[189]

There might be some dangers here. For example, Middleton and Walsh urged that "There is a sense, then, in which genuine faithfulness to the authority of Scripture means that we must go not only beyond the biblical text but sometimes even *against* the text."[190] Does this imply that postmodern thinking is to be used as an external "control" in biblical hermeneutics? By reinterpreting Scripture in the light of postmodern thinking, Christians can perhaps gain a platform for effective apologetics. However, the risk is that in so doing Christians may take on board too much of the new trends and end up with nothing distinctive to say, somewhat like many of the classic theological liberals.

For many Christians, the hermeneutical issues raised by postmodernists are particularly sensitive, since Christian faith is largely defined in relation to a specific text, the Bible. Some more orthodox Christian thinkers have claimed that postmodernist approaches to hermeneutics tend to be

---

183. Allen, "Christian Values," 20–55.
184. Ibid., 21–25.
185. Ibid., 25–27.
186. McGrath, *Passion for Truth*, 188.
187. Ibid., 189.
188. Grenz, *Primer*, 174. Cf. Grenz and Franke, *Beyond Foundationalism*, 10.
189. Grenz, *Primer*, 167. The prefix "post-" is probably more for effect (and parallels with postmodernism, etc.) than because all of these stances are *after* the opposite view.
190. Middleton and Walsh, *Truth Is Stranger*, 184.

destructive of meaning. For example, Kevin Vanhoozer, in his lengthy monograph provocatively entitled *Is There a Meaning in This Text?*,[191] criticized the various postmodernist approaches to the interpretation of texts. Summing up the postmodernist approach as "incredulity toward meaning,"[192] Vanhoozer classified[193] the postmodernist thinkers about interpretation as either "Undoers" (deconstructionists such as Derrida), "Users" (pragmatists such as Rorty or Fish), "Unbelievers" (hermeneutical nihilists following in the steps of Nietzsche),[194] and "Usurpers" who use a text "to propound one's own ideology."[195] For Vanhoozer, theories of hermeneutics do not stand alone: "*textual meaning will only be as determinate and decidable as the conception of reality that it ultimately presupposes*";[196] and, "Behind these debates about the nature of interpretation lie conflicting visions of what it is to be authentically human . . . whether there is determinate meaning to human life."[197]

For Vanhoozer,

> Two contrasting interpretations of interpretation now compete for the soul of Western culture. One seeks to decipher and to locate a stable determinate meaning; the other affirms the freeplay of signs and gives up the search for some vantage point outside language. The one seeks understanding; the other seeks to avoid being taken in.[198]

In other words, Vanhoozer saw a clash of worldviews in the changes involved in postmodern hermeneutics. Nowhere is this clash more significant than in the interpretation of the Bible itself.[199]

---

191. An obvious parody of Fish's *Is There a Text in This Class?*

192. Vanhoozer, *Is There a Meaning?*, 16.

193. Somewhat less than neatly. Deconstruction ends up fitting into two of Vanhoozer's categories: Undoers and Unbelievers.

194. Vanhoozer, *Is There a Meaning?*, 38, 52–58.

195. Ibid., 185.

196. Ibid., 123 (italics original).

197. Ibid., 138.

198. Ibid., 135. Thus, "For Undoers the 'best' reading is the one that challenges and overturns the dominant ideology by exposing and dismantling it, even if that means reading against the apparent sense of the text" (ibid., 167). Comp. the polemical attack on postmodernist views of truth in Groothuis, *Truth Decay*, 10.

199. Compare the extended discussion of similar issues in Sutcliffe, *Is There an Author?*

Postmodernism and Interpretation of the Bible

"In recent years a diverse host of literary and cultural criticisms have migrated into the land of modern biblical studies,"[200] claimed a group of postmodernist biblical scholars and theologians in 1995. They contended that Enlightenment approaches to biblical hermeneutics were influenced by the same mindset as other discourses of modernity.[201] The independent individual interpreter stood as the subject over against the Bible as the object of study, bringing their critical analysis to bear on the issues of interpretation, "mastering" the text by a process of critical examination,[202] assuming that there was a "right" answer to every question raised, corresponding with the actual facts,[203] which could be established by scientific and historical study conducted by objective, unprejudiced scholars.

The degree of objectivity and "scientific" results that flowed out of such critical study was probably more asserted than real, as illustrated by Tyrell's famous criticism of nineteenth-century critics like Adolf von Harnack: "The Christ that Harnack sees, looking back through nineteen centuries of catholic darkness, is only the reflection of a liberal Protestant face, seen at the bottom of a deep well."[204]

Many recent critics have drawn attention to significant weaknesses in such modern approaches to biblical hermeneutics. First, they pointed to the difficulty for contemporary interpreters, with their own cultural, ideological, and/or theological baggage, in seeking to enter into the mindset of the ancient authors.[205] Further, it was argued that an objective, disinterested, neutral interpretation of the Bible is impossible,[206] for "every biblical reader comes to the text with expectations and preconceptions, with hope and imagination."[207] Even scientific, "objective" analysis involves "a creative construction of the reader," at least in part.[208] Thus, "the widespread

---

200. Collective, *Postmodern Bible*, 12.

201. Cf. ibid., 139.

202. Cf. McKnight, *Post-Modern Use*, 106.

203. Cf. Hatina, "Intertextuality and Historical Criticism," 30.

204. George Tyrell, as quoted in McGrath, *Passion for Truth*, 29.

205. Collins, ed., *Feminist Perspectives on Biblical Scholarship*, 3. Cf. Collective, *Postmodern Bible*, 277–78.

206. Fowler ("Postmodern Biblical Criticism," 22) calls this line of criticism "one grand index of the postmodern."

207. Collective, *Postmodern Bible*, 278.

208. McKnight, *Post-Modern Use*, 175.

philosophical and political turn in recent literary studies has had the effect of discrediting terms such as *disinterested* and *objective*."[209]

Postmodern developments in hermeneutics suggest that there is not necessarily one true meaning of the text—the author's intention or the grammatical/literal meaning of the text.[210] For postmodernist interpreters, the only condition of readers making meaning was that they do not claim totality of understanding and they acknowledge that "our representations of and discourses about what the text meant and how it means are inseparable from what we *want* it to mean, from how we *will* it to mean."[211]

As McKnight points out, the perception of biblical texts has been affected by the different worldviews of readers as well as developments within a particular worldview.[212] Recent critics have been willing to accept multiple meanings, seeing every interpretation as colored by the reader's perspective, even if that perspective is "historical-critical." Thus, "the contemporary reader's 'intending' of the text is not the same as that of the ancient author and/or the ancient readers. This is not possible, necessary, or desirable."[213] In fact, modern criticism tended to turn the Bible into "an historical relic, an antiquarian artifact"[214] unrelated to contemporary culture. As Sandra Schneiders wittily asserted, "the scholars seemed to be caught in an infinite historical regress, tracing the ever more remote explanation of the ever more fragmented text into an ever receding antiquity that was ever less relevant to the concerns of the contemporary believer."[215]

Finally, "postmodern readings demonstrate that traditional interpretations are themselves enactments of domination or, in simpler terms, power plays."[216] This problem has particularly been highlighted by feminist critics. For example, T. Drorah Setel wrote, "As a scholarly pursuit, contemporary

---

209. Anderson and Moore, eds., *Mark and Method*, 15. Cf. Fiorenza, "Remembering the Past," 47.

210. Jack, *Texts Reading Texts*, 21.

211. Collective, *Postmodern Bible*, 14.

212. Such as the understanding of Romans before and after Augustine, as traced by Krister Stendahl (McKnight, *Post-Modern Use*, 145–47).

213. McKnight, *Post-Modern Use*, 150. Cf. Fiorenza, "Remembering the Past," 51. Fiorenza points out, however, that this does not mean that historical judgments are "totally relativistic": "They are open to and necessarily subject to scholarly scrutiny" (ibid., 53).

214. Collective, *Postmodern Bible*, 2. Cf. McKnight, *Post-Modern Use*, 173–74.

215. Schneiders, "Postmodern Message," 61

216. Collective, *Postmodern Bible*, 3. Cf. ibid., 4.

work supports assumptions that are reflective of the patriarchal nature of our society."[217]

As a result of such critiques of modern analysis of the Bible, many recent biblical scholars and critics have turned to postmodernism for new approaches.

Alison Jack, for example, approached biblical studies with explicit postmodernist presuppositions. "The original form of a text, its author's intention and the context of its intended readers all lose their privileged position as guarantors of the text's meaning." Rather meaning is located in "the history of the discourse: the author-text relationship is replaced by the reader-text relationship." Moreover "the unavoidable role of ideology in this relationship is acknowledged, and the politics of any reading is laid bare." There is no center or presence, but "only the multiple meanings of each reader . . . inevitably conditioned by their experiences and all the other texts they have encountered."[218]

Similarly, *The Postmodern Bible*,[219] a series of essays on criticism of the Bible by a collective of postmodernist scholars, called for

> a foundational shift in biblical criticism *away* from a hermeneutical project whose goal is to find the correct key to unlock the unitary truth of the text and *towards* projects focused on multiplicities of meanings, interpretations examining layers of ideology and shifting meanings—in short, toward cultural critique.[220]

Such projects have included the use of postmodernist hermeneutical approaches in biblical studies: reader-response criticism; deconstructive criticism (which involves "very close readings of specific texts" and "makes explicit what is hidden, repressed, or denied in any ordinary reading");[221] rhetorical criticism ("the study of 'the means by which a text establishes and manages its relationship to its audience in order to achieve a particular effect,'"[222] applicable to both biblical texts and the work of biblical scholars);[223] psychoanalytic criticism (based on the insights of Freud, Lacan,

---

217. Setel, "Feminist Insights," 35.
218. Jack, *Texts Reading Texts*, 28–29. Cf. ibid., 89.
219. Collective (George Aichele et al.), *Postmodern Bible*.
220. Ibid., 225–26.
221. Ibid., 130. Cf. Jack, "Out of the Wilderness," 151; Moore, "Deconstructive Criticism," 86–87.
222. Collective, *Postmodern Bible*, 158.
223. Ibid., 159–68, 182–83.

Kristeva and Irigary, among others);[224] various forms of feminist criticism[225] (exposing both traditional biblical criticism and the Bible itself as "narratives of male mastery")[226] and ideological criticism, which was described by the *Postmodern Bible* as "a deliberate effort to read against the grain,"[227] "concerned with theorizing and critiquing... processes of meaning production as social and political realities,"[228] driven especially by liberationist theologies[229] or perspectives.[230] Following this stream of thinking, prominent late twentieth-century theologian and biblical scholar Elisabeth Schüssler Fiorenza argued that "*the* litmus test for invoking Scripture as the Word of God must be whether or not biblical texts and traditions seek to end relations of domination and exploitation."[231] Once again we see here the privileging of politically "progressive" perspectives.

Intertextuality is another postmodernist approach being employed in biblical criticism. Postmodern intertextuality emphasizes the ubiquity and instability of intertextual relationships, the reader's role in constructing them, and consequently the multiplicity of possible ways of interpreting a text,[232] and "the bias of individual interpreters" in an ideological sense.[233]

All such readings may be labeled "postmodernist" since they tend to produce "multiple rather than singular meanings, an open rather than closed narrative structure, textual tensions and ambiguities as an alternative

---

224. For instance, Moore ("Deconstructive Criticism," 98) follows Derrida in positing "a 'textual unconscious,' an unpredictable and hence uncontrollable excess of meaning that simmers within any linguistic production, ever ready to spill over."

225. Collective, *Postmodern Bible*, 225–71. Cf. the classification of feminist approaches to biblical studies in Osiek, "Feminist and the Bible," 100–103.

226. Collective, *Postmodern Bible*, 14. Cf. Schneiders, "Postmodern Message?," 65–71; Anderson, "Dancing Daughter," 106–11; Abraham, "Feminist Hermeneutics and Pentecostal Spirituality," 6–7; Brooten, "Early Christian Women," 65, 82.

227. Collective, *Postmodern Bible*, 275.

228. Ibid., 272.

229. Much of the chapter in *The Postmodern Bible* on ideological criticism is about liberation theologies which "attempt to interpret the Bible out of their own concrete political, economic and social circumstances" (ibid., 281).

230. Postcolonial criticism, which reads the Bible and its interpretation in the light of the experience and perspective of those subjugated by modern empires, is an example of this. Cf. Sugirtharajah, *Postcolonial Reconfigurations*, 3–4.

231. As quoted in Collective, *Postmodern Bible*, 248. Cf. Fiorenza, "Words of Prophecy," 4.

232. Moyise, "Intertextuality and Old Testament," 17–18. Cf. Hatina, "Intertextuality and Historical Criticism," 28–43; Jack, *Texts Reading Texts*, 89.

233. Moyise, "Intertextuality and Old Testament," 41.

to resolution and clarity."[234] For example, "ideological criticism is an affirmation of difference as a principle that precludes univocal, singular readings of texts, cultures, interests and ideologies."[235] But not all readings are legitimate. For example, Jack criticizes another reader for "accepting the text even when its message is, for example, misogynist," and trying to *understand* it, so that "he can never judge it by the standards of today."[236] In a similar fashion, *The Postmodern Bible* notes with respect to feminist criticism that "Such an argument shifts the location of an interpretation's authority to values *external* to the text."[237]

These frank statements imply that, just as modern criticism of the Bible tended to impose its set of values on the process—valorizing modern science, for example, and dismissing the supernatural—so postmodernists also have installed their agendas, values, and politics, within which they view every question of interpretation. One kind of mastery of the Bible has been replaced by another. In other words, both modernist and postmodernist criticism of the Bible involves a clash of worldviews; the difference is that postmodernists are more honest about it. However, are they any more tolerant of other possibilities than the modernists were? And how do their approaches affect the reading of Revelation?

Postmodernism and the Book of Revelation

The Book of Revelation was affected, like every other part of the Bible, by the passage from premodern to modern hermeneutics. As Christopher Rowland explains, "There comes a moment at the beginning of the Enlightenment when there is a real parting of the ways over the interpretation of the Apocalypse."[238] Many biblical scholars influenced by the Enlightenment were highly critical of Revelation and its teachings,[239] and, according to Wainwright, "By the end of the nineteenth century, contemporary-historical criticism dominated scholarly approaches to the book."[240] On the other hand, fundamentalists, who rejected these approaches, adopted a similar epistemology to the modernists in their search for a literal hermeneutic that

---

234. Collective, *Postmodern Bible*, 135.

235. Ibid., 301–2.

236. Jack, *Texts Reading Texts*, 31

237. Collective, *Postmodern Bible*, 248 (italics added).

238. Rowland, Foreword in Moyise, ed., *Studies in Revelation*, ix. Cf. Wainwright, *Mysterious Apocalypse*, 108–9.

239. Wainwright, *Mysterious Apocalypse*, 109–15.

240. Ibid., 134.

would make Revelation speak a clear *predictive* word to the modern era and thus justify itself as Holy Scripture.

More recent critical studies of Revelation have started to take a somewhat different approach to the book, while not necessarily discarding "modern" methods. The failure of modern critics to come to a consensus on its meaning, the unusual use of language (especially symbolism) in the text, the endless variety of approaches and interpretations of even the most apparently straightforward passages, the incredibly rich and varied impacts the book has had on literature and the arts over the centuries, and the ethical difficulties it raises for contemporary readers all seem to beg for new approaches to be taken. And such readings have gradually been forthcoming.

Rejecting the traditional Protestant view of the "perspicuity of Scripture"[241] and the traditional Catholic emphasis on an authoritative interpretive tradition, postmodern critics of Revelation have tended to place emphasis on the many conflicting interpretations offered of this text over the centuries, concluding that a single correct interpretation is an impossible, and perhaps undesirable, goal.

Earlier twentieth-century scholars who saw Revelation as somewhat incoherent in its present form often explained this on the basis of sources and the process of redaction.[242] This was based on the assumption that a clear meaning must be obtainable somehow.[243] More recently, for example, A. Y. Collins argued that Revelation "is a very carefully planned work with clear indications of its overall plan which have very seldom and never adequately been noticed."[244] Gregory Linton, however, commented, "One may wonder how its plan can be so clear and yet never noticed before her study."[245] He suggested that the many *different* "clear and recognizable" structures argued for by scholars have been imposed on the text rather than discovered there.[246] The gaps in a text like Revelation, which are at times "yawning chasms," were not then to be resolved by the process of composition (source criticism) but rather seen as possibilities in the reader's reception of the work:

---

241. The idea that the Bible can be understood clearly by any reader, at least in its main teaching. This was a key plank of the Reformation agenda.

242. E.g., novelist D. H. Lawrence saw Revelation, along source-critical lines, as "a multi-layered text, which has gone through many reworkings and revisions" (Jack, *Texts Reading Texts*, 169).

243. E.g., Caird, *Revelation of St. John*, 3.

244. Collins, *Combat Myth*, 1.

245. Linton, *Intertextuality in Revelation*, 179.

246. Ibid., 185.

"Where are places of silence, contradiction, and incoherence that demand the active participation of readers if they are to make sense of the text?"[247]

Whereas modern interpretation of biblical texts tended to see the author's intention as the key to a correct or valid interpretation of the text, postmodern readers put the weight on the perspective of the reader.[248] Thus Tim Long called for a focus on "real readers" reading Revelation, who honestly declare who they are and what motivates them, and share their readings with us in an egalitarian way, as individual readings that make no pretense to objectivity, though they take the text seriously and use whatever skills and training they have to enhance their reading.[249]

The postmodern idea of intertextuality has also been used in similar ways to provide new insights into Revelation. For example, G. L. Linton[250] argued that Revelation is highly intertextual because "it has motivated readers to find many and far-ranging intertexts."[251] Highly intertextual texts that mix generic conventions are "writerly" or "open," allowing the readers greater space to construct their own meanings from the text. Revelation is "highly intertextual" and "open to multiple interpretations,"[252] the reader must decide which genre to use to interpret it,[253] and "its meaning is inexhaustible."[254]

Steve Moyise started a lively argument on the use of the Old Testament in Revelation, involving particularly Greg Beale and Jon Paulien, with his monograph on this topic published in 1995.[255] The debate began with Moyise's introduction of several concepts associated with postmodernist hermeneutics into the study of the use of the Old Testament in Revelation—specifically intertextuality, but also reader-response and deconstruction.[256]

According to Moyise,

> The task of intertextuality is to explore how the source text [in this case, the Old Testament] continues to speak through

---

247. Ibid., 205. Cf. Jack, *Texts Reading Texts*, 176; Pippin, *Death and Desire*, 87–88.

248. Cf. Moyise, ed., *Old Testament in the New*, 132.

249. Long, "Real Reader," 89–90.

250. Linton, *Intertextuality in Revelation*. A shorter version of Linton's views is found in his paper presented at the 1991 Society of Biblical Literature seminar, titled "Reading the Apocalypse as an Apocalypse."

251. Linton, *Intertextuality in Revelation*, 61.

252. Ibid., 141–42.

253. Ibid., 148–49.

254. Ibid., 163.

255. Moyise, *O.T. in Revelation*.

256. Moyise, "Intertextuality and Old Testament," 14, 41.

the new work [in this case, Revelation] and how the new work forces *new meanings* from the source text.²⁵⁷

Material taken from the source text (whether by quotation, allusion, or just echo) is placed in a new context in the new work; consequently, the original context is not totally determinative of its meaning and new meaning is found in (or created from) the source text by this process. For example, because Revelation does not signal allusions to the Old Testament by explicit quotation, "the reader is unsure whether he or she is reading John's words or words from another context."²⁵⁸ Thus the intention of the original source's author is also not determinative for its meaning:

> if an allusion points the reader to something outside of the text, it inevitably sets up a relationship between the two contexts which is in some sense unpredictable (*and out of the hands of the author*).²⁵⁹

This whole process illustrates that meaning is made by the reader of a text, not just its (original) author.²⁶⁰ Hence the meaning of any text is capable of multiple, even unlimited, extension by its readers and reusers.²⁶¹ Thus Moyise calls for a more dialectical or "interactive" approach to interpretation, whereby the reader enters into a dialogue with the text and its intertexts.²⁶² Clearly here the reader is king!

Many other postmodernist critics have emphasized the apparently negative position taken by Revelation towards the values and dominant discourses of its day.²⁶³ Brian Yhearm, for example, argued that John was obsessed with persecutions and overreacted strongly as an alienated sectarian. He "polemicizes against power, honor and wealth"²⁶⁴ and promotes a lifestyle incompatible with the culture of Asia and probably with that of most Christians there. Yhearm contrasted Revelation with the more eirenic attitude of Paul to the empire and the attitudes of *1 Peter* and *Ignatius*; these

---

257. Moyise, *O.T. in Revelation*, 111 (italics added).
258. Ibid., 137.
259. Ibid., 135 (italics added).
260. Ibid., 142–43. Comp. Mathewson, "Assessing Old Testament Allusions," 321.
261. Beale (*John's Use*, 31, 32, 33, 35, 37, 39, 40, 56, 57, 59) reacts strongly to this aspect in his critique of Moyise and others, especially Ruiz, repeatedly referring to them as generating the possibility of "new, endless meanings," "endlessly multiple meanings," "a fathomless pit of interpretative possibilities," "countless interpretations," and similar phrases.
262. Moyise, *O.T. in Revelation*, 145–46.
263. Cf. Jack, *Texts Reading Texts*, 103.
264. Yhearm, *Sitz im Leben*, 377.

writings "highlight the non-normative nature of Revelation"[265] in early Christianity. Similarly, Robert Royalty set up John's strong opposition to food offered to idols against the supposedly more lenient position of Paul.[266] These writers stressed the differences between Revelation and the rest of the New Testament, unlike some modernist interpreters who tried to reinterpret Revelation so as to minimize such differences, often in violation of the textual evidence.[267]

Many postmodern critics were also concerned about the tension between Revelation and contemporary Western values. For example, Jack argued that Revelation is a violent and anti-female work: "for women the text always needs deconstruction rather than reconstruction,"[268] and she called on readers to "reject the text as Scripture."[269]

Some critics influenced by liberation theology, however, saw in Revelation a cry for justice from the oppressed and a vision of a just new world. Pablo Richard, for example, contended that "Revelation is a liberating book, one full of hope; its utopia is political and unfolds in history." However, "within the church its function is one of critique of, and resistance to, the Hellenization of Christianity and its authoritarian and patriarchal institutionalization."[270] And Long saw Revelation as a kind of battleground, declaring that he wanted "to foreground the political polemic of Revelation" and expose "the readings of the North American Right."[271] Many recent commentators on Revelation, partly influenced by postcolonial reading, have seen it at least partly as a protest against, or exposé of, the unjust Roman Empire, and they frequently go on to draw parallels with modern imperialism, particularly that of the USA.[272] In fact, the idea that John's main target was imperial Rome is now almost a scholarly consensus.

The sensitivity of postmodern thinkers to issues of power in the creation and interpretation of texts has been exemplified by practices such as

---

265. Ibid., 354.

266. Royalty *Streets of Heaven*, 30–31. Cf. Fiorenza, "Words of Prophecy," 172. The emphasis on John's role in church conflicts, and particularly the idea that he was an antagonist of Paul, probably goes back to the work of nineteenth-century theologians like Ferdinand Christian Baur and Ernst Renan (Wainwright, *Mysterious Apocalypse*, 128–29).

267. Moyise, "Does the Lion?," 181–84.

268. Jack, *Texts Reading Texts*, 196. Cf. Jack, "Out of the Wilderness," 149–62.

269. Jack, *Texts Reading Texts*, 204.

270. Richard, *People's Commentary*, 3.

271. Long, "Real Reader," 90.

272. Some examples are Howard-Brook and Gwyther, *Unveiling Empire*, and Friesen, *Imperial Cults and the Apocalypse*.

"resisting reading" and rhetorical criticism. Here the reader exposes, resists, or rejects the values and aims of the author and seeks to recover "suppressed" or "rejected" voices alluded to in the text. Postmodern critics have often used rhetorical criticism as a means of understanding, and often resisting, the purposes of Revelation. However, in so doing they have inadvertently allowed the author's intention to reclaim center stage in interpretation, as the following examples demonstrate.

Yhearm, for example, saw the literary features of Revelation as part of John's rhetorical strategy to establish his authority over the seven churches of Asia. Hence John structured his vision report in Rev. 1 in such a way as to resemble commissioning narratives of both Old Testament prophets and New Testament apostles.[273] W. G. Carey suggested that John used extreme polemic and even imperialistic rhetoric, coupled with features of apocalyptic genre,[274] to establish his authority with his audience. Carey criticized other scholarly readers who "lack the rhetorical sensitivity to recognize John's use of standard apocalyptic resources—self-characterization, dialogues with heavenly beings, and the like—as literary devices," as opposed to describing real experiences.[275] According to Carey, John used a range of rhetorical devices to undermine the position of his opponents,[276] such as disidentification and remythologisation, identifying his enemies with persons, places, or concepts with negative connotations (such as Balaam).[277]

Robert Royalty Jr. agreed that "Revelation is a highly rhetorical text that tries to *do something*."[278] He argued that John combined all his opponents (including other Christians) into one group of Satan-deceived enemies in order to force the reader to choose between just two sides.[279] John used rhetorical strategies to undercut his opponents in the churches,[280] such as his "slanderous" attacks on "Jezebel";[281] because he felt threatened

---

273. Yhearm, *Sitz im Leben*, 94. According to Max Weber (*Economy and Society*, 1:440), a personal call was a crucial distinguishing feature of prophets.

274. Carey, "Ambigous Ethos," 173.

275. Carey, *Attention-Seeking Behavior*, 113.

276. Ibid., ch. 5.

277. Ibid., 207–10.

278. Royalty, *Streets of Heaven*, 10, 14. Royalty specifically describes Revelation's language as "epideictic rhetoric" (ibid., 126–28).

279. Ibid., 15, 28–29.

280. Ibid., 30–32, 152–54.

281. Ibid., 31–33.

by "the very presence of diversity in ethical and theological matters."²⁸² Thus Royalty set John up as an enemy of postmodern values.²⁸³

Other postmodernist writers focused on the question of genre in a different way. Rather than just studying Revelation in the light of genres of its time (prophecy, apocalyptic, letters, drama, liturgy), they related it to genres of other times. Pippin, for instance, saw Revelation as a form of fantasy, with elements of horror (such as the terrifying beasts), picking up a whole range of desires in the reader²⁸⁴ and expressing a utopian vision of the future.²⁸⁵ This does not just mean a "fairy story": "Fantasy literature does not claim to mirror reality directly; rather it illuminates the real world. . . . Its rhetoric is unreal, not providing escape, but allowing silent voices to speak and unconscious desires to be enacted."²⁸⁶

Alison Jack, however, read Revelation as a nightmare. Jack first pointed to the anarchy of the text, where "Nothing is stable and fixed: the scene changes rapidly from one sphere to another, as does the perspective of the watcher."²⁸⁷ She described the role of Jesus (such as his threats to break in on the unprepared) as mercurial, even sinister, rather than reassuring. Moreover no one could escape being branded by either God or the devil, "each person's eternal fate is ultimately outwith [sic.] their control," and "the warnings and admonitions of the figures who are met in the world of the nightmare only heighten the anxiety of the reader."²⁸⁸

All these critics were thus self-consciously interpreting and addressing Revelation in the light of the values of the end of the second millennium. At times, they tried to co-opt the text to serve their own social-political positions; alternatively they rejected Revelation because its values are in conflict with theirs. However, this process has thrown up useful insights into the text, and the critics concerned would argue that all readers follow similar strategies in responding to texts.

According to Steve Moyise, postmodern interpreters of Revelation basically have two choices. If they simply want to understand the text more, they should allow multiple interpretations, just as modern physics has had to realize that light behaves both like waves *and* particles. But if they have

---

282. Ibid., 28. Comp. ibid., 33; Fiorenza, "Words of Prophecy," 17.

283. For a more sympathetic rhetorical analysis of Revelation, see DeSilva, *Seeing Things John's Way*.

284. Pippin, *Death and Desire*, 89–91.

285. Ibid., 92–96.

286. Ibid., 95–96. Cf. ibid., 100.

287. Jack, *Texts Reading Texts*, 198.

288. Ibid., 199–201.

some other goal ("promote the Christian faith, empower oppressed people or some other ideological purpose"), they should resist readings that contradict that goal, even though some might "call this an imposition on the text,"[289] provided that they do not pretend that their ideologically informed reading is the only true interpretation.

But what we are seeing in postmodern reading of Revelation, I believe, is an interaction of worldviews. Modernist readers sought to play down, if not eliminate, the supernatural or spiritual aspects of this text, such as John's claim to have seen a vision of real angels and the like, and to reinterpret the text sympathetically to bring it into line with the ethic of nonviolence perceived in, say, the Sermon on the Mount, thus reclaiming Revelation for a liberal viewpoint. Postmodernist readers have also resisted John's claims to spiritual or supernatural experience, interpreting them as rhetorical and political strategies, and have openly condemned the extreme positions and ethically dangerous language they found in Revelation, criticizing Revelation from their own progressive position. Wainwright's comments seem to apply to both modernist and postmodernist scholars:

> a large number of theologians and scholars evaluate the Apocalypse by standards that are not wholly derived from its contents. They read it in the light of ideas of love, justice and peace that are more clearly stated in other parts of the Bible. . . . They treat the teaching of other parts of the Bible or the dictates of their own consciences as a superior authority to the Apocalypse.[290]

But what would happen if we took the worldview and perspective of Revelation as a starting point, rather than evaluating it wholly from a modern or postmodern standpoint? Is it possible to construct a dialogue between Revelation and the emerging postmodern worldview?

---

289. Moyise, "Does the Lion?," 193.
290. Wainwright, *Mysterious Apocalypse*, 115–16.

CHAPTER 2

Revelation in Context

THE PROJECT IN WHICH I am engaged in this book involves defining or constructing a Christian worldview for a postmodern era, through a dialogue with an ancient Christian text, the Book of Revelation. In order for such an attempt to have any credibility, I need to establish that a distinctly Christian worldview exists, as opposed to one that is premodern, modern, postmodern, or derived from a particular period or place. So, for example, does Revelation itself unveil or imply a distinctly Christian worldview—distinct, that is, from worldviews of the late first century, when Revelation was written?

Is there anything new in this worldview compared to the worldviews common in the first century AD? To what extent may John's thinking on reality and knowledge be explained successfully by the influence of Judaism, perhaps apocalyptic Judaism in particular, or the influence of the wider Mediterranean world in which this text was produced? Is the worldview of Revelation just another class of what might be called a "premodern" or ancient worldview, which was basically made out of date by the rise of modernity or modern science, or is there something in it that compels us to take it seriously in the twenty-first century?

John was not, of course, writing in a vacuum, but against a background of worldviews that he had inherited, been indoctrinated in, or become acquainted with, well before he "set pen to papyrus" in Revelation.[1] Therefore we must investigate to what degree the worldview expressed in Revelation is

---

1. Most likely John dictated his manuscript to a scribe.

the same as what we know of those first-century worldviews that John could reasonably be expected to have been influenced by.

It is well beyond the scope of this book to explore all the possible influences on Revelation from other worldviews, religions, and cultures of the ancient world.[2] All I can attempt is to examine the possible influence on John's worldview of the dominant worldviews he would have known, in particular the Hellenistic, Jewish, and Jewish apocalyptic worldviews, because all of these must have been part of his heritage as a Jew living in the Roman Empire, speaking Greek, and moving in a Hellenistic world (such as the cities of Asia to which Revelation is addressed).

REVELATION AND THE ANCIENT MEDITERRANEAN WORLDVIEW

The Ancient Mediterranean Worldview

In spite of the diversity in thinking across different cultures of John's day, there does seem to have been a broad worldview consensus common to the various peoples of the first-century Mediterranean world, often called "premodern" by today's scholars, which had several defining characteristics. Many of these were also reflected in what is called "Hellenism," the specific worldview of the Greeks that virtually took over the Mediterranean and Ancient Near East after the conquests of Alexander the Great.

Belief in Spiritual and Supernatural Realities

First, they took spiritual realities very seriously. Most of them saw a strong relationship between spiritual things and earthly, natural events, and accepted supernatural and paranormal experiences and revelation as valid "windows" on reality. Thus people tended to attribute many "natural" events to supernatural or theological causes. For example, Vermes asserts,

---

2. Influences have been posited from Iran, Babylon, and other cultures that John probably had little direct contact with. This does not mean that such influences can be dismissed, but they are probably influential indirectly, that is through one of the worldviews I will attempt to examine in this chapter. For example, the Hellenistic worldview had clearly been influenced by cultures and religions of the East (Hengel, *Judaism and Hellenism*, 1:107-8) and the Jewish worldview had been developed in interaction with such cultures as the Babylonian and Iranian during the period before its clash with Hellenism.

> Instead of ascribing physical and mental illness to natural causes, Jesus' contemporaries saw the former as a divine punishment for sin instigated by the devil, and the latter as resulting from a direct demonic possession.[3]

This belief was not unique to Jews. In all cultures, similar ideas led many sick people to seek divine healing. For example, many (non-Jews) slept in temples of the Greek healing god Asclepius, hoping for a dream or vision promising healing.[4] The city of Pergamum, one of the cities whose church is addressed in Revelation, was a particular center of this cult.[5] In a different context, when lightning struck a section of the grounds of Octavius Augustus Caesar, this was interpreted by some as meaning that the god Apollo wanted a temple in that place.[6] Having little faith in technology or progress, ancient societies ascribed all events (good or bad) to persons, human or nonhuman.[7] A common example of this was belief in the "evil eye," meaning "the conviction that certain individuals, animals, demons or gods have the power to cause some negative effect on any object, animate or inanimate, on which they may look," which needed to be warded off by amulets, miniature phalluses, etc.[8]—a belief similar to the ideas of Papua New Guineans mentioned in chapter 1.

Aune writes that, "The world of the ancients was populated by multitudes of gods and daimones"[9] (including spirits of the deceased).[10] With some major exceptions, this Mediterranean worldview was polytheistic and syncretistic in religion. People tended to believe in the reality of all the gods worshiped by the various nations of the ancient world, and sometimes in their identity with gods of different names worshiped elsewhere. Thus, for example, the Hellenistic musical and gymnastic festival founded by Alexander the Great and held every five years in Tyre "included sacrifice to the guardian deity of the festival, the Tyrian Heracles-Melkart,"[11] the design of Greek temples "traditionally permitted different gods and mortals to

---

3. Vermes, *World of Judaism*, 8.

4. Aune, *Prophecy in Early Christianity*, 26; Green, *Alexander to Actium*, 487; Keener, *Miracles*, 1: 37–40.

5. Thomas, *Apocalypse*, 133.

6. Veyne, *Bread and Circuses*, 251.

7. Malina, *New Testament World*, 102–3; Fox, *Classical World*, 51.

8. Malina, *New Testament World*, 120–30.

9. Aune, *Prophecy in Early Christianity*, 33; Hengel, *Judaism and Hellenism*, 1:233.

10. Aune, *Prophecy in Early Christianity*, 26.

11. Hengel, *Judaism and Hellenism*, 1:73. This deity was identified with the Greek god Heracles (Portier-Young, *Apocalypse Against Empire*, 119).

share the temple with the main deity,"[12] and some early Hellenistic Jews even identified their God with the Zeus of the Phoenicians and Greeks.[13] The Greeks "had long been ready to accept alien forms of the divine into their pantheon,"[14] usually giving them Greek names, so they found "the exclusiveness of the Jewish conception of God strange and presumptuous."[15]

The gods were believed to be able to communicate with people. As David Aune argues,

> All cultures of the ancient Mediterranean world and the Near East had a revelatory worldview. It was assumed that communication between the human and divine worlds was necessary for achieving and maintaining social and individual welfare.[16]

Such communication took the form of divination,[17] prophetic oracles,[18] and narratives of miracles, dreams, visions, and journeys to otherworldly places,[19] sometimes conveyed in a state of inspired ecstasy.[20] Most people believed such oracles to be "truly messages from the gods,"[21] especially if received in "altered states of consciousness" or "ecstatic frenzy"[22]

---

12. Price, *Rituals and Power*, 146.

13. Hengel, *Judaism and Hellenism*, 1:94. This was one example of the "mass syncretization known as *theokrasia*," which took place during the Hellenistic era in respect of Zeus especially (Green, *Alexander to Actium*, 397).

14. Hengel, *Judaism and Hellenism*, 1:261. Cf. Walbank, *Hellenistic World*, 120. New gods were also "invented" where needed, for socio-political purposes, such as the cult of Sarapis, developed out of Egyptian and Greek antecedents under King Ptolemy I, which subsequently spread throughout the Greek and Roman world, supported by stories of miracles and visions experienced by his followers (Walbank, *Hellenistic World*, 121; Green, *Alexander to Actium*, 406–8).

15. Hengel, *Judaism and Hellenism*, 1:261.

16. Aune, *Literary Environment*, 231. Comp. Hengel, *Judaism and Hellenism*, 1:217, which claims that the "common basis" of the "spiritual milieu" of "the Hellenistic period from the beginning of the second century BC" is "the idea of '*higher wisdom by Revelation.*'" This explains why "During the Hellenistic and Roman periods there was a great respect for revelatory literature of all types," including the Septuagint (Aune, *Prophecy in Early Christianity*, 114).

17. Aune, *Prophecy in Early Christianity*, 23, 45, 82–83.

18. Cf. ibid., 23–79; and Green, *Alexander to Actium*, 593–95, on some of the forms these took.

19. Hengel, *Judaism and Hellenism*, 1:210.

20. Ibid., 216. An example of this is the "*engastrimythoi*," literally "ventriloquists," but in fact "mediums in a state of possession trance who spoke with a strange voice" (Aune, *Prophecy in Early Christianity*, 40–41).

21. Aune, *Prophecy in Early Christianity*, 32.

22. Ibid., 47.

and expressed in poetry.[23] It was believed that these oracles would always be fulfilled, but often in an unexpected way, as they were couched in ambiguous language.[24] Some of these oracles, however, were political in content,[25] and therefore could be a danger to the state, hence Augustus had over two thousand anonymous oracles collected and burnt.[26] Also, people who were dying were believed capable of foreseeing what would happen to their kindred, and hence their testaments were full of predictions and advice.[27]

The religious practices of most peoples were a combination of public, traditioned civic rituals[28] and more private, voluntary cults.[29] The Hellenistic period (after Alexander) witnessed significant shifts in the religious arena, however. Traditional Greek religion was in decline,[30] especially among the educated elite,[31] though there was at least nominal respect given to the Greek gods[32] and an ongoing belief in omens and the like.[33] Green points out that "the original force of the old myths was rapidly being lost in an increasingly secular, skeptical, and commercial age. Yet the emotional

---

23. Ibid., 50–51. According to Pieter Craffert, this way of thinking is normal for a "polyphastic" culture, which takes such states seriously as a source of understanding of "the mind, humankind, and the cosmos" (Craffert, "Altered States of Consciousness," 127).

24. Aune, *Prophecy in Early Christianity*, 51.

25. Ibid., 74–77.

26. Hengel, *Judaism and Hellenism*, 1:185–86; Aune, *Prophecy in Early Christianity*, 79.

27. Malina, *New Testament World*, 115. There are numerous examples of this in the Bible (e.g., Gen 49:1–28) and other Jewish literature, such as the *Testament of the Twelve Patriarchs*.

28. "Ancient religions were primarily public religions," says Price (*Rituals and Power*, 120).

29. Fox, *Classical World*, 55–56.

30. Walbank (Walbank, *Hellenistic World*, 209) alleges that "many people were at bottom agnostics or even atheists." The rise of Epicureanism tended to distance people from the gods, who had no interest in humanity (Green, *Alexander to Actium*, 207).

31. "We sometimes forget the stubborn, glacial resistance, at a lower level, to what must seem, in retrospect, a general collapse of faith" (Green, *Alexander to Actium*, 399, see also 588). For further discussion of skeptical attitudes to the supernatural among the ancients, see Keener, *Miracles*, 1:87–91.

32. For example, offering of sacrifices in connection with gymnasia (cf. Walbank, *Hellenistic World*, 183) or claiming traditional gods as patrons of a kingdom (ibid., 210–11). Similarly, the Roman games were officially religious festivals and gods were invited to banquets where sacrifices were offered to them (Veyne, *Bread and Circuses*, 210, 235).

33. As instanced by the way that King Seleucus supposedly obtained confirmation for the locations he had chosen for the new city of Antioch and its port by the flight of an eagle with sacrificial meat (Green, *Alexander to Actium*, 162).

need was as strong as ever," and was seeking satisfaction through assimilation of foreign cults, ruler worship, and astrology.[34] As a result, there was a great interest in the religion and wisdom of the East (mainly Babylon, Iran, and Egypt).[35] In the later Hellenistic period, there was a "resurgence of religious enthusiasm (in particular by way of magic and the more exotic foreign cults)"[36] and "a proliferation of private religious clubs."[37]

Another growing factor was the rise in ruler cults, also derived from the Greek contact with the East. This began as early as Alexander, who encouraged his court to practice an act of obeisance repulsive to Greeks and Macedonians of the era, but common for Persians, whose empire he was conquering.[38] Ruler cults subsequently became "an institution common to most of the hellenistic kingdoms"[39] and subsequently taken over by Rome.[40] Green argues that ruler worship helped fill the vacuum left by declining confidence in the traditional gods, as expressed in a paean given to one king (in 291):

> The other gods are far away,
> Or cannot hear,
> Or are nonexistent, or care nothing for us;
> But you are here, and visible to us,
> Not carved in wood or stone, but real,
> So to you we pray.[41]

---

34. Green, *Alexander to Actium*, 174, see also 206, 398.

35. Hengel, *Judaism and Hellenism*, 1:212–14; Green, *Alexander to Actium*, 396–97, 586. A famous example is the spread of the cult of Isis from Egypt across the Mediterranean world to the point where "By the Graeco-Roman period Isis had become the most influential and emotionally potent deity known to the ancient world" (Green, *Alexander to Actium*, 410, 590). Similarly, the worship of the Anatolian goddess Cybele became almost universal in the Roman Empire (Green, *Alexander to Actium*, 590). Comp. Georgi, "Propagandistic Pattern," 35–37.

36. Green, *Alexander to Actium*, 481.

37. Ibid., 589.

38. Walbank, *Hellenistic World*, 38. Alexander had previously been recognized as divine in Egypt, called "son of Zeus" (or Amon, following the common Greek practice of identifying foreign gods with their own), and had demanded to be voted a god in Greece (ibid., 41–42).

39. Ibid., 121, see also 212–18. Cf. Green, *Alexander to Actium*, 55, 195; Portier-Young, *Apocalypse Against Empire*, 51–54.

40. Though even then "the Greek cults were largely independent of Roman practice, being rooted in Greek traditions" (Price, *Rituals and Power*, 77). For example, Romans tended only to worship dead emperors subsequent to their apotheosis, whereas Greek tradition allowed for living rulers to be worshiped (ibid., 75).

41. Green, *Alexander to Actium*, 55; cf. Price, *Rituals and Power*, 38.

S. R. F. Price, on the other hand, sees the ruler cults as a response to changing political realities "as the Greeks attempted to represent to themselves first the Hellenistic kings and then the power of Rome."[42] The architecture of the temples carefully subordinated the emperors to the traditional gods,[43] but Hellenistic ruler cults went further than the imperial cult of Rome in terms of actual direct sacrifices to/for the king.[44] They were able to be easily accommodated into Greek religion because its central distinctive features were "the nexus of temple, anthropomorphic cult statue and sacrifice"[45] and the general humanism of ancient Greek religion.[46]

Ancient civilizations, of course, did not differentiate between sacred and secular, or between religious, economic, and political spheres of society, as modern societies have tended to do. Human rulers were mostly seen as somehow representatives of the gods, if not gods themselves, functioning in a kind of high-priestly role. And the help of the gods was invoked in every aspect of life.[47]

On the other hand, Hellenism tended to be secular and humanistic in philosophy. In spite of its ability to accept, absorb, and respect not only Greek gods but also those of other cultures, Hellenism was not in itself a religion. It also placed more emphasis on human thinking[48] (such as philosophy)[49] and reason than most ancient worldviews, as illustrated by this comment from the historian Polybius (writing about the Achean League): "It is clear that we should not say that it is the result of chance, for that is a poor explanation. We must rather look for a reason, for every event, probable or improbable, must have a reason."[50] Many Greek philosophers were obsessed with mathematical reasoning: "God, Plato is said to have declared, always

---

42. Price, *Rituals and Power*, 47.

43. Ibid., 146–56.

44. Ibid., 223.

45. Ibid., 201.

46. "Even Hellenistic ruler cults had their roots in the secular humanism of the Periclean *polis*," claims Green (*Alexander to Actium*, 57). Such cults were greatly assisted by the theory of Euhemerus that "the gods themselves had originally been great monarchs honored for their achievements on earth" (ibid., 398).

47. Fox, *Classical World*, 54–55.

48. A consequence of this was a tendency among intellectuals, at least, to claim only provisional and probable knowledge (Green, *Alexander to Actium*, 607–9).

49. Especially in Athens, "renowned as the home of philosophy," with its academy founded by Plato and other rival schools (Walbank, *Hellenistic World*, 178–80; Green, *Alexander to Actium*, 60), but more popular forms of philosophy flourished throughout the Hellenistic world (Walbank, *Hellenistic World*, 181).

50. Walbank, *Hellenistic World*, 156.

geometrizes."⁵¹ In a similar way, the gradual rejection of magical-religious causes for illness was often replaced by an "arbitrary philosophical system" that could be even worse.⁵² Hellenistic medicine was a mixture of rational thinking, superstition, primitive observation, and traditional concepts such as the "four humors."⁵³

Fate, Astrology, and Sorcery

Two practices widely prevalent across the ancient Mediterranean world were magic and astrology. These were rooted in the worldview of the ancient Greeks and others. For example, it was assumed that the gods' behavior (or Fate) determined events on earth and there was a "widespread conception of a '*sympatheia*' between earthly and heavenly events."⁵⁴ This concept was easily harnessed as the basis for magic and alchemy, by which people sought to manipulate the powers for their own ends⁵⁵ and protect themselves from harm.⁵⁶ Even Jews and Christians⁵⁷ were not exempt from such influences. Among the Jews there were tortuous attempts to separate legitimate practices from illegitimate,⁵⁸ and both Judaism and Christianity had to respond to the tendency of Hellenistic magicians to adopt their divine names for magical purposes, as illustrated by the account of Jewish exorcists in Acts 19:13–20, who tried to use the name of Jesus in a quasi-magical formula.⁵⁹

Then there was a universal interest in astrology.⁶⁰ As Hengel observes, astrological literature "made a decisive contribution to the world picture and the religion of educated citizens in late antiquity."⁶¹ This was rooted in four related aspects of Hellenistic thinking. First, the concept of fate, a central part of Hellenistic thinking from ancient times, gradually became

51. Green, *Alexander to Actium*, 455. The ancient Greeks made incredible advances in mathematics, especially geometry (ibid., 462–66).

52. Ibid., 486.

53. Ibid., 483–90.

54. Hengel, *Judaism and Hellenism*, 1:232; cf. Green, *Alexander to Actium*, 454, 482.

55. Green, *Alexander to Actium*, 482–83, 586–87.

56. For example, people used an oracle about a plague in A.D. 166 as magical amulet to ward off the plague (Aune, *Prophecy in Early Christianity*, 67).

57. Aune, *Prophecy in Early Christianity*, 45.

58. Goldin, "Magic and Superstition," 115–37; Achtemeier, "Miracle Workers," 152–56.

59. Cf. Fiorenza, "Miracles, Missions, and Apologetics," 13.

60. Cf. Green, *Alexander to Actium*, 595–97.

61. Hengel, *Judaism and Hellenism*, 1:214–15.

dissociated from belief in the traditional Greek pantheon as this lost credibility among thinking Greeks, so that by the third century BC[62] it enabled what Hengel calls "the victorious progress of *astrology*."[63]

Second, the Greeks enthusiastically believed in "the regularity and perfection of the heavenly order."[64] As Green argues, "Plato, Aristotle, and the Stoics all posited a divine and mathematically ordered cosmos, revolving round earth—itself unmoving—as a central focal point."[65] While some thinkers, such as Aristarchus of Samos, ventured to suggest that the sun was the center of the universe, this idea did not win much support from his contemporaries or successors, even being seen as impious.[66] Also some schools such as Stoicism tended to pantheistic and monistic ideas of reality,[67] which offered an intellectual foundation for astrology.[68]

Third, associated with this was a cyclical view of history, sometimes expressed in the idea of "great world year" governed by the movements of the stars and producing repetition of historical events and catastrophes, derived probably from Babylonian astrological thinking.[69] Thus, as Green argues,

> The divinity and life of the heavenly bodies, their supposedly regular, circular, uniform movement, the geocentric postulate that underlay almost all astronomical theory: these emerge as aspects of a Weltanschauung so deeply rooted in the Greek psyche that even seemingly contrary evidence could not eradicate it.[70]

---

62. Ibid., 125, 236. There was also in the increasing obsession with Fortune or Chance (Tyche), personalized even as a god (Green, *Alexander to Actium*, 53–54, 271, 400, 634). Belief in Fate also stimulated a new interest in oracles about the future (ibid., 593–94). However, the determinism that this implies was balanced by a belief in free will, as advocated by the anti-fatalist Epicureans and even the fatalist Stoics (ibid., 621, 645).

63. Hengel, *Judaism and Hellenism*, 1:236. Green (*Alexander to Actium*, 185–86, 596) notes that "the Hellenistic period witnessed a great advance in scientific astronomy" but many were more interested in what the stars demonstrated about "cosmic order and morality."

64. Hengel, *Judaism and Hellenism*, 1:235.

65. Green, *Alexander to Actium*, 454.

66. Walbank, *The Hellenistic World*, 185–86.

67. Hengel, *Judaism and Hellenism*, 1:147–49; Green, *Alexander to Actium*, 238, 633–34.

68. Green, *Alexander to Actium*, 400–401, 587, 595–96, 635.

69. Hengel, *Judaism and Hellenism*, 1:191–92. This is opposite to the Jewish and Iranian linear conception of history (ibid., 192–93).

70. Green, *Alexander to Actium*, 454, see also 462.

Finally, ancient Mediterranean people envisaged light as a positive entity, not derived from any source, emanating (for example) from the eye; hence stars were living animate beings, which explained why they moved while the earth stood still.[71]

Humanity, Honor-Shame, and Death

All the ancients held to some kind of belief in a life after death. This was a subject people were almost obsessed with in the Hellenistic period.[72] However, the exact nature of such expectation varied from an underworld (Hades) to reincarnation. Hellenism was also dualistic in at least some senses, especially in its view of human nature. Greeks distinguished sharply between body and soul[73] and their concept of life after death was centered on the fate of the (disembodied) immortal soul.[74] Perhaps partly because of this, and partly due to the roots of Hellenism in Homeric mythology and syncretism, many Greeks had a strongly permissive attitude to most forms of sexual behavior.[75] For example, Zeno, the founder of Stoicism, the most moralistic philosophical school, at least for a time "upheld sexual freedom between men and women [and] . . . was against monogamy, and firmly tolerant of homosexual relations,"[76] an attitude entirely common in the Hellenistic world.[77]

However, this worldview did not see the individual human being as primary. As Bruce Malina writes, there was a "nonindividualistic, strongly group oriented, collectivistic self-awareness that seems to have been typical of the first-century people in our New Testament."[78] Such group-oriented

71. Malina, *New Testament World*, 120–21.

72. Hengel, *Judaism and Hellenism*, 1:212.

73. As in the Orphic doctrines that influenced Plato, according to which the body was a prison or tomb of the soul or spirit, leading to a strong teaching of abstinence (Green, *Alexander to Actium*, 592–93).

74. Cf. Hengel, *Judaism and Hellenism*, 1:201, 246; Sanders, *Paul and Palestinian Judaism*, 53; Veyne, *Bread and Circuses*, 112. Veyne (ibid.) points out the length some wealthy Greeks went to in order to provide sacrifices on their behalf after they died—"The fate of the dead depended . . . not on their conduct in this world but on the care of them taken by the living." On the other hand, the progressive secularization of the Hellenistic world was undermining even the belief in Hades (Green, *Alexander to Actium*, 176).

75. Cf. Green, *Alexander to Actium*, 100, 175–76, 182, 246, 388–89, 569–71.

76. Green, *Alexander to Actium*, 63.

77. Cf. Fox, *Classical World*, 44–45, 89, 173, 296–97.

78. Malina, *New Testament World*, 60. Malina describes how conscience functioned mainly as an index of one's reputation in the eyes of others (ibid., 58–59) and

identity meant that members of a group were presumed to act alike—what we today would call "stereotyping."[79] Social values were governed by concepts such as honor and shame, as befits an "agonistic" society.[80] Thus a person's (or a group's) standing in their community was governed by both conferred honor (perhaps inherited) and their behavior as measured by their conformity to expectations related to these values.[81] People could thus gain or lose honor by their response to challenges to their honor, and "love of honor" drove people to compete with others to gain it.[82] Religion was also centered on showing honor or respect to the deity,[83] and doing so in public, in front of one's peers.[84]

Later Hellenism modified this worldview by placing the individual human being more at the center of concern[85] (as opposed, say, to the group, state, or gods), and this was associated with the belief in democracy as the ideal form of government.[86] Moreover, the more Hellenistic culture declined, the more "the individual was thrown back on himself."[87] This trend is also reflected in the growing attention of philosophers to questions of peace of mind as opposed to intellectual enquiry:[88] "this self-searching for the idea of spiritual liberation . . . is the most noticeable feature that all Hellenistic systems of thought have in common."[89] This was partly due to the decline in confidence in traditional Greek religion and to the loss of

---

people showed little or no interest in the inner workings or motives of other individuals (ibid., 66).

79. Ibid., 63–65.

80. Cf. ibid., 27–53.

81. For example, honorable people went to great lengths to avoid giving the impression that they were threatening the good of others in their community (ibid., 91–93), which could lead to envy (ibid., 113–14). People like tax collectors, money lenders, and traders were seen as dishonorable because they got rich by defrauding others (ibid., 98).

82. Ibid., 111–12.

83. Ibid., 30, 186.

84. Price, *Rituals and Power*, 120–21.

85. An example of this is the increasing emphasis in Jewish literature on "the personality of the individual teacher," which, according to Hengel (*Judaism and Hellenism*, 1:79), "derived from Greek custom and was probably a sign that the individualism of the Hellenistic period was also gaining influence among the Jewish people."

86. Cf. Walbank, *Hellenistic World*, 156–57. The forms of democracy persisted well after the loss of self-government by the Greek cities (cf. Green, *Alexander to Actium*, 155, 196–98, 382).

87. Green, *Alexander to Actium*, 587.

88. Walbank, *Hellenistic World*, 196.

89. Green, *Alexander to Actium*, 53, see also 58, 603.

political freedom in the cities, first under the Hellenistic monarchs and then under Rome.[90] As Green comments, "men were driven, more and more, if they could not be masters of their fate, at least to remain captains of their souls."[91] The dominant philosophical schools of the Hellenistic and Roman eras (Stoicism, Epicureanism, Cynicism, and later Neoplatonism) were all individualistic and inward focused.[92]

But ancient Mediterranean culture was also strongly hierarchical, as exemplified in its attitude to work. For example, in the ancient Greek world, work as a necessary part of life was disdained: "the essence of a notable was that he was a man of leisure, independent and *fully human*,"[93] whereas "to be a merchant, or to work for others, remained by and large anathema."[94] This attitude hindered economic progress. For example, in Hellenistic society, craftsmen and scientific theorists were unable to communicate with each other and thus develop technology as much as they could have if the intellectuals had not despised craftspeople.[95] It was also reflected in the political systems of the day (even in democracies, power was held by the aristocracies,[96] and a large class of people—slaves—had no rights at all) and in their religious thinking.[97]

Backward-Looking Traditionalism

The ancient Mediterranean world was backward looking rather than forward looking, with a tendency to idealize a past "Golden Age"[98] and to value stability in the face of potential chaos. As Green argues, "the predominant economic ideal in antiquity was not growth at all, but rather stability; one more instance of the ubiquitous cast of mind that regarded change of any kind as degeneration."[99] The Bible itself reflects this: it starts with

90. Cf. Green, *Alexander to Actium*, 53.

91. Ibid., 605.

92. Ibid., 56–64, 605.

93. Veyne, *Bread and Circuses*, 46 (italics added). Similarly Aristotle denied that any person who had to work of necessity could possibly be happy (ibid., 47) and similar attitudes were common right up to the Industrial Revolution (ibid.) Traders were also held in contempt (ibid., 52). See also Green, *Alexander to Actium*, 363, 470–71.

94. Green, *Alexander to Actium*, 471.

95. Ibid., 481.

96. Malina, *New Testament World*, 83.

97. Cf. ibid., *New Testament World*, 104–5.

98. Cf. Green, *Alexander to Actium*, 392, 470; Price, *Rituals and Power*, 99.

99. Green, *Alexander to Actium*, 363, see also 458–59, 472. "Even for rebels stability remained the basic ideal" (Ibid., 388). Because of the limited goods available in

God bringing order out of chaos (Gen 1:2–31), followed by the loss of the original Edenic conditions (Gen 3). This is a pattern followed repeatedly in the Old Testament (e.g., chaos–Flood–new order in Gen 6:1—9:17, or the cyclical patter of Judges 1). Revelation itself can be read as the final stages of bringing an eternal order out of the satanic chaos, not without its struggles. Most ancient societies lived in danger of invasion, collapse, food shortages, epidemics, or other forces of chaos, and their religions and political behavior were especially aimed at preserving or restoring a measure of stability in the face of these dangers. There was little or no hope of progress, for people saw "their existence as determined and limited by the natural and social resources of their village, their preindustrial city, their immediate area and world, both vertically and horizontally."[100]

Thus even the Hellenists, for all their intellectual vigor, did not share the modernist faith or interest in progress or scientific method. Green points to a certain ambivalence in Greek thinking: on the one hand, there is "the indomitable inventiveness and originality of Greek intellectual thought," but on the other, "the ingrained Greek conservatism that never felt the world should be changed, merely analyzed and explained."[101] Hence "the remarkable scientific advances of the Hellenistic period contributed virtually nothing to society's technological or economic betterment,"[102] partly due to the "intellectual elitism and acute social snobbery inherent in Greek society"[103] and the reverence for logical reasoning as opposed to observation and experiment, which in any case were crippled by a lack of good instruments.[104] And Walbank reports that in the later Hellenistic period there seemed to be "a general weakening . . . in the rational outlook which seems essential for progress in both theoretical science and technology."[105]

In a similar way, the Hellenistic attitude to the economic side of life seems irrational to (post-)modern people. As Oswin Murray writes,

---

society, "most people would be interested in maintaining things just the way they are" (Malina, *New Testament World*, 90).

100. Malina, *New Testament World*, 89.

101. Green, *Alexander to Actium*, 458–59, see also 612.

102. Ibid., 363.

103. Ibid., 456.

104. Ibid., 457, 470, 481–82. The one exception to the lack of interest in new technology was in the area of warfare (ibid., 474–78).

105. Walbank, *Hellenistic World*, 195. Similarly, Green writes of the "slow but ineluctable shift away from the freethinking rationalism that had marked the late archaic and early classical periods [in Greek history] . . . , the reversion to authoritarian modes of thought. . . in every socially conditioned aspect of Hellenistic culture" (Green, *Alexander to Actium*, 481). This led increasingly to a conformist syncretic belief system (ibid., 609).

> The amount of effort great thinkers of the ancient world spent on the fundamental questions of human morality and social and political organization is nowhere matched by any close and well informed discussion of the principles of economic organization: even the very word 'economy,' Greek though it was, denotes the low esteem in which such activity was held . . .[106]

Economic progress driven by such modern concepts as productivity improvement, long-term capital investment, and labor-saving machinery is noticeably lacking in the Hellenistic world because its worldview prized stability and feared idleness of cheap human workers as a threat to the "divinely established order on which the world's harmony depended."[107]

The ancients placed strong confidence in tradition and the wisdom of the ancients was highly valued. Even among the Greeks, there was what Green calls "a ubiquitous dead-weight conservatism . . . that habitually sought precedent and authority in every area from religion to literary criticism, from ethics to politics."[108] The Hellenistic worldview was grounded in Greek mythology, especially as found in Homer:[109] "constant reading of Homer [in the gymnasia] kept alive knowledge of Greek mythology, and favored the *interpretatio graeca* of the Oriental world of the gods."[110] Similarly, in Ptolemaic Egypt (and later) the corpus of myths was "regularly employed as a kind of exotic secular Bible, to provide precedents, exempla, warnings, or moral guidelines for human activities on earth,"[111] even if this Bible was given only lip service at times[112] and the interest in Homer was more a matter of nostalgia for past roots and certainties, along with the idealization of rural life.[113]

Summing up, the ancient Mediterranean worldview in general was:

---

106. Veyne, *Bread and Circuses*, xiii. Cf. also Green, *Alexander to Actium*, 362–63, 369.

107. Green, *Alexander to Actium*, 469. Most thinkers in the Hellenistic period valued the maintenance of the status quo (ibid., 605). One of the exceptions was the group known as the Cynics, though even they were inconsistent (ibid., 612–17).

108. Ibid., 482. Similarly Green contends that "the nostalgic systematization of previous knowledge" was the "widespread and ultracharacteristic habit" of the Hellenistic era (ibid., 605).

109. Hengel, *Judaism and Hellenism*, 1:66–67, 75; cf. Walbank, *Hellenistic World*, 182; Price, *Rituals and Power*, 181.

110. Hengel, *Judaism and Hellenism*, 1:67.

111. Green, *Alexander to Actium*, 177. Even in the Greco-Roman period Homer "often came to be used as a final arbiter, an irrefutable court of appeal" (ibid., 482).

112. Ibid., 206.

113. Ibid 207, 233–35.

1. Open to spirits and the supernatural
2. Dominated by concepts of Fate and a geocentric universe
3. Postmortem obsessed
4. Group oriented
5. Backward looking

Revelation and the Ancient Mediterranean Worldview

In many ways, Revelation reflects this common worldview of its day, as we might expect. But there are other points where it diverges from that worldview, which I will now try to identify.

Clearly, Revelation reflects the prevailing openness among ancient Mediterranean people to supernatural and paranormal experiences and revelation, and their tendency to attribute earthly events to spiritual causes. For example, not only does the whole book constitute an outstanding example of the experiences and revelation valued by the ancients,[114] but it also accepts such experiences as real: both positive (from the Spirit) and negative (from the devil), as in the case of the signs performed by the land beast in 13:13–15 and by demonic spirits in 16:14.[115]

Moreover Revelation clearly shares the belief that natural events are ultimately explicable in terms of supernatural or theological factors. For example, the five earthquakes mentioned in Revelation are explained as the result of "acts of God" (to quote the phrase that still lingers in insurance terminology today), frequently in response to human sin (6:12–17; 8:5; 11:13; 19; 16:18–19.)

However, at some points John's thinking diverges from that of his contemporaries in significant ways that reflect his Christian faith and Jewish roots. For example, Revelation follows the Jewish worldview in rejecting all gods but the one true Creator, as illustrated by the response the text expects from the natural disasters it describes: a turning away from their polytheism to the true God (9:20; 14:7), which would represent a major shift in the worldview of most ancient Mediterranean dwellers. It specifically condemns magic practices (21:8; 22:15) and puts a very different construction on the influence of stars. It is also frequently skeptical of claims to spiritual experiences such as prophecy. For example, Jezebel's claim to be a prophet is not accepted uncritically (2:20), nor is the claim of her followers to have

---

114. See further discussion in chapter 4.
115. See chapter 3.

"learned what some call 'the deep things of Satan'" (2:24.) John's spirituality is not undiscerning or indiscriminate, but rather conflicts with the syncretistic attitude of most people of his day.

Second, while Revelation accepts the common idea of a geocentric, "triple-decker" universe, with the heavens (including the stars) above, the earth in the middle, and the underworld below (5:3), sometimes adding the sea as a separate realm (5:13; 14:7),[116] it tends to use this picture more metaphorically. Unlike some other Jewish apocalypses, Revelation does not indulge in cosmological speculation and makes no specific statements about the relationship of the earth to the heavenly bodies. Instead, it uses spatial language more to indicate moral and spiritual relationships: thus heaven is "up" because God and his angels are more powerful than, and superior morally and spiritually to, earth-dwellers; the "bottomless pit" is "down" because it consistently represents forces of chaos and evil.[117] The text does not contest the geocentric cosmology of its contemporaries but shows little interest in defending or building on it either.[118]

Third, Revelation clearly shares the common expectation of its contemporaries in life beyond the grave, as expressed not only in eschatological hope and promise (such as the promises of Jesus to the overcomers in Rev 2–3) but in statements about the state of the physically dead. For instance, the "souls of those who had been slaughtered for the word of God" are "under the altar" in heaven and crying out to God (6:9–10). Similarly "the souls of those who had been beheaded for their testimony to Jesus . . . came to life and reigned" (20:4). The dead are now, it seems, in one of three places—Death, Hades, or the sea—and will be recovered from there to face judgment (20:13). However, Revelation is set apart as a Jewish-Christian text by its confidence not just in life after death, but in a bodily resurrection, of which Jesus was the precursor (1:5, 18; 20:4–6, 12–15).

---

116. Thus Jesus' second coming will be from *above*, from the realm of the clouds (Rev 1:7; comp. 14:14); the New Jerusalem also "comes *down* from my God out of heaven" (3:12; comp. 21:2, 10); John goes *up* to heaven in the spirit (4:1), the "stars of the sky *fell* to the earth" during the sixth seal (6:13), another star *falls* "from heaven to earth" and "opened the shaft of the bottomless pit" (9:1–2), from which smoke *rises* onto the earth's surface (9:2), and a beast "comes *up* from the bottomless pit" to kill the two prophets (11:7), who later are raised to life and go *up* to heaven in a cloud (11:12).

117. "Divine forces come down from heaven, and evil forces come up from the abyss" (Thompson, *Apocalypse and Empire*, 76).

118. In a similar way, John commonly uses language about the sun metaphorically (Rev 1:16; 10:1; 12:1), but when the literal sun is in view, it is subject to God's sovereign judging power (6:12; 7:16; 8:12; 9:2) and not ultimate, for in the New Jerusalem it is no longer needed to give light (21:23; 22:5). This last statement reflects the ancient belief in light as a force independent of "light-sources."

Fourth, as I will argue at greater length in chapter 5, Revelation makes a serious break from the prevailing hierarchical, group-oriented view of human persons, modifying its stereotyping of, say, non-Christian Jews (2:9; 3:9) and merchants (18:11–24) by accentuating the value of individual non-conformity within the local churches, as in the prophecy to the church in Thyatira, where "the rest . . . who do not hold this teaching" (2:24) are commended for not following the teaching of Jezebel. In fact, the heroes of the book are those dissenters who stand up for Jesus *against* the pressure of the group, such as those who did not worship the beast or take its mark (13:8–10,15; 14:12–13; 15:2; 20:4–6).

Similarly, the low status accorded to traders and craftspeople in the ancient Mediterranean world, especially in comparison with aristocrats or intellectuals, is not found at all in Revelation. It is true that traders and craftspeople are condemned as part of the Babylon system in 18:11–24, but this has nothing to do with a hierarchical view of society, instead being attributed to their participation in a system of injustice, persecution, exploitation, and deception (18:4, 7, 13, 20, 23, 24). The only distinction made between people has to do with their relationship to God and Christ: the faithful witnesses are the future aristocracy (20:4–6), but otherwise everyone is equal before God's judgment (20:12).[119]

Finally, how traditional and backward looking is Revelation? The epistemology of Revelation is certainly based on the revelation of God to his prophets; here John is building on the tradition of revelation to the Old Testament prophets (a point that will be taken up further in chapter 4). But in many ways John's thinking is quite radical and untraditional compared to his contemporaries. He certainly does not follow the traditions of the polytheistic cultures of his day (such as the Homeric canon). Moreover he is quite prepared to break with Jewish tradition and precedent in embracing the revelation of Jesus Christ. This is exemplified by the fact that, although he uses and refers to the Old Testament frequently, he applies it in very different ways to his Jewish contemporaries.

Revelation reflects the fear of chaos and instability that formed part of the ancient Mediterranean worldview: each of the series of sevenfold judgments in the text represents a lapse into chaos or an invasion of chaos (chs. 6, 8–9, 16); angelic beings are restrained for a time from releasing chaos (7:1–3; 9:13–15); the fall of the dragon represents the imminent threat of chaos (12:12); and the fall of Babylon the whore represents the kind of instability and chaos feared by all in the Roman Empire (chs. 17–18), though

---

119. And those who worship God and Christ constitute "an egalitarian *communitas*" since "worship is a radical equalizer" (Thompson, *Apocalypse and Empire*, 69–71).

the final outcome is a stable world order (22:1-5). On the other hand, we cannot but notice that it is largely *God's* hand that produces chaos! For example, it is the opening of the seven seals *by the Lamb* that unleashes conquest, slaughter, famine, pestilence, and cosmological disasters (ch. 6), and it is God's prophets who consume people with fire and cause droughts and plagues (11:5-6).

Revelation is largely hostile to the stability of the Roman order, because of its oppressive anti-God nature, and rejoices in its fall. The attempts of the empire to impose a stable political, religious, symbolic, and economic order (13:3-4, 7-8, 16-18), in defiance of the threat of chaos (13:3), are seen as derived from the dragon (12:18—13:4), antagonistic to God (13:6) and his people (13:7), and ultimately deceptive (13:14). Similarly, the global civilization produced by Roman rule and exemplified in the city of Rome itself is pictured as a whore (ch. 17) held together only by oppression and injustice (18:13, 19). Like Babylon of old, she is doomed to destruction (14:8; 18:2). Christians are not to participate in this world order (13:7-8; 14:9-12; 18:4) and are to rejoice in its fall (18:20; 19:1-3). Thus Revelation sees the Pax Romana as a false stability, somewhat like the Babel of old (Gen 11), which is destined to be destroyed by the judgment of God just as Babel was undone by the confusion of languages.

It's also important here to note that Revelation does not primarily look back or glorify the past. There is a note of "paradise regained" in the promises to the overcomers (2:7) and in the ultimate new world order (22:1-2, 14), but the ultimate perspective is progressive! John is looking forward rather than backward to paradise, and moreover it is a city, not a garden, that the narrative moves towards (21:2, 10; 22:2, 14, 19), which amounts to a partial endorsement of urban life.

In conclusion, Revelation shares many features of the general worldview of its region in the first century, but (in keeping with its Jewish roots and the revelation of Jesus in the New Testament as a whole) dissents from this worldview in significant ways. In fact, Revelation (with the rest of the New Testament) begins a shift in the ancient world, making it more individualistic, forward looking, and egalitarian—in a word, more modern— while contending for a rather Jewish version of the ancient belief in the supernatural.

Revelation and Ancient Hellenism

How much influence of Hellenism in particular can be seen in Revelation? Certainly there are some Hellenistic features in it. It is written in Greek, even though the Greek has been described as "barbarous," in a form or genre typical of the Hellenistic world:[120] revelatory literature, framed as an epistle. Second, the dualism that is part of Revelation's worldview has some commonalities with Orphic, Platonic, and Neoplatonic thinking,[121] which tended to view the body as the prison of the soul or spirit, though Revelation's belief in physical resurrection cuts against these ideas. Third, unlike the *Jewish* worldview, Revelation sees the world of its day as a unified whole, with no special privileged place given to any one ethnic group. Fourth, Revelation, like Hellenism, draws on ancient myths, for example, in the story of the woman, the baby, and the dragon in 12:1-6. It also gives some credence to astrology, at least in the broad sense common to most cultures of the ancient world, which would all see predictive significance in the movements of the heavenly bodies, especially unusual movements (cf. 1:16, 20; 6:12-14; 8:10-12; 9:1; 12:1-4).

Finally, the ultimate paradise in Revelation takes the form of a Greek-like city, a "polis" (3:20; 21; 22:2,14,19) with walls, gates, a river, a street, and trees (21:12—22:2), and a king's throne (22:3), albeit with some significant differences to any actual Greek city—for example, no temple (21:22) and a much stricter moral code: "dogs and sorcerers and fornicators and murderers and idolaters, and everyone who loves and practices falsehood" (22:15) are excluded.

On the other hand, the differences between the worldviews of Hellenism and Revelation are profound. As already noted, Revelation is not at all given to syncretism but is committed to the Jewish view of God as the sole deity and creator of all, and it divides the world into two distinct groups, not on the basis of ethnicity but on the basis of loyalty to God and Jesus. Its worldview therefore has little in common with secular humanism. Moreover the worldview of Revelation is not at all dominated by Fate; rather its view of history is centered on the sovereignty of God and Jesus—that is, it is a personal rule, grounded in justice, and open to influence by prayer (6:10-11; 8:3-5). Consequently its superficial interest in astrology comes from an entirely different viewpoint than the worldview of Hellenism. The stars are not alive, nor are they ruling, nor symbolic of gods; rather they are totally under the sovereign rule of the one true God and their movements have predictive significance only as portents displayed by him. I will explore this further below in chapter 7.

---

120. Cf. Hengel, *Judaism and Hellenism*, 1:112. More explicitly, one critic has proposed that Revelation is a kind of Greek tragedy and that its structure is modeled on the sevenfold stage arrangements of the theatre in Ephesus (cf. Bowman, *Drama of Revelation*; Bowman, "Dramatic Structure and Message"; Smalley, *Thunder and Love*, 103-4).

121. Cf. Green, *Alexander to Actium*, 592.

Revelation is also hostile to many values of Hellenistic culture, for example, the cult of Caesar and the state (13:1—14:11) and the economic system of the ancient Mediterranean world (13:16–17; 18:11–23). Unlike participants in the Greek gymnasium, John sees nakedness as shameful (Rev. 3:17–18; 17:16), a viewpoint that is drawn from the Torah (e.g., Gen 3:7–12, 21; 9:21–27; Lev 18), and follows the Jewish standard on sexual morality as opposed to the more permissive Hellenistic attitude to sexual behavior (Rev 2:20, 22). While it draws on a number of ancient myths, Revelation always puts them at the service of a Judeo-Christian worldview and never gives them credence in a Hellenistic sense. It never adopts the Hellenistic perspective on either Homer or oriental mythology.

In conclusion, one would have to say that the worldviews of Hellenism and Revelation are fundamentally different and opposed. The individualism, forward-looking attitude, and egalitarianism in Revelation's worldview have little or no connection with Hellenistic thinking. But perhaps the worldview of Revelation owes a lot more to the influence of the Jewish worldview of its day.

REVELATION AND THE ANCIENT JEWISH WORLDVIEW

Hellenism and the Jews

The response of Judaism to Hellenism has a strong bearing on the subsequent development of Christianity and provides a useful case study for how adherents of one worldview negotiated the challenge of a rival worldview or ideology. Space does not permit a full discussion of this topic,[122] but we can observe that the Jews were strongly affected by Hellenism at least from the time of Alexander's conquest of the Persian Empire. This influence resulted from the political-military dominance of Hellenistic kingdoms (the Ptolemies of Egypt and the Seleucids of Syria) in the area, the growth of Greek colonies in Palestine, the increasing growth of Koine Greek as the lingua franca of the region,[123] and the increasing influence of Greek forms of literature and knowledge. This was magnified by pressure from the Seleucids on the Jews to adopt Greek ways (at least alongside the traditional Jewish

---

122. See Borgen and Giversen, eds., *The New Testament and Hellenistic Judaism*.

123. Beginning at least as early as the third century B.C. in Judea. By the time of the New Testament, many in Jerusalem even spoke Greek as their mother tongue, and there were many other Jews (especially in the Diaspora) who had two languages and cultures (Hengel, *Judaism and Hellenism*, 1:103–5, see also 60–65).

forms) and to see themselves as one people with the other subjects of the Seleucid kingdom.[124]

The response of the Jews to this situation varied. Some, especially the aristocratic high-priestly families in Jerusalem, moved towards assimilation to Hellenism, that is, the (partial) adoption of Greek ways and thinking.[125] This is illustrated by the apocryphal Jewish book 1 Maccabees, which deplores the move towards Hellenism by some of the Jews under the rule of the Hellenistic king Antiochus Epiphanes in the second century BC: "they built a gymnasium in Jerusalem, such as the pagans have, disguised their circumcision, and abandoned the holy covenant, submitting to the heathen rule as willing slaves of impiety" (1 Macc 1:13-16 JB).[126] As this implies, the Hellenizers were mainly the upper classes of Jewish society, who stood to gain most from cooperation with the Hellenistic rulers and who ignored the effects of their system of government on the poorer rural Jews. As a result, Jewish literature from both the apocalyptic and wisdom streams both "regarded the growth in the power of the aristocracy and the penetration of Greek customs into Jerusalem [in the Ptolemaic period] with the utmost distaste."[127]

Other Jews rejected Hellenism as hostile to true Judaism. For example, the scribal movement tried to counteract the inroads of Greek influence[128] in the cultural and religious life of the Jews,[129] giving rise ultimately to the Maccabean revolt.[130] But the Hellenistic worldview could not be ignored

---

124. How strong such pressure was is a matter of debate. For example, Peter Green alleges that Antiochus Epiphanes had no interest in "stamping out local culture" or "acting as a proselytizer for Hellenism" (*Alexander to Actium*, 505) and attributes his attacks on Judaism to political and especially financial difficulties and the fierce resistance of Jews to his plundering of their temple (ibid., 515). This at least shows that their worldview was somewhat different to those of other subject peoples in the Seleucid Empire, in spite of Green's tendency to play down the differences. For an extended discussion of the growing Seleucid pressure, see Portier-Young, *Apocalypse Against Empire*, 49-216.

125. Hengel, *Judaism and Hellenism*, 1:56,71-74; Wright, *People of God*, 199-200; Collins, *Between Athens and Jerusalem*, 109-10; Portier-Young, *Apocalypse Against Empire*, 91-104.

126. See also 1 Macc 1:41-45; 2 Macc 4:7-20; 5:15.

127. Hengel, *Judaism and Hellenism*, 1:50; see also 56-57, 73-74.

128. One of areas of conflict was over sexual morality. The Jewish Scriptures were not prurient (that is, they did not seek to hide references to sex, nor did they present sex as dirty in itself; see for example the erotic *Song of Solomon*), but they took a strong stand against the sexual immorality that was often strongly associated with polytheistic religion (e.g., Num 25; Lev 18; 19:20-22; 20:10-21).

129. Partly through the establishment of Jewish schools (Hengel, *Judaism and Hellenism*, 1:78-83).

130. At one point in this struggle, the Seleucid regent Lysias published a decree

and in the post-Maccabean situation, Greek forms were even used to resist Greek thought: as Hengel explains, "knowledge of Greek language and literature, indeed training in rhetoric, were put completely at the service of the defense of the Jewish tradition against the dangers of Hellenistic civilization."[131] In fact, Hengel argues that "From about the middle of the third century B.C. *all Judaism* must really be designated '*Hellenistic Judaism*' in the strict sense."[132]

Other Jews took a mediating position with respect to Hellenism,[133] which included an attempt at assimilation of some aspects of Hellenism to a Jewish worldview. For example, some Jewish writers sought to assimilate Greek myths to the storyline of the Bible, even ascribing ancient intellectual breakthroughs to ancient biblical figures (such as astrology to Enoch or Abraham, or writing to Moses).[134] In such literature, "The ideals of Judaism are the popular ideals of the Hellenistic world: to be first in everything that is beneficial to mankind."[135] In some Greek cities, the Jews were thoroughly integrated into Greek culture; for example, in Sardis, one of recipients of Revelation, the great synagogue was part of a building complex including the gymnasium.[136] In some cases, there was a clear intent to convert Hellenists to Judaism by proving the superiority of the Jewish faith, so that Hengel speaks of some of this literature as "an expression of the missionary expansion of Greek-speaking Judaism of the Hellenistic and Roman period."[137]

"admitting the incompatibility of the Mosaic Law and Hellenism" (Green, *Alexander to Actium*, 440).

131. Hengel, *Judaism and Hellenism*, 1:102; see also 112, 150. This was also true of the Septuagint translation of the Jewish scriptures into Greek: "fundamentally the translators were very little influenced by the Greek spirit" (ibid., 114). Some anti-Hellenistic writings, such as Ecclesiasticus (or Sirach), were perhaps influenced subtly by Stoicism, which in turn had "a great deal in common with the thought world of the Old Testament" (ibid., 149; cf. Green, *Alexander to Actium*, 502).

132. Hengel, *Judaism and Hellenism*, 1:104 (italics original).

133. Cf. Portier-Young, *Apocalypse Against Empire*, 111.

134. Hengel, *Judaism and Hellenism*, 1:95. In a different way, the Hellenist Jewish philosopher Aristobulus argues that Greek philosophers and poets had taken over some ideas from Moses, but were still inferior to him (ibid., 165; see also Green, *Alexander to Actium*, 501).

135. Collins, *Between Athens and Jerusalem*, 42. Similarly, the emergence of apocalyptic literature in Judaism, especially with its encyclopedic wisdom based on ancient revelations, was in part a response to the challenge of Hellenistic education invading Judea (Hengel, *Judaism and Hellenism*, 1:208).

136. Hengel, *Judaism and Hellenism*, 1:68.

137. Ibid., 169. Compare Jesus' comments on the Pharisees who "cross sea and land to make a single convert" (Matt 23:15). Cf. Fiorenza, "Miracles, Missions, and Apologetics," 2–3.

Whatever response the Jews made, the encroachment of Hellenism could not be ignored and it inevitably influenced Judaism and its worldview irreversibly.

The Jewish Worldview/s of John's Day

The phrase "Jewish worldview" raises several issues. First of all, is there such a thing as a uniform Jewish worldview in the first century, or must we rather speak of varying Jewish worldviews and varying Judaisms?[138] Can anything uniform profitably be said about a religious group that encompassed such diverse parties as the Pharisees, Sadducees, various kinds of Zealots, and the Essenes,[139] and which was spread throughout the Mediterranean and Middle Eastern world with all the differences in culture that would imply? And second, which sources will best give us a window on that/those worldview(s)?

In response to the first point, the evidence seems to show that there was a commonly held worldview discernible among first-century Jews, in spite of their many differences in belief and practice. John Collins, for example, has argued that "Judaism in the Hellenistic age was not nearly as uniform" as some scholars have thought, and he has distinguished between traditional covenant Judaism and the forms found in the apocalyptic literature and the wisdom literature, where the obligations of people are grounded in higher revelation or universal wisdom as opposed to the history of Israel. However, even Collins still identifies such practices as refusal to worship other gods, separation from the Gentiles, Sabbath keeping, circumcision, and dietary laws as "hallmarks of Judaism"[140] and identifies common features of Jewish identity: the law, ethnic continuity, and relations with the land.[141] In other words, there were things that made Jews distinctive, however much diversity there was among them. Collins speaks of "the common Jewish heritage" appealed to by the author of 2 Maccabees, for example, as against "those issues which might prove to be divisive" in the story of the Hasmoneans.[142]

138. As argued, for example, by Jacob Neusner (Neusner, Green, and Frerichs, eds., *Judaisms and Their Messiahs*, ix). But even he speaks of "a group of religious systems that form a distinct family" (ibid.).

139. As Neusner (ibid., xiii) argues, "books so utterly remote from one another as the Mishnah and Philo and Fourth Ezra and Enoch should not contribute doctrines to a common pot: Judaism." For an account of the variations within Judaism held by these different groups, see N.T. Wright, *People of God*, 181–214.

140. Collins, *Between Athens and Jerusalem*, 14, 7.

141. Ibid., 15.

142. Ibid., 80–81. Sanders (*Paul and Palestinian Judaism*, 239, see also 423) too

Limitations of space prevent me from studying this in depth, but with the help of primary and secondary sources we can establish at least a preliminary picture of how the first century Jews thought *as Jews*, however much they were also influenced by other worldviews held by their neighbors. For, as Christopher Rowland observes, "For all Jews living in the midst of pagans the conflict of two world-views was inevitably awkward and sometimes profoundly difficult."[143]

Taking up the second question, the best way to establish the nature of this common Jewish worldview is to examine as wide a range of sources as possible. The main primary sources for a first-century Jewish worldview would be, in no particular order: the Hebrew Scriptures (especially the Torah[144] and the books written late, such as Daniel and Zechariah[145]); other Jewish religious literature of the period 200 B.C.–A.D. 100 (such as the apocryphal books,[146] the apocalyptic and pseudonymous literature,[147] and the literature of the Qumran community[148]); Jewish literature of a broader provenance (such as the work of Philo of Alexandria); Jewish history (such

---

writes that the evidence inclines him "to think of a close and positive relationship among the various forms of Judaism of the period (despite the obvious inter-group hostilities)." And Rowland isolates "Temple and Torah" as the key elements that "distinguished [a Jew] from his pagan neighbors" (*Christian Origins*, 11) even though "the nature of Judaism was a complex of competing and conflicting opinions and beliefs" (ibid., 66).

143. Rowland, *Christian Origins*, 8.

144. Perhaps the only authoritative Scripture that all Jews would have accepted without qualification (cf. ibid., 10).

145. Many scholars agree that certain books were written, completed or edited as late as the fourth to second century B.C. Among these would be 1 and 2 Chronicles, Deuteronomy, Ezra, Nehemiah, Esther, parts of Proverbs, Ecclesiastes, Ezekiel, Daniel, Haggai, Zechariah, Malachi and the second part of Isaiah (cf. Hengel, *Judaism and Hellenism*, 1:115-16, 153; Goldstein, "Authors of 1 and 2 Maccabees," 72).

146. Largely those included in the Septuagint (Greek) Old Testament but not accepted into the Jewish canon when it was finalized. The books are Tobit, Judith, 1 and 2 Maccabees, Wisdom, Ecclesiasticus, and Baruch. There is also extra "apocryphal" material found in Esther and Daniel. In any quotations I have made from this material, I have followed the Jerusalem Bible.

147. Discussion of apocalypses will be deferred to the next section.

148. Sanders (*Paul and Palestinian Judaism*, 423-24) comments on this, "The general type of religion found at Qumran is not exceptional, although there are noteworthy and unique aspects." Thus the Qumran people shared the same basic worldview as all Jews. There is a vast literature about Qumran and the Dead Sea Scrolls, so I have mainly consulted the following secondary sources about the Qumran community and the Scrolls: Pate, *Communities of the Last Days*; and the relevant sections of Hengel, *Judaism and Hellenism*, vol. 1. Quotations from the primary sources (the Scrolls themselves) have been taken from Vermes, *Dead Sea Scrolls in English*.

as the writings of Josephus); the New Testament (largely written by first-century Jews); and the later rabbinic literature, which may preserve the thinking of earlier Jews.[149]

By examining such primary sources, and with the guidance of modern scholars referred to *inter alia*, we can confidently sketch the broad outlines of a first-century Jewish worldview. In other words, nearly all Jews carried certain strong convictions in the depths of their minds.

Monotheism

First, they all held a strong monotheism: the belief that there was one personal deity who created all things[150] and who stood in sovereign control of the whole universe.[151] As N. T. Wright points out, Jewish monotheism was creational (the one true God made the world), providential (this God is involved with the world), and covenantal (this God is committed to working through his people Israel).[152] Hence the Jews had no respect for the gods worshiped by others[153] and no desire to participate in their religious observances, however much such acts might have led to peace[154]—"they were not willing to accept the kind of syncretism that was so common in the ancient

---

149. This literature "tells us a good deal about the period before A.D. 70. But in its present form it reflects the culture and agendas of a much later time" (Wright, *People of God*, 151).

150. Cf. Gen 1:1; Ps 24:1–2; Neh 9:6. Hengel (*Judaism and Hellenism*, 1:157) comments that the creation account of Gen 1–2 represented "the genuinely Jewish answer to the 'principle of form' of the visible world."

151. As expressed in the famous "Shema" of Deut 6:4: "Hear, O Israel: YHWH our God, YHWH is one" (Wright, *People of God*, 248) and by the (sometimes syncretistic) Hellenistic Jewish writer Artapanus calling God "the master of the universe" (Collins, *Between Athens and Jerusalem*, 35). Artapanus had a positive attitude to the local pagan gods and cults, but still did not regard them as truly gods (ibid., 35, 37, 39, 63). See also Judith 9:4; Esth 4:17; 8:16; Dan 4:34–35.

152. Wright, *People of God*, 248–52. Thus the military victories of the Maccabean revolt were attributed to God's power rather than the strategy or courage of the Jewish fighters (Mendels, *Jewish Nationalism*, 173).

153. See, for example, the ringing affirmations of monotheism and satirical denunciations of idolatry in Isa 40:12–31; 43:8—44:28; 45:9—46:13; 48:1–22. Comp. Wis 13:10—14:11.

154. Cf. Wright, *People of God*, 156. Cf. Esth 3:8, 13. Mendels (*Jewish Nationalism*, 197–98, see also 289–300) comments, "The fact that Yahweh was an indigenous nationalistic God who could not tolerate other cults and other gods created most of the friction that occurred in the first century C.E. between the Jews and non-Jews living in the Land, as well as between the Jews and the Roman authorities." Cf. Collins, *Between Athens and Jerusalem*, 7, 103.

Near East at the time."[155] While there was a growing emphasis on angels and demons in Jewish literature of this period,[156] such beings were very much subordinated to the sovereign God,[157] though this did not prevent many Jews from turning to angels for help in a quasi-magical way,[158] showing that they were open to some influence from other cultures.

The Jewish worldview included a firm belief in God's self-revelation in theophanies,[159] miracles,[160] oral prophecy,[161] and written scripture.[162] This did not mean that all revelation was necessarily supernatural in form. There was room in the Jewish worldview for intelligent reflection; as Hengel comments, "we find rational, critical, speculative and universalist tendencies"[163] in Judaism and its scriptures[164] well before it encountered the rationalistic Hellenistic civilization.[165] Moreover the canon of the Hebrew scriptures was far from settled until at least the council of Jabneh,[166] and there was even less agreement about the status of oral law. The aristocratic high priests and their followers tended to accept only the Torah as scripture, whereas groups like the Pharisees and Essenes placed more confidence also in prophecy, including the more recent apocalyptic works.[167] However, all saw the scriptures as basic to their faith and utterly trustworthy as to fact, so that Judaic learning could be described as "a system that shamelessly invokes *a priori* facts of history, and that knows things before proof or without proof."[168] There was an emphasis on the significance of each detail of the Torah, even each letter—

---

155. Mendels, *Jewish Nationalism*, 198. See also the repeated warnings against syncretism in places like Exod 20:3–6; 1 Kgs 18:21–40; 2 Kgs 21:1–15; Isa 2:6–20.

156. E.g., Tob 3:8,17; 5:5; 6:8; 8:3; 12:15; Dan 6:22; 8:15–16; 9:21–22; 10:4–21; 12:5–9. Cf. Hengel, *Judaism and Hellenism*, 1:154–55, on the trend to both "hypostatizations" (e.g., of wisdom) and extensions of the doctrine of angels.

157. Cf. Rowland, *Christian Origins*, 30–31, 33–38.

158. Cf. Goldin, "Magic of Magic," 131–37.

159. E.g., Exod 3:1–6; Isa 6:1–5; Dan 10: 1–9.

160. E.g., Exod 4; Josh 6:20; 10:12–14; 1 Kgs 18:36–39; 2 Kgs 19:35.

161. E.g., Deut 18:15–22; 1 Kgs 17:1–5; 2 Kgs 20:1–11; 2 Chr 20:14–20; Isa 7:3–9. Aune (*Prophecy in Early Christianity*, 104) argues that prophecy "was alive and well" during the Second Temple Era, "though in a form considerably different from that of classical OT prophecy."

162. E.g., 2 Chr 34:14–21; Jer 36; Dan 9:2.

163. Hengel, *Judaism and Hellenism*, 1:113, see also 147, 157.

164. E.g., Job, Jonah, Proverbs.

165. Cf. Hengel, *Judaism and Hellenism*, 1:116–28..

166. Though Aune (*Prophecy in Early Christianity*, 106) puts it as early as the first century B.C.

167. Hengel, *Judaism and Hellenism*, 1:176.

168. Neusner, Greeen, and Frerichs, eds., *Judaisms and Their Messiahs*, xiii.

"each omission of a letter in copying the Torah meant in principle an attack on the divine structure of the world, formed by the Torah."[169] This emphasis on written scripture was unique in the ancient Mediterranean world.

Election, Covenant, and Torah

All Jews shared a strong consciousness of being a people set apart by God as his own, distinct from all other races and nations,[170] brought into covenant with God[171] by his sovereign will and responsible to keep that covenant as an act of gratitude to God's grace.[172] Thus the faithfulness or otherwise of Israel to the covenant, as expressed in Torah observance, was the key to their enjoyment of God's blessing or curse.[173] These convictions were particularly expressed in the story of the Hebrew Scriptures, especially in Genesis and Exodus, which laid the foundations for the storyline of Israel as a self-conscious people.[174] However, some sects (particularly the one based

---

169. Hengel, *Judaism and Hellenism*, 1:172.

170. Maintaining the identity and purity of this people in the midst of a multiethnic world was, of course, a challenge, and there were many controversies over issues such as marriage with non-Jews, as reflected in texts such as Ezra 9–10; Neh 13:1-3, 23-29; and Tob 4:12-14. This did not mean that God had no plan for the Gentiles; Jewish writers oscillated between seeing this as beneficent or punitive, but they always connected it with God's work with Israel. Collins points to "a persistent hope for the conversion of the gentiles" in some Jewish literature, specifically 2 Maccabees (Collins, *Between Athens and Jerusalem*, 78, see also 70, 216-17; cf. Tob 14:6; Jud 14:10; 2 Macc 3:35-40; Dan 2:46-47; 3:28-29; 4:34-37; 6:26-27; Jon 3-4), and the presence of proselytes and "God-fearers" in most cities (ibid., 163-68). A whole kingdom converted to Judaism for a period, before being conquered by Rome (ibid., 164).

171. E.g., Gen 15:18; 17; Exod 24; Josh 24; Ezra 10:3-5; Neh 9:7-8, 32; Jud 9:18; 1 Macc 2:20; 4:10; 2 Macc 1:1; 7:36; 8:15. "Covenant theology was the air breathed by the Judaism of this period" (Wright, *People of God*, 262).

172. The Jews did not see themselves as earning the covenant by good works but they did see covenant keeping as essential to their inheritance of God's covenant promises. Thus Israel's plight in the first century was to be explained as "punishment for her sin" (Wright, *People of God*, 271). Cf. Sanders, *Paul and Palestinian Judaism*, 75, 106, 110, 175-77, 420-22, 426-27; Rowland, *Christian Origins*, 25-27.

173. So failure on the part of the Jewish people to keep the Torah might postpone their deliverance from foreign (i.e., pagan) rule, whereas a faithful observance of Torah might hasten their redemption (Wright, *People of God*, 237; cf. Mendels, *Jewish Nationalism*, 122, 301). This was certainly the conviction of the Qumran community, who explained the failure of the Maccabean revolt to lead to a pure Israelite kingdom by the failure of the Jews to repent and adhere faithfully to the Law (Hengel, *Judaism and Hellenism*, 1:226-27) or even to their own sinfulness (cf. Talmon, "Waiting for the Messiah," 121).

174. As Wright (*People of God*, 215) explains, stories function "as an index of the worldview of any culture" and first-century Judaism "quite obviously thrived on stories"

at Qumran)[175] saw themselves as the true Israel and thus the true heirs of the covenant.[176]

The Jews all shared a firm attachment to the Torah or Law[177] as revealed to Moses, and a determination to practice at least the main rudiments of that Law, especially those controversial elements that made them stand out as a "peculiar people": circumcision, Sabbath observance, abstinence from unclean foods (such as pork), and refusal to participate in worship of other gods or idols.[178] Some Jews, of course, did compromise in these areas, especially under pressure, but these were seen as "fraternizers with the enemy."[179] At the other extreme, some sects demanded a far higher standard of their followers than required for ordinary lay people[180] in the Law, but their main source of laws was still the Torah. The Torah could function as a focal point for Jews in exile from their land and temple,[181] as the growth of synagogues for its study demonstrated,[182] though some Diaspora writers

---

founded on the "basic story, told in the Bible, of creation and election, of exodus and monarchy, of exile and return." But some Hellenistic Jews found ways to integrate pagan-Greek myths into the story as well (Hengel, *Judaism and Hellenism*, 1:73-74).

175. Hengel, *Judaism and Hellenism*, 1:48-52.

176. Wright, *People of God*, 205; Hengel, *Judaism and Hellenism*, 1:244; Sanders, *Paul and Palestinian Judaism*, 425; Vermes, *World of Judaism*, 117.

177. Cf. 1 Macc.2:50; 3:48, 56; Neh 8:1—9:3. "For all groups which claimed affinity with Judaism, these five books formed the central pillar of their faith" (Rowland, *Christian Origins*, 46). Some scholars argue that the apocalyptic literature represents a countervailing view that minimizes, or even opposes Torah and Moses, but, as Portier-Young (*Apocalypse Against Empire*, 305) concludes, "there is no evidence that the early Enochic literature rejects the Pentateuchal laws" or Moses.

178. Wright, *People of God*, 168. These aspects of Jewish observance were under strong pressure throughout their history, but especially in the crisis period of Hellenisation referred to in 1 and 2 Maccabees, under the reign of Antiochus Epiphanes (cf. 1 Macc 1:41-53, 60-67; 2 Macc 6:1-11; 7:1-42; 11:24-25; 13:9-14; 14:26-36; 15:1-5,17; Dan 1:8-17). A subsequent rebellion against the Romans in the time of emperor Hadrian was also provoked by a ban on circumcision and the construction of a pagan altar on the site of the destroyed Jewish temple in Jerusalem (Wright, *People of God*, 165-66; Mendels, *Jewish Nationalism*, 387). Emphasis on such "boundary-markers" is also found in at least some Hellenistic Jewish sources, such as Theodotus, though his narrow Judaism is perhaps in the minority among Hellenistic Jews (Collins, *Between Athens and Jerusalem*, 47-48).

179. Wright, *People of God*, 168.

180. For example, both the Pharisees and the Qumran community seem to have aimed for a piety and purity similar to that required for priests (Wright, *People of God*, 195, 208; Rowland, *Christian Origins*, 70; Sanders, *Jesus and Judaism*, 20; cf. Hengel, *Judaism and Hellenism*, 1:178; Pate, *Communities of the Last Days*, 46; Vermes, *World of Judaism*, 116).

181. Collins, *Between Athens and Jerusalem*, 12, 15.

182. Cf. Wright, *People of God*, 228. Such synagogues and attached schools were

tended to explain it or reinterpret it in Hellenistic categories,[183] either to present a positive picture to Greeks or to help Jews feel good about their religion (or both).[184]

Holy Places

All Jews shared a strong attachment to the "Promised Land" of Canaan,[185] even though many Jews of the Diaspora might never set eyes on it[186] and even though it was under the control of heathen (Roman) rulers. According to Doron Mendels, all the Jews of the Hellenistic and Hasmonean period "shared a great passion for the Land, as well as the technique of recourse to the past to justify their holding of the Land."[187] This changed somewhat after the Romans took over their homeland, and for some Jews it lost its political significance, but most still saw the Promised Land as holy,[188] and during the war of A.D. 66–70 "the Land as an ideal within the national awareness was *common* to all groups."[189]

---

also found in Judea, including Jerusalem, and were a major part of a conscious effort by Jews to preserve their worldview in the face of the increasing influence and pressure from Hellenism (Hengel, *Judaism and Hellenism*, 1:82–83). However, this also meant that the meaning and requirements of the Torah needed to be carefully defined, which led to the rise of a large body of orally transmitted case law, now recorded in the *Mishnah* (Wright, *People of God*, 229; cf. Sanders, *Paul and Palestinian Judaism*, 76–81, 111).

183. Collins, *Between Athens and Jerusalem*, 42, 44–45, 51, 151, 157, 163, 180, 185, 190, 199, 215; Hengel, *Judaism and Hellenism*, 1:164–66. Sometimes this meant reducing the Law to a series of ethical principles (Collins, *Between Athens and Jerusalem*, 167). But even the Jewish Hellenistic philosopher Philo, while seeing "the letter of the laws" as symbols, stressed the need to pay heed to them (ibid., 112) and "we have no reason to believe that any strand of Diaspora Judaism abandoned circumcision" (Collins, *Between Athens and Jerusalem*, 167, cf. 189).

184. Ibid., 46; cf. Hengel, *Judaism and Hellenism*, 1:1, 70.

185. Cf. Gen 12:7; 15:7, 17–21; Josh 1:2–4; Jub 13:2–7, 19–21 (which acts as a midrash on passages about Abraham in Genesis, reminding the reader of the second century B.C. or later of the promises given to Abraham and inherited by the Jews his descendants); the Qumran *War Scroll* (which extended claims to almost all the Near East); Ecclesiasticus 46:1–10 (a poem on the conquest of the Land by Joshua). Cf. Mendels, *Jewish Nationalism*, 92–98, for comments on these passages and others.

186. Cf. Collins, *Between Athens and Jerusalem*, 78–85.

187. Mendels, *Jewish Nationalism*, 92.

188. "For religious Jews this behavior [of the Romans, treating the Land as their property and dividing it up] was a transgression against their scriptures, because in it [sic] the Land was considered to be one holy entity" (ibid., 246), though not necessarily the site for a Jewish state (ibid., 258).

189. Ibid., 263.

There was an even stronger attachment to Jerusalem and its temple. Jerusalem was seen as the center of the earth[190] and the temple represented all that was central to Jewish faith.[191] Hence Josephus wrote, "Whoever was master of these [the city and the Temple] had the *whole nation* in his power, for sacrifices could not be made without (controlling) these places, and it was impossible for any of the Jews to forego offering these, for they would rather give up their lives than the worship that they are accustomed to offer God."[192] This applied to the Diaspora Jews, for whom "the Jerusalem temple was certainly held in high honor,"[193] as well as the Jews who lived near Jerusalem. Even if Jews could not travel there, they might pray towards it.[194] Those Jews who disapproved of the high priests and other aspects of the running of the temple, and who even (as in the case of the Qumran group) withdrew from it, still held to the ideal of an actual purified temple being

---

190. Cf. Ps 122, 132; Malina, *New Testament World*, 184–85. Hengel points out that "The significance of Jerusalem grew with the growth of the western Diaspora, though it continued to remain *the center of world Judaism*" (Hengel, *Judaism and Hellenism*, 60, italics added; cf. Wright, *People of God*, 247).

191. Cf. Tobit 1:4; 13:9–12,21–23; 14:5; Jud 4; 1 Macc 1:21–41; 4:36–61; 7:36–37; 2 Macc 1:12, 18–36; 2:16–18, 22; 3:6–40; 5:15–17; 14:31; 15:17. Most Jews "looked to Jerusalem, and its Temple, as the centre of their homeland, and as their very *raison d'être* as a people" (Wright, *People of God*, 157; comp. Collins, *Between Athens and Jerusalem*, 111; Mendels, *Jewish Nationalism*, 135, 148, 150–51). However, it is also true that "the Temple became the focus of many of the controversies which divided Judaism in this period" (Wright, *People of God*, 225) and its legitimacy was questioned by many because of their rejection of the Hasmoneans, Sadducees, and Herod (ibid., 225–26).

192. *Antiquities* 15:247–48, as quoted in Mendels, *Jewish Nationalism*, 285. Cf. Sanders, *Jesus and Judaism*, 63–65.

193. Collins, *Between Athens and Jerusalem*, 81. Of course, in practice, Diaspora Jews could not participate in the life of the temple, and its role was "largely symbolic," so that their "practical allegiance . . . was to the law" (ibid., 111.) Nonetheless the temple was still central to their identity and worldview as Jews and they continued to pay the half-shekel temple tax until A.D. 70 (Rowland, *Christian Origins*, 81).

194. E.g., Dan 6:10. There was also a replica established at Leontopolis in Egypt, under the Ptolemies, by a member of the high priestly line, as a result of disputes about the valid priesthood. Its status, of course, was somewhat controversial, especially in view of the prohibition of other sacrificial centers in Deut 12:5–14. Collins (*Between Athens and Jerusalem*, 72, and see 78–79) argues, "there is no record that his temple was ever a bone of contention," but Mendels (*Jewish Nationalism*, 150) contends that the Jews "felt uncomfortable with other Jewish religious centers such as Leontopolos" since "they knew that the uniqueness of Jerusalem and its Temple along with its role as a unifying symbol for all Jewry, was crucial for Jewish existence."

established.[195] And this hope did not entirely die even when the second temple was destroyed by the Romans in A.D. 70.[196]

The Jewish worldview was characterized by a strong concern for purity or holiness viewed in terms of maintaining boundaries. This conviction undergirded and bound together the previously mentioned aspects of the Jewish worldview. David Rhoads concludes that, "What gave the whole system [of Jewish life in the first century] coherence was the concept of holiness," which was "a core value of the Jews,"[197] in fact "the major concept by which the nation-culture structured and classified everything in its world—people, places, objects, and times."[198] Jews were devoted to preserving the holiness of God and his temple and themselves as his people. Later they even constructed "maps" of comparable holiness of places and people, excluding Gentiles who were not holy at all.[199] Crossing the boundaries (cosmological, bodily, or social)[200] drawn by such a worldview brought defilement. The degree of seriousness and extensiveness accorded to the ritual and moral purity rules in the Hebrew Scriptures was what differentiated the different groups within Judaism,[201] but the overall concept was shared by nearly all Jews.

Future Hope

Finally, Jews shared a hope of future deliverance and vindication by God in some form or other. Not all Jews held to a uniform "messianic" hope.[202]

---

195. Cf. Wright, *People of God*, 206–7; Mendels, *Jewish Nationalism*, 146–48, 203; Goldstein, "Authors of 1 and 2 Maccabees," 70; Vermes, *World of Judaism*, 118–19.

196. Mendels, *Jewish Nationalism*, 201. Later, after the two failed attempts to throw of the yoke of Rome, rabbinic Judaism's theory, that the study of the Torah could serve as a kind of substitute for temple worship, grew in influence (ibid., 199; Sanders, *Paul and Palestinian Judaism*, 163–64).

197. Rhoads, "Social Criticism," 145.

198. Ibid., 147.

199. Ibid., 146–47, Rhoads draws on the work of Jerome Neyrey. These "maps" originate from the third century A.D. or later, but the ideas they represent may be found in the Old Testament and other Jewish literature.

200. Cf. ibid., 153.

201. Ibid., 147–48.

202. Wright points out that the places in Jewish literature "where Messianism is made explicit" are "comparatively rare" (*People of God*, 300) but that "the idea of a Messiah was at least latent in several varieties of Judaism" (ibid., 308; see 307–20 for a full discussion of this theme). Comp. Mendels, *Jewish Nationalism*, 225–29; Green, "Messiah in Judaism," 1–10; Goldstein, "Authors of 1 and 2 Maccabees," 88; Nickelsburg, "Salvation without and with a Messiah," 63–65; Kee, "Christology in Mark's Gospel," 187–93;

Some looked for two messiahs: a kingly messiah from the tribe of Judah (the line of David) and a priestly one from the tribe of Levi.[203] But nearly all believed that the logical implication of all their other convictions had to be that they would be restored to their former "glory days,"[204] much as in the reigns of David and Solomon,[205] or perhaps even better, and thus that their God and their faith would be vindicated before the nations.[206] As Wright explains it,

> The hope of Israel, and of most special-interest groups within Israel, was not for post mortem disembodied bliss,[207] but for a national liberation that would fulfil the expectations aroused by the memory, and regular celebration, of the exodus, and, nearer at hand, of the Maccabaean victory. Hope focused on the coming of the kingdom of Israel's god.[208]

This hope was stimulated by the past actions of Israel's God in times when his people were in bondage, and supported by the pattern expressed most clearly in Deuteronomy and Judges and subsequently reiterated by Israel's prophets: "the trajectory of sin-exile-restoration."[209] Of course, the Jews of the first century were not precisely in exile, being in the land and relatively free to practice their religion until (and even after) the war of A.D. 66–70, but they were under the oppressive rule of pagan Rome, a parallel

---

Charlesworth, "Jewish Messianology to Christian Christology," 225-31, 248-51.

203. Such as the Qumran community (Wright, *People of God*, 208; Pate, *Communities of the Last Days*, 48; Talmon, "Waiting for the Messiah," 125–26) and the *Testaments of the Twelve Patriarchs* (e.g., *T. Levi* 8; *T. Dan* 5:6).

204. Wright, *People of God*, 247, see also 268–72; Rowland, *Christian Origins*, 101–2; Aune, *Prophecy in Early Christianity*, 122–29.

205. Mendels, *Jewish Nationalism*, 227. The promises recorded in the Hebrew Scriptures about David fueled this hope as against the frustrating experience of living under pagan rule (cf. 2 Sam 7:8-16; Ps 89; 132:11–18; Jer 23:5–6; Ezek 34:23–30; Isa 11:1–10; Rowland, *Christian Origins*, 27, 92–94).

206. Cf. Rowland, *Christian Origins*, 31.

207. Though by the first century, most Jews had come to believe in some kind of life after death, at least in the form of a physical resurrection at the end. Cf. Isaiah 26:19; Dan.12:2, 13; 2 Macc.7:9, 14; 12:43–45; Wisdom 3:1–7; 4:7–17; Matt.22:23–33; Acts 23:8.

208. Wright, *People of God*, 169–70; cf. ibid., 300–301; Goldstein, "Authors of 1 and 2 Maccabees," 69. The Qumran community believed that the hope of restoration was in its early stages of realisation among them (Pate, *Communities of the Last Days*, 42–44).

209. Pate, *Communities of the Last Days*, 19. "According to Deuteronomy 4:29, 31; 30:1–10 (cf. Lev. 26:40–45), the promise is held out to Israel that, if she will return to the Mosaic law in exile, then God will restore Jews, the chosen people, to their land and will exalt them above the nations (see Deut. 7:6–7; 10:14–15; 14:2; 26:19; 28:1)" (ibid., and see also 24–29).

situation to the low points of the period of Judges and the uncertainties following the return from Babylon in the fifth century B.C. In this situation, such books as Judges (with its repeated cycle of sin-oppression-repentance-restoration), 1 and 2 Samuel (in which the Israelites gradually gain a clear independence of their enemies and even come to dominate their immediate region), Ezra, Nehemiah, Esther (all of which tell how God favored, supported, and vindicated the Jews under the conflicts with pagan enemies in the Persian Empire), and even more particularly 1 and 2 Maccabees (which tells the story of the successful revolt against the Syrian Greek rulers in the second century B.C.) would have alternately encouraged, challenged, and provoked the Jews of the first century. Thus there was also a common view that if the Jews obeyed the Law strictly they would be restored.[210]

This then was a nationalistic hope:[211] it meant the restoration of Israel[212] to her land, full restoration of her temple,[213] priesthood, and cult in all its purity, freedom to practice all the requirements of the Torah,[214] and independence of (even domination over) the pagan nations while living under the rule of God. As the Tefillah, a prayer reformulated after A.D. 70, pleads,

> Bring quickly the year of our final redemption.... Proclaim the liberation with the great trumpet and raise a banner to gather together our dispersed. Restore our judges as in former times ... and reign over us, thou alone.... Be merciful ... to Israel thy people and to Jerusalem thy city; and to Zion the dwelling place of thy glory; and to thy Temple and thy habitation; and to the kingship of David thy righteous Messiah.[215]

And in the case of sects such as the Qumran community, it meant a special role and place for them in bringing this about.[216]

---

210. Ibid., 48.
211. Mendels, *Jewish Nationalism*, 3; comp. Rowland, *Christian Origins*, 18.
212. That is, the full twelve tribes (cf. Sanders, *Jesus and Judaism*, 96–97).
213. Cf. Sanders, *Jesus and Judaism*, 87–88.
214. Mendels, *Jewish Nationalism*, 130; comp. Rowland, *Christian Origins*, 102.
215. Rowland, *Christian Origins*, 105. Cf. Wright, *People of God*, 302. Mendels (*Jewish Nationalism*, 6) writes of the four "national symbols of temple, territory, army and kingship (or rulership)" as the key issues in Jewish nationalism at this time, 200 B.C.– A.D. 132.
216. Cf. Talmon, "Waiting for the Messiah," 120–21.

The Jewish Worldview and Revelation

Clearly there were marked similarities between the worldview of first-century Jews and that of John, the author or redactor of Revelation, who himself was probably a Jew.

To begin with, Revelation has a very similar idea of monotheism to that held by the Jews. At the outset of his book, John has God say, "I am the Alpha and the Omega . . . who is and who was and who is to come, the Almighty" (1:8). He portrays a scene in heaven where every heavenly being worships the "one seated on the throne" (4:2) who "created all things" (4:11). Like a typical Jewish prophet, he calls the Gentiles to turn away from idols and worship only the true creator God (14:7; 9:20; 2:14, 20). His worldview is God-centered and his view of God owes much to the Hebrew Scriptures. Revelation also follows mainstream Judaism in forbidding worship of angels (19:10; 22:8-9).

Second, Revelation shares the Jewish belief in revelation. Indeed the accounts of God's revelation of himself, and his purposes in Revelation are frequently similar to accounts in the Old Testament and other Jewish literature. For instance, the initial account of John's revelatory experience (Rev 1:10-20) has strong similarities with Daniel 10:4-11 and his vision of heaven in Revelation 4 resembles that of Ezekiel 1. Revelation shows a commitment to revelation in the forms of theophanies (Rev 4), miracles (Rev 11:11-13), oral prophecy (Rev 10:11), and written scripture (Rev 22:18-19), like the Jewish viewpoint.

Revelation also shows a strong awareness of and respect for the distinctive features of Jewish faith and practice. There are frequent references to heaven using the language of the temple, for example: "golden bowls full of incense" (5:8), incense smoke (8:4-5), the ark of the covenant (11:19), the tent of witness (15:5), and the altar (16:7; 6:9). Positive references are also made to the tribes of Israel (7:4-8; 21:12), the temple and altar (11:1-2), the holy city (11:2; see also 20:9), the commandments (12:17; 14:12), Mount Zion (14:1), ritual purity (14:4),[217] and Moses "the servant of God" (15:3). The final paradise is described as "the holy city, the new Jerusalem" (21:2, 10), its gates are inscribed with the names of the tribes of Israel (21:12), and the glory of the nations is brought into it (21:24-26).

Revelation supports the idea of a distinct, elect, Israelite nation whose people are sealed by God and protected from His plagues in a way

---

217. A very similar reference occurs in the Qumran literature, where "the only explicit reference to the separation of the sexes . . . appears in a context of ritual cleanness" in connection with a holy war in the document 1 QM 7.3-6 (Vermes, *World of Judaism*, 123).

reminiscent of Exodus (Rev 7:3–8; 9:4). The names of the tribes are part of the New Jerusalem (Rev 21:12.) It shares the storyline of the Hebrew Scriptures,[218] as seen for example in the reappearance of motifs from the early chapters of Genesis in Revelation 2–3 and 22 (the paradise of God, the tree of life). It clearly subscribes to the hope of Israel in a strong messianic form: a world-ruling Messiah (11:15) of the tribe of Judah and line of David (5:5), defeating and subduing the nations (19:15), and a new glorious Jerusalem (21:2,10). It supports the idea of a resurrected body of saints ruling with the Messiah (20:4).

However, while there are strong features in common between the common Jewish worldview of the day and that expressed in Revelation, there are also undeniable and quite fundamental differences.

First, Revelation's messianic view is distinctly Christian. It is not just that John believes that Jesus is the promised Messiah; he also reworks the whole concept of Messiah. He is comfortable with the Messiah being a military figure who will "strike down the nations, and . . . rule them with a rod of iron" (19:15). But this person is also "a Lamb standing as if it had been slaughtered" (5:6) and his conquest is attributed to his blood and the courageous witness (even to martyrdom) of his followers (5:9–12; 12:10–11).[219] In fact, it is these witnesses who rule with him for a thousand years (20:4). This also implies that John's understanding of the storyline of Israel, as found in the Hebrew Scriptures, is different to the way many Jews of his day understood it, especially about where the story is heading. Revelation reworks the hope of Israel quite radically, placing no emphasis on the restoration of the physical temple and its sacrificial system or the hope of the Land, and instead highlighting the centrality of the Lamb (21:22–23; 22:1, 3–4), the immediacy of God and the Lamb (21:3, 22; 22:3–5), and the openness of the city to everyone "written in the Lamb's book of life" (21:24–27) when it describes the New Jerusalem.

It follows that Revelation has a different view of what constitutes the people of God. While there is continuity with the Jewish thought, not all Jews seem to be included in John's view of Israel (only "one hundred forty-four thousand, sealed *out of* every tribe of the people of Israel," Rev 7:4)[220]

---

218. Cf. Wright, *People of God*, 150, where Wright claims, "first-century Judaism and Christianity have a central worldview-feature in common: the sense of a story now reaching its climax. And, most importantly, *it is the same story*" (italics original).

219. In contrast to the Jewish remembrance of the Maccabaeans who inspired the armed resistance to Rome in A.D. 66–70 by their willingness to lay down their lives rather than compromise on the Law's demands.

220. There are parallels here with the beliefs of the Qumran community who saw themselves as the true Israel and an alternative temple to that in Jerusalem (Wright,

and there seem to be an overwhelming number of Gentiles (7:9). Moreover, while there is mention of keeping the commandments of God (12:17; 14:12), there is no emphasis on (or even mention of) the Jewish "identity markers" of Sabbath, circumcision, and food laws. It seems that John's view of God's people is similar to that found in Paul's writings (e.g., Eph 2–3) or in Acts 15, where Gentile believers are admitted as equals, provided only that they abstain from idols and fornication, things strangled, and eating blood (Acts 15:19–20, 28–29). Overwhelmingly John characterizes God's saints as those from every nation who follow Jesus and hold fast to his testimony (2:3,10; 3:8; 7:9–17; 11:8; 12:11,17; 13:10; 14:1–5,12; 15:2–3; 17:14; 19:7–10; 20:4–6; 21:7–8, 27; 22:3–5, 14). Hence Revelation radically challenges or redraws the boundaries of holiness central to the Jewish worldview.[221]

Revelation even modifies the monotheism of the Jewish worldview. As we saw above, John takes a strongly Jewish stance towards idols and in defense of a monotheistic worldview. However, his portrayal of Jesus begins to modify this stance and raise questions about the implications of his Christology. This is a complex issue and has been well debated by others.[222] But it is worthwhile to make a few salient observations. Certainly, in many places in Revelation, Jesus, while honored as Messiah, is still clearly subordinated to God. For example, the revelation of the book is given to Christ by God (1:1), he receives his authority to rule from his Father (2:28), he refers to "my God" (3:2, 12), he approaches God's throne and receives the sealed scroll from "the one who was seated on the throne" (5:7), the song of the Lamb glorifies God as almighty and worthy of worship from all nations (15:3–4), and John is commanded to worship only God as he holds the testimony of Jesus (19:10).[223]

But there are other places where God and Jesus are associated as apparent equals. For example, they are praised together (5:13), they are both feared as agents of wrath (6:16), salvation is attributed "to our God who is seated on the throne, and to the Lamb" (7:10), at the seventh trumpet voices in heaven say, "The kingdom of the world has become the kingdom of our Lord and of his Messiah" (11:15), the children of the woman are "those who keep the commandments of God and hold the testimony of Jesus" (12:17; cf. 14:12; 20:4), the 144,000 are "firstfruits for God and the Lamb" (14:4) and

---

People of God, 205–6). Like the Qumran community, John saw many other Jews as false claimants (Rev 2:9; 3:9), however, there was nothing in Qumran thinking to parallel John's inclusion of an uncountable number of Gentiles in God's people (7:9).

221. Compare Rhoads' analysis of Mark, in which "The Jesus movement . . . treated boundaries as lines to cross, redraw, or eliminate" (Rhoads, "Social Criticism," 154).

222. E.g,. Bauckham, *Theology of Revelation*, 54–65.

223. Stramara, *God's Timetable*, 80.

have "his name and his Father's name written on their foreheads" (14:1), the risen martyrs are "priests of God and of Christ" (20:6), the temple in the New Jerusalem is "the Lord God the Almighty and the Lamb" (21:22), its light is "the glory of God . . . and its lamp is the Lamb" (21:23), and its river flows "from the throne of God and of the Lamb" (22:1; cf. 22:3).

Sometimes divine titles are given to Christ, for example, "I am the first and the last" (1:17; also 2:8; 22:12-13; cf. "'I am the Alpha and the Omega,' says the Lord God" in 1:8), "the holy one" (3:7; cf. 16:4), and "Lord of lords and King of kings" (17:14; cf. 19:16). Revelation doesn't spell out the implications or meaning of these things, but clearly Jewish monotheism is being modified here.

Finally, Revelation is hostile to at least some Jews (2:9; 3:9), calling them a "synagogue of Satan." They are seen as false Jews who "slander" the followers of Jesus (2:9), perhaps inciting persecution against them (Rev 2:10; 3:8; cf. Acts 18:12-13).

Thus Revelation follows the Jewish worldview to a large extent but not completely. It cannot be said that John's worldview was the same as that of (non-Christian) Jews of his day. In fact, I will later seek to show that John is undermining significant aspects of the Jews' worldview. But perhaps there was a closer affinity with one sector of Judaism: the people who produced the Jewish apocalypses.

REVELATION AND THE APOCALYPTIC WORLDVIEW

Revelation and the Genre Apocalypse

There is now a reasonable consensus among scholars that Revelation is a member (perhaps the paradigmatic member) of an ancient genre of Jewish-Christian literature known[224] as apocalyptic.[225] While there is still a live debate about the genre of this book, enough similarities have been identified with books usually accepted as apocalypses to lead us to the conclusion that Revelation may best be seen as a member of the apocalyptic family. Most commentators would concur with Aune's conclusion that "The production of Revelation . . . is consistent with the hypothesis that the author was him-

---

224. Known to us, that is. There is no evidence that such a genre was formally identified before the production of Revelation (Linton, "Reading the Apocalypse as an Apocalypse," 174; Collins, "Morphology of a Genre," 4).

225. "The notion that there is a class of writings that may be labeled 'apocalyptic' has been generally accepted since Friedrich Lücke published the first comprehensive study of the subject in 1832" (Collins, *Apocalyptic Imagination*, 2). This does not mean that there is no dissent from this view.

self nourished on Jewish apocalypticism and regarded the apocalyptic genre as an entirely appropriate literary vehicle to communicate his theological agenda."[226]

But what is an apocalypse? In one sense, it is a book like Revelation,[227] which makes the argument that Revelation is an apocalypse somewhat circular. But more seriously, the standard definition is that proposed by John Collins and the Society of Biblical Literature working group:

> "Apocalypse" is a genre of revelatory literature with a narrative framework, in which a revelation is mediated by an otherworldly being to a human recipient, disclosing a transcendent reality which is both temporal, insofar as it envisages eschatological salvation, and spatial insofar as it involves another, supernatural world.[228]

Revelation seems to fit this definition quite neatly. Its title implies this: "The Revelation . . ." (Gk. ἀποκαλυψις), from which the name of the genre was derived. Its emphasis on being a "revelation" of hidden reality originating in God, mediated through angels and visions to a legitimate spiritual leader, also fits the genre. Revelation also apparently claims to be predicting events even into the distant future, like one of its apocalyptic predecessors, the Book of Daniel.

Like other works classified as apocalypse, Revelation is a prose narrative[229] of a human being "transported" into heaven "in the spirit" to see heavenly realities and the true causes of history from "behind the scenes." Its style, its identification of itself as a testimony (1:3, etc.), and its language—especially the use of symbolism and weird imagery and the use of numbers symbolically—are similar to other apocalypses.

Its content also implies apocalypse, beginning with its interpretation of earlier prophecies: apocalypses characteristically provided "inspired" interpretation of earlier prophecy (such as Dan 9:2, 24-26 with Jer 25:11-12;

---

226. Aune, *Revelation 1-5*, lxxxix.

227. After all, the very name of the genre is derived from the Greek name of our text, *apokalypsis*.

228. Collins, "Morphology of a Genre," 9. Cf. Collins, "Jewish Apocalypses," 28. Subsequently, Collins accepted an addition to this definition, that "an apocalypse is 'intended to interpret present earthly circumstances in the light of the supernatural world and of the future, and to influence both the understanding and the behavior of the audience by means of divine authority'" (Collins, "Genre, Ideology and Social Movements," 19). Some alternative definitions may be found in Hellholm, "Problem of Apocalyptic Genre," 22; Beale, *Use of Daniel*; and Aune, *Prophecy in Early Christianity*.

229. This contrasts with the emphasis on oral communication and oral tradition in the classical prophets and the rabbis (cf. Morris, *Apocalyptic*, 56).

29:10),[230] and Revelation continues this tradition, particularly with reference to Daniel, probably the earliest extant apocalypse. Its emphasis on the end of history—the final judgment, the resurrection and a new world order including a restoration of paradise to God's faithful people[231]—is very similar to the other apocalypses. And therefore it seems to function as a theodicy, like many other apocalypses; that is, it seems to function to justify belief in a God who is sovereign and good to his people, in the face of evidence to the contrary in their experience.[232]

On the other hand, Revelation is unlike other apocalypses[233] in several significant ways.

First, it lacks some generic features that are almost ubiquitous in Jewish apocalypses: it is not pseudonymous;[234] it does not present itself as an ancient prophecy of a long-dead godly hero, like Enoch, Moses, or Ezra, but simply as the testimony of a contemporary person called "John" (1:1, 9);[235] and it does not present a review of history from the earliest times in the guise of prediction (so-called *ex eventu* prophecy, which located the reader near the time of the end and made the actual predictions in the apocalypse seem more credible).[236] Rather Revelation is explicitly focused primarily on "what must *soon* take place" (1:1). Unlike Daniel, who was told "keep the words secret and the book sealed until the time of the end" (Dan 12:4, see also 12:9), John sees a scroll being unsealed (Rev 5–6) and is told, "Do not

---

230. Cf. Hengel, *Judaism and Hellenism*, 1:206.

231. Cf. Sanders, "Palestinian Jewish Apocalypses," 459.

232. Cf. Wall, *Revelation*, 18; Rowland, *Revelation*, 19–20.

233. Edith Humphrey ("Sweet and the Sour," 451) argues that the differences "give the work the appearance of an 'anti-apocalypse,' or at least an apocalypse in reaction against certain traditional details of the genre."

234. Of the apocalypses studied by the Society of Biblical Literature Genres Project, "All fifteen of the Jewish apocalypses and nineteen out of twenty-four of the early Christian apocalypses . . . are pseudonymous" (Linton, "Reading the Apocalypse as an Apocalypse," 180).

235. H. B. Swete (*Apocalypse of John*, cxxxi, as quoted in Walvoord, *Revelation of Jesus Christ*, 24) comments, "This abandonment of a long-established tradition is significant; by it John claims for himself the position of a prophet who, conscious that he draws his inspiration from Christ or His angel and not at second hand, has no need to seek shelter under the name of a Biblical saint."

236. Collins, "Pseudonymity, Historical Reviews and Genre," 332, 335; Hengel, *Judaism and Hellenism*, 1:184. There is a kind of historical review in 17:9–12, but it is not presented as long-term future prediction (Collins, "Pseudonymity, Historical Reviews and Genre," 339). Interestingly, John places the seven messages to the churches (Rev 2–3) where some apocalypses had this review (Fiorenza, *Justice and Judgment*, 51).

seal up the words of the prophecy of this book, for the time is near" (Rev 22:10; see also 1:3, but also 10:4).[237]

Revelation also shows little interest in supplying missing information from Old Testament stories. All the other Jewish apocalypses spend much time filling out such Old Testament (especially Genesis)[238] accounts as those of Adam and Eve and the Fall,[239] antediluvian times,[240] and the life of Joseph and his brothers,[241] to take the most prominent examples. In contrast, Revelation rarely quotes directly from the Old Testament, though it is full of Old Testament language and allusions, and it rarely discusses Old Testament stories explicitly.[242]

Finally, John places his revelations in a letter framework (1:4-8; 22:21.) While prophetic letters are not unknown, "*no other apocalypse is framed by epistolary conventions.*"[243]

The Apocalyptic Worldview

However, it is the comparison between the apocalyptic worldview and that of Revelation that is my main concern here. As Aune rightly observes, it is wise to distinguish "between 'apocalypses' (as literature), 'apocalyptic eschatology' (as a world view), and 'apocalypticism' (as a socio-religious

---

237. Humphrey, "Sweet and the Sour," 451. John Collins, however, contends that "the contrast between Daniel, who is commanded to seal his book (12:4), and John, who is forbidden to do so, is more apparent than real. Daniel intends that the revelation be made public in the time of Antiochus Epiphanes (i.e. in the time of the real author)" (Collins, *Apocalyptic Imagination*, 211). I would argue that the contrast still stands. Revelation is *explicitly* about the near future and this reveals a different way of looking at the future compared to Daniel or the other apocalypses.

238. Of course, Revelation is very interested in Genesis, as we will discuss in chapter 5 below, but it does not indulge in speculation or amplification of these ancient stories.

239. For example: *2 En.* 13; *2 Bar.* 48:42,46; 54; 56; *3 Bar.* 4; *4 Ezra* 3:5-8, 20-22, 26; 7:116.

240. Especially the explanation of Gen 6:4, the story of the "Watchers" (e.g., *1 En.* 6-9; 69; 86; *2 En.* 7; 18; *T. Reu.* 5:6-7; *T. Naph.* 3:5; *2 Bar.* 56:12; *3 Bar.* 4:10).

241. The main theme of *The Testaments of the Twelve Patriarchs*.

242. One of the exceptions is Rev 2:14, which refers to the story of Balaam and Balak (cf. Num 25.) However, John simply uses the story illustratively to attack the Nicolaitans, and makes no attempt to add to (or explain) the Old Testament story itself.

243. Aune, *Literary Environment*, 240 (italics original); cf. Krodel, *Revelation* , 47, 51-56. However, Collins ("Early Christian Apocalypses," 71) argues, "the use of the letter form is quite superficial."

movement)."[244] A study of the works normally called Jewish apocalypses[245] and composed approximately 200 B.C.–A.D. 120 reveals a rather similar worldview to that found in Revelation, and distinct from the thinking of other streams in Judaism,[246] though Wright contends, "The worldview to which many apocalyptic writings give voice is the worldview shared by many other Jewish writings of the period."[247]

First, the worldview of the apocalypses may be described as apocalyptic in the most literal sense of the word. That is, they see the spiritual (invisible) world as the center of reality, which can only be truly perceived by spiritual people. By their nature as apocalypses, these works are an attempt to take the reader "behind the scenes" to see the true workings of the universe and history otherwise hidden to normal observers.[248] For example, several of these works contain heavenly journeys in which the protagonist (and implied author) is taken up to see how things look in and from heaven. Enoch, for instance, is caused to fly into heaven where he sees two great houses, then the throne of God with its attendant angels; from this vantage-point he is taken on journeys through the earth and Sheol and shown such things as the angels who rule over different aspects of reality.[249]

Second, for the apocalyptic writers, God is the fundamental reality in the universe, the ultimate director of all things and all history, and the ultimate source of true knowledge. So in the heavenly journeys just referred to, for instance, the climax is the revelation of God and his throne. In 2 *Enoch*, for example, the prophet journeys through successive heavens, seeing such things as the atmosphere, apostate angels, paradise, hell, the sun and moon, giants, angels, and the zodiac, but not until he arrives at the tenth heaven

---

244. Aune, "Problem of Genre," 67. For some scholars, however, the whole idea of an "apocalyptic worldview" is suspect in the light of the great variety among the apocalypses (e.g., Glasson, "What Is Apocalyptic?," 98–105).

245. I am leaving explicitly Christian apocalypses out of this discussion, since they came after Revelation. Rather the works labeled "apocalypses" in Charles, ed., *Apocrypha and Pseudepigrapha of the Old Testament in English*, vol. 2, have been studied, together with the canonical book of Daniel, about the dating and authorship of which there is some controversy (e.g., Collins, *Apocalyptic Imagination*, 68–72; Morris, *Apocalyptic*, 76–81).

246. Cf. Collins, "Genre, Ideology and Social Movements," 16–17.

247. Wright, *People of God*, 298. Comp. Portier-Young, *Apocalypse Against Empire*, 282–84.

248. "The existence of another world beyond what is accessible to humanity by natural means is a constant element in all the apocalypses" (Collins, "Morphology of a Genre," 9). Cf. Portier-Young, *Apocalypse Against Empire*, 291–92.

249. *1 En.* 14–20, etc. Comp. *2 En.* 3–22 (journey to the ten heavens); *3 Bar.* 2–11 (journey to five heavens); and Rev 4–5.

does he see the terrible and glorious face of God and receive through an archangel books in which to write about the destinies of human souls and the secrets of God's creation. The revelations he then receives about the original creation, the nature of humanity, and the early history of the world (up to the flood) all reveal a God who is directing all things, even when things go astray through sin.[250] And in *4 Ezra*, the protagonist's repeated questioning of God's ways in the light of the destruction of Jerusalem are met with an insistence that history must proceed according to God's timetable[251] and an assurance that the world is getting old and hastening to its final end.[252]

Third, the apocalyptic worldview is in some sense messianic. Almost without exception, the Jewish apocalypses have a significant, even central role for the coming Messiah or a similar figure.[253] *1 Enoch*, for instance, speaks of the coming of "the Elect One," predicting that "righteousness shall prevail in his days,"[254] and prophesies about "the Son of Man" alongside God—probably modeled on Daniel's vision.[255] In *The Testaments of the Twelve Patriarchs* Judah predicts the rise of a star of peace, a person of righteousness of Judaic descent, "a rod of righteousness to the Gentiles."[256] The *Sibylline Oracles* testify to a hope of "blessed man" who "has won fair dominion over all" and who destroys the Gentile cities before restoring Jerusalem to a new level of glory and righteousness.[257] *2 Baruch* explicitly says, "when the time of the advent of the Messiah is fulfilled, that He shall return in glory,"[258] raise the dead,[259] and bring a new golden age to the Israelites.[260] And *4 Ezra* talks of "my Son the Messiah" rejoicing the survivors

250. *2 En.* 1–35.

251. *4 Ezra* 5:41–49.

252. *4 Ezra* 14:10–17.

253. Several of these apocalypses show evidence of subsequent Christian interpolations, such as the reference to "the blood of God" and "Jesus Christ the Immanuel" in *3 Bar.* 4:15. But even allowing for this, the messianic hope is very prominent in all this literature. Cf. Aune, *Prophecy in Early Christianity*, 122.

254. *1 En.* 39:6, see also 49:2–4.

255. *1 En.* 46:1–3, see also 48:2; Dan 7. Thus *1 Enoch* goes beyond other Messianic texts in its Parables section (*1 En.* 37–71) in its "identification of the messianic figure with the traditional transcendent exalted figures" (Nickelsburg, "Salvation without and with a Messiah," 63).

256. *T. Jud.* 24, esp. vv. 5–6.

257. *Sibylline Oracles* 5:414–33.

258. *2 Bar.* 30:1. He also speaks of the revelation of "the principate of My Messiah" (39:7), which will stand forever (40:3).

259. *2 Bar.* 30:2.

260. *2 Bar.* 72–74.

of the last days' trials for four hundred years, then dying before the general resurrection.[261]

Fourth, the worldview of the apocalypses is strongly dualistic in that truth, reality, power, and religion are all contested areas between good and evil, truth and deception, God and Satan. However, it is a limited, Jewish dualism[262] like that of Revelation. God is ultimate in power, but there is real opposition to him from both human beings and spiritual beings.[263] In several apocalypses there is a contest for the human soul between the Lord and Beliar.[264] There are warnings against Satan and his spirits[265] and prophecies of his future doom.[266] *2 Enoch* has a succinct summary about the devil, his names and origin, and his role in the sin of Adam and Eve.[267] A number of the apocalypses contain a legend about heavenly beings (sometimes called "Watchers") coming down to earth, procreating with women and begetting giants (an elaboration and explanation of an enigmatic passage in Gen 6:4); these angels are imprisoned somewhere as punishment.[268] Daniel also has overtones of conflict on an angelic as well as human level.[269]

Fifth, the worldview of the apocalypses may also be described as prophetic, in that the truth about reality and history can only be known by revelation, which God grants to his prophets and through them to all believers.[270] Each of the apocalypses contains prophecy (albeit pseudonymous) in

---

261. *4 Ezra* 7:28–30. Subsequently this book pictures the Messiah as a lion, reproving the final earthly empire (symbolized by a strange eagle) for its wickedness (*4 Ezra* 11:37–46; 12:31–32), and later still, as a man coming up from the sea, overcoming the enemy nations and gathering the ten lost tribes of Israel (*4 Ezra* 13). Michael Stone ("Messiah in 4 Ezra," 217), however, argues that in *4 Ezra* the Messiah "was conceived of primarily as acting in legal terms rather than military ones; his coming as king was not expected."

262. See the discussion of different kinds of dualism in Wright, *People of God*, 252–59, and my discussion in chapter 3 below.

263. Cf. Collins, "Genre, Ideology and Social Movements," 22. George Nickelsburg ("Salvation without and with a Messiah," 51) sees the "Book of Watchers" as teaching that the human race is the victim of superhuman powers warring against God. If this is so, it is at variance with Gen 6 (where the blame for the deteriorating situation in the world is laid at the feet of humans, e.g., Gen 6:5–7) and Revelation (e.g., 12:11.) Cf. Portier-Young, *Apocalypse Against Empire*, 288.

264. For example, *T. Dan* 4:7; 5:1; *T. Naph.* 2:6; *T. Asher* 1:8; *T. Ben.* 3:3–5.

265. For example, *T. Dan* 3:6; 6:1.

266. For example, *Ass. Moses* 10:1.

267. *2 En.* 31:4–6, also 29:4–5.

268. Cf. *1 En.* 6–10, 69, 86; *2 En.* 18; *T. Naph.* 3:5; *2 Bar.* 56:12–13; *3 Bar.* 4:10. There are veiled references to these ideas in the NT: cf. 2 Pet 2:4; Jude 6.

269. Cf. Dan 10:12–13, 20–21.

270. Cf. Hengel, *Judaism and Hellenism*, 253.

which the protagonist(s) foretell events and their meaning into the distant future,[271] often as a result of dreams and visions[272] and/or with the assistance of angels,[273] sometimes using highly symbolic language.[274]

Sixth, most of the Jewish apocalypses have a highly speculative and detailed cosmology that goes beyond what we find in the Hebrew canonical scriptures, drawn from ancient knowledge and speculation and influenced by Hellenistic ideas.[275] The most outstanding of these speculations occurs in 2 *Enoch* 11–16, which gives a detailed explanation of the courses of the sun and moon, how the calendar is calculated and some of the background to this. The author describes angels who attend to such duties, names and describes the "Phoenixes and Calkydri," who are "flying elements of the sun," appearing like lions-cum-crocodiles,[276] and describes the gates of the sun. He subsequently attributes encyclopedic knowledge, and a literal encyclopedia, to Enoch.[277] Similarly, the author of 1 *Enoch* explains the winds coming from the portals of heaven[278] and subsequently devotes a whole section of his book to "the book of the luminaries," containing accounts of the sun, moon, seasons, winds, mountains, rivers, and the order of the year.[279]

---

271. To the protagonist, that is. The historical position of the actual author is often closer to the end of the sequence of events predicted. A prime example is the "animal apocalypse" in 1 *Enoch*, which "foretells" history from the Flood to the Maccabean period (cf. 1 *En.* 89), all of which would be future to the biblical Enoch but mostly past to the actual author(s.) A different case is found in 2 *Baruch*'s interpreted vision of human history from Adam to the Messiah (2 *Bar.* 53–74); in this case the protagonist, an associate of the prophet Jeremiah, stands fairly late in the sequence, but the actual author would be just before the end.

272. Such as 1 *Enoch*'s "animal apocalypse" (cf. 1 *En.* 85:1–3), the appearance of two giant angels to the sleeping Enoch in 2 *En.* 1:2–5, 2 *Baruch*'s dream account of a forest, vine, fountain, and cedar (2 *Bar.* 36:1), the strange symbolic woman seen by Ezra in the field (4 *Ezra* 9:38—10:28), Daniel's own visions and his interpretations of Nebuchadnezzar's (Dan 2; 4; 7; 8; 9:20–27; 10–12), and Levi's dream of the heavens (*T. Levi* 2). Cf. Rowland, *Open Heaven*, 218, 228–39; Russell, *Method and Message*, 132–39.

273. Either speaking a direct message to the protagonist (such as Ezra's dialogues with the angel Uriel, for example 4 *Ezra* 4), or interpreting his dreams or visions (e.g., 2 *Bar.* 55:3—56:1; 4 *Ezra* 10:29–57), or opening up a fresh sight to him (e.g., *T. Levi* 5:1), or taking him on a journey (e.g., 2 *Bar.* 6:3).

274. As in 1 *Enoch*'s "animal apocalypse" (cf. 1 *En.* 85–91), 2 *Baruch*'s account of a forest, vine, fountain, and cedar (2 *Bar.* 36–40,) and Ezra's vision of the strange three-headed eagle (4 *Ezra* 11). Comp. Dan 2:31–45; 7; 8.

275. Though adapted to a Jewish worldview and even used to resist Hellenism (cf. Portier-Young, *Apocalypse Against Empire*, 286–90, 306).

276. 2 *En.* 12:1; comp. 3 *Bar.* 6–8.

277. 2 *En.* 40.

278. 1 *En.* 34–36, see also 41:3–7.

279. 1 *En.* 72–82.

Both *2 Enoch* and *3 Baruch* contain detailed (and inconsistent) accounts of the different levels of the heavens,[280] partly to explain events on earth and partly to explain what happens after death. Rival systems of knowledge sometimes come under attack, such as the *Sibylline Oracles'* praise of the Jews for not studying portents and astrology, and even astronomy, because of their tendency to deceive.[281]

Seventh, the worldview of the apocalypses is eschatological and teleological. History is drawing to a climax and final resolution with the ultimate victory of good over evil. Virtually all the apocalypses look forward to a final consummation of world history,[282] which will include such elements as the appearance of the Messiah figure,[283] the final judgment of all people and nations,[284] the resurrection of all people,[285] the vindication and exaltation of the Jews and/or Jerusalem,[286] a future paradise for the faithful people of God,[287] punishment and torment for the wicked,[288] destruction of the earth as we know it,[289] and the end of the devil/Beliar/Satan.[290]

---

280. *2 En.* 3–22; *3 Bar.* 2–11. Compare the less systematic account in *1 En.* 17–36 and the simpler, shorter one in *T. Levi* 3. Hengel (*Judaism and Hellenism*, 1:205) comments, "the spatial conception of the spheres of heaven laid one on top of the other. . . belongs just as much to the mythical world-view of the Palestinian Jews as to the conceptual sphere of Hellenistic mysticism."

281. *Sib. Or.* 3:221–33. This stands in contrast to the cosmological speculation in some other apocalypses and even the mention of the zodiac in *2 En.* 21:6 and 30:6.

282. Cf. Collins, "Morphology of a Genre," 9; idem, *Apocalyptic Imagination*, 9, 205. Comp. Aune, *Prophecy in Early Christianity*, 110. Hengel (Hengel, *Judaism and Hellenism*, 1:194–95) argues that the rise of apocalyptic literature owed much to the Hellenistic crisis of the second century B.C., which produced "a new interpretation of history" and "burning expectation of the end." Cf. Aune, *Prophecy in Early Christianity*, 110–12.

283. *1 En.* 38:2; 45:3–4; 51:3–5; 62:1–2,5; *Sib. Or.* 5:14–17.

284. *1 En.* 38:1–4; 45:3; 62:3; 104: 5–6; *Sib. Or.* 4:41–42, 83–84; *2 En.* 44:5; 52:15; 65:6; *2 Bar.* 24; *4 Ezra* 7:33–35, 39–44, 70–74, 102–15.

285. *1 En.* 51:1; *T. Jud.* 25:14; *T. Zeb.* 10:1–2; Ezra 7:32; *Sib. Or.* 4:81–82; *2 Bar.* 30:2–5; 50:2–3; Dan 12:2.

286. *As. Moses* 10:8–9; *T. Dan* 5:10–13; *Sib. Or.* 5:249–52, 260–68.

287. *1 En.* 11; 25:5–6; 45:4–5; 62:14–16; *Sib. Or.* fragment iii:46–49; bk. 3:702–31, 44–60, 72–94; bk. 4:187–92; *T. Dan* 5:12; *2 En.* 65:8–10; *4 Ezra* 8:52–54.

288. *1 En.* 45:6b; 62:11–12; 91:9; *T. Zeb.* 10:3; *Sib. Or.* fragment iii:43–45; bk. 4:43–44, 183–86; *As. Moses* 10:10; *4 Ezra* 7:36, 38; Dan 12:2.

289. *Sib. Or.* 3:77–92. On the other hand, Wright (*People of God*, 299) argues strongly that most apocalyptic writing "does not suggest that the space-time universe is evil, and does not look for it to come to an end. An end to the *present world order*, yes. . . . The end of the space-time world, no."

290. *T. Jud.* 25:3.

In this future hope, however, as in other areas, the apocalyptic literature, is decidedly Jewish in orientation, largely preoccupied with the hopes, fears, tragedies, and triumphs of the Jews. These authors spend a lot of time amplifying the stories of the Jewish Scriptures. They celebrate Jewish heroes. They compare Jewish ways and the Law favorably with the lifestyles of the Gentiles.[291] They retell the story of the Jews, as found in the Old Testament.[292] Their Messianic and eschatological hopes are centered primarily on the Jews[293] and the Jewish nation, capital, and temple.[294] The future of the Gentiles is also mentioned[295] (how often is a textual problem with the probability of some instances reflecting Christian interpolation), but Israel is at the center of focus.[296] Thus, for example, the author of *4 Ezra* faces a challenge to his Jewish attitude of superiority over the nations when he sees Gentiles lording it over the Jews.[297]

This does not mean that the apocalypses endorse every aspect of mainline Judaism or the Jewish worldview described above. Clearly some of their criticism is directed at Jewish leaders (for example, *1 En.* 89:68-71, 74-75). Most of the apocalypses seem to reflect a particular stream within Judaism of 200 B.C.-A.D. 100: there is a lot of commonality in their views and several of the others apparently refer to *1 Enoch*.[298] According to David Aune, there were two broad streams in postexilic Judaism, one of which was the "prophetic-eschatological." This stream was never dominant and stood aloof from the state and the priestly cult. Their future hope lay in the end

---

291. E.g., *Sib. Or.* 3:573-600; *2 Bar.* 77:15-16; 84:2, 6, 8, 9.

292. For example: *1 En.* 89:1—90:15, and ch. 93 (which "foretell" the story from the flood to Maccabean times); *As. Moses* 2-9 (from the division of the kingdom after Solomon to first century A.D.); *2 Bar.* 54-68 (from Adam to rebuilding the temple).

293. See for instance *T. Sim.* 7:2; *T. Levi* 2:10; *T. Jud.* 22:2; *Sib. Or.* 5:249 ("the godlike heavenly race of the blessed Jews") *4 Ezra* 13 (including all twelve tribes).

294. E.g. *1 En.* 90:28-29; *As. Moses* 10:8-9; *T. Dan* 5:10-13; *T. Ben.* 9:2-4; *Sib. Or.* 4:115-16; 5:249-52, 260-68, 420-27; *2 Bar.* 1-4; 31-35; 67-68; *4 Ezra* 3, 10.

295. E.g., *T. Levi* 4:4 speaks of God visiting "all the Gentiles in His tender mercies forever" (cf. 8:14 and 18:9); *T. Naph.* 8:3 says that God will "save the race of Israel . . . and . . . gather together the righteous from among the Gentiles" (cf. *T. Asher* 7:3).

296. For instance, the author of *2 Baruch* prophesies that the coming Messiah will spare nations that have not "trodden down the seed of Jacob" but destroy "those who have ruled over you" (*2 Bar.* 72:4-6).

297. *4 Ezra* 6:55-59.

298. E.g., *T. Sim.* 5:4; *T. Levi* 10:5; *T. Jud.* 18:1; *T. Dan* 5:6; and *T. Ben.* 9:1 explicitly mention Enoch; *As. Moses* 10:3-4 parallels *1 En.* 1:4-6 and there are several parallels between *1 Enoch*, *2 Baruch*, and *4 Ezra*. Cf. Charles, *Apocrypha and Pseudepigrapha*, 2:179. However, their worldview was still Jewish, for example in its attachment to the covenant and Torah (cf. Sanders, *Paul and Palestinian Judaism*, 424).

of history rather than in the restoration of an independent temple-centered state.[299]

Finally, the implication of many of these strands in apocalyptic thinking seems to be a strongly deterministic view of history. The apocalyptic view of history and the future, as expressed in the use of *ex eventu* prophecy and perhaps also influenced by it, was much more deterministic than that of the classical Old Testament prophets,[300] though not fatalistic in the Hellenistic sense.[301]

In classical Hebrew prophecy, long-range predictive prophecy is very much the minority: most of the material in, say, Isaiah or Jeremiah, is exhortation, comment on current events, or short-range prediction. This at least gives the impression of a reasonably "fluid" future, especially in those places where it is clear that the outcomes are dependent on the response of the hearers (a point made explicitly in Jer 18:7–10).[302] But in most of the apocalypses there is so much that purports to be long-range prediction[303] that the future seems very much set. Passages which set out the future ages of world or Jewish history, such as *1 Enoch*'s ten "weeks"[304] and animal apocalypse,[305]

---

299. Aune, *Prophecy in Early Christianity*, 110. However, he cautions, "All attempts to link apocalyptic literature to *specific* sects or movements have proven unsuccessful" (ibid., 111). Collins ("Genre, Ideology and Social Movements," 23) argues that "it is a gross over-simplification to speak of 'the apocalyptic movement'" and supports many of Aune's reservations, but contends that the worldview of the Qumran community "is quintessentially apocalyptic, in its orientation to the supernatural world and its eschatological expectation" (ibid., 24).

300. Collins, "Pseudonymity, Historical Reviews and Genre," 335.

301. Fatalism in that sense is far from the worldview of Revelation, the apocalypses or the canonical Scriptures (cf. Travis, *Christian Hope*, 38–39). According to Wright's (*People of God*, 200–201) interpretation of Josephus, the Essenes were content to wait for God to bring Israel's liberation to pass, the Sadducees believed in "seizing and maintaining political power for themselves" and the Pharisees looked for God to act but "loyal Jews may well be required as the agents and instruments of that divine action." One argument for identifying the DSS community with the Essenes is their shared determinism (Pate, *Communities of the Last Days*, 73).

302. See Collins, "Pseudonymity, Historical Reviews and Genre," 336–37.

303. Cf. Russell, *Method and Message*, 96–100. Russell argues that the apocalyptists were motivated to clarify and systematize unfulfilled predictions made by the classical prophets, particularly those of the glorious future of Israel, especially in the hazardous times of the Maccabean Revolt and later Roman domination. As he points out, the apocalypses are not really making long-range predictions at all; the actual authors see themselves as close to the end.

304. *1 En.* 93; 91:12–17. Hengel (*Judaism and Hellenism*, 1:189; italics original) comments that here "the *determinism* and *periodization* of the whole of world history emerges more strongly than in the book of Daniel . . ."

305. *1 En.* 89–90.

or *2 Baruch*'s night vision of history from Adam to the Messiah,[306] seemingly leave little room for human action or choice.

Moreover there is little obvious challenge to the readers of these apocalypses to involve themselves in creating a new future with God. In fact, there is little direct address to the reader at all in these works, though there is in some apocalypses a strong ethical undertone that anticipates parts of Jesus' teaching in the New Testament.[307] And as Collins comments, "apocalyptic language is *commissive* in character: it commits us to a view of the world for the sake of the actions and attitudes that are entailed."[308]

An exception to this is the canonical apocalyptic Book of Daniel, where God's people have a significant role to play as witnesses and "history-makers," as suggested by the career of Daniel and his three friends (Dan 1–6),[309] promises such as Dan 7:18 and 12:3,[310] and the role of prayer and fasting in the narrative.[311] On the other hand, Daniel's prophecies of four empires (Dan 2, 7) suggest that the broad outline of the future is determined, and his detailed prophecies of events surrounding the career of Antiochus Epiphanes (Dan 11) imply a strong determinism, as does his use of predictive dates (Dan 9:24–27; 12:11–12).

However, perhaps because of such features in Daniel, this characterization of the Jewish apocalypses has been challenged by several recent writers. N. T. Wright, for example, contends it is not true that apocalypses "believed in a dualistic or deterministic world while Isaiah and Ezekiel believed in free will." He continues, "To analyze these writings in such a way is to capitulate to a Josephus-like Hellenization of categories." Rather all biblical writers believe in a divine plan that is "working its way out in history."[312] In other words, Wright is attributing to all the apocalyptic authors the worldview that he also (correctly) attributes to the canonical prophets, which balances a strong belief in God's sovereignty over all events in history with a conviction that human beings (especially God's people) have a vital part to play in creating the future that God wants.

More recently, Anathea Portier-Young, in *Apocalypse Against Empire*, has argued that the apocalyptic literature advocates "theologies of resistance"

---

306. *2 Bar.* 53–74.

307. This is most strongly seen in the *Testaments of the Twelve Patriarchs*; e.g., *T. Gad* 6:3 (love and forgiveness to others).

308. Collins, *Apocalyptic Imagination*, 215.

309. Cf. Portier-Young, *Apocalypse Against Empire*, 258–62.

310. Cf. ibid., 231–33.

311. Cf. ibid., 243–47.

312. Wright, *People of God*, 298.

towards the Seleucid Hellenistic empire, basing her argument on both Daniel and sections of *1 Enoch*. According to her, "in the apocalyptic writings revelation provides a theological framework for action,"[313] either in the form of "nonviolent resistance and covenant obedience," as in Daniel, or in armed resistance (as in the Apocalypse of Weeks and the Book of Dream).[314] This assumes a strong conviction of human freedom and responsibility, not a uniform determinism.[315]

Revelation and the Apocalyptic Jewish Worldview

The worldview of these Jewish apocalypses and that of Revelation look decidedly similar, so much so that John J. Collins, one of the leading scholars on apocalyptic literature, could state that "Revelation, then, shares the typical apocalyptic view of the world as the arena of angels and demonic powers in the present and subject to a definitive eschatological judgment."[316]

Certainly there is a literary and theological relationship between Revelation and several other apocalypses. For example, there are a number of parallel passages and phrases as shown in this table.[317] Some may have been derived from Old Testament sources. This shows that either John borrowed somewhat from the other apocalypses or they both drew from a common stock of ideas within the Jewish world.

Phrase	Apocalyptic Source	Revelation Reference	Possible OT Parallel
Spirits (plural) going out from God	1 *En.* 39:12	4:5	
Defeating accusations of Satan	1 *En.* 40:7	12:10	Zech. 3:1
Blood of righteous ascending to God	1 *En.* 47:1	6:9–10	Gen 4:10
Messiah recognized in God's presence	1 *En.* 48:2	5:5	Dan 7:13–14
Word of Messiah's mouth slaying sinners	1 *En.* 62:2	19:21	

313. Portier-Young, *Apocalypse Against Empire*, 218, 314, 323.
314. Ibid., 219, 262, 277–78, 326, 337–40, 351, 370, 376–79.
315. Cf. ibid., 288.
316. Collins, *Apocalyptic Imagination*, 213.
317. Charles (ed., *Apocrypha and Pseudepigrapha*, 2:180) has a longer list of parallels between Revelation and *1 Enoch*.

Son of Man seated on throne of glory	1 En. 69:29	1:5; 7:17	Dan 7:13–14
Blood to the horse's breast (bridle)	1 En. 100:3	14:20	
Names being blotted out of book of life	1 En. 108:3	3:5	Exod 32:32–33
Giving the saints to eat of the tree of life	T. Levi 18:11; 1 En. 25:5	2:7; 22:2	
Tribe of Dan alienated from Israel	T. Dan 7:3	7:5–8 (Dan omitted from list of tribes)	Jer 8:16?[A]
Lamb of God (sinless sacrifice)	T. Benj. 3:8;	5:6, 9, 12	
Codes for Caesars of Rome	Sib. Or. V:1–51	13:18; 17:9–11	
New Jerusalem	Sib. Or. V:20–33	21:9–27	Isa 54:11–13
Two monsters (sea and land)	2 Bar. 29:4	ch. 13	Dan 14 (Bel and the Dragon)[B]

A. Cf. Stramara, God's Time*table*, 121–23.
B. Apocryphal addition to Daniel, from the Greek version.

However, there are also some significant theological differences between Revelation and the other apocalypses, some of which imply a difference in worldview. The first difference arises from John's Christian claims. While both Revelation and the Jewish apocalypses are strongly Messianic, John makes a claim that the other authors either did not foresee or would probably have rejected: he states that the Messiah has arrived, has suffered for the world's sins, and has already been vindicated and exalted as the world ruler to whom all must submit (1:5–6; 5:5–13).

Defining the difference between John's Christology and that of the other apocalyptists is not a simple task, not least because of the textual difficulties and probability of Christian interpolations in some of the Jewish apocalypses. However, if we take a mediating position on the texts (not accepting sections that are likely to reflect Christian editing but not rejecting Messianic references out of hand), there are certainly phrases in the apocalypses just as open to Christian interpretation as similar texts in the canonical Old Testament. These would include 1 En. 39:6–7, which speaks of "the Elect One of righteousness and of faith" and predicts that "the righteous and the elect shall be without number before Him forever and ever" (cf. Rev 7:9).

However, the general flavor of Messianic hope in these apocalypses is more Jewish nationalistic than what we find in the New Testament, including Revelation. Compare, for example, *4 Ezra* 13 with Rev 19:11–21. In both of these passages, we see a Messianic figure (a Man coming up out of the sea in *4 Ezra*; a rider on a white horse called "the Word of God" in Revelation) who faces warlike opposition from a large multitude (*4 Ezra* 13:5, 34; Rev 19:19). In both passages the Messiah's only weapon is his mouth, out of which comes fire in *4 Ezra* 13:9–11 (later interpreted as symbolizing the Law—4 Ezra 13:38) and a sword in Rev 19:15. With this he annihilates his foes (4 Ezra 13:11; Rev 19:20–21). In both cases there is a sequel: a gathering of a people (4 Ezra 13:12–13; Rev 20:4). But here the resemblance ends, for the people gathered by the Messiah in *4 Ezra* are the ten tribes taken captive by Assyria (*4 Ezra* 13:39–48), whereas for John they are the martyrs for Jesus (Rev 20:4).

Moreover even those (Jewish) apocalypses written in the first century A.D. or later still see the coming of Messiah as a future (perhaps near future) event, which means the authors have either rejected Christian claims or been unaware of them. In other words, John's Christology—that is, his concept of what the Messianic hope means, how it is fulfilled, and who the Messiah is—contrasts strongly with what these apocalypses envisaged and cannot be attributed primarily to their influence,[318] though it is likely that John knew at least some of these books[319] and shaped his material to appeal to their readers to some extent. I do not agree with Collins when he argues that "Historical references to Christ [in Christian apocalypses] . . . do not modify the apocalyptic paradigm in any significant way";[320] at least in Revelation, I see a substantial reworking of this paradigm in the light of John's conviction that Jesus is the promised Messiah.

A second major difference in worldview between Revelation and other Jewish apocalypses relates to ancient cosmology. While both Revelation and the Jewish apocalypses see God as the primary reality and ruler of the universe, the speculative and detailed cosmology found in the apocalyptic literature is largely absent from Revelation.

An important example of the difference in cosmology between Revelation and the other apocalypses relates to the place and role of angels. The

---

318. Krodel (*Revelation*, 50) suggests that John was implicitly criticizing "certain apocalyptic traditions that were circulating in his churches" by reworking apocalyptic traditions "in the light of Jesus' death and resurrection"; e.g. he ditched the apocalyptic idea of tribulation as persecution in favor of a Christian model of redemptive suffering.

319. As implied by the table of parallels above.

320. Collins, "Morphology of a Genre," 13; cf. Collins, *Apocalyptic Imagination*, 213; Krodel, *Revelation*, 47–49.

action in the apocalypses is very much heaven-directed and a significant amount of this is carried out mainly by (good or evil) angels. For example, in *1 Enoch* it is the fallen angels, led by Azazel, who teach people how to make weapons and metallurgy as well as occult practices, whereas in the parallel passages in Genesis, these things are attributed to fallen people.[321] Similarly, in *2 Baruch* it is four angels who destroy the walls of Jerusalem to allow the Chaldean army to enter the city, quite a different picture to that given in the relevant Old Testament passages.[322]

Now, Revelation is like the apocalypses in the prominent role given to angels not only as bearers of revelation but also as actors in the drama, carrying out the will of God. There are angels associated with the churches, for example, and the messages to the seven churches are actually addressed to them (Rev 2–3). Angels hold back the four winds and are addressed by another angel to delay damage to the world (Rev 7:1–3; cf. *1 En.* 66). Angels take part in heavenly wars (Rev 12:7). An angel gathers the vintage of the earth (Rev 14:19). A series of angels execute the final stage of God's wrath (Rev 15:1; 16:1–21). An angel binds the devil for a thousand years (Rev 20:1–3). In both Revelation and *1 Enoch*, for instance, angels present the prayers of the saints to God (Rev 8:3–4; *1 En.* 47:1–2, 4), though *1 Enoch* takes it a step farther, when angels are said to represent the righteous before God.[323]

But the angelology of Revelation is rudimentary compared to some of the apocalypses. Virtually none of the angels in Revelation are named,[324] for instance, whereas both good and evil angels are carefully named in *1 Enoch* 8 (fallen angels—Azazel, etc.); 10 (Uriel, Raphael, Gabriel, Michael); 20 (God's seven holy angels); 40 ("the four angels of the Lord of Spirits," v. 10, are named); 69:1–15 (all the fallen angels are named and their crimes detailed); *2 Enoch* 21:3 (Gabriel); 22:6–12 (Michael and Pravuil); *2 Baruch* 55:3 (Ramiel); *3 Baruch* 11–15 (Michael); Daniel 9:21 (Gabriel); 10:13, 21; 12:1 (Michael). Angels are attributed major roles in the ordinary workings of the cosmos by several apocalypses.[325] They also report that angels came

---

321. Comp. *1 En.* 8 with Gen 4:17–24. These versions are not necessarily incompatible, but the emphasis is certainly different.

322. Comp. *2 Bar.* 6–8 with 2 Kgs 25:1–4; 2 Chr 36:17; and Jer 39:1–4. The Old Testament passages clearly attribute what happened to God's judgment, but they make no mention of angels directly intervening.

323. *1 En.* 104:1. Elsewhere an angel intercedes for Israel (*T. Levi* 5:6; *T. Dan* 6:2) and angels come into heaven presenting the merits of the righteous (*3 Bar.* 12).

324. The exception is Michael (Rev 12:7).

325. *1 En.* 82:10–20 (the sun and the year's calendar); *2 En.* 11–16; *3 Bar.* 6:13.

down and cohabited with women,[326] that evil spirits torment the wicked after their death,[327] that one angel tried to become equal to God and was thrown out,[328] and that angels are assigned to particular people, both the righteous and the ungodly,[329] which may be a genuine parallel to the angels of the churches in Revelation 2–3. The apocalypses are clearly very conscious of the presence and activity of angels in the universe and much more willing to see their agency in events on earth than the author of Revelation.

Third, while both Revelation and the Jewish apocalypses share common hopes centered on the coming resurrection of the dead and the rewards of the faithful, Revelation is far less exclusively concerned with the Jews. In fact, in Revelation, "The narrow sphere of Jewish national hopes has been exchanged for the life and aims of the society whose field is the world and whose goal is the conquest of the human race."[330]

Fourth, Revelation and the Jewish apocalypses have a different view of history and the role of human beings in it. All the apocalypses see that there is conflict between good and evil, and real wills independent of and even opposed to God's, but John calls his readers to a much more activist role in creating the future and sees the future as more open than other apocalypses.

From almost the opposite viewpoint, John J. Collins urges that Revelation is just as deterministic as the other apocalypses, as shown by 1:1 ("what must soon take place").[331] Certainly there is a stress in Revelation on the predetermined direction of history. But Revelation resembles classical Old Testament prophecy whenever it addresses the churches and calls Christians either to repentance or to faithful endurance or to disassociation from the enemy state (e.g., 2:5; 13:10; 18:4). In such cases, the future is truly open within the bounds of God's overall plan. Even Collins concedes that because of the victory of Christ over the dragon by his death and exaltation (ch. 12), Christians have a model:

> They too can defeat the dragon if they are 'washed in the blood of the lamb' and are prepared to lay down their lives.... Detachment from this world, in the hope of the glory that is above or is to come, is a common characteristic of the Jewish apocalypses....

---

326. *1 En.* 6, 86; *2 En.* 18:1–6. However, in one pseudepigraphal text this is at least partly blamed on the women who beguiled the Watchers (*T. Reu.* 5).

327. *T. Asher* 6:5.

328. *2 En.* 29:4–5; cf. Isa 14:12–15; 9:1; 12:9.

329. *2 Bar.* 12–13.

330. Swete, *Apocalypse of John*, cxxxix, as quoted in Walvoord, *Revelation of Jesus Christ*, 25.

331. Collins, "Pseudonymity, Historical Reviews and Genre," 339.

The difference in Revelation is that the impulse to martyrdom, and to the rejection of this world, is intensified by the example of Jesus, who achieved his victory by his crucifixion.[332]

In other words, according to Revelation, Jesus' followers have a real role to play in creating the future. However, while this is clearly true of Revelation, it is largely only implied in most of the other apocalypses.[333]

The evidence just explored shows, therefore, that Revelation has a similar but not identical worldview to the authors of the main Jewish apocalypses written previous to or contemporary with it. Some of the differences between them are differences largely in degree (as in the emphasis on angels), whereas others seem to suggest that John has made a more or less decisive break with at least some elements in the kind of worldview expressed in this stream of Judaism, such as in his acceptance of Jesus as Messiah, his adoption of a less Jewish-centered focus, and his move away from (or avoidance of) apocalyptic determinism towards a worldview in which human beings, especially God's people, play a significant part in the direction of history. His failure to emphasize the ancient cosmologies specifically embraced by some other apocalypses suggests either a lack of interest in such questions or perhaps an unwillingness to be committed to speculation not particularly associated with his Hebrew roots or his Christian faith.[334] For twenty-first-century readers, this makes his writing less archaic than most of the apocalypses we have considered.

Comparative Chart of Worldviews

Feature	Hellenism	Judaism	Apocalyptic	Revelation
Theology	Syncretism	Monotheism	Monotheism	Modified monotheism
Central people	Hellenes	Jews	Jews	Church of all nations

---

332. Collins, *Apocalyptic Imagination*, 213–14.

333. See also Hill, "Prophecy and Prophets," 405–6. Though see also the discussion above with Portier-Young, who views the other apocalypses as more activist in goal.

334. Even Collins ("Genre, Ideology, and Social Movements," 16), who usually emphasizes the similarities between Revelation and the Jewish apocalypses, allows that "we need to distinguish between the 'historical' type of apocalypticism, typified by Daniel and Revelation, and the more cosmic orientation of the heavenly ascents."

Feature	Hellenism	Judaism	Apocalyptic	Revelation
Scriptures	Homer	Torah & prophets	Torah & prophets, including apocalypses	Torah & prophets, including apocalypses & Christian writings
Spiritual center	Olympus	Jerusalem Heaven	Jerusalem Heaven	New Jerusalem Heaven
Political center	Polis	Jerusalem	Jerusalem	Heaven
Political authority	King/emperor	Sanhedrin	God	God and Christ Local church
Mission	Spread Greek culture	Hold to Torah and God	Hold to Torah and God	Spread gospel & hold to it
Education	Gymnasium	Synagogue	Apocalyptic sect?	Local church
Entry	Admission to gymnasium	Circumcision	Circumcision	Conversion to Jesus (baptism)
Driving force of history	Fate	Covenant	God's Plan	God's Plan & Christ (ians)
Hope	Hellenized civilization	Freedom to practice Torah	Triumph of Judaism	Overcoming opposition New Jerusalem

PRELIMINARY CONCLUSIONS

As we conclude this extended comparative study of Revelation and other worldviews of the first century, certain things stand out. First, John was a man of his time and assumed certain features of the worldviews he had inherited. Revelation makes no clear and decisive break with the ancient worldview of the Mediterranean or the particular thinking of the Greeks or Jews. He accepts the geocentric worldview of his day, for example, and accentuates such common beliefs as supernatural revelation and supernatural agency in human affairs. His worldview has many similarities to that of the Jewish apocalypses in particular.

Second, John wrote in the midst of clashing and competing worldviews. The Hellenistic and Jewish worldviews in particular were clearly at loggerheads, even to the point of violence.[335] John sometimes tends towards

---

335. The Maccabean wars were strongly focused on the worldview clash between Hellenism and Judaism and this was also central in the rebellion against Rome, even

the worldview or ideology of the Hellenists (such as in their internationalism or preference for Greek language) but more frequently adopts the mindset of the Jews (such as in his support for monotheism as against syncretism). However, this clash does not in itself feature largely in his text. He is more concerned with the clash between the Christian faith and all the competing worldviews of his day.

Third, John struck out in new directions as a result of his Christian faith. While he clearly owes a lot to his predecessors and contemporaries in his thinking about many issues, he shows evidence of a developing worldview that is in important respects new and different. This emerging worldview is based on acceptance of Jesus as the Jewish Messiah and Lord of the whole earth, contrary to the beliefs of both Jews and Gentiles (especially Romans). It tends to take a middle ground between Judaism and Hellenism—not a compromise, however, but a new direction rejected by both Jews and Greeks alike.[336] It is strongly monotheistic, but the monotheism of Judaism is modified by the way Jesus is portrayed. It rejects the anthropocentric theology of Hellenism but glorifies a man who died as (at least) God's agent and Lord of the nations. It is particularist in terms of its monotheism and Christology but universalist in its view of the people of God as drawn from all peoples. It has a Jewish view of history (linear rather than cyclical) but an unorthodox (to the Jews) view of where that history is going and what stage it was up to by the first century. It is these new directions that make Revelation a promising source for developing a postmodern Christian worldview.

As will become more apparent in chapter 7, Revelation is very conscious of the conflict of worldviews triggered off by the emergence of Christianity, and of specific conflicts between Christian and other worldviews. In fact, the whole structure and plot of Revelation represents Christians and their worldview in conflict with existing worldviews of that era. Revelation represents its rival worldviews by pictures, symbols, and caricatures, some of them derived from apocalyptic literature, and undermines its rival worldviews by its use of such language rather than attacking them verbally or with rational arguments. It uses generic features associated with rival worldviews in order to reinterpret or undermine those worldviews. It points up the flaws in its rivals' claims and their oppressive nature, but does so from a Christian stance rather than one that is generally skeptical.

The ultimate point of such a strategy is not just negative: John's purpose in undermining rival views is to promote Christianity and the new

---

though there were other factors.

336. Cf. 1 Cor 1:22–24.

worldview it represents as more satisfying and comprehensive than the alternatives. As Elisabeth Schüssler Fiorenza proposed some time ago, "the early Christian movement and its literature should be viewed as rooted in the attempt to attract and convince the persons of the Hellenistic world, be they already Christians, Jews, or pagans."[337] Revelation is no exception to this.

How this conflict and strategy plays out in terms of intellectual issues, both in John's day and in our postmodern world, will be explored in the rest of this book.

---

337. Fiorenza, "Miracles, Missions, and Apologetics," 1–2.

CHAPTER 3

The Reality of the Spirit World

Wʜᴀᴛ ɪs ʀᴇᴀʟ? Fᴇᴡ of us spend any time thinking about the question, but our implicit answer to it shapes everything we do, every decision we make. For example, most countries of the world suffer periodic natural disasters. People's response to these, what they attribute them to, how they act to prevent or manage them tells one a lot about their worldview.

On a much more trivial level, we all take attitudes that relate to what is real and what is only make-believe or superstition. Is there a Santa Claus? Are fairies real?[1] What about extra-terrestrials or angels or ghosts? How do we decide about these questions? None of us only believes in what we see with our literal eyes. Not only do we accept the reality of invisible forces like electricity and radio waves, nearly everyone believes in such abstractions as love and justice and beauty, even though some philosophers have tried to reduce all these to feelings about the world.

Therefore the first question I want to consider in the light of postmodernism, and my goal of identifying a Christian worldview for postmodern times, is the nature of reality, what philosophers call ontology. The question can be framed like this: Is it plausible that reality includes not just those features studied by science or analyzable in terms of our physical senses and human reason, but also another dimension that has room for God, spirits, angels and the like?

---

1. One of Richard Dawkins' common rhetorical points is that belief in God is equivalent to belief in "fairies at the bottom of the garden," an old English superstition. He implies that Christians are superstitious and gullible.

ANCIENT, MODERN, AND POSTMODERN ONTOLOGY

Ancient and Modern Thought

As I demonstrated in the previous chapter, in the first-century Mediterranean world everyone accepted that the spirit world was just as real as the physical world, including both gods and demons,[2] and spirits of the deceased.[3] There was also a universal interest in astrology,[4] based on such widespread beliefs as "'*sympatheia*' between earthly and heavenly events,"[5] and people sought to manipulate the powers for their own ends[6] and protect themselves from harm. Because ancient societies had little faith in technology or progress, they ascribed all events (good or bad) to persons, human or nonhuman,[7] hence the attention given to prodigies in the ancient world.[8]

Christianity spoke into such a universal worldview, not having to prove that gods and spirits were real, but rather that there was only one true God and that the other gods of the day were either fictions or evil spirits.[9] And indeed this is still the case in much of the world today,[10] where Christianity is flourishing the most.

However, the rise of modernity from the Enlightenment onward changed all this for the West, as illustrated by the wave of witch burnings in the sixteenth and seventeenth centuries (in North America) and their abrupt cessation at the beginning of the eighteenth century.[11] People had become more tolerant, but also they had ceased to take seriously the idea that people could be agents of Satan, or even that such a being as the devil exists—though Karl Barth draws attention to the irony that the rationalistic eighteenth-century thinkers were also fascinated with mysteries and became founders of Freemasonry in "the form of an introduction to a mystery religion."[12]

---

2. Aune, *Prophecy in Early Christianity*, 33. Cf. Hengel, *Judaism and Hellenism*, 1:233; Wink, *Unmasking the Powers*, 108.

3. Aune, *Prophecy in Early Christianity*, 26.

4. Cf. Green, *Alexander to Actium*, 595–97.

5. Hengel, *Judaism and Hellenism*, 1:232; cf. Green, *Alexander to Actium*, 454, 482.

6. Green, *Alexander to Actium*, 482–83, 586–87.

7. Malina, *New Testament World*, 102–3.

8. Cf. Aune, *Revelation 6–16*, 416–19.

9. See, for example, 1 Cor 8:4–6; 10:20–22.

10. Cf. Boyd, *God at War*, 11–17, for some modern examples of this worldview.

11. Hekman, *Gender and Knowledge*, 116.

12. Barth, *Protestant Theology*, 35.

As chapter 1 explained, post-Enlightenment modernity looked especially to science as the paradigmatic form of human knowledge.[13] At its most extreme, represented best perhaps by logical positivism,[14] modern thought had no room for God or any invisible spiritual realm not able to be accounted for or mastered by the norms of science or technology. Empirical science was the only true model of truth to such philosophers and statements about metaphysical questions (such as the existence of God or the ultimate nature of reality) tended to be dismissed as meaningless or nonsense.[15]

Postmodernist Responses

However, as I explored in chapter 1, postmodernists question the privileging of natural science over other forms of knowledge and investigation, as a result of the work of philosophers such as Husserl, Kuhn, Gadamer, and Lyotard. Science has had a lot of success in studying the world "out there" and bringing it under human control. But scientific "laws" are often now seen as a representation of reality rather than exactly how reality works, and the limitations of natural science in studying human beings and societies are realized.[16]

This thinking has implications for the concept of the spiritual. For instance, Kevin Hart questions the common assumption that Derrida, and poststructuralism generally, are necessarily hostile to belief in God.[17] He finds support, or at least sympathy, in Derrida's work for a negative theology, the kind of approach to theology that underpins the *via negativa* in traditional Christian mysticism,[18] which refuses to make positive affirmations about God because God is essentially unknowable and no description of God in human language can ever capture God's essence. In Hart's view, deconstruction is not against theology as such, but rather seeks to make way for a "non-metaphysical theology"; or at least "negative theology may deconstruct positive theology."[19] Hart thus sees postmodernism as opening the door to God-talk, though perhaps of a very different kind to that of

13. Hekman, *Gender and Knowledge*, 4.
14. Cahoone, ed., *Modernism to Postmodernism*, 6.
15. Cf. MacIntyre, "Moral Philosophy," 2–3.
16. Hekman, *Gender and Knowledge*, 13.
17. Hart, *Trespass*, esp. 22–34.
18. As opposed to the *via positiva*, which sees everything in the world as a symbol of God's goodness and grace and is willing to make positive affirmations about what God is like.
19. Hart, *Trespass*, xi.

traditional Christianity. For example, he argues that "Derrida's quarry is the notion of totalization, and he closes on God only to the extent that God has been taken to function as a means of totalization."[20]

McKnight points out that in the discourses of modernity God-talk was ruled out because the word "god" has no correspondence with anything in the natural world. The postmodern phase may be seen as showing the limits of such rationality and opening the possibility of conceptualizing God again.[21] Spiritual reality becomes conceivable again, as is shown by the increasing respect shown by postmodern anthropologists towards the spiritual practices and beliefs of premodern cultures[22] and the openness of popular culture in the west to such ideas as exorcism, spirit guides, angels, and astrology.

So might even an ancient text like Revelation have something to say about the nature of reality and the validity of spiritual reality in particular?

SPIRITUAL REALITY IN REVELATION

The Spiritual World in Revelation

As stated in chapter 2, Revelation is shaped by an apocalyptic worldview. By this is meant not just that its worldview resembles that found in the Jewish apocalypses of that era,[23] but that it is a worldview centered on the idea of revelation of invisible realities, a literal "revelation worldview." As John Collins writes, "The existence of another world beyond what is accessible to humanity by natural means is a constant element in all the apocalypses."[24]

According to Revelation, all reality is grounded in God, who is the most permanent reality there is—"him who is and who was and who is to come" (1:4). Moreover God's heavenly realm is as real as—even more fundamentally real than—the visible world. We may not be able to see "the seven spirits who are before his throne" (1:4; 4:5), for example, or the "Lamb standing as if it had been slaughtered" (5:6), but in John's revelation all this is a fundamental part of how the universe operates. In fact, as Friesen argues, "In John's text the true center of space is the throne of God

---

20. Ibid., 29–30.
21. McKnight, *Post-Modern Use*, 196–203.
22. E.g. Taussig, *Mimesis and Alterity*; Sullivan, *Icanthu's Drum*; see especially Sullivan's closing comments (ibid., 681–82.)
23. As discussed in the previous chapter.
24. Collins, "Morphology of a Genre," 9; see also Thompson, *Apocalypse and Empire*, 31.

in heaven."[25] Moreover his universe is not empty (unlike that of modernity) but populated by all sorts of spirits (1:5; 2:7; 3:1; 4:2,5; 5:6; 14:13; 16:13,14; 19:10; 21:10; 22:6,17).

This spiritual reality is invisible to the natural senses; it can only be seen by revelation, to those who are "in the spirit" (1:10; 4:2), and can only be described in highly symbolic language, though the effects of events in this realm can be experienced in natural ways (for example, the plagues of 6:7-8 or the destruction of Babylon in ch. 18). In Revelation the language of sense perception is used primarily of seeing "in the spirit" (for example, 1:12-13; 5:1-2; 7:1-2), as opposed to using the physical senses.[26]

The author of Revelation also shares the perspective of all peoples of the ancient Mediterranean regarding the causes of events. As Paul Minear writes, for John "it was axiomatic that all earthly happenings, whether present or future, derive from what happens in heaven."[27] Examples of this include the drama of the opening of the seven seals in heaven (chs. 5–6) with the consequences in human life (war, famine, and the like) or the political and religious consequences that flow out of the war in heaven (12:7—13:18). In fact, Revelation may be seen as an exposé of world events, taking us "behind the scenes" to the real causes of things seen and heard by humankind[28]—though in this case (as in much of the Bible) the direction is not just one way; earth affects heaven as well as heaven affecting earth.

The Place of Angels

The reality and role of angels is a significant part of the apocalyptic worldview. In the Jewish apocalypses the action is very much heaven-directed and a significant amount of this is carried out mainly by (good or evil) angels, as I explained in chapter 2. In the apocalypses, angels are seen as having major roles in the ordinary workings of the cosmos[29] and are assigned to particular people, both the righteous and the ungodly.[30] In a similar way, the Qumran documents speak of two opposing spirits or angels controlling their human followers.[31] The Old Testament also speaks regularly of angels

25. Friesen, *Imperial Cults*, 163.
26. The epistemological issues involved here are picked up in the next chapter.
27. Minear, "Cosmology," 24–25.
28. Cf. Malina, *Genre and Message*, 47, 254; Hurtgren, *Anti-Language*, 89.
29. *1 En.* 82:10-20 (the sun and the year's calendar); *2 En.* 11–16; *3 Bar.* 6:13.
30. *2 Bar.* 12–13.
31. Cf. *Community Rule* 1QS ch. 3, and comments in Hengel, *Judaism and Hellenism*, 1:218.

and "the experience of angels seems to have been common throughout the Mediterranean."[32]

In Revelation too, a prominent role is given to angels, not only as bearers of revelation but also as actors in the drama, carrying out the will of God, as explained in chapter 2. For example, angels hold back the four winds (7:1–3) and an angel gathers the vintage of the earth (14:19). Revelation 12:7–9 describes an angelic battle that it presents as lying behind, or related to, events on earth, perhaps events of the Jewish-Roman war of A.D. 66–70 in particular; this idea is similar to aspects of Jewish apocalypses and the Dead Sea Scrolls.[33] On the other hand, the angelology of Revelation is rudimentary compared to some of the apocalypses.

In Revelation, angels are mostly either serving God (as in most cases in the text) or fighting God and on the side of Satan (as in 12:7 and 16:13–14). However, Walter Wink has argued that not all angels are just "black or white." If we take seriously John's language of the angels of the seven churches (Rev 2–3), which seem to represent the spiritual state of their congregations,[34] then we must allow that God's angels can be compromised and defeated just as much as humans.[35] Similarly, Loren Stuckenbuck argues that the portrayal of angels in Revelation 2–3 "involves a demotion from views of angelic functions held by the intended readers."[36]

Whether or not this argument is accepted—and it is clearly controversial—it seems that John's view of angels is not entirely compatible with traditional (including Christian) views. It seems that John, rather than trying to enhance or enlarge the role of angels, is consciously "bringing them down to size." In two episodes where John attempts to worship an angel (19:10 and 22:8–9), the angel resists being worshiped, not just because angels are not divine and only God should be worshiped, but because an angel is *equal* to the comrades of John:

> "I am a fellow servant with you and your comrades who hold the testimony of Jesus." (19:10)

> "I am a fellow servant with you and your comrades the prophets, and those who keep the words of this book." (22:9)

---

32. Malina, *Genre and Message*, 61.
33. Cf. Aune, *Revelation 6–16*, 691–93.
34. Cf. Wink, *Unmasking the Powers*, 70.
35. Ibid., 72–73.
36. Stuckenbuck, *Angel Veneration and Christology*, 238. Cf. Carrell, *Jesus and the angels*, 20–21.

Angels seem to know much more than human beings like John. They are portrayed frequently as glorious and powerful, even to the point of being described in terms like those used of God or Christ.[37] But John wants to insist that they are actually the equals of believers in Christ,[38] or at least of prophets of Christ.

Moreover the word "angel" (Gk. ἀγγελος, angel, messenger) is itself ambiguous. While clearly denoting a heavenly spiritual being in most cases, it is used by other New Testament authors to denote a human messenger.[39] This is why some interpreters understand the "angels" of the seven churches (Rev 1–3) as their leaders or bishops.[40] After all, we normally (and probably correctly) take the behaviors described in Revelation 2–3 as ascribed to the believers, not the angels, which is why some other interpreters see the "angels" as in some sense as "personifications of the life or spirit of the churches."[41] There is even an ancient Arabic commentary on Revelation that reflects a variant text of 1:1 identifying John as the angel to whom Jesus made known the prophecy, rather than an angel mediating it to John.[42] This text is probably unreliable and the usual textual reading fits the rest of the narrative better, but it shows that the boundaries between angels and humans (at least prophets) can be quite blurred.

There is also another episode in Revelation where angels and Christians play parallel roles: the story of Satan's downfall from heaven in Revelation 12. While the heavenly aspect of the story tells of a battle between two armies of angels (12:7–9) in which the devil is defeated and expelled from heaven, the prophetic commentary announced by "a loud voice in heaven" (12:10) attributes the victory not to Michael and his angels but to "our comrades" (Gk. τῶν αδελφῶν ἡμῶν, our brothers), who "have conquered him by the blood of the Lamb and by the word of their testimony, for they did not cling to life even in the face of death" (12:10,11).[43] Here the (human) comrades are the primary actors and the angels are secondary.

---

37. Cf. Filho, "Visionary Experience," 216; Stuckenbruck, *Angel Veneration and Christology*, 228–30; Carrell, *Jesus and the Angels*, 75.

38. Cf. Brighton, *Revelation*, 343.

39. E.g., Matt 11:10; Mark 1:2; Luke 7:24, 27; 9:52; Jas 2:25.

40. Cf. Aune, *Revelation 1–5*, 111–12.

41. Carrell, *Jesus and the Angels*, 20. Aune (*Revelation 1–5*, 109–12, 120, 131–32) calls it a "literary device" and describes the angels as an "alter ego" of each congregation but asserts they are still angels consistent with John's usage elsewhere in the book. Fiorenza (*Justice and Judgment*, 146) refers to them as "visionary counterparts of the prophets in the communities."

42. Davis, "Arabic Commentary," 91–92.

43. Cf. Pattemore, *People of God*, 93–96; Aune, *Revelation 6–16*, 699–703; Beale,

Spiritual Experience in Revelation

If angels, spirits, and God are real, as is assumed in Revelation, then it follows that human experience of these realities must be possible. In Revelation such experience is mediated by the Spirit who speaks to the churches (2:7 and parallels; 14:13) and is especially felt by those who are "in the spirit" (or "Spirit";[44] 1:10; 4:2; 21:10), which seems to imply some kind of altered state of consciousness. As Malina writes, "Whether one translates this phrase by ecstasy or trance, the point is that John himself insists he fell into an altered state of awareness and came to experience an alternate reality."[45] Such experiences were usually rejected by followers of the Enlightenment, but were (and are) common to premodern societies[46] and are being sought out by followers of new spiritualities in the Western world with increasing seriousness.

Forms of spiritual experience or practices described in Revelation include communication with angels (1:1; 10:1, 9; etc.), visions (1:2, 12–20; 4:1; etc.), auditions or voices (1:10; 4:1; 10:4; etc.), prophesying (1:3; 2:20; 11:3, 6; 19:10; 22:6, 7, 10; etc.), anointed seeing (3:18), communion with Jesus (3:20), worship and singing (5:9, 12, 14; 11:16; etc.), prayer (5:3, 4; 22:17), visionary acts such as eating a scroll (10:9, 10), miracles (11:5, 6, 11; 13:13–15; 16:14; 19:20), portents (12:1; 15:1; etc.), sorcery (18:23; 22:15), healing (22:2), and partaking of the "water of life" (22:17). Some are more likely symbolic, such as eating a scroll, but others are meant to be taken as literal fact.

Monotheism in Revelation

The difference between Revelation, as a Christian text, and the generally accepted worldview of its day lies in its attitude to the spirits of the universe. As discussed in chapter 2, people in the ancient Mediterranean tended to

---

Commentary on the Greek Text, 663–66; Resseguie, *Narrative Commentary*, 91, 131, 173–74; Fee, *Revelation*, 162–63, 168–73.

44. The Greek allows for either punctuation.

45. Malina, *Genre and Message*, 27. Cf. ibid., 31–34, and compare the discussion of the phrase in Aune, *Revelation 1–5*, 82–83. Aune suggests three possibilities: an ecstatic state (which he leans towards), divine inspiration apart from ecstasy (the common use elsewhere in the NT; cf. Luke 2:27; John 4:23f.; Acts 1:2; Rom 8:9; 1 Cor 14:2, 15, 16; Eph 3:5), and use of apocalyptic language to fabricate the vision report, which he finds the weakest suggestion.

46. Cf. Malina, *Genre and Message*, 28; Wink, "Demons and DMins," 506; Sullivan, *Icanthu's Drum*, 651–60.

believe in the reality of all the gods worshiped by the various nations of the ancient world, and sometimes in their identity with gods of different names worshiped elsewhere. They also saw the stars as "living, personal, beings," gods in fact.[47] But Revelation is strongly monotheistic and in John's world spirits are interpreted very differently.

The position of God as creator and governor of the universe is a central feature of John's cosmology. From the point of view of Revelation, all other reality derives from God as creator (4:11; 10:6; 14:7) and is subject to him and dependent on him. This is illustrated by his control of food supplies (6:5–6, 8; 18:8), wild animals and birds (6:8; 9:3–10; 19:17–18, 21), plagues and diseases (6:8; 11:6; 16:2, 9, 11; 18:8; 22:18), the heavenly bodies (6:12–13; 8:12; 16:8, 10),[48] mountains and islands (6:14; 16:20), the winds (7:1), the sea and other bodies of water (8:8–11; 16:3–4, 12), and the rain (11:6.) Also he is able to send down hail, fire, lightning, burning mountains, and stars onto the earth (8:7–11; 16:18, 21) and to cause earthquakes (6:12; 11:13; 16:18); he is sovereign over time (10:6; 6:10–11) and the underworld (9:1–2; 17:8; 20:1–3, 13–14); and he is even able to raise the dead (11:11; 20:4–6, 13), control and defeat the devil and his angels (12:9; 20:2–3, 10), and sway the hearts of people (17:17). As Malina puts it, "if John has any message at all, it is that the one God is in control of the universe."[49]

Revelation thus reflects a very similar idea of monotheism to that held by the Jews. At the outset of John's book, God says, "I am the Alpha and the Omega . . . who is and who was and who is to come, the Almighty" (1:8). He portrays a scene in heaven where every heavenly being worships the one sovereign creator (4:2, 11). Like the Jewish prophets, he calls the Gentiles to turn away from idols and worship only the true creator God (14:7; 9:20; 2:14, 20) and follows mainstream Judaism in forbidding worship of angels (19:10; 22:8–9). The existence of other spiritual beings is not denied, but "Any cosmic beings regarded as deities by John's contemporaries are regarded simply as sky beings in God's entourage."[50] The stars may be personal or spiritual, but not independent;[51] in fact, they may rather serve as images of underlying realities such as kingdoms (1:16, 20; 2:1, 28; 6:13; 8:10–12; 9:1; 12:4; 22:16).

---

47. Malina, "How a Cosmic Lamb Marries," 76; Malina, *Genre and Message*, 6–7.

48. This conviction made the predictions of disasters involving the sun, etc. meaningful as poetic imagery (cf. Minear, *New Testament Apocalyptic*, 52–55).

49. Malina, *Genre and Message*, 78.

50. Ibid., 261.

51. Ibid., 15.

"Religion" as a Key Issue

John sees the whole arena of religion as the central key to what happens in history. In the plot of the book everything turns on people's religious beliefs and decisions. This may seem obvious when the context is the life of the local churches of Asia (Rev 2–3), but as John portrays it, the whole of history is governed by "religious" events, particularly those to do with people's response to God and Jesus Christ. This is seen, first, in the nature of the sins in response to which disasters are experienced. John attributes these disasters to people's decision to resist the will of God, especially in the areas such as idolatry (worship of false gods), sorcery, and moral defects such as theft, murder, and fornication (9:20–21; 16:9–11).

John's tendency to give central place to religious factors also appears in the story of the two witnesses (11:1–13). This is told in the context of a threat to God's temple (11:1–2), the place of true worship of the true God, and follows the recommissioning of John in chapter 10 and the refusal to repent in 9:20–21. The content of the witnesses' message is not given but we are meant to infer that it is centered on worship of God in view of this context, the parallels with Elijah and Moses (11:4–6), the reaction of the world to their death (11:7–10), and the result of their public resurrection and ascension (11:11–13). Hence, the events that unfold in the city (11:8, 13) are governed by people's choices about whom to worship.

The tale of the three beasts (the dragon, the sea beast, and the land beast) in Revelation 12–14 obviously has a strong political and economic dimension. But the central issue is religious: who is to be worshipped?[52] The beasts' followers worship the dragon and the beast (13:4, 8, 12–15; 14:9–11), stimulated by the beast's healing (13:3,12), signs performed by the land beast (13:13–14), and the construction of an image of the sea beast (13:14–15). The economic decisions of the beast's regime are designed to get people to give allegiance, and even worship, to the beast (13:16–17). In opposition to this, the gospel calls for people to worship God (14:6–7; 15:4). And it is because religious decisions are so ultimate that the consequences of them are also ultimate (14:9–13).

The crimes of the whore of Babylon are also described in moral or religious terms such as "fornication" (17:2; 18:3, 9; 19:2), "sorcery" (18:23), corruption (19:2), and "sins" against God (18:4–5.) Of course, one of her chief crimes is persecution of believers (17:6; 18:24; 19:2). Though the martyrs' cause is made political by the government powers who persecute them (13:15), their death is attributed to their witness to Jesus (12:11; 20:4). In

---

52. Thus also worship has political consequences and dimensions (cf. Ruiz, "Politics of Praise," 376–85).

other words, the issue is religious, though it clearly has political or legal implications, since the declaration of the lordship of Jesus over all the kings of the earth (1:5; 2:26–28; 17:14; 19:16) is a clear challenge to the claims of Caesar. It is, of course, anachronistic to speak of "religion" and "politics" as separate spheres in the ancient world; my point in differentiating between them here is to show the primacy of "religious" issues—that is, questions about who to worship—in John's worldview. Most other ancient people would, in fact, agree with him on this priority, though they would violently disagree about whom people should worship.

John highlights these issues because there is ambiguity, confusion, and dissension among the churches of Asia over the boundaries and concepts of worship and religion. For example, the church in Ephesus seems to see religion as primarily a matter of orthodoxy (rejecting false apostles and "the works of the Nicolaitans," 2:6), but John sees this as inadequate if love[53] is missing (2:4.) At the other end of the spectrum, some believers in Pergamum saw no problem with eating food sacrificed to idols (2:14, 15), and some in Thyatira even wanted to explore "the deep things of Satan" (2:24), but John sees this as unacceptable compromise with worship of the one true God, even using words like "fornication"[54] (2:20, 21) and "adultery"[55] (2:22) to describe it. Perhaps he has literal sexual sin in mind here,[56] or else there is a deliberate double meaning, in that polytheistic worship often included sacred prostitution and Israel was enjoined not to participate in this as it would involve a less than total commitment to their "jealous" God (Exod 20:5). Worship of God was often compared in the Old Testament to marital devotion and fidelity; going after other gods and alliances with ungodly nations were likened to adultery (e.g., Jer 2:2; Ezek 23; Hos 1:2; 2:1–20; 3:1). Revelation has a similar view (17:1–5; 18:3, 9; 19:2).

God's Control of History

Revelation declares that "the Lord our God the Almighty reigns" (19:6). Right at the beginning this is made clear to John. He is shown "what *must* soon take place" (1:1; repeated in 22:6). Later God is portrayed as seated on

---

53. Love to God or love for one another. Commentators differ here; I take it in the sense of devotion to God and Jesus, because this is more emphasized in Revelation and fits the storyline, as will be argued in chapter 6. Cf. Beale, *Book of Revelation*, 230; Caird, *Revelation of St. John*, 31–32; Sweet, *Revelation*, 81.

54. Gk. πορνεια, used of "illicit sexual intercourse in general" (*Thayer's Greek-English*, 532).

55. Gk. μοιχάω, commit adultery (*Thayer's Greek-English Lexicon*, 417).

56. Cf. Aune, *Revelation 1–5*, 204–205; Beale, *Book of Revelation*, 262.

a throne (4:2, 9)[57] and his plans are described as a sealed scroll that no one (except the Lamb) is able to open (5:1–5).

The aorist passive form of *didōmi* (*edothē*, ἐδόθη, given)[58] is used to indicate authority and power to act in certain prescribed and limited areas. Thus the rider on the red horse "was permitted (Gk. *edothē*) to take peace from the earth" (6:4). The fallen star is "given the key to the shaft of the bottomless pit" (9:1) and thus allowed to release smoke and locusts onto the earth (9:2–3), which are "given authority (Gk. *exousia*) like the authority of scorpions of the earth" (9:3), but within strictly circumscribed boundaries (9:4–5). The beast from the sea is "given a mouth uttering haughty and blasphemous words" and "allowed to exercise authority for forty-two months" (13:5, 7). The beast from the land is "allowed" to perform signs on behalf of the first beast and give breath to its image (13:14–15).

There are other expressions that carry the same idea. God "grants"[59] two witnesses "authority to prophesy" for a set period (11:3). Four angels are "released"[60] at the exact predetermined time "to kill a third of humankind" (9:15). The rise and rule of the "ten horns" is for a limited time, "one hour" (17:12). The actions of the beast and its horns are attributed to God's sovereignty (17:17) and the devil is bound for a thousand years, after which "he must[61] be let out for a little while" (20:3, 7).

God's sovereign control is demonstrated by his determination of the time limits for events (6:10–11; 7:3; 10:6–7). Moreover the whole movement of the storyline in Revelation implies that God is directing everything and that there are no uncertainties or deviations possible. Here the perspective of Revelation is similar to that of the Jewish apocalypses,[62] though not entirely, as I showed in chapter 2 and will explore further below and in chapter 5. They also share a certain dualistic perspective.

Dualism and Binary Thinking in Revelation

Various forms of dualism were common in the ancient Mediterranean. For example, the Hellenistic worldview often distinguished sharply between

---

57. Cf. Rissi, *Time and History*, 51.

58. Described by Rienecker and Rogers (*Linguistic Key*, 831–32) as "the theological or divine passive indicating that God is the one who gives." See also McIlraith, *Reciprocal Love*, 98.

59. Gk. δώσω, future active of δίδωμι.

60. Gk. ἐλύθησαν, aorist passive of λύω, "loose," "untie," or "release."

61. Gk. *dei*=, "it is necessary that."

62. As in 4 *Ezra* 5:41–49.

body and soul, as in the Orphic doctrines, which influenced Plato and according to which the body was a prison or tomb of the soul or spirit.[63] Their concept of life after death was centered on the fate of the (disembodied) immortal soul.[64]

Mainstream Jewish thinking was different. According to N. T. Wright, the Jewish worldview embraced such "dualisms" as the existence of heavenly beings such as angels and the differentiation between Creator and creation, good and evil, this age and the age to come. It also entertained such dualisms as that between human knowledge and revelation, between members of different religions, and between opposite tendencies in human beings.[65] According to Doron Mendels, "The author of Revelation shows how strongly dualism was imbued in the Jewish mind of the day. The only army that counts for him is transcendental and universal, rather than earthly and national."[66] However, Jews were suspicious of dualisms that tended to postulate "two ultimate sources of all that is";[67] a Platonic dualism of matter and spirit, or body-soul in humans, could end up threatening their creational or providential monotheism.[68]

As I explained in chapter 2, Jewish apocalypses had a bolder form of spiritual dualism, seeing God as ultimate in power, but with real opposition to him from both human and spiritual beings.[69] In several apocalypses there is a contest for the human soul between the Lord and Beliar.[70] There are warnings against Satan and his spirits[71] and prophecies of his future doom.[72] George Nickelsburg sees the "Book of Watchers" in *1 Enoch* as teaching that the human race is the victim of superhuman powers warring

---

63. Green, *Alexander to Actium*, 592–93.

64. Cf. Hengel, *Judaism and Hellenism*, 1:201, 246; Sanders, *Paul and Palestinian Judaism*, 553; Veyne, *Bread and Circuses*, 112.

65. Wright, *People of God*, 252–59.

66. Mendels, *Jewish Nationalism*, 348.

67. Wright, *People of God*, 253.

68. Cf. Collins, *Between Athens and Jerusalem*, 160–61.

69. Cf. Boyd, *God at War*, 172–80.

70. For example, *T. Dan* 4:7; 5:1; *T. Naph.* 2:6; *T. Asher* 1:8; *T. Ben.* 3:3–5.

71. For example, *T. Dan* 3:6; 6:1.

72. For example, *As. Moses* 10:1. Cf. *2 En.* 31:4–6; also 29:4–5.

against God.[73] The Book of Daniel also has overtones of conflict on an angelic as well as human level.[74]

Revelation seems to reflect the Jewish dualisms distinguished by Wright, with the possible exception of the postulation of two opposing tendencies in human beings. There is also some evidence of matter-spirit and body-soul dualities (6:9–11 apparently speaks of disembodied souls), but not with the assumption that spirit or soul is more real or good than matter or body. Revelation envisages a bodily resurrection at the end (20:13) and a new world described in physical, even sensuous, terms (21:1–22:5). Revelation is not negative about the natural realm as such and neither does it see it as "unreal." For example, John himself is located in a natural geographical location, the island of Patmos (1:9), when he starts to see his vision, and he is told to direct it to seven churches in real first-century cities of Asia (1:11).

Dualism in Revelation is more ethical and soteriological in nature, resembling the dualism of the Jewish apocalypses. It shows strong binary thinking in terms of such opposites as good/evil and chosen/rejected. In fact, for John the whole of history is driven by a conflict between the forces of good (God, Jesus, the angels, Jesus' true followers, the faithful churches) and evil (Satan/the devil/the serpent/the dragon and his angels, the beasts, Babylon, unbelievers, and false believers). John does not see the two sides as equally ultimate and powerful; rather he sees God as in control and governing the outcome of all historical events *in detail*. However, since he does see freewill beings as having some ability to withstand and oppose God, within limits set by the deity, he takes this struggle very seriously.[75] In this sense, Revelation subscribes to a dualistic view of reality and history[76] expressed in his attitude to the Roman Empire: "The political dualism relates to the present visible rule of Rome and the future visible rule of the Almighty,"[77] or the present visible rule of Rome contrasted with the present "invisible" rule of God and Christ.

---

73. Nickelsburg, "Salvation without and with a Messiah," 51. However, Gen 6 lays the blame for the deteriorating situation in the world at the feet of humans and in another Jewish text this incident is at least partly blamed on the women who beguiled the Watchers (*T. Reu.* 5).

74. Cf. Dan 10:12–13, 20–21.

75. According to Boyd, "the dualism of the Bible is a free will dualism, not a metaphysical dualism," derived from the idea that "God chose to create a quasi-democratic cosmos in which dualism could result" (Boyd, *God at War*, 176.)

76. Contra Kallas, "The Apocalypse—An Apocalyptic Book?," 69–80. Collins calls it "cosmic dualism" in *Combat Myth*, 158–61.

77. Yhearm, *Sitz im Leben*, 304.

The reality and influence of the devil is a vital part of the worldview of Revelation. Satan is portrayed as a strong anti-God force among the seven cities of Asia. He influences some of the Jews (2:9; 3:9), persecutes Christians (2:10, 13), dominates the life of some cities (2:13), and leads some Christians into false doctrine and practice (2:24). The war between Satan's angels and Michael's (12:7-9) implies that there is real opposition to God, as do the ongoing machinations of the dragon, both directly (12:13-17) and through his agents the beasts (ch. 13). Their devilish power over the whole inhabited world is real and therefore so is their effect on history, as illustrated by the healing of the beast's head wound (13:3, 14), the universal worship given the beast (13:8), the powers exercised by the land beast promoting a universal and compulsory "beast religion" (13:12-18), and their final battle against God's forces (19:19-21). But while the devil is real, his doom is sure (20:2-10).

Revelation's soteriological dualism is seen in John's theology about the death of Jesus. While he does not have such a developed theory of atonement as seen in Paul or *Hebrews*, he sees Jesus' death as both a crime (for which the perpetrators are accountable, 1:7) and an achievement. That is, his death frees believers from their sins and enables them to take their place in God's plans (1:5-6), it has ransomed people from all ethnic backgrounds (5:9), it brings cleansing to those who came out of "the great ordeal" (7:14), and it provides the basis for the victory of the martyrs over the dragon, especially the dragon's accusations against them (12:11). Each of these claims presupposes that there is a conflict between good and evil, that people need to be set free from sin against God in order to be able to serve him, and that this freedom has been achieved by Jesus' death, which has liberated believers from the accusations of Satan and the judgments of God upon sin.

But this effect was only for those who chose God's side against Satan's, those whose names were written in "the book of life of the Lamb that was slaughtered" (13:8; cf. 3:5; 17:8; 20:12, 15; 21:27). John has a constant tendency to divide all people into two exclusive groups—those *for* and *against* God—and to assign them to opposite fates. For example, in the messages to the seven churches, true "overcoming" believers are contrasted with both "outside" enemies like the false Jews (2:9; 3:9) and false Christians or infiltrators into the church (2:2, 6, 14-15, 20-23). The seal of God (7:2-4) divides people into two camps with opposite fates (9:4); in a similar but opposite way, so does the mark issued by the land beast (13:16-17; 14:9-12; 16:2; 20:4), in what Royalty calls "polemical parallelism" and "dualism of decision."[78] Only those who are written in the Lamb's book of life will be

---

78. Royalty, *Streets of Heaven*, 185.

able to resist the beast and avoid the eternal punishment resulting from following it (13:8; 14:9–11; 17:8); throughout Revelation, having one's name in this book separates the followers of Jesus from those doomed to destruction (3:5; 20:12–15; 21:27). People belong either to "the holy city" (11:2) or "the great city" (11:8), two sides that are constantly at war.[79] Finally, there is a permanent separation at the end between those who enjoy the blessings of the new order and those who are clearly "outside," in the lake of fire (21:7–8, 27; 22:14–15).

Revelation is thus a war story, predicated on struggle.[80] The faithful witnesses/martyrs are opposed to their persecutors and murderers (2:9–10, 13; 6:9–10; 16:6). Most people oppose the prophetic witnesses of God and delight in their death (11:9–13). The political "powers that be" (Roman and local authorities) are consistently seen as opposed to Christians and to God himself (13:6–7; 16:6; 17:6,13–14; 18:24), and as coming under his judgment (16:10–11, 19–21; 18:6, 8, 20, 21; 19:2); believers are thus called on to "come out" of their control and loyalty (18:4; comp. 13:7–10; 14:9–12). There are several out-and-out wars between Christ and his followers, on the one side, and the earthly authorities stirred up by the dragon, on the other (12:17; 13:7; 16:12–16; 17:14; 19:11–21; 20:7–10).

Because of his soteriological dualism, John has a strong emphasis on maintaining boundaries between the church and the surrounding culture, as many commentators have pointed out.[81] However, John's identity markers are different to those of Judaism, with its strong emphasis on purity viewed in terms of maintaining boundaries.[82] There is mention of keeping the commandments of God (12:17; 14:12), but otherwise the identity markers mentioned are abstaining from eating food sacrificed to idols and fornication (2:14, 20), worshiping only the one true God (13:8; 14:9–12), and abstaining from other sins of the world in general (21:8, 27; 22:15). Overwhelmingly, John characterizes God's saints as those from every nation who follow Jesus and hold fast to his testimony (2:3, 10; 3:8; 7:9–17; 11:8; 12:11, 17; 13:10; 14:1–5, 12; 15:2–3; 17:14; 19:7–10; 20:4–6; 21:7–8, 27; 22:3–5,14). Hence Revelation radically challenges or redraws the boundaries of holiness central to the Jewish worldview.[83]

---

79. Cf. Minear, "Ontology and Ecclesiology," 94–100.
80. Cf. Minear, "Cosmology of the Apocalypse," 28.
81. Cf. Minear, "Ontology and Ecclesiology," 102.
82. Rhoads, "Social Criticism," 145–48.
83. Compare Rhoads' analysis of Mark, according to which "The Jesus movement . . . treated boundaries as lines to cross, redraw, or eliminate" (ibid., 154).

Thompson therefore suggests that the dualism of Revelation needs some qualification,[84] as the boundaries between good and evil, present and future, heaven and earth are much more porous, much less impenetrable, than we might first think.[85] He points to parallels in language between good and evil entities (such as the feminine language applied both to Babylon and the New Jerusalem), the dependence of evil on God's sovereignty, the possibility of entities changing from one sphere to another (such as the fall of the dragon in ch. 12), and the call to repentance as a means of moving through the boundaries.

Thompson is attempting to avert too strong a dualism:

> If there was irreconcilable contradiction among religious, social, biological, and cultural dimensions of Christian existence, the seer would be affirming that at the most fundamental level of reality there is an eternal, fixed metaphysical dualism. Such a view is antithetical to John's.[86]

Thompson is alert to a real danger. However, he seems to press the case too far, as when he claims that even in the new order of Revelation 21–22 "the unfaithful may still have the possibility of repentance";[87] there seems to be no hint of this in the text.[88]

From another perspective, James Kallas argues strongly that Revelation is radically *different* to the other apocalypses,[89] since Revelation rejects the apocalyptic dualism that sees Satan as behind the sufferings of the elect and returns to the view of the Old Testament that "suffering is the work *of God* . . . due to man's failure to stay true to the will of God."[90] While it is true that the themes of God's sovereignty and judgments are very prominent in Revelation, it is a gross overstatement to suggest that these overturn the dualism in John's worldview. For example, Kallas insists that the seven churches "have merited their suffering."[91] While this is true in some cases, it overlooks the persecution of the Smyrnans by the devil that they are not to fear (2:9–10) and the successful endurance of suffering by the Philadelphians (3:8–10).

84. Thompson, *Apocalypse and Empire*, 74–91.
85. Ibid., 81.
86. Ibid., 91.
87. Ibid., 84.
88. Comp. the critique of Thompson's argument in Gilbertson, *God and History*, 70–71; and also Friesen, *Imperial Cults*, 161–65.
89. Kallas, "Apocalypse—An Apocalyptic Book?," 69–80.
90. Ibid., 78.
91. Ibid.

Later Kallas urges that Satan "is not independent, a God-opposing figure working out his own designs, but is instead a tool in the hands of the omnipotent God. . . . He is forced to execute God's will. Demonology has disappeared. . . . All true dualism, positing a foreign will opposed to God and exercising its own independent desires, is gone."[92] This assumes a false antithesis. Revelation clearly places Satan and sinful humanity under the sovereign hand of God, but it equally clearly sees them as pursuing their own agendas in opposition to him. To put it another way, Revelation is not at all dualistic in the sense of evil being equal to good—but neither are the other apocalypses! Rather it is dualistic in the sense of seeing real conflict in the moral and spiritual universe, though under God's control and destined to be resolved in his victory.

In conclusion, we see a limited but definite dualism of thought in Revelation. John eschews any ontological dualism in his view of the basic makeup of the universe. He holds to the strongly monotheistic concept of a sovereign God who controls all things. On the other hand, he has an equally strong concept of spiritual warfare reflected in human struggles but grounded in a cosmic battle between good and evil, God and Satan—what Boyd calls a "warfare worldview."[93] This leads him to a firm soteriological dualism that places all human beings on one side or the other in this battle and assigns to each person a final destiny in the New Jerusalem or the lake of fire—not, however, based on ethnicity, gender, or other human (even traditional religious) boundaries, but solely on one's response to God and Jesus.

Binary Thinking about Spiritual Realities

Because of his ethical, spiritual, and soteriological dualism, John does not accept all spiritual reality as valid in the sense of right or good. The criteria he uses for distinguishing between valid and invalid claims to spiritual revelation will be examined in the next chapter. However, it needs to be noted here that he believes in true and false spiritual claims. For example, one of the major themes in the messages to the seven churches is the need to discern between the two: seeing through the claims of "those who *claim* to be apostles but are not" (2:2), "those who *say* they are Jews and are not, but are a synagogue of Satan" (2:9; 3:9), "Jezebel, who *calls herself* a prophet" (2:20), churches that "have a *name* of being alive" but are dead (3:1; italics

---

92. Ibid., 80.
93. Boyd, *God at War*, 11–22, 55–72, 75–79.

added), and those which *think* they are rich and prosperous but are actually "wretched, pitiable, poor, blind, and naked" (3:17).

Later in John's narrative, the land beast uses signs to deceive "the inhabitants of the earth" (13:13–14). These signs appeal to the senses and cause people to *think* they are perceiving or experiencing spiritual reality when they are actually worshiping a false god (false not necessarily in the sense of non-existent, but in the sense of opposed to the one true Supreme Being). This beast is described as having "two horns like a lamb" while speaking "like a dragon" (13:11), and later it is called "the false prophet" (16:13; 19:20; 20:10). Similarly, in 16:13–14 signs are specifically attributed to "demonic spirits" and it is said of the whore that "all nations were deceived by your sorcery" (18:23).

For John, as I argued above, this all goes back to the devil, who is called "the deceiver of the whole world" (12:9; 20:3, 7–8, 10). This does not necessarily imply that false claims to experience of spiritual realities always originate in evil spirits. For example, the deceptive signs performed by the land beast in 13:13–15 may be genuinely supernatural or may be fakery; the evidence suggests that both possibilities were quite common in that day, though not often in the imperial cult.[94] Scherrer thinks that for John the signs are real but satanic,[95] and other ancient Christians certainly take this perspective,[96] but the text of Revelation is not so explicit.

John's call for discernment is quite relevant, as it provides a safeguard against superstition and general animism, and protects his monotheism. Yhearm argues,

> While monotheism was very rare in the ancient world, John advocates a pervervid monotheism where other gods are not merely dismissed but repudiated with scorn through a very simple dualistic antithesis which says that there is one true God and claims to the contrary are demonically inspired and dangerously counterfeit.[97]

But does John follow any *guidelines* for discerning between true and false spiritual reality? It seems that several are implied in his language: some kind of testing process is implied by 2:2 ("you have tested those who claim to be apostles but are not, and have found them to be false"). Symptoms of false spirituality may include opposition to the church, verbal ("slander")

---

94. Cf. Scherrer, "Signs and Wonders," 599–610. See also Botha, "God, Emperor Worship," 95–96.

95. Scherrer, "Signs and Wonders," 602.

96. Ibid., 603.

97. Yhearm, *Sitz im Leben*, 373.

or physical (2:9, 10; 11:9, 10; 12:10; 16:6; 17:6; 18:24; 19:2), propagation of teaching that involves compromise with the non-Christian culture, especially in the area of idolatry (9:20; 18:4; 21:8; 22:15),[98] moral impurity (2:14, 20; 3:4?; 9:21; 17:4; 18:3,9; 19:2; 21:8, 22; 22:11, 15), attachment to material luxury (3:17; 18:3, 7, 9, 14), and spiritual lassitude and/or self-satisfied complacency (3:1–2, 15–17).[99] More explicitly, false spirituality is revealed in worship of the beast and receiving his mark (13:4-6, 8, 15–18; 14:9–11; 16:2; 19:4), blasphemy (13:5; 17:3), and cursing God during the plagues of his judgment (16:9, 11, 21).

True spirituality, on the other hand, is shown by moral purity (3:4; 14:4; 18:4; 22:11), repentance (3:19; 11:13), good deeds (2:5, 26; 14:13; 19:8), keeping God's commands (12:17; 14:12; 22:14), worship and fear of the true God only (4:8, 11; 11:13, 18; 14:7; 15:3, 4; 19:5, 6, 10; 22:9), prayer (8:3, 4), and persevering faith in and fervent love for Jesus, expressed in open testimony, even under pressure (1:9; 2:3, 4, 10, 13, 25; 3:8, 10, 11, 20; 5:9–13; 6:9–11; 11:7, 15; 12:11, 17; 13:10; 14:4, 12; 16:15; 17:14; 19:10; 20:4).[100] Poverty is also commended as a mark of spirituality (2:9).

This way of discipleship is open to all, without distinction of race (5:9; 7:9; 14:6; 15:4), and on the basis of Jesus' blood (1:5; 5:9; 7:14; 12:11; 22:14?), as a gift (21:6; 22:17), but John does not seem to envisage any alternative path. Rather he calls the Christians to spiritual discernment and to rejection of other ways that may involve compromise with idolatry and the non-Christian culture (2:2, 6, 14–16, 20–24; 13:8; 14:9–11; 18:4). Tolerance for other views and practices is *not* one of the values the text espouses; in the only place where the word "tolerate" occurs it is negative (2:20). As John sees it, the danger for these beleaguered believers is of being swallowed up by the surrounding culture (represented by the whore), if not eliminated by its oppression (represented by the beast). John divides all people into two camps, where the dividing mark is loyalty to God and Jesus.

This distinction is brought out particularly clearly in the two female metaphors of the whore and the bride. The whore's name is "a mystery: 'Babylon the great, mother of whores and of earth's abominations'" (17:5). She represents false spirituality that has its origins in literal Babylon,[101]

---

98. This is the problem with the Nicolaitans and Jezebel (Rev 2:14, 15, 20). Such may even explicitly call for openness to Satan (2:24), though the language here is quite ambiguous.

99. Cf. Moberly, *Prophecy and Discernment*, 225–26.

100. Compare the tests for genuine "perceptions" of God developed by mystical theologians and spiritual directors in the Catholic tradition (Alston, *Perceiving God*, 202–3).

101. Cf. Isa 47:8–13; this passage mentions sorcery, enchantments, love of pleasure,

or maybe further back in Babel.¹⁰² Her spirituality is blasphemous (17:3), impure (17:4), sensual and material (17:4; 18:7, 14, 16), intolerant of the witness of Jesus (17:6, 14; 18:20),¹⁰³ It is summed up in one word: sorcery (18:23), the ultimate misuse of spiritual power for personal gain.

In contrast, the spirituality associated with the bride is pure and righteous (19:8) and totally focused on the Lamb (19:9; 21:2, 9, 22, 23; 22:3–5). It is anchored in both Israel (21:12) and the church (21:14). Both women are pictured as having extreme wealth (compare 21:11,18–21 with 17:4 and 18:3, 9, 12, 13, 16), but John skillfully paints one as pure and the other as tainted.¹⁰⁴ The bride's influence is also international (21:24–26), bringing healing to the nations (22:2). Her spirituality is open to all (21:25, 26), but it is also exclusive: "nothing unclean will enter it, nor anyone who practices abomination or falsehood, but only those who are written in the Lamb's book of life" (21:27). In other words, followers of other spiritual ways are welcome, but only on condition that they abandon those ways for Christianity.

REVELATION'S WORLDVIEW AND TODAY'S WORLD

Postmodern Problems with John's Thought

Postmodernists are almost always suspicious of dualistic or binary thinking. For instance, Mark Taylor argues,

> most of the Christian theological network rests on a dyadic foundation that sets seemingly exclusive opposites over against each other. Furthermore, these paired opposites form a hierarchy in which one term governs, rules, dominates, or represses the other.¹⁰⁵

This leads many commentators to be very uncomfortable with Revelation's dualisms, especially when applied to his female figures. For example, Schüssler Fiorenza writes,

---

wisdom and knowledge, arrogance, and astrology as features of Babylonian spirituality—quite an accurate picture.

102. Gen 11, the futile attempt to reach into heaven by united human technology for the glory of man.

103. According to Stramara (*God's Timetable*, 93–96, 111–12), this picture may be based on the real historical figure Julia Agrippina, wife of Emperor Claudius and mother of Nero.

104. Cf. Royalty, *Streets of Heaven*, 71–78, 208–9, 225–34.

105. Taylor, *Erring*, 108.

> Rather than envision political powers and social realities, they displace the Apocalypse's emphasis and construe femaleness in dualistic terms of good and evil, pure or impure, divine or demonic, helpless or powerful, bride or temptress, wife or whore. Rather than instill "hunger and thirst" for a just world such dualistic feminine symbolizations perpetrate prejudice and injustice against wo/men if they are not adequately translated.[106]

Her point seems to be that John's dualism tends towards stereotypes, which in turn create a black and white world, without the shades of grey we experience in human life, and can provide a foundation for prejudice.[107] Tina Pippin argues that Revelation's view of women is sexist: the female characters are portrayed in traditional stereotypes, either as dangerous erotic seducers (ch. 17), chaste pure submissive brides (ch. 21), or mothers giving birth (ch. 12).[108]

This is certainly a danger with dualistic and absolutist thought like John's; on the other hand, John does show awareness of the mixed nature of human experience, especially in his critiques of the seven churches, who are approved in some points and denounced on others (2:2–6, 13–16, 19–20), and he balances his group judgments with awareness of individuality (as in 2:14, 15, 24; 3:4, 20), as will be explored further in chapter 5.

Thompson explains John's dualism as the response of a "cognitive minority" holding to a "deviant knowledge" that is struggling against the "public knowledge" of the "cognitive majority" of his day.[109] As Thompson points out, members of the cognitive minority tend to be hostile to the majority for rejecting their view of reality, and their rhetoric may become very intense as they seek to explain why others do not accept their story.[110] This does not mean that the minority is necessarily wrong, however: frequently in history, minority perceptions have been justified by subsequent developments—indeed this is often how worldviews get changed.

Others view the way John analyzes reality as a rhetorical strategy. For example, Royalty argues that Revelation "tries to unite the 'opposition' into one diabolical unity"[111] as part of John's strategy to outflank his rivals within the churches of Asia and suppress diversity of thinking among

106. Fiorenza, "Words of Prophecy," 13. Cf. Fiorenza, "Followers of the Lamb," 142.

107. Fiorenza ("Words of Prophecy," 14–15) also argues this with respect to John's language about some of his Jewish opponents.

108. Pippin, "Eros and the End," 200.

109. Thompson, *Apocalypse and Empire*, 193.

110. Ibid., 193. Cf. Yhearm, *Sitz im Leben*, 230–33; Hurtgren, *Anti-Language in the Apocalypse*, 139–44.

111. Royalty, *Streets of Heaven*, 14.

the Christians.¹¹² But this approach is in danger of judging Revelation anachronistically, according to values like diversity and tolerance that are privileged in postmodernist thought. If "Jezebel" really is a false prophet, for instance, who is leading Christians astray into "deep things of Satan" (2:24)—a claim quite compatible with the worldview of John and his readers—John would feel he has the duty to denounce her, provided that he is discerning correctly.¹¹³ Moreover, Royalty is himself drawn into John's dualism: he accepts that there is a two-way battle between John and his rivals, while criticizing John for contesting it, thus creating a new dualism—Royalty versus John of Patmos. This is the difficulty in all postmodernist (indeed all) thought: it is impossible not to think dualistically (or use binary thinking) in some sense; indeed it is difficult not to create enemies and give them appropriately derogatory labels, even while criticizing those enemies for doing the same.

Other readers of Revelation see all the spiritual realities in the text as literary *fictions* created by John for his rhetorical and political purpose.¹¹⁴ Such a position may simply be an implication of the reader's own worldview, particularly that of modernity, which rules out the possibility of spirits, or a form of postmodernism that is highly suspicious of the author. However, it raises the question: to what extent are the speaking characters in Revelation meant (by John) to be viewed as true communicators or mediators of God's revelation and to what extent are they rather characters in a drama, playing out a role?

For example, the angel who carries John away "in the spirit into a wilderness" to see the whore (17:3), and then gives him an extended analysis of the meaning of this vision (17:7–18), is probably meant (by John) to be seen as a real spiritual person communicating truth from God about the meaning of what John was seeing and the coming events implied (real history). However, the kings and merchants who wail over the fall of Babylon (18:9–20) are fictionalized, representative figures playing parts in a drama. We are not meant to treat them as mediators of God's voice, or to expect to hear their literal words in history, though their speeches are probably meant to convey *something* about real history and *something* of its meaning. Many of the voices in Revelation, however, are in between these alternatives, and some cases are difficult to classify precisely, even if we read with sympathy to John's perspective.

---

112. Ibid., 28–33.

113. I will take up the epistemological issues involved here in the next chapter.

114. This seems to be the stance of, for instance, Greg Carey ("Ambiguous Ethos," 174–75, 178–79; *Attention-Seeking Behavior*, 172).

Another problem lies in the authoritarian nature of John's claims.[115] For example, it must be acknowledged that one of the key criteria for true spirituality in Revelation is loyalty to John and the tradition of the apostles as interpreted by him. Thus the Christians in Sardis are called back to "what you received and heard" (3:3), the language of an emerging tradition (cf. 2:5); the Ephesians are commended for testing and rejecting false apostles (2:2); and the New Jerusalem is founded on the twelve apostles (21:14.) This implies perhaps that the ranks of the apostles are closed, but also suggests that there is no true salvation outside the faith founded on them—an idea that had many unfortunate consequences in later years, once the apostles and the city became identified with a visible organization with very earthly powers.[116]

Furthermore, in Revelation a key test of true spirituality is one's response to the book's prophecy: those who respond to it positively are blessed (1:3; 22:7), as are those who "listen to what the Spirit is saying to the churches" (through John) (2:7 and parallels), those who make this prophecy available (22:10), and those who accept the words of the prophets of God generally (10:7); while anyone who tampers with the manuscript is warned of dire consequences (22:18, 19).[117] These forms of language are authoritarian in the literal sense: they make the authority of the church, apostles, prophet, or tradition the criterion of truth or true spirituality.

Moreover, as some commentators have noticed, John hardly argues his case but just proclaims it in a kind of "take it or leave it" fashion. Instead of engaging his opponents or arguing why they are wrong, he is more likely to call them names such as Balaam and Jezebel;[118] his intention seems to be to reveal the spiritual nature of the opponents or their practices, for the names used are deliberately intertextual, calling forth the associations attached to their original use in the Old Testament. Thus John forces the reader to take sides: for or against him and his prophecy, as well as for or against Jesus. I'll take this up more in the next chapter.

Whatever else we may conclude from this, it certainly shows that a Christian worldview informed by Revelation will tend both to affirm the reality of the spirit world and to want to classify spiritual reality according to an ethical and soteriological dualism. The first point is close to the

---

115. Cf. Long, "Real Reader," 92–98.

116. Richard (*People's Commentary*, 3) sees Revelation as anti-authoritarian, resisting "the Hellenization of Christianity and its authoritarian and partriarchal institutionalization." This is also plausible, given the way John critiques the Asian churches.

117. Cf. Carey, "Ambiguous Ethos," 174.

118. Cf. Fiorenza, "Words of Prophecy," 8, 17; Carey, "Ambiguous Ethos," 177–79; Royalty, *Streets of Heaven*, 28, 31–33.

thought of some kinds of postmodernism. The second is in strong tension with postmodernist pluralism.

Revelation's Worldview and Today's World

Can the worldview of Revelation make any useful contribution to our idea of reality in the twenty-first century, in the light not only of modern science but also of postmodernist criticism of its dualism and authoritarianism? Can John's claims to have experienced the spirit world be trusted? Is his dualistic way of understanding the makeup of that world relevant or acceptable in a postmodern era?

Certainly the survival of belief in spiritual realities throughout the modern era can be read as a witness to a hunger of the human spirit and its intuitive sense of spiritual reality. Religious belief, for instance, has survived the pressures of modernity and even totalitarian opposition in the twentieth century. And even where traditional forms of religion have declined, other spiritual practices have arisen to fill the vacuum.

So can a Christian perspective emerge that can speak with power to postmodern people yet have some continuity with a worldview such as what we find in Revelation? Such a perspective, to be convincing in the postmodern era and still be authentically Christian, will need to take the spirit world seriously again, rather than dismissing it as antiquated or unscientific. A reductionist attitude to spirits and spiritual experience is now open to challenge, in spite of developments in neuro-psychology.[119]

But this perspective will also need to listen to Revelation's insistence on discernment and its dualism of good and bad spirits; otherwise a Christian worldview will be in danger of becoming indistinguishable from other forms of spirituality. Criteria need to be developed for distinguishing authentic Christian spiritual experiences from those that are humanly engineered[120] or demonic. Otherwise we may well end up with an undiscerning superstitious worldview somewhat like animism. As I argued earlier, Revelation gives us a model here with its emphasis on monotheism versus idolatry, moral purity, fervent confession of Jesus, resistance to "the mark of the beast," and true spiritual authority, including the authority of Scripture itself.

However, a Christian mindset appropriate to the postmodern era will not be able to uncritically follow the worldview found in Revelation and

---

119. See discussion in Green, *Body, Soul, and Human Life*.
120. As illustrated by the kind of spiritual chicanery portrayed in the movie *Leap of Faith*.

other parts of the Bible, in at least two points. First, the insights and models produced by modern science cannot simply be ignored, as some fundamentalists have been tempted to do. Christians should confidently affirm the reality of the spiritual world without denying the regularity and value of the natural order. I will come back to this in the next chapter. Second, the dualism of true/false or godly/demonic, which I argued is at work in Revelation, and which I believe must be preserved, must not be interpreted in such a way that Christians demonize their contemporaries or each other. Postmodernists have rightly pointed out the dangers in an uncritical dualism that degenerates into prejudice, stereotyping, and a political program that presumes that "we"[121] are right and "everyone else" is of the devil.[122] More subtly, one of Derrida's insights was that such opposites are unstable, since "one term relies on and inheres within the other."[123] Hence, "A characteristic feature of postmodern debates in a variety of cultural arenas is the insistence on the hearing of alternative voices."[124] While Christians need to hear other voices with discernment, in keeping with a belief that the demonic realm is real, postmodernism challenges us not to be closed-minded either. Moreover belief in a real God and a real devil does not ensure that Christians of any stripe can always be certain which is which in the specific complex situations of our day. Thus we should follow the more sophisticated postmodernists in being self-conscious and critically aware of our dualisms, aware that "our struggle is not against enemies of blood and flesh" (Eph 6:12) and "the wind blows where it chooses" (John 3:8).

I now want to briefly examine two possible variations on a Christian worldview for the postmodern world, one found in the work of theologian Walter Wink and the other in the fastest growing form of Christianity worldwide, the Pentecostal movement.

Walter Wink: Shifting from Modernity

Walter Wink's writings[125] represent a classic case of a Christian scholar whose thinking has shifted from being strongly influenced by the discourses

---

121. Whoever "we" may be.

122. Cf. Penner, *End of Apologetics* for a critique of forms of contemporary Christian apologetics that fall into this trap.

123. Sarup, *Post-Structuralism and Postmodernism*, 38.

124. Middleton and Walsh, *Truth Is Stranger*, 13.

125. Dr. Wink is a theologian and writer, currently Professor Emeritus of Biblical Interpretation at Auburn Theological Seminary in New York City. Previously, he was a parish minister and taught at Union Theological Seminary in New York City.

of modernity to a position that makes room for the spirit world, albeit in a new postmodern form. For instance, he writes that "angels had no place in my worldview,"[126] but subsequently, as result of Bible study and experiences as a minister,[127] his worldview has shifted.[128]

Wink contends that we are living through "a vast sea change in the metaphors with which we describe and make our home in the world."[129] The modern materialist or secularist worldview "which systematically excludes God from reality"[130] is "terminally ill" and therefore "many people sense an acute spiritual hunger and are reaching out, at times blindly and in every direction, for adequate sustenance."[131] While he thinks that the "biblical worldview" is "in many ways beyond being salvaged," due to its relativity to "its historical epoch,"[132] he wants to "contribute toward a new, postmaterialist cosmology, drawing on biblical resources,"[133] "a worldview capable of honoring the lasting values of modern science without succumbing to its reductionism."[134]

Wink's project involves the recapturing of biblical categories describing spiritual realities and experiences, such as angels, spirits, and demons, but reinterpreting them in a way compatible with true science and credible in the present day, in terms of "the interiority of earthly existence."[135] He sees the "principalities and powers"[136] found in the New Testament not as spirits in the air but as representing both the inner souls or cultures and the outward form of human power structures.[137]

For instance, Satan is not so much the personal devil of traditional belief but "the very specific spirituality of domination,"[138] created (or at least enhanced) by humanity's bad decisions over many millennia, to the point that it threatens our future and that of the planet.[139] Similarly, the old gods

126. Wink, *Unmasking the Powers*, 69.
127. E.g., ibid., 73–86.
128. Ibid., 170.
129. Ibid., 7.
130. Ibid., 5.
131. Ibid., 2.
132. Ibid., 5.
133. Ibid., 6.
134. Ibid., 2.
135. Ibid., 172.
136. The term is Paul's but such concepts are found all through the New Testament.
137. Wink, *Unmasking the Powers*, 4, 172–73; "Demons and Dmins," 507.
138. Wink, "Demons and Dmins," 505.
139. Wink, *Unmasking the Powers*, 39.

suppressed by Christianity are still "alive" and should be respected but not worshipped, not demonized but subordinated to the one true God over all, for they are "the 'within' of instinctuality or the collective compulsions of society."[140] Thus Wink calls for an openness to the gods of other religions and their myths, subordinated to God and "the foundational myth of the Judeo-Christian tradition";[141] not a revival of polytheism but a new form of henotheism,[142] resembling in some aspects the pre-exilic theology of Israel.

Many aspects of his project incorporate forms of postmodern thinking, for example his call for a different "participative" human relationship with nature[143] and his post-individualist concept of the person as a network of relationships, seen as a deduction from the new developments in science.[144] Wink seems to be attempting to create a Christian spirituality for the postmodern age. This attempt should be commended for its openness to the spirit world, its efforts to integrate spirituality and science, its reanimation of the environment, its insight into the "incarnation" of spirits,[145] its openness to traditional practices such as exorcism,[146] *and* its skeptical approach to traditional Christian spiritual concepts in modern dress, as in Winks' critique of Frank Peretti (who wrote a series of novels which attempted to create an apocalyptic cosmology of angels and demons loosely based on the Bible).[147] Wink shows us that a Christian cosmology must avoid slipping into a kind of "super-spiritual" dualism that *misuses* texts like Revelation.

However, it seems to me that his approach to the spirit world is still infected with reductionism. His reinterpretation of Satan and the gods, while capturing a vital part of their reality not perceived by traditional Christianity, makes them too impersonal and too sociological in nature to form part of a Christian worldview that can explain reality as we experience it and equip us against evil,[148] as illustrated by his refusal to give a straight answer to the question, "Are spirits real?"[149] He seems to lurch between an attraction to animism and a kind of pantheism, with his combination of spirits

140. Ibid., 125. Influence of Jungian psychology may be seen here.
141. Ibid., 124.
142. Ibid., 124.
143. Ibid., 159.
144. Ibid., 160.
145. Ibid., 4; idem, "Demons and Dmins," 504.
146. Wink, "Demons and Dmins," 506–7.
147. Ibid., 503–4.
148. See, for example, the mini-debate between Wink and C. Peter Wagner about whether the demonic can be redeemed. Wagner seems closer to the worldview of Revelation on this point in that he unhesitatingly affirms the reality of spirits (ibid., 507–12.)
149. Wink, *Unmasking the Powers*, 71.

and an underlying impersonal "unitary view of reality."[150] Having come a long way in his worldview shift, he still understates the spirit world.

With these reservations, however, Wink has explored the reality and duality of the spirit world as expressed in the Bible with refreshing candor and a new perspective that sets up all sorts of possibilities for a Christian worldview for postmodern times, as well as showing the dangers involved.

Pentecostalism: A New/Old Christian Worldview

I argued earlier that postmodern people are often hungry for some form of spiritual reality or experience. As one writer puts it,

> Many in society are seeking religious expressions that value pragmatic, experiential practices and intuitive, mystical ways of knowing, they are seeking religious practices that allow them to be active participators in God's unfolding purposes rather than remaining as detached observers of God's completed work.[151]

This helps explain why Pentecostal-charismatic Christianity is now the fastest growing form of Christianity in the world,[152] having grown from nothing to around half a billion adherents in a century.[153]

For example, the key spiritual phenomena reported by Pentecostals are spiritual gifts, in particular speaking in tongues. Emphasis on such a non-rational experience brings Pentecostals into collision with modernity, including modern Christianity, which tends to privilege rational-intellectual approaches to God. However, speaking in tongues tends to be consistent with a more postmodern "non-referential" view of language. Moreover Pentecostals frequently tend to take the spirit world seriously, expecting to experience spiritual realities (such as healing, angels and prophecy) and to fight with evil spirits, unlike many Christians who are influenced by modernity and see such language as either superstitious or purely theoretical.

---

150. Ibid., 162; cf. ibid., 170.

151. Hey, "Contemporary Developments," 3; cf. Ma, "Biblical Studies in the Pentecostal Tradition," 63.

152. Anderson, *Introduction to Pentecostalism*, 1.

153. The Pentecostal movement was born at the beginning of the twentieth century. Estimates of the number of Pentecostals vary, partly because of the difficulties in defining who Pentecostals are, but a conservative estimate of Pentecostal-charismatic Christianity would put the figure at around 450 million (cf. Dempster, Klaus, and Petersen, eds., *Globalization of Pentecostalism*, xiii).

There also seems to be a growing consensus that a distinctly Pentecostal[154] worldview may be delineated, as opposed to the *doctrines* expressed by the various Pentecostal movements, though most of the work in this area seems very preliminary in nature.[155] For example, Jackie Johns contends, "At the heart of the Pentecostal worldview is affective experience of God which generates an apocalyptic horizon for reading reality."[156] Margaret Poloma describes the Pentecostal worldview as characterized by "its belief in and experience of the paranormal as an alternate *weltanschauung* for our instrumental rational modern society."[157] Kenneth Archer writes of "this experiential worldview" in which "the essence of Pentecostalism is its persistent emphasis upon the supernatural within the community."[158] And James K. A. Smith, a Pentecostal philosopher, speaks of a Pentecostal worldview that includes five key elements: a "radical openness to God," "an 'enchanted' theology of creation and culture" that takes seriously the idea that the creation is "charged" with the presence of both God's Spirit and "other spirits," "a nondualistic affirmation of embodiment and materiality," an "affective, narrative epistemology," and "an eschatological orientation to mission and justice."[159]

Julie Ma studied the interaction between a Pentecostal worldview and that of an animist tribe in the Philippines and concluded that, since a Pentecostal worldview included belief in the reality of the spirit world,[160] Pentecostals and animists "share many worldview features" though there are also "several fundamental differences."[161] The similarities may explain how the Pentecostal churches there are growing.[162] Similar conclusions have been drawn about Africa, where Pentecostal and other similar churches are exploding in growth, partly due to their ability to communicate with

---

154. I am using this word in a non-denominational sense. Many Christians outside the Pentecostal churches would share their worldview in whole or in part. In fact, some have been in the forefront of articulating or defining such a worldview (e.g., Charles Kraft, Peter Wagner, Jack Deere). Cf. Pratt, "Need to Dialogue," 7–32.

155. For example, Steven J. Land's study of Pentecostal *spirituality* intermittently makes comments on worldview; he seems to see the Pentecostal worldview as placing the affections in a central position unlike the more cerebral emphasis of other churches (Land, *Pentecostal Spirituality*, 55, and ch. 3).

156. Johns, "Pentecostalism and the Postmodern Worldview," 87, 91–95.

157. Poloma, *Assemblies of God at the Crossroads*, xix.

158. Archer, "Pentecostal Hermeneutics," 65, 64.

159. Smith, *Thinking in Tongues*, 11–13, 22–47. See also Smith, "Advice to Pentecostal Philosophers," 235–47; "What Hath Cambridge to Do with Asuza Street?," 109–10.

160. Ma, "Two Worldviews," 265–88.

161. Ibid., 288.

162. Ibid., 289. Cf. Menzies, "Frontiers in Theology," 37–38.

traditional African worldviews.¹⁶³ As Smith concludes, "all commentators agree that the implicit cosmology assumed by spiritual warfare is one of the primary factors in the explosion of Christianity in the majority world."¹⁶⁴

Thus a Pentecostal worldview would at least include belief in the ongoing reality and experience of the supernatural order, unrestrained by the scientifically oriented view of modernity,¹⁶⁵ and in a supernatural interventionist God as a practical reality that everyone can experience.¹⁶⁶ It would also include an ethical or spiritual dualism of God versus Satan/spirits, as represented in various forms of spiritual warfare common among Pentecostal-charismatic Christians.¹⁶⁷

Scott Ellington urges that Western Pentecostals allow their openness to experience of God to modify their worldview as moderns:

> By confessing and believing the words of God in Scripture, words which are couched in a worldview different to our own, we are invited to imagine a God that transcends our worldview, not so much destroying it as expanding and transforming it to include the spiritual world. The Bible invites us to see beyond our own worldview and to catch a glimpse of the world as God sees it.¹⁶⁸

This will continue to be relevant in a postmodern era. As Gerald Sheppard argues, the experience of Pentecostals may place them in a unique position to take part in the challenging task of reinterpreting Christianity in the light of the changes of postmodern times.¹⁶⁹ Margaret Poloma sug-

---

163. Cf. Anderson, "Stretching the Definitions?" 101–2; cf. Ellington, "Pentecostalism and the Authority of Scripture," 23 n. 8.

164. Smith, *Thinking in Tongues*, 41. Of course, there are other factors—social, economic, even political—that help explain the strong growth of Pentecostal-style churches in the Majority World. Cf. Martin, *World Their Parish*.

165. Ellington, "Pentecostalism and the Authority of Scripture," 22.

166. For example, one Pentecostal scholar told Harvey Cox (*Fire from Heaven*, 71) that "the experience of God has absolute primacy over dogma and doctrine." Cf. Yong, "'Not Knowing Where the Wind Blows,'" 93–94; Ellington, "Pentecostalism and the Authority of Scripture," 17–19.

167. Cf. Smith, *Thinking in Tongues*, 41. Some Pentecostals are aware of the risk of an ontological dualism here which would make God and the devil more or less equal. Cf. Pratt, "Need to Dialogue," 22; Robeck, "Signs, Wonders, Warfare, and Witness," 4; Taylor, "Worldviews in Conflict," part 1, 8–20.

168. Ellington, "Pentecostalism and the Authority of Scripture," 35.

169. Sheppard, "Pentecostals, Globalization, and Postmodern Hermeneutics," 290. However, elsewhere he makes it clear that "we can never return to a premodern *or submodern* perspective" (Sheppard, "Biblical Interpretation after Gadamer," 129, italics added).

gests that "The charismatic world-view is a curious combination of the premodern and modern that may paradoxically be a good fit for the emerging postmodern world while simultaneously protesting its seeming chaos."[170] And Timothy Cargal argues that Pentecostalism has something distinctive to contribute to postmodern discussions of the Bible, provided that Pentecostals are also willing to listen to other postmodern voices.[171]

Pentecostalism may then be the form of contemporary Christianity most able to express the insights I have discerned in Revelation and speak to the needs of the postmodern world, though its attitude to postmodernism is ambivalent, and it is in constant danger of slipping into a fundamentalist, rejectionist type of reaction that will make it less relevant to our times. For example, while the openness of Pentecostals to the spirit world is similar to the worldview of Revelation, they have not always used the discernment found in John's thinking, so that they have oscillated between an uncritical acceptance of all claims to spiritual experience and a tendency to demonize their rivals. Nonetheless, the emergence of Pentecostalism indicates one possible direction for a Christian response to the issues raised in postmodernity.

---

170. Poloma, "'Toronto Blessing,'" 381.
171. Cargal, "Beyond the Fundamentalist-Modernist Controversy," 186–87.

CHAPTER 4

The Validity of Revelation

WE ARE DEFINED TO some degree by what we think is real, as the previous chapter noted. But we are also defined by our epistemology, by how we think we know anything and what we understand by truth. This has been one of the key areas debated by postmodernists and their critics, especially those who are conservative Christian believers.

As a young university student in Sydney, Australia, in the late 1960s, I was taught epistemology by a wonderful atheist professor named David Armstrong. Professor Armstrong loved to provoke and challenge his teenage students, especially those with religious beliefs. But he also had a great ability to teach clearly and engage his students in thinking about the big questions of philosophy. I still remember the first few lectures he gave us, in which he gradually led us deeper and deeper into the intricacies of epistemology as we searched for answers to the simple question, "How do we know anything?" Such questions refuse to go away.

Everyone in the world has implicit answers to such questions, even if they rarely or never articulate those answers. For many cultures, there is a very simple answer: we simply believe what has been handed down to us from our ancestors, who found out (either by hard experience or by some form of spiritual revelation) all that we need to know. For these cultures, truth equals tradition. For modern Western intellectuals, however, tradition is no answer at all. We must discover or work out for ourselves what is true; we can only know anything by the exercise of our rational minds. In our schools we teach students to think independently, critically, "for themselves," though often we then criticize them for doing so if we don't like the answers they come up with. But *in practice*, even most Western people rarely criticize what they hear from respected authorities such as mass media, universities, textbooks, and especially scientists, if for no other reason that the work involved in checking out every assertion is too great and demands much more learning than most of us have.

In some respects, this is the core chapter of this book. For what Revelation can teach us about truth and knowledge is really the foundation of a Christian worldview. But just the word "foundation" raises a lot of questions, because much of the discussion has revolved around the issue of "foundationalism." A Christian worldview for a postmodern era must address these questions.

EPISTEMOLOGICAL PROBLEMS TODAY

Challenges to Assumptions of Modernity

Enlightenment thinkers usually accepted the correspondence theory of truth. They clearly assumed that there is a reality existing outside and independent of us (metaphysical realism)[1] and that our knowledge of it is reliable to the extent that our beliefs correspond to what is really there (epistemological realism.)[2] Modernists also embraced a form of foundationalism as defined by Wolterstorff:

> Simply put, the goal of scientific endeavor, according to the foundationalist, is to form a body of theories from which all prejudice, bias, and unjustified conjecture have been eliminated. To attain this, we must begin with a firm foundation of certitude and build the house of theory on it by methods of whose reliability we are equally certain.[3]

---

1. Cf. Gregersen, "Contextual Coherence Theory," 198.

2. Or what Gregersen (ibid., 200) calls "scientific realism," the claim that "there exists some sort of correspondence between our scientific theories and the actual entities and structures of the real world." Another contemporary version of this is "critical realism," which affirms that "Valid knowledge of the real world can only be acquired through critical reflection upon experience," as opposed to "naïve realism," which assumes that "the external world is as we experience it" (Niekerk, "Critical Realist Perspective," 51, see also 55–58).

3. Wolterstorff, *Reason within the Bounds of Religion*, 28. Other useful summaries of foundationalism are found in Plantinga, "Belief in God as Basic," 9; and Grenz and Franke, *Beyond Foundationalism*, 30–31. See also Plantinga, *Warranted Christian Belief*, ch. 3, part IIA.

Such a firm foundation was usually sought by modernity in self-evident truths or the evidence of the human senses, but the foundationalist model was also shared by medieval thinkers who sought a foundation in Scripture or the church.

Modernists contended for the power of human reason to investigate truth, establish ethics, solve human problems, and create a better world unfettered by tradition, prejudice, superstition, passions, or authority (especially religious authority).[4] Thus Kant wrote, "Have courage to use your *own* understanding!"[5] and "to criticism everything must submit."[6] Modernists were keen to eliminate bias, prejudice, and tradition from their minds and think rationally, because "unwarranted" belief was an epistemological "sin."[7] As W. K. Clifford claimed, "it is wrong, always, everywhere, and for anyone to believe anything upon insufficient evidence,"[8] and according to Richard Dawkins it still is wrong.[9]

The epistemology of the Enlightenment was fundamentally humanistic: its starting point was not revelation from God (through the church or the Bible) but individual human beings discovering truth for themselves. In this way, according to Ernest Gellner, a contemporary defender of the Enlightenment project, humans can attain to "external, objective, culture-transcending knowledge."[10]

The correspondence theory of truth, however, has been problematized by postmodern thinkers. How can we ever know if our ideas "correspond" to reality? As Cupitt puts it, "what kind of exercise is it to lay out a proposition alongside a fact to see if they are the same shape?"[11] In practice, reality is always one step removed. We can only have ideas about things through language[12] and words do not refer directly to outside realities, but to other words.[13] Thus postmodernists argue that we do not simply discover the ex-

---

4. Cf. Lyotard, *Postmodern Condition*, 31.

5. Kant, "What Is Enlightenment?" 51.

6. As quoted by McGowan, *Postmodernism*, 32.

7. Cf. Plantinga, "Belief in God," 1–2, and his discussion of Locke in *Warranted Christian Belief*, ch. 3, part IA; MacIntyre, *Whose Justice?*, 6.

8. Clifford, *Lectures and Essays*, 183, as quoted in Plantinga, *Warranted Christian Belief*, ch. 3, part IIB.

9. Cf. Dawkins, *God Delusion*, 51, 282.

10. Gellner, *Postmodernism, Reason, and Religion*, 75.

11. Cupitt, *Leap of Reason*, 17. Cf. MacIntyre, *Whose Justice?*, 357–58; Dewitt, *Worldviews*, 20–23.

12. "We can never say what is independent of all saying" (Cahoone, *From Modernism to Postmodernism*, 14). See also Lyotard, *Postmodern Condition*, 24.

13. Eagleton, *Literary Theory*, 111. See also Collective, *Postmodern Bible*, 124.

ternal world, but in a sense "construct" a world by our use of language.[14] For example, Rorty describes "truth, goodness and beauty . . . as artifacts whose fundamental design we often have to alter."[15]

The same considerations[16] tend to undercut foundationalism. If reality as we encounter it is actually based in language, then neither self-evident propositions nor sense perception will provide us with an absolute foundation for knowledge.[17] What counts as "self-evident" will vary from culture to culture and what our senses perceive (or at least how our minds interpret it) will depend on the way they are trained by language and culture. In other words, "facts are always already theory-laden."[18] Thus the critique involved in postmodernism is both anti-foundationalist and anti-absolutist.[19] Truth and knowledge are seen as provisional and uncertain rather than absolute and objective.[20]

The central place of the subject is likewise being questioned. The Enlightenment view of knowledge pictured the individual "knower" or subject as studying reality outside himself (the object) as an impartial observer who had freed himself from the trammels of tradition or religion and could apply his unbiased reason to the object of study. As Susan Hekman puts it, "the modern episteme is defined by the Cartesian dichotomy between subject and object" and "the subject is the self-conscious guarantor of all knowledge."[21] Moreover the masculine gender used earlier in this paragraph is deliberate: the observer was most likely seen as male—"the 'I' has always had a phallic character in western thought," according to Hekman.[22]

However, postmodernists point out that the subject is not standing "outside" the world but in a specific place in space, time, culture, and

---

14. Cf. Grenz, *Primer on Postmodernism*, 41.

15. Rorty, *Consequences of Pragmatism*, 92. Cf. Miller, "Emerging Postmodern World," 11.

16. And others (cf. Plantinga, *Warranted Christian Belief*, ch. 3, part IV), but I'm concentrating on postmodern thinking.

17. Perhaps the problem is in the word "absolute." Eagleton argues that many postmodernists are attacking a "straw target"; scientists never imagined there were "absolute grounds" for truth, except nineteenth-century positivists (Eagleton, *Literary Theory*, 125).

18. Kirk, "Confusion of Epistemology," 139.

19. McGowan, *Postmodernism*, ix. Cf. Hekman, *Gender and Knowledge*, 1.

20. Though some other philosophers like Jürgen Habermas have attempted to construct a new form of rationalism that preserves the basic thrust of modernity without depending on a foundationalist epistemology (cf. Bertens, *Idea of the Postmodern*, 114–16).

21. Hekman, *Gender and Knowledge*, 62. Cf. Grenz, *Primer on Postmodernism*, 3.

22. Hekman, *Gender and Knowledge*, 68.

history.²³ Knowers cannot help but see things from their own perspective, which can never be totally objective and will differ from the perspective of every other knower, including and *excluding* different factors.²⁴ Postmodernists thus reject the idea that there is an "Archimedean point" from which the knower can study the known.²⁵

Christian Responses

Christians have been varied in their responses to these shifts in thought. John Thornhill accurately states their dilemma when he argues,

> The fundamental challenge faced by Western thought today is the reconciling of a recognition of objective truth with a full acknowledgement of the vast range of subjective factors which condition our access to that truth.²⁶

Many Christian thinkers worry that postmodernism threatens the concept of objective truth, which seems essential to Christian doctrine. For example, Stanley Grenz declares himself to be "in fundamental agreement with the postmodern rejection of the modern mind" and "the postmodern discovery that no observer can stand outside the historical process,"²⁷ but on the other hand he contends,

> rejection of the correspondence theory not only leads to a skepticism that undercuts the concept of objective truth in general; it also undermines Christian claims that our doctrinal formulations state objective truth.²⁸

Philip D. Kenneson, however, drawing on postmodernist thought, especially that of Richard Rorty, debunks the assumptions of the Enlightenment with a view to rescuing Christianity from its categories. He urges Christians to consider taking trust, rather than doubt, as their starting point

---

23. Eagleton, *Literary Theory*, 203. Cf. Westphal, *Whose Community?*, 23–26.
24. Cf. Cahoone, *From Modernism to Postmodernism*, 16.
25. Cf. Hekman, *Gender and Knowledge*, 12. Cf. MacIntyre, *Whose Justice?*, 367.
26. Thornhill, *Modernity*, 127.
27. Grenz, *Primer on Postmodernism*, 165–67.
28. Ibid., 163 (italics added). Cf. Kirk ("Confusion of Epistemology," 144–46, 154–56), who argues for "a moderate foundationalism, supported by a robust realism," in which God is the foundation, and McGrath (*Passion for Truth*, 132, 192), who dismisses foundationalism but sees the need for some criteria by which to "exclude certain viewpoints as unacceptable."

in knowledge, unlike Descartes,[29] and to throw out the dichotomy between objective and subjective truth.[30]

Problems with foundationalism are also explored by the Christian "Reformed epistemologists." Wolterstorff, for example, argues that simple statements based on observation are fraught with problems due to the uncertain state of human observation, and amount to statements about human consciousness.[31] Moreover inductive reasoning rests on the unprovable assumption of uniformity in the natural world.[32] Even the less difficult empiricist theory—"falsificationism," the assertion that valid scientific propositions must be falsifiable—is unworkable because this process rarely causes a theory to be rejected: somehow or another, most contrary evidence can be "explained away."[33] Meanwhile, "deductivism" is virtually obsolete because it cannot account for many seemingly rational theories and is not easily applicable to the physical world.[34] Hence Wolterstorff concludes, "Our future theories of theorizing will have to be nonfoundationalist ones,"[35] though he hastens to add that this does not rule out the existence of objective reality or our ability to know such reality. Meanwhile Plantinga points to the logical problem in the foundationalist foundations: their foundational proposition is not itself either self-evident or evident to the senses.[36]

More recently, Pentecostal philosopher James K. A. Smith has joined the critique of modernist epistemology for its overconfidence in an objective, neutral, and universal human rationality, contending that "the lineaments and conclusions of universal reason are, at the end of the day, only one particular perspective writ large as if it were not a perspective but 'just the way things really are.'"[37] After commending postmodernism's affirmation of perspectivalism, he argues for an epistemology that brings the hearts or affections to the fore: "the point is to affirm the primacy of the heart and affections as the basis for a rational, intellectual engagement with and interpretation of the world."[38]

---

29. Kenneson,, "No Such Thing," 157–58.
30. Ibid., 159.
31. Wolterstorff, *Reason within the Bounds of Religion*, 46.
32. Ibid., 38–40.
33. Ibid., 41–45.
34. Ibid., 37–38.
35. Ibid., 56–57.
36. Plantinga, "Belief in God," 9–10. Cf. Nash, *Faith and Reason*, 86.
37. Smith, *Thinking in Tongues*, 57. Cf. Westphal, *Whose Community?*
38. Smith, *Thinking in Tongues*, 59.

But if foundationalism is in difficulties, what are the alternatives?

Alternative Starting Points

What is the ultimate source of reliable knowledge about truth for human beings? Foundationalists have sought for a set of propositions that are both certain and known non-inferentially as a starting point for knowledge.[39] More broadly, however, the ultimate source of knowledge comes down to a choice among these possibilities or a combination of them:

- Self-evident propositions
- Experience (either of the senses or the spirit)
- Tradition or community
- Revelation from God (mediated through scriptures, experience, reason, and/or tradition)

The postmodernist criticism of Enlightenment foundationalism has made some of the other options live again; for instance, religious experience,[40] tradition,[41] community, and revelation. But they can only be taken seriously if we abandon true foundationalism: none of these options could stand the weight required by that position; that is, none of these sources can act as the foundation from which all other knowledge can be derived. For example, we can no more derive the whole truth about God from the study of science than we can derive all scientific truths from the Bible.

Alternative Models

So if foundationalism will not work, what possible alternative models or pictures can best help us understand how truth and human knowledge functions? According to Grenz and Franke,[42] the alternative models available are:

1. Coherence: all the different kinds of knowledge act as a mutually reinforcing web of truth, so any claims to knowledge should cohere with

---

39. Cf. Wolterstorff, *Reason within the Bounds of Religion*, 46.
40. E.g., Alston, "Religious Experience," 31–51.
41. E.g., MacIntyre, *Whose Justice?*; Westphal, *Whose Community?* 22–23, 90–91.
42. Grenz and Franke, *Beyond Foundationalism*, 29–32, 38–42.

our existing knowledge.[43] No beliefs are more basic than others but the whole set of beliefs we have "must carry 'explanatory power.'"[44]

2. Pragmatism: knowledge is what advances inquiry, what is verified by subsequent events or discoveries—what "works" in that sense.[45]

3. Language games: truth or knowledge claims are those that "win" in the contest with other claimants according to the rules of a particular discourse (science, history, theology, etc.).

JUSTIFICATION FOR RELIGIOUS KNOWLEDGE

The Special Case of Religious Knowledge

Enlightenment foundationalism tended to either discredit religious knowledge or at least sideline it. In early modern thought, religion had to be grounded in the acceptable foundations of self-evident propositions or sense experience. Thus Descartes built a proof of God from his foundation of the mind's experience of itself and Locke attempted to show the reasonableness of a Christianity unburdened of too much doctrinal baggage.[46] But the result, as Voegelin argues, was that, "the God for whose answer we are hoping and waiting is turned into the object for an ontological proof of his existence";[47] hence the growth of deism (a religion grounded in natural theology)[48] and a general drift to skepticism and atheism.[49]

In the following century, Christian thinkers tried to find a better foundation for theology that would preserve its uniqueness while re-establishing its intellectual credentials.[50] One project was liberalism: Schleiermacher, the father of liberal theology, sought to establish religion on the founda-

---

43. For a more complete defense of coherentism and an explanation of its differences to foundationalism, see Gregersen, "Contextual Coherence Theory," 181–231, esp. 192–93. For a more skeptical response, see Dewitt, *Worldviews*, 17–19, 25–27.

44. Grenz and Franke, *Beyond Foundationalism*, 39.

45. J. Andrew Kirk's ("Confusion of Epistemology," 134) "Reliabilism," "a belief is justified just in case it is based on reasons that are reliable indicators of the truth, produced by cognitive processes that are generally reliable," sounds like a variation of pragmatism.

46. Grenz and Franke, *Beyond Foundationalism*, 33.

47. Voegelin, "Gospel and Culture," 143.

48. The Deistic trend is still strong among some who privilege natural processes and scientific knowledge in the area of religion (cf. van Huyssteen, "Postfoundationalism," 17).

49. Grenz and Franke, *Beyond Foundationalism*, 33.

50. Ibid., 33–37.

tion of a feeling of absolute dependence.[51] Another project was evangelical fundamentalism, which took its name from an attempt to rescue the foundational doctrines of Christian faith from skeptics and tried to ground religion in an infallible Bible.

In late modernity, religious knowledge was often not accepted as proper knowledge at all, because it was not acceptably "grounded" or not able to be proved or falsified. For instance, the logical positivists argued that religious propositions were meaningless because they were not grounded on empirical observation of natural realities. Alternatively, anthropologists, psychologists, and sociologists explained (away) religion as a function of social control or an effect of psychological functions.

Even today, religious knowledge has still seemed second-class compared to science especially. As van Huyssteen itemizes the contrast in current stereotypes,

- Scientific statements are hypothetical, fallible, and tentative, while statements of religious faith are dogmatic, ideological, and fideistic.
- Scientific thought is always open to critical evaluation, justification, or falsification, while religious faith goes against the facts and often defies empirical evidence.
- Scientific thought delights in critical dissent and constructive criticism, while faith more often than not depends on massive consensus and uncritical commitment.
- Scientists therefore seem to base their beliefs on evidence and rational argument, while religious beliefs appear to be founded on "faith" only.[52]

The postmodernist turn has at least opened the door to alternative rationalities to science, even allowing for the possibility of mystical experience as a pathway to knowledge, as found, for example, in the later work of Paul Davies.[53]

Justifying Religious Knowledge

All this raises the broader question: are religious beliefs groundless or irrational, and if not, how may they be established? Or to put it another way,

---

51. Erickson, *Christian Theology*, 19.

52. van Huyssteen, "Postfoundationalism," 15. This view is prominent among some of the New Atheists, especially Richard Dawkins. For a short critique, see Plantinga, *Where the Conflict Really Lies*, 122–23.

53. Cf. van Huyssteen, "Postfoundationalism," 17–19.

is true religious knowledge possible, and if so, how can it be justified? What are the alternative positions?

First, religious epistemological foundationalism proposes that individual items of religious knowledge are grounded in such realities as religious experience or Scripture. There are problems with both of these. William Alston argues that "experiential awareness of God, or . . . the *perception* of God, makes an important contribution to the grounds of religious belief."[54] However, there is no *generic* religious experience (in spite of older pluralists like John Hick);[55] even if there were, it would have to be interpreted. Rather there are the varied experiences of different kinds of believers and religious communities, which are to some degree created, or at least structured, by their existing beliefs.[56] And as Wolterstorff argues,[57] Scripture cannot be used as a foundation, for three significant reasons: much of our knowledge cannot be deduced from the Bible; we cannot know *indubitably* that it is an inspired text, especially in its presently-available form;[58] and knowledge of what it says is subject to hermeneutical difficulties.

Second, we could explain religious beliefs in cultural, anthropological, or psychological terms, leaving their epistemological status uncertain.

Third, religious beliefs can be explained in terms of their function within a Christian community or tradition, as in the postliberal position, drawing on Wittgenstein's "language games" theory.[59] This approach has been attacked for its lack of epistemological realism and its inability to handle questions from outside the Christian community or tradition, such as "Is God real?"[60] Alasdair MacIntyre, however, has provided a vigorous defense of his version of this model, arguing that traditions, while having their own "account of and practices of rational justification," can be assessed by how well they handle epistemological challenges.[61] A specific histori-

---

54. Alston, *Perceiving God*, 1.

55. Cf. Lindbeck, *Nature of Doctrine*, 32, who argues that attempts to define such an experience have tended to be vacuous.

56. Grenz and Franke, *Beyond Foundationalism*, 49. I return to the notion of experiencing God being a source of justification below.

57. Wolterstorff, *Reason within the Bounds of Religion*, 58–62. Cf. Grenz and Franke, *Beyond Foundationalism*, 34–35, 37.

58. Due, for example, to questions about the reliability and origins of the text as we have it today.

59. Cf. Grenz and Franke, *Beyond Foundationalism*, 45–46. For a critical summary of how language games can be used to explain religious belief, see Nielsen, "Religion and Groundless Believing," 19–21.

60. Nielsen, "Religion and Groundless Believing," 21–27. See also Fackre, *Doctrine of Revelation*, 83.

61. MacIntyre, *Whose Justice?*, 366.

cal tradition of enquiry will face its own crises of belief, generated either internally or externally to the tradition, and either make progress thereby, falter, or be modified (or even taken over) by a rival tradition able to solve the problems concerned.

A fourth, similar alternative put forward by the "Reformed epistemologists" involves taking religious beliefs or revelation from God as a starting point in the epistemological process, while avoiding foundationalism. For example, Wolterstorff writes about "control beliefs," beliefs that guide our thinking and cause us to reject certain hypotheses that are either inconsistent with or "do not comport well with those beliefs."[62] Common examples include elementary arithmetic, confidence in my sense experience as a guide to reality, and the belief that there are other persons in the world and there is a real past; what all these have in common is that, not only are they not provable, but we would never attempt to prove them.[63] Control beliefs are not self-evident or indubitable, nor are they immune from criticism or revision, but they are, to use Plantinga's vocabulary, "properly basic," and both Plantinga and Wolterstorff argue that Christians are justified in using their Christian beliefs in God as "control beliefs" in this sense, without taking them to be foundationalist certitudes.[64]

This is a bold move to overturn the subject-oriented humanistic epistemology of the Enlightenment without returning to medieval authoritarianism. However, it is open to the charge of being arbitrary. For example, this view means that our warrant for accepting any theory "will have to be *relative* to a body of beliefs."[65] Put another way, this means that our rationality is relative to our community, as Plantinga concedes when he says, "The Christian community is responsible to *its* set of examples, not those of non-believers."[66] Or to put it a different way again, what we see as properly basic will depend on our worldview.[67] But if this is so, is there any convincing reason to privilege Christian "control beliefs" over, say, Buddhist or atheist ones?[68] And if not, is there any reason to be a Christian rather than a Buddhist or atheist?

62. Wolterstorff, *Reason within the Bounds of Religion*, 68.

63. Cf. Plantinga, *Where the Conflict Really Lies*, 124.

64. Wolterstorff, *Reason within the Bounds of Religion*, 70, 76–84, 92–97; Plantinga, "Belief in God," 1–16; idem, *Where the Conflict Really Lies*, 46. Cf. Nash, *Faith and Reason*, 87–91.

65. Wolterstorff, *Reason within the Bounds of Religion*, 102 (italics added).

66. Plantinga, "Belief in God," 16 (italics added).

67. Cf. Nash, *Faith and Reason*, 91.

68. Wolterstorff seems to admit this problem in the preface to the first edition of *Reason within the Bounds of Religion*, 11–12. Gregersen and van Huyssteen (eds.,

In response to such questions, a fifth possibility would be to explain religious beliefs in terms of postmodernist categories or within an explicitly pluralistic mindset, accepting that there are many possible religious beliefs that are justifiable within the communities of faith they have arisen from, and that we cannot adjudicate between them as we don't have an objective standpoint from which to do so.[69] It could be argued that the previous two alternatives *implicitly* accept a pluralistic worldview and Gregersen and van Huyssteen are probably correct to assert that "Cognitive pluralism has . . . become one of the primary challenges to both science and theology."[70] The main problem with such a pluralist view is the difficulty of handling the contradictory notions of competing religious traditions; it gives up any confidence that we can know anything definite about God. Choice between religious belief systems then comes down to personal preference or tradition.[71]

A sixth possibility would consist in justifying religious beliefs by using a different epistemology to foundationalism, such as coherentism or pragmatism.[72] Grenz and Franke, for example, describe Christian beliefs as a "belief-mosaic" and see theologizing as "leading to a mosaic of interlocking pieces that presents a single pattern."[73] Such a strategy helps to integrate religious beliefs with the conclusions of science, for example,[74] and sees all truth as ultimately originating in God. But all forms of coherentism tend to have difficulty with circularity: that is, I may hold a set of consistent but false beliefs; so indeed might a whole community. As Plantinga argues,

> Coherentism . . . is unsuccessful because it sees warrant as involving only the relation between beliefs; but the fact is the relation between experience and belief and between environment and belief is also crucial to warrant.[75]

Rethinking Theology and Science, 5–6) rightly, in my view, take issue with an "intra-communal" view of theology that amounts to its "re-tribalization," the weakness of the post-liberals and "Reformed epistemologists."

69. MacIntyre's (*Whose Justice?*, 352–69) argument referred to above is specifically targeted at this argument.

70. Gregersen and van Huyssteen, eds., *Rethinking Theology and Science*, 4.

71. Further discussion of pluralism is found in chapter 7.

72. According to Grenz and Franke (*Beyond Foundationalism*, 43), this was the strategy of theologian Wolfhart Pannenberg: "At the heart of Pannenberg's theological agenda is the task of demonstrating the internal coherence of the doctrines and the external coherence of Christian doctrine with all knowledge."

73. Ibid., 51.

74. As argued by Gregersen in his article "A Contextual Coherence Theory."

75. Plantinga, *Warrant and Proper Function*, vii. Cf. also Cupitt, *Leap of Reason*, 17; Yong, *Beyond the Impasse*, 71; Dewitt, *Worldviews*, 25–27.

A seventh view posits an eschatological view of truth, arguing that Christian beliefs will be justified in the long run (at the final revelation of the last judgment),[76] paralleling a trend observable in some epistemological history for "truth to win out." Certain knowledge is deferred to the eschatological future, until which truth claims will be provisional and contestable.[77] This leaves the current state of claims to religious truth very uncertain, however, and opens Christians to the charge of an irrational leap of faith.

It seems to me that all these proposals fail to address the concept of revelation. Modernity explicitly rejects (external) authority as a basis for belief, partly deriving from the Enlightenment's reaction against medieval Catholic authoritarianism,[78] but a postmodern Christian epistemology must address the question of revelation and authority afresh. Plantinga speaks of "sources of knowledge in addition to reason";[79] revelation seems to me to be a better source than belief. Perhaps exploration of the epistemology of the Book of Revelation can help us address this issue.

KNOWLEDGE AND TRUTH IN REVELATION

When we read Revelation in the light of issues discussed so far in this chapter, what light does this shed on them? It seems to me that at least five basic positions emerge from a study of the epistemology implicit in this text.[80]

1. Limitations of Human Knowledge

The project of the Enlightenment tried to establish human knowledge on a solid human foundation. It sought to enable human knowledge to become encyclopedic.[81] However, according to Revelation, as well as many postmodernists, the nature of fundamental reality is not obvious to human beings. It is not "present" to us. If the spiritual/heavenly order is more fundamentally real than the observable realities of earthly life, as I suggested was John's view in the previous chapter, then our senses are not able to ap-

76. On the eschatological aspect of revelation, see Bloesch, *Holy Scripture*, 54-55.
77. Grenz and Franke, *Beyond Foundationalism*, 44.
78. Cf. Cupitt, *Leap of Reason*, 21.
79. Plantinga, *Where the Conflict Really Lies*, 46
80. A version of the following material has been published online by *Heythrop Journal* as "The Epistemology of the Book of Revelation" (2013).
81. The development of Google and Wikipedia may amount to a postmodern project along similar lines.

prehend the nature of fundamental reality, which has serious implications for empiricism.

Human beings can and do experience the spiritual or heavenly realm in a number of ways, according to John. For example, Jezebel and her followers, who were operating in the spiritual realm illicitly, would experience God's judgments empirically in the form of sickness, distress, and death (2:20–23). But frequently they may fail to interpret these experiences correctly or to see the spiritual factors behind apparently "natural" events in their lives. Those who profited from Babylon would lament her downfall without necessarily seeing it as a result of God's judgments (Rev 18); in fact, many Romans in later centuries saw the decline of their empire to be the result of the growth of Christianity among them and the subsequent affront to the traditional gods.[82]

Some philosophers have argued that the spiritual or heavenly realm presumed in Revelation simply does not exist. This argument is based on the lack of observable evidence for spiritual things. However, this argument seems to me to assume what it wants to prove. If, by definition, only things observable by human beings using their senses (enhanced perhaps by various forms of technology) are real, then the existence of spiritual things (God, angels, devils, ghosts, miracles) is ruled out. But this conclusion owes more to the worldview of modernity, or a particular modern school of thought, than to specific evidence.

John does not specifically describe or argue the points just made about human limitations. To the extent that he explains why humans do not perceive spiritual things (or why they misperceive them), he tends to attribute this to deception, ultimately from the devil, whom he calls "the deceiver of the whole world" (12:9). This deception takes several forms in Revelation: the whore Babylon is accused of deceptive sorcery (18:23); false apostles and false prophets attempt to deceive the churches, with some success (2:2,6,14–15,20–24); false Jews also contribute to religious confusion (2:9; 3:9); and some churches are self-deceived by their own reputations (3:1–2, 17). It is probably because of deception that people do not repent even when visited by plagues from God that should "open their eyes" to the truth of their situation (9:20–21; 16:9, 11, 21).[83]

This problem of deception has similarities to some insights of postmodernism. People become deceived, or deceive themselves, because of their own limited, self-interested, power-driven perspective on issues of

---

82. Cf. Wilken, *As the Romans Saw Them*, 63; Heschel, *Prophets*, 1:197.

83. Perhaps due to judicial hardening on the part of God, as in the account of the exodus (Exod 7:3).

truth. However, John attributes this also to spiritual factors and sees that it can be overcome, at least in part, by revelation.[84] There is a moral dimension to human failure to know God and his will in the Bible (Prov 1:7; Rom 1:18–32; Rev 21:27).[85] In a Christian worldview, this is the result of the Fall of humankind related in Genesis 3[86] and adopted in the story assumed by Revelation.[87] Such a position is also implied when Revelation portrays humanity as hostile to God.

2. The Importance of Revelation

The second insight that Revelation offers about epistemology is this: since (according to Revelation) the fundamental, spiritual-heavenly realities are not perceived by the senses, or even by reason (though John nowhere discusses this),[88] they must be disclosed to us by revelation from heaven.[89] This is illustrated by John's own experience, as we will see.

Revelation everywhere traces back all knowledge of spiritual reality to God's revelation. Of course, John is not making a radical statement for his day. According to Martin Hengel, Jewish apocalyptic literature had a similar perspective:

> In Hasidic apocalyptic . . . the receipt of supernatural revelation . . . is meant to be fundamentally superior to the traditional wisdom won from "primal revelation" and empirical experience and to the rational thought of the Greeks.[90]

And as noted in chapter 2, according to David Aune, "All cultures of the ancient Mediterranean world and the Near East had a revelatory worldview."[91] Similarly, Eric Voegelin points out that Plato was just as conscious of revelation as any Christian theologian.[92]

---

84. Cf. Friesen, *Imperial Cults*, 188.

85. This was developed most comprehensively by the theologian Augustine with his elaboration of the role of the will in human life and rationality (cf. MacIntyre, *Whose Justice?*, 156–58). See also Descartes, *Meditation 4*; Fackre, *Doctrine of Revelation*, 45.

86. Fackre, *Doctrine of Revelation*, 43–58.

87. See chapter 6 on the centrality of this story in a revelation worldview.

88. Paul is less reticent here: cf. 1 Cor 1:18–2:16; Col 2:8.

89. Wall, *Revelation*, 16.

90. Hengel, *Judaism and Hellenism*, 1:253.

91. Aune, *Literary Environment*, 231. Cf. Hengel, *Judaism and Hellenism*, 1:217.

92. Voegelin, "Gospel and Culture," 153.

Because of the widespread revelatory worldview identified by Aune, people of that time held revelatory literature in great respect, including the Septuagint.[93] The Book of Revelation is, of course, a prime example of such literature, as its title indicates (1:1).[94] John describes his initial experience as that of a recipient of a divine communication and revelation (theophany) similar to that experienced by Old Testament prophets such as Isaiah and Ezekiel (1:10–20). Similarly, in his heavenly journey, he describes being taken up by supernatural power to experience the heavenly spiritual world (4:1–2; 17:3; 21:10). Moreover he himself frequently cannot interpret what he sees and needs help from angelic beings (7:13–14; 17:6–7).

Various literary features of Revelation also indicate that it is produced as a revelatory text and emphasizes revelation as a means of conveying truth. For instance, John's effective claim to a kind of prophetic copyright is made in the name of God (22:18–20) and may be said to be motivated by his conviction that his prophecy is the word of God himself (1:2; 22:6).

Revelation also uses the literary forms of some ancient oracles,[95] such as the "oracular beatitudes" or "makarisms" (1:3; 19:9; 22:7, 14),[96] "didactic oracles" (18:4–8),[97] "oracles of doom" (18:2–24),[98] and "legitimation oracles" (1:8,17f; 22:16,20);[99] it is also framed like an "oracular letter."[100] The messages to the seven churches (chs. 2–3) are styled in the manner of Hebrew prophecy.[101]

The scene of the seven-sealed scroll (ch. 5) dramatically underlines the need for revelation. The scroll clearly contains information of great moment concerning the future and God's purposes. However, "no one in heaven or on earth or under the earth was able to open the scroll or look into it" (5:3); its contents can only be revealed by the Lamb, who alone is worthy to open the scroll's seals (5:5–9) and thus reveal the progress of God's judgments on the earth (ch. 6).

Could the events described in 6 have been "foreseen" by human prognostication? Some of them are common events of the ancient world, so perhaps any informed person could foresee such possibilities. What has to be

---

93. Aune, *Prophecy in Early Christianity*, 114.
94. See discussion of the genre of apocalypse and Revelation in chapter 2 above.
95. Aune, *Prophecy in Early Christianity*, 279–88.
96. Cf. ibid., 64, 279.
97. Cf. ibid., 63.
98. Ibid., 75–76.
99. Ibid., 68–72.
100. Ibid., 72–73.
101. Ibid., 275–79.

revealed therefore, as John sees it, is not just the events themselves, but their meaning, their origin, and therefore the outcome of what is happening.[102] John claims to have insight from Jesus into these things, as he emphasizes through the story of the opening seals, leading up to the world-shaking crisis of the sixth seal (6:12–17).

The role of the Spirit in transmitting revelation is a key focus of Revelation. In order to receive this revelation, John must be "in the spirit" (Gk. *en pneumati*, 1:10; 4:2; 17:3; 21:10)[103] so that he can effectively tune in to the world of spiritual and heavenly realities. As Bauckham argues, "The Spirit does not give the content of the revelation, but the visionary experience which enables John to receive the revelation."[104] In the case of the initial messages to the individual churches, John presents himself almost as a faithful secretary taking dictation from Jesus or the Spirit. Each message begins, "These are the words of [Christ] . . ."[105] and concludes with reference to "what the Spirit is saying to the churches" (2:7, 11, 17, 29; 3:6, 13, 22). Moreover the prophetic dimension is a realm of the spirit (19:10; 22:6).

John thus presents the subject matter of his text not as created by him as author, but as received in the Spirit. Whatever the precise nature of his experience was, to him it involved an inbreaking of God into his consciousness. This claim, of course, is controversial. But Christopher Rowland argues, "We should pay John the compliment of accepting his claim unless there are strong reasons for denying it."[106]

However, such comments raise epistemological issues. For instance, there is the question of genre. No scholar would question that Revelation is an ancient revelatory text, and most accept that it is an apocalypse.[107] In these genres, we expect the literary features found in Revelation. Such genres of writing have never disappeared altogether and are reappearing in

---

102. Cf. Gilbertson, *God and History*, 163.

103. For discussion of what "in the spirit" means phenomenologically see chapter 3.

104. Bauckham, *Theology of Revelation*, 116. Cf. Snyder, "Triple-Form and Space/Time Transitions," 445–47.

105. The phrase τάδε λέγει (lit. "thus says . . .") is found in the NT only in Rev 2–3 and Acts 21:11, but commonly translates in the Septuagint prophetic introduction formulae in the Old Testament (Boring, "Apocalypse as Christian Prophecy," 45; cf. Aune, *Prophecy in Early Christianity*, 275).

106. Rowland, *Revelation*, 23. Elsewhere Rowland (*Open Heaven*, 235–36) reports the findings of J. Lindblom on the extent of "authentic visionary experience" in Revelation. See also the defense of the genuineness of the visions in Rissi, *Time and History*, 18–21, compared to the more measured opinion of Aune (*Prophecy in Early Christianity*, 274–75).

107. Cf. Aune, *Revelation 1–5*, lxx–xc. See chapter 2 for more discussion of this point.

the postmodern era. Are their stories of mystical or supernatural experiences simply a literary tradition or should we take them as making truth claims?

Many recent critics see John's claim to a revelatory experience as just a rhetorical strategy. Thompson argues that John minimizes his role in the revelation in order to minimize "the possibility of considering this revelation to be a partisan, idiosyncratic view of the world"[108] and to encourage the idea that "the vision is self-authenticating."[109] And Robert Royalty argues that John's presentation of himself as a prophet is a strategy designed "to increase the authority of the text among its audience,"[110] and that the visions are designed as "external proofs" of John's message.[111] However, this perhaps puts the alternatives too starkly. Even if we accept that John uses his experience to his advantage, this does not mean that the experience was fictional or illusory. To really do justice to John's text, we must at least be open to the possibility that he had the vision he describes, whether or not we accept the content as true.

What, then, about the experiences claimed by the authors of pseudonymous apocalyptic books like *1 Enoch* or *4 Ezra*? Were they real? Various answers have been offered to this. Perhaps their claims *are* merely a literary device, or they represent a genuine experience on the part of the real author (even though ascribed to a past figure), or the authors felt themselves to be identified with their pseudonyms in some psychological way (through "corporate personality" or prophetic tradition or the Hebrew sense of "contemporaneity" with the past), and/or the experiences were to some degree "self-generated" (perhaps by meditation on a passage of Scripture, lamenting to the point of emotional exhaustion, or fasting).[112] However, the worldview of the authors and readers of apocalypses would appear to make a claim to some genuine experience, even experience of divine revelation, credible to them.[113]

Nonetheless, this case clearly draws attention to the need for some kind of testing mechanism to differentiate between true and false claims to divine revelation, if the concept is to have any epistemological value. Phenomenology and sincerity will not be sufficient. Both the reality of such

---

108. Thompson, *Apocalypse and Empire*, 178.

109. Ibid., 179. See below.

110. Royalty, *Streets of Heaven*, 18.

111. Ibid., 132.

112. E.g., Dan 9:2–3; 10:2–3; *2 Bar.* 35:1—36:1; 43:3; 47:2—48:1; *4 Ezra* 5:13–22. Cf. Aune, *Prophecy in Early Christianity*, 109–10.

113. Rowland, *Open Heaven*, 218; cf. ibid., 228–39; Russell, *Jewish Apocalyptic*, 132–39; Craffert, "Altered States of Consciousness," 127.

visions and their content need to be evaluated by some kind of accepted criteria. Revelation accepts revelatory experiences as real—both positive (from the Spirit) and negative (from the devil, 13:13–15; 16:14)—but it is skeptical in places. For example, Jezebel's claim to be a prophet is not accepted uncritically (2:20), nor is the claim of her followers to have "learned what some call 'the deep things of Satan'" (2:24). How does John distinguish between them? I will return to this shortly.

The Channels and Language of Revelation

Revelation opens by calling itself a revelation that originated in God and was intended for "his servants," but would not be given to them directly (1:1.) This mediated method of revelation is characteristic of the whole book. God himself is said to speak directly only twice (1:8 and 21:5–8). Jesus speaks more frequently; indeed the whole book is also entitled "the testimony of Jesus Christ" (1:2). Occasionally direct speech is attributed to the Spirit (14:13; 22:17).

Between the beginning and the end of the book, however, much of the communication comes from angels. A particular angel is given the biggest role (1:1; 22:6, 8, 16), but many other angels play a part in the communication, verbally (5:2; 10:1–10; 17:1–2, 7–18; 21:9–10, 15, 17; 22:1, 6, 8)[114] or by taking part in the action of the story.[115] At times, the whole choir of heavenly beings breaks into song (5:11–13; 7:11–12; 19:1–3, 6–8).

The final link in the "revelatory chain"[116] is John himself. He receives "the revelation" (1:1), also described as "the word of God" and "the testimony of Jesus Christ" (1:2), from Jesus' angel (1:1) and by vision (1:2). John presents himself as a somewhat passive recipient of revelation, but not as a mere cipher. He takes part in the drama: he falls (1:17; 19:10; 22:8), weeps bitterly (5:4), converses with heavenly beings (17:6, 7, 13, 14; 10:8–9), and even eats a scroll (10:10). He also acts as the mediator of seven communications to the

---

114. See also Rev 7:2–3; 14:5–11,15,18; 16:5; 18:1–3, 21–24; 19:17–18.

115. There is also a lot of anonymous communication from heaven in the form of voices (Rev 1:10–12; 4:1; 9:13–14; 10:4, 8; 11:15; 12:10; 14:2, 13; 16:1,17; 18:4; 19:5; 21:3) or unattributed statements (7:4; 10:11; 11:1; 13:9–10) and sometimes other heavenly beings, such as the four living creatures (4:8–9; 5:9–10, 14; 6:1, 3, 5, 7; 19:4) and the elders (4:10–11; 5:5, 8–10; 7:13–14; 11:16–18; 19:4), even the altar (16:7), have messages too. See also 5:13; 6:9–10, 15–16; 8:13; chs. 11–12; 13:3–4; 15:2–4; 16:9, 11; 18:9–20.

116. Boring, "Apocalypse as Christian Prophecy," 54.

angels of seven Asian churches (2:1, etc.), if indeed these ἄγγελοι are to be understood as literal angels.[117]

Most importantly, John edits and compiles "the words of the prophecy of this book" (22:18), giving them their final and unalterable form (22:18–19). Thus he shares in the authorship of the text. As Bauckham argues, "Whatever John's visionary experiences were, he has transformed them, by a long process of reflection, study and literary composition, into a literary work which communicates their message to others."[118]

What sort of language is appropriate for writing about revelatory experiences? The Bible as a whole uses a range of literary genres and forms to express the revelatory experiences and messages of its authors, including argument, poetry, and narrative. Revelation itself uses a variety of different forms of speech, generic features, and literary devices. To study them all would be outside the scope of this book, but two prominent features of the text need to be noted.

First, it is largely written in prose as a straightforward autobiographical account of the experiences of a single person, John. This is standard for most Jewish apocalypses, except that their authors usually present themselves in pseudonyms. But it emphasizes John's stance as a witness, which will be discussed shortly.

Second, the "foreign," "hidden" nature of the reality to be revealed is such that it must frequently be communicated in strange symbolic and pictorial language. Here again, Revelation resembles the Jewish apocalypses, each of which is some form of prophecy (albeit pseudonymous) in which the protagonist(s) foretell events and their meaning into the distant future,[119] often as a result of dreams and visions[120] and/or with the assistance of angels,[121] sometimes using highly symbolic language.[122] However, as a result, this "revelation" conceals as much as it reveals.

---

117. Cf. Aune, *Revelation 1–5*, 108–12.

118. Bauckham, *Theology of Revelation*, 116–17. Cf. Heschel, *Prophets*, 1:25.

119. To the protagonist, that is. The historical position of the actual author is often closer to the end of the sequence of events predicted. A prime example is the "animal apocalypse" in *1 Enoch*, which foretells history from the flood to the Maccabean period (cf. *1 En.* 89), all of which would be future to the biblical Enoch but mostly past to the actual author(s).

120. E.g., *1 En.* 85:1–3; *2 En.* 1:2–5; *2 Bar.* 36:1; *4 Ezra* 9:38—10:28; Dan 2; 4; 7; 8; 9:20–27; 10–12; *T. Levi* 2.

121. E.g., *4 Ezra* 4; *2 Bar.* 6:3; 55:3—56:1; *4 Ezra* 10:29–57; *T. Levi* 5:1; 6:3.

122. As in *1 Enoch*'s "animal apocalypse" (cf. *1 En.* 85–91). Cf. *2 Bar.* 36–40; *4 Ezra* 11; Dan 2:31–45; chs. 7–8.

3. The Role of the Witness

Enlightenment epistemology pictures the knower of truth as an independent discoverer, as opposed to the recipient of tradition in the medieval worldview. In contrast, many postmodernists are more likely to picture the knower as a constructor of truth, though not necessarily deceitfully so. But John sees himself neither as a subject/discoverer nor as an inventor/constructor, but as a witness, in continuity with much Jewish and Christian thought before and contemporary with him.[123]

As noted above, John sees and hears continually, not with his natural senses, but in vision. The phrases "I saw"[124] and "I heard"[125] frame most of the pericopes of the vision,[126] but even when they are missing John relates "seen" images or "heard" voices. In fact, throughout his vision he presents himself as a spectator or experiencer of spiritual realities. The language of sense perception is used, but not of scientific investigation; rather John is claiming a form of spiritual eyewitness testimony, perhaps not dissimilar to the perception of God discussed by Alston.[127] Moreover John does not apparently go looking for this vision or seek answers to particular questions (except within the visionary experience itself); the vision comes to him.[128]

From the outset, John takes the standpoint of a witness. 1:2 states that he "testified[129] to the word of God and to the testimony[130] of Jesus Christ, even to all that he saw." John's testimony is based on that of Jesus (as in 1:9; 19:10; 22:16, 20), who is himself described as a witness (1:5; 3:14).[131] Like a witness in a court of law, John vows that "these words are trustworthy and true" (21:5; 22:6). As Hill observes, such witness bearing is "witness communicated through speech," not martyrdom.[132] However, John implies that

---

123. E.g., Isa 43:9–12; Acts 1:8. Cf. Trites, *New Testament Concept of Witness*.

124. Gr. εἶδον, aorist of ὁράω, see or observe, or occasionally, a form of βλέπω, see or look, as in 22:8.

125. Gr. ἤκουσα, aorist of ἀκούω, hear, receive news of.

126. He sees (1:12; 4:1; 5:1, 2, 6, 11; 6:1, 2, 5, 8, 9, 12; 7:1, 2, 9; 8:2, 13; 9:1, 17; 10:1, 5; 13:1, 11; 14:1, 6, 14; 15:1, 2, 5; 16:13; 17:3, 6; 18:1; 19:11, 17, 19; 20:1, 4, 11, 12; 21:1, 2, 22; 22:8) and hears (1:10; 4:1; 5:11,13; 6:1, 3, 5, 6, 7; 7:4; 8:13; 9:13; 10:4, 8; 11:1; 12:10; 14:2, 13; 16:1, 5, 7; 18:4; 19:1, 6; 21:3; 22:8), and even tastes (10:10) in the vision.

127. Alston, *Perceiving God*.

128. Many apocalyptic visions were sought for, often with prayer and fasting (e.g., Dan 10:2, 3, 12).

129. Gr. ἐμαρτύρησεν, aorist of μαρτυρέω, bear witness, testify, be a witness.

130. Gr. μαρτυρίαν, testimony, witness, evidence.

131. Compare John 3:31–33; 18:37. Cf. Hill, "Prophecy and Prophets," 411; Trites, *Concept of Witness*, 155–59.

132. Hill, "Prophecy and Prophets," 412. However, it may result in martyrdom (Rev

he was suffering for his witness (1:9) when he speaks of sharing "persecution" with his readers and being on Patmos "because of the word of God and the testimony of Jesus" (cf. 1:2 and 20:4).[133]

The whole text of Revelation is replete with the language of witness and courts.[134] The witnesses of Jesus are effectively the heroes of the book: Antipas "my witness, my faithful one" (2:13), the souls "slaughtered for . . . the testimony they had given" (6:9), the two witnesses-cum-prophets of chapter 11 (11:3), "your comrades who hold the testimony of Jesus" (19:10), and others.[135]

John's comrades are said to win the divine court battle against the dragon "who accuses them day and night" by "the word of their testimony" (12:10, 11), though this requires them to lay their lives on the line (12:11)[136] in keeping with the later sense of *marturia*.[137] The dragon makes war on those who "hold the testimony of Jesus" (12:17), who are placed in the power of the beast and called on to endure in faith (13:7, 10; 14:12). Similarly, the whore was drunk with "the blood of the witnesses to Jesus" (17:6), but later "God has given judgment for you against her" (18:20). The unbelieving world is condemned for shedding the blood of "the witnesses to Jesus" (17:6), but those "beheaded for their testimony to Jesus" are vindicated finally: they sit on thrones and have "authority to judge" (20:4).

This witness is seen as costly because there is a real contest between God's people and their foes. John, as I pointed out, portrays most people as living in a state of deception. Thus the witnesses to Jesus are opposed, persecuted and even killed for their testimony.[138] Jesus commends those in the

---

2:13; 6:9; 12:11; 17:6; 20:4).

133. Of course, the text does not explicitly state that John was in Patmos as a punishment for his witness to Jesus. However, I think the reference to persecution earlier in the verse tips the balance in favor of the view that John was in Patmos as a punishment. Cf. Hill, "Prophecy and Prophets," 411-12; Thompson, *Apocalypse and Empire*, 172-73; Howard-Brook and Gwyther, *Unveiling Empire*, xxvii; Witherington, *Revelation*, 9; Friesen, *Imperial Cults*, 136.

134. E.g., the final court scene where people are judged according to "their works, as recorded in the books" (Rev 20:12).

135. Cf. Bauckham, *Theology of Revelation*, 118-21; Trites, *Concept of Witness*, 159-70. This is one reason why the dispensationalist reading of Revelation, which assumes that true believers have been raptured to heaven before most of this witness takes place, distorts the meaning of the text. The true heroes of the book are those who are very much on earth!

136. Cf. Trites, *Concept of Witness*, 170-71.

137. Cf. Aune, *Revelation 1-5*, 185; and Trites, *Concept of Witness*, 13, on the process through which this word took on its modern meaning.

138. Cf. Trites, *Concept of Witness*, 155-56.

churches who are enduring patiently (2:2–3, 19; 3:10), suffering affliction and slander (2:9), or refusing to deny him under pressure (2:13). He warns the faithful believers that they will be persecuted, even thrown into prison (2:10), and urges them to be "faithful until death" (2:10), like Antipas (2:13), in view of "the hour of trial" (3:10.)

The concept of witness as evidence for truth is not, of course, unknown: in fact, from ancient times, it has been central to our courts and in disciplines such as history.[139] What is required for testimony to be accepted in such cases?

Obviously, the witness must be in a position to testify due to having seen or heard the events under consideration, as opposed to secondhand reports or rumors.[140] Second, the witness must be reliable, that is, a good observer.[141] Third, the witness must be honest, faithful, given to telling the truth without distortion, embellishment, or exaggeration, and certainly not deliberately lying.[142] Fourth, their testimony must "ring true" and be consistent.[143] To the extent that a witness is not totally reliable, consistent, or faithful, or their story seems improbable, contradicting most people's observation and experience, their testimony will be discounted unless corroborated by other reliable witnesses.[144] Finally, in a court, the witness must be present for cross-examination. However, in the case of historical testimony, this lack of "presence" has not ruled out the use of testimony as a central kind of evidence; instead, other testimony and other forms of evidence are used to test the testimony under consideration.

So are there criteria that could be applied in order to assess the credibility of a testimony like John's, even in the absence of the witness himself? Does John himself show awareness of any such criteria? Many critics allege that he in fact supports a weak testimony, with authority-building devices designed to impress his readers/hearers and silence doubters. Elisabeth Schüssler Fiorenza, for example, explains John's claims of divine authority and his "vilification of his prophetic rivals" as due to "a great anxiety about the authority of his work."[145]

---

139. Cf. Coady, *Testimony*, 7–8, 26–27; Trites, *Concept of Witness*, 4–15.

140. Coady, *Testimony*, 27–30. However, Coady points out that we frequently accept second-hand reports as evidence for facts in everyday life (ibid., 38–40, 48–49).

141. Ibid., 35–36.

142. Thus false witness is seen as a serious vice in all codes of morality (Ricoeur, *Essays in Biblical Interpretation*, 128–29).

143. Cf. Coady, *Testimony*, 47.

144. On the place of corroboration in testimony, see ibid., 34–35.

145. Fiorenza, "Words of Prophecy," 8.

John does not appear to consider tests for testimony. And if we apply the tests for ordinary testimony to Revelation, we get mixed results. If John can be believed, he *is* a firsthand witness of his experiences (as opposed to telling someone else's experiences), but the experiences are not of external realities, as opposed to the original eyewitness testimony of the apostles (Luke 1:2; Heb 2:3; 1 Pet 5:1; 2 Pet 1:16–18; 1 John 1:1–3). He tells the story like an observer with an eye for detail, but it is almost impossible to translate his descriptions into pictures, since the details are often bizarre and even incoherent.

It is impossible for us, 1900 years later, to be sure whether or not he is exaggerating or distorting his story in order to serve his political goals (as some commentators claim), but at least he does not try to hide his own ignorance and fallibility (as in the references to him attempting to worship angels).[146] The story he tells would not ring true to many outside the Christian community, although the apocalyptic language would perhaps appeal to some Jews familiar with other apocalypses, and parts of his description of current events and the nature of the Roman Empire would be coherent with common experience of the day. He is at least consistent in the overall thrust of his testimony.

However, the testimony of John and of his fellow witnesses is strongly commended by their willingness to die rather than change or deny their witness to Jesus. In an era when torture was widely accepted as part of the legal process (the testimony of slaves was only accepted if obtained under torture, for example),[147] such steadfastness added credibility to the testimony of the Christians.[148] As I discussed above, John himself makes this point strongly (12:11). And in fact, the resoluteness of the testimony of Christian martyrs strongly impressed Greco-Roman observers and won many of them over in the centuries after Jesus, leading Tertullian to talk of "the blood of the martyrs" being "the seed of the church."[149]

Many modernists and postmodernists practice a stance of suspicion towards witness as a path to truth. Modernists frequently insisted that we investigate all such claims for ourselves by reason and observation or experience.[150] Postmodernists doubt the ability of any subject to manage this challenge, due in part to our own standpoint and bias.

---

146. Friesen, *Imperial Cults*, 188. Cf. Stuckenbuck, *Angel Veneration and Christology*.
147. Trites, *Concept of Witness*, 6.
148. Cf. Swinburne, *Metaphor to Analogy*, 94.
149. Cf. Chadwick, *Early Church*, 29; Bauckham, *Theology of Revelation*, 151.
150. E.g. David Hume's discussion of this topic, powerfully criticized in Coady, *Testimony*, 79–100. See also ibid., 101–13; and Keener, *Miracles*, 1:107–70.

Yet the basic stance of suspicion is impractical and unworkable in real life, where mostly we do not have the time, the resources, or the need to investigate everything, and we rely happily on trusted credible authorities or witnesses to tell us what is true.[151] In fact, most of what we know, we know on the basis of testimony of authorities.[152] For example, in spite of its proven bias, selectivity, and frequent unreliability, most of us rely on the mass media to provide us with the "facts" about current events; our only check (if any) is to choose the media outlet that seems the most credible to us, perhaps because its reporting has been fairly reliable and balanced in cases we have personally experienced.

Some recent philosophers have sought to re-establish witness as a valid path to truth,[153] and argue that testimony may be just as useful a method for finding the truth as observation, for instance.[154] In fact, Derrida argues that relationship, communication, and society are impossible without testimony and trust (in others).[155] But if testimony is a valid source of truth in daily life and in courts of law, then there is no logical reason why testimony to spiritual realities must be rejected out of hand; nor must revelation be ruled out as a valid source of truth, for it consists of the ultimate infallible expert, witness, and authority telling us what is true.

It can, of course, be objected that in the case of spiritual (or other extraordinary) experiences there are much greater difficulties with testimony than usual, because corroboration is unlikely and the testimony may not ring true to people who have not had similar experiences. For example, so-called near-death experiences or stories of alien encounters are difficult to assess, even though they are increasingly told and believed[156] in our postmodern world. This objection must be accepted, but it is not fatal to belief in testimony, provided that the realities testified to by a witness are *in principle* able to be experienced by others or tested in some way.[157] I have suggested

---

151. Thus trust, not criticism or skepticism, may be a valid stance in deciding the truth of a matter (cf. Coady, *Testimony*, 46–47, 112–15). Complete suspicion is an unworkable stance (ibid., 85–95).

152. Cf. ibid., 6–7.

153. Ibid.; Vanhoozer, *Is There a Meaning?*, 290–92; Plantinga, *Warrant*, 77–88; Cartledge, *Practical Theology*, 52–61; Ricoeur, *Biblical Interpretation*, 110–54.

154. Cf. Coady, *Testimony*, 143–48.

155. Caputo, ed., *Deconstruction in a Nutshell*, 22–23; cf. Derrida, "Faith and Knowledge," 63–64.

156. Probably due at least in part to the number of such testimonies.

157. Cf. Coady, *Testimony*, 52–53 for a brief discussion of "religious" testimony, and ibid., 179–98 on "astonishing reports" generally. See also the arguments in Nash, *Faith and Reason*, 151–56; and Alston, *Perceiving God*, 209–10 against the view that religious experiences are less able to be checked than nonreligious ones, and the extended

how this might be the case above, and will return to this point when I take up the question of revelation in a more general way.

Another important qualification must be noticed, however. Ricoeur's essay "The Hermeneutics of Testimony" explores the question of to what extent absolute truth can be established by testimony, in the light of the fact that testimony has the context of a dispute and conflicting opinions, and in law and history only strong probability can be established thereby. Moreover testimony is inherently interested: it is testimony on behalf of a person or a cause; thus it can be biased and slanted by rhetoric in order to cause the hearer or reader to accept the desired conclusion.[158] It must therefore be conceded that absolute certainty cannot be obtained by testimony; of course, postmodernists point out that such certainty is a chimera in any field of knowledge and rhetoric is a feature of all forms of argument.

Ricoeur also points out the hermeneutical issues raised by testimony. As a form of text, witness statements must be interpreted. This is a real problem, though no more so than the problem of interpreting any other evidence. In fact, if such problems ruled out testimony as grounds for truth claims, both law and the study of history would be impossible.

Finally, we need to return to the question of martyrdom. In his essay "Toward a Hermeneutic of the Idea of Revelation," Ricoeur comments,

> When this proof becomes the price of life itself, the witness changes names. He becomes a martyr.... I am well aware that any argument from martyrdom is suspect. A cause that has martyrs is not necessarily a just cause. But martyrdom precisely is not an argument and still less a proof. It is a test, a limit situation. A person becomes a martyr because first of all he is a witness.[159]

In other words, while martyrdom does not prove the truth of the testimony, it does at least enhance the credibility of the witness in terms of sincerity or consistency. Early Christian teaching, as found in the Gospels, Acts, and Revelation, speaks of a willingness to be killed rather than to kill, which makes these Christians true martyrs as opposed to warriors who risk their lives for a cause.

---

arguments in Keener, *Miracles*, vol. 1, esp. 148–53. Comp. also Smith, *Thinking in Tongues*, 62–64.

158. Coady, *Testimony*, 124–27.

159. Cf. ibid., 113.

4. The Insights and Authority of Prophets

Closely allied to the concept of a witness, especially when spiritual realities and revelation are concerned, is that of a prophet, one who purportedly tells others what God is saying about a situation. John clearly presents himself as such a person[160] and he attempts to present a prophetic view of history.

As many postmodernists have pointed out, there is no such thing as an objective—in the sense of value-free—interpretation of history.[161] All human interpretations of history come from a particular standpoint and bias. However, a Christian worldview allows for the possibility of an interpretation that comes from God's standpoint as history's governor and which is mediated through God's chosen messengers, the prophets. In fact, this is the understanding not only of Revelation but of nearly all the Bible.[162]

John certainly believes in the validity of a prophetic perspective on history and positions himself as the successor to Old Testament prophets. For example, according to him, God's prophets know what "must soon take place" by the process of revelation (Rev 1:1, 3; cf. Amos 3:7). Prophets are commissioned to speak or write the true history of the past, present, and future (Rev 1:19; cf. Jeremiah). Prophets foretell the consequences of human choices (Rev 2:5, 10, 16, 22–23, 26–28; 3:3, 8–10, 16, 20–21; 14:9–11; cf. Isa 8:5–8). Prophets like John are taken into the throne room of God to see the way the universe really operates and how God's plans for history are progressively unveiled (Rev 4–6; cf. 1 Kgs 22:19–23).[163] God fulfills what he has announced previously to his prophets (Rev 10:7; cf. Dan 9:2). Prophets even come to embody God's message for history, as when John eats the small scroll (Rev 10:8–10; cf. Ezek 3:1–3).

John also views prophets as being able to take an active role in the history they interpret (Rev 11; cf. 1 Kgs 17–18). Their words of prophecy can influence the course of events (Rev 11:3) and what happens to them can ultimately vindicate their perspective on what has happened (Rev 11:7–13). Prophets also authoritatively interpret portents seen either in vision or in the visible heavens (Rev 12, 15, 17; cf. Dan 10).

According to John, prophets make authoritative judgments of the ethical significance of events in history since, as Heschel explains, "their

---

160. E.g. 1:1–3,19; 2:1; 4:1; 22:7, 10, 18, 19. Cf. Aune, *Prophecy in Early Christianity*, 274.

161. See chapter 6.

162. Cf. Heschel, *Prophets*, vol. 1, chs. 9–10. Comp. Weber, *Economy and Society*, 1:450, where Weber argues that prophets articulated "a unified view of the world derived from a consciously integrated meaningful attitude toward life."

163. Cf. Heschel, *Prophets*, 1:21–22.

concern is not with facts, but with the meaning of facts."[164] There are many examples of this in Revelation, but one clear case is the heavenly commentary on the turning of the waters into blood in 16:4–7, which is seen as God's judgment on those who killed the "saints and prophets" (Rev 16:6) and is also justified as a due vengeance for this persecution (Rev 16:5–7; cf. 1 Kings 21). Modern and postmodern critics may view this as violent and vengeful,[165] but in John's thinking it is God's justice at work.[166]

In John's thought, prophets see the final outcome of historical trends whose results cannot always be predicted humanly. John, for example, sees the ultimate fall of Babylon (Rev 18; cf. Jer 50–51) and the ultimate triumph of Christianity (Rev 20–21). In summary, prophets give God's or Jesus' perspective on and interpretation of events.

Postmodernist commentators often seek to explain John's perspective on the issues facing the seven churches in terms of his political struggles as a church leader with rival prophets and leaders.[167] Tim Long, for instance, is suspicious about John's motives, labeling his "threats" as "stratagems of control," and urging that "Ephesus becomes an image of every disempowered community, bowing its head under an all-controlling authority."[168]

Whatever the truth of this political or psychological perspective may be, John is being consistent with *his* worldview in claiming a prophetic perspective on the issues. For example, the "false Jews" referred to in 2:9 clearly did not see *themselves* as a "synagogue of Satan," and others in Smyrna would have had all kinds of opinions on them, but John attributes his judgment of them to the words of Jesus (2:8) and the Holy Spirit (2:11). And obviously the devil himself did not *literally* throw some Smyrnan believers into prison (2:10). This action was taken by local authorities, perhaps at the urging of the Jewish leaders in the city, and it may have been seen by some as vindicating their opposition to Christians or showing loyalty to the gods they served or to the empire. But John attributes their actions to an evil supernatural influence, in the name of Jesus and the Spirit.

Similarly, John claims he has God's point of view when he explains the actions of political leaders as governed both by opposition to the Lamb (17:14) and by the sovereign purpose of God (17:17), which includes his purpose to punish Babylon for her sins (17:1; 18:5.) So is there any way we can test such claims?

---

164. Ibid., 1:14.
165. E.g., Pippin, *Death and Desire*; Yhearm, *Sitz im Lebe*.
166. Cf. Peters, "Politics of Violence in the Apocalypse of John."
167. Cf. Royalty, *Streets of Heaven*, 28, 30.
168. Long, "Real Reader Reading Revelation," 96–98.

The special claims made for prophets in Revelation do not mean that prophets were unchallengeable, nor that they had "almost unlimited authority . . . as the sole possessor of the Spirit . . . [standing] above the community," as David Hill claimed.[169] Old Testament prophets were subject to tests because there were false prophets as well as true (Deut 13:1-5; 18:20-22; 1 Kgs 22:5-28; Jer 14:13-16; 23:9-40; 28:1-17; 29:8-32), and their authority was only to be accepted if genuine (Deut 18:18-20). The methods used to distinguish true and false prophets in the Old Testament were not without problems; in fact, Aune claims that "No distinction between 'true' and 'false' prophets can be made on the basis of objective, historical criteria."[170] However, this does not mean there were no methods at all or no concept of true and false prophets.[171] A similar principle applies to New Testament prophets (Matt 7:21-23; 1 Cor 12:2-3; 14:29-33; 1 John 4:1-6).[172] John upholds this principle explicitly (Rev 2:2) and in his own practice (2:20). As Fiorenza notes, "the church in Asia Minor has the right to test the itinerant apostles and prophets,"[173] and other ancient Christian documents agree.[174]

One possible test relates to validation of prophets and their message by supernatural signs or miracles, a form of confirmation widely appealed to in the Bible.[175] However, John is somewhat ambivalent here: his two prophetic witnesses (ch. 11) are empowered to work miracles of judgment (11:5, 6) and are raised from the dead publicly (11:11), but elsewhere he stresses the possible deception caused by "false signs" (13:13-15), following other trajectories in the Bible.[176]

---

169. Hill, "Prophecy and Prophets," 410. See also ibid., 414-17, and Aune's response in *Prophecy in Early Christianity*, 5, 11-12.

170. Aune, *Prophecy in Early Christianity*, 87.

171. Cf. Strauss, "Jerusalem and Athens," 135. In my "Holding Prophets Accountable" I set out some of the criteria used to decide between true and false prophecy in both the Old and New Testament. See also the extended discussion of this issue in Moberly, *Prophecy and Discernment*. Moberly argues that the key means of discerning between true and false prophets was by looking at their behavior, and to some extent their confession of Christ.

172. See the extended discussion of how prophecy and prophets were evaluated, both in the Old Testament and in Christianity, in Aune, *Prophecy in Early Christianity*, 217-29.

173. Fiorenza, *Justice and Judgment*, 144. Cf. Friesen, *Imperial Cults*, 188.

174. E.g., *Didache* 11-12 (in Staniforth, ed. and trans., *Early Christian Writings*, 232-34).

175. Cf. Mark 16:20; 2 Cor 12:12; Heb 2:4; Swinburne, *Metaphor to Analogy*, 94, 97.

176. E.g., Deut 13:1-3; Exod 7:8-12; Matt 7:22, 23; 24:24; 2 Thess 2:9-11. Many of the New Testament warnings are eschatologically oriented.

What criteria does John himself seem to follow in distinguishing between true and false prophecy, then? First, he may well think that true prophecy must be fulfilled by events happening as predicted within a reasonable space of time (cf. Deut 18:21-22; Isa 43:9).[177] John emphasizes the closeness of the events he is predicting (Rev 1:1, 3; 22:6, 7, 10, 12, 20), with some exceptions (such as the thousand years of Rev 20), apparently inviting his hearers to test his prophecy.

Second, he seems to believe that true prophets uphold the name of God and have no compromise with idols, other deities, or immorality (see Deut 13:1-5). This is the criterion John uses to undermine the claims of the prophet Jezebel (Rev 2:20). It is also implied by John's consistent rejection of other religions and gods (Rev 9:20; 14:7).

Third, and related to the second point, John seems to think that prophets must speak consistently with the existing beliefs and teachings of the church (cf. 1 Cor 12:1-3; 1 John 4:1-3). Here again Jezebel is faulted (by implication) for teaching practices rejected by the representatives of the whole church in Jerusalem (cf. 2:20, 14-15 with Acts 15:19-20, 29). Of course, she might well have replied that her teaching is consistent with, say, Paul's, at least on the subject of food offered to idols (cf. 1 Cor 8-11).[178]

Fourth, there is the test of the consensus of the church, either locally (cf. 1 Cor.14:29; 1 Thess 5:19-21) or universally (especially in the case of texts being considered for recognition as Scripture). I have already mentioned the testing of claims to be apostles (Rev 2:2); clearly John is urging the churches to subject Jezebel and her prophecies to close scrutiny (Rev 2:20-23) and not blindly accept anyone who claims to be a prophet.[179]

These implied tests are, of course, largely internal to John's Christian tradition, with the exception of the test of events fulfilling prophetic forecasts. John's own claims to have God's authoritative word were also subject to testing, and we know that not everyone immediately accepted Revelation as truly prophetic or qualified for admission to the canon of Scripture.[180] But once having passed the test,[181] a prophecy was accepted as an authoritative word from God,[182] a word of revelation that ought to be believed and obeyed.

177. Compare examples of Jewish prophecy that were/were not fulfilled in the very late Second Temple Period, including Josephus (Aune, *Prophecy in Early Christianity*, 135-41).

178. Cf. Royalty, *Streets of Heaven*, 30-32.

179. Cf. 1 John 4:1.

180. Cf. Wainwright, *Mysterious Apocalypse*, 30; Witherington, *Revelation*, 10-11.

181. Cf. Weber, *Economy and Society*, 1:458-60 on this process.

182. The philosophical issues implicit in such a claim of "divine discourse," whether

In the messages to the seven churches there is the repeated exhortation, "Let anyone who has an ear listen to what the Spirit is saying to the churches" (Rev 2:7, 11, 17, 29; 3:6, 13, 22; cf. 13:9; Matt 13:9). This implies that in order to receive this revelation it is necessary to "have an [spiritual] ear" and to use it to "listen to what the Spirit is saying" through the prophet. In other words, the hearer needs to be spiritually attuned and open to the message, willing to believe it and act on it (Rev 1:3; 22:7). But it also implies that some of the hearers either do not "have an ear" (are unable to receive the revelation) or will not choose to listen. This would include the Nicolaitans and their followers (2:6, 15), members of the "synagogue of Satan" (2:9; 3:9), Jezebel and her followers (2:20-23), and some blind though otherwise faithful Christians (3:16-17).

John sees it as taking some level of spiritual discernment to actually receive God's revelation through the prophetic witnesses. Thus John calls on his hearers to "calculate"[183] (13:18) and think wisely (17:9). Many professed Christians, he implies, will fail to receive the revelation, not because of any natural inability, but because they have been deceived by the many competing voices (2:6, 9, 14–16, 20–24), or lulled into a false sense of security by their achievements (2:3-4, 19-20; 3:1-3, 15-17)—all as a result of what Minear calls "the invasion of demonic deceptions within the churches."[184] However, such believers are apparently *capable* of hearing the voice of the Spirit and repenting of their ways (2:5, 16, 22; 3:3, 18–20). Yet those "outside" will fail to perceive what God is revealing and doing (9:20-21; 16:9, 11, 21) even though, as typical ancient Mediterranean dwellers, their worldview allowed them to perceive the hand of God in disastrous events; thus they inconsistently curse God because of what they suffer (16:9, 11, 21).

Prophets and prophecies, almost by definition, are meant to carry authority as channels of revelation from an omniscient and omnipotent God. But it is important to clarify the nature of this authority, because both modernism and postmodernism are suspicious of authority when it comes to questions of truth and ethics. For example, it is important to note that prophets do *not* carry institutional authority. Their authority does not originally derive from a position or title conferred by an organization, unlike later teaching authority in the institutional church.[185] Hence John does not

---

in terms of a specific prophecy or a whole text (or even the whole Bible), are examined in some depth in Wolterstorff, *Divine Discourse* in terms of speech-act theory. Wolterstorff distinguishes sharply between divine discourse and divine revelation.

183. Gr. ψηφισάτω , figure out or count.

184. Minear, "Ontology and Ecclesiology," 102.

185. In later generations, the words of the prophets may be canonized and become authoritative in that sense, but contemporary prophets are usually controversial, as

introduce himself as an apostle (unlike Peter and Paul) or bishop, or even an elder (cf. 2 John 1 and 3 John 1). He has no organizational sanctions to threaten his opponents with, and he cannot enforce his instructions to the churches.

Rather, prophets' authority is "author-ity." As Paul Ricoeur argues,

> The prophet presents himself as not speaking in his own name, but in the name of another, in the name of Yahweh. So here the idea of revelation appears as identified with the idea of a double author of speech and writing.[186]

Thus prophets' authority depends on their hearers recognizing their words as coming from God or Jesus, partly due to their previous credibility and partly due to the power of the prophecies themselves. The final decision lies with the hearers (and subsequently with the interpretive community of the church). Even John's threats in the name of Jesus are only effective to the degree that they are seen as credible by the Christians of Asia, that is, to the degree that he is seen as a true prophet of God. For example, Jesus' threat to the church of Ephesus to "remove your lampstand from its place" (2:5) could be taken to mean that John will shut the church down or excommunicate them, but it is questionable whether *he* could have done that.

Now I argued above that one of the key tests of prophecy is fulfilled prediction.[187] But it is just here that John's credibility as a prophet may be questioned,[188] for he seems to predict the destruction of Rome,[189] and yet this did not happen in the time scale implied; in fact, the city of Rome was never destroyed completely, even after the fall of the Western Empire. Hence, Tina Pippin argues that Revelation cannot have value as a predictive prophecy because its dream has not been fulfilled: even when Christianity triumphed in the Roman Empire, nothing really changed.[190]

How may this be explained? Perhaps John was just mistaken, and thus a false prophet in that sense, even if he has a valuable insight and message

---

Revelation makes clear. Compare the comments on this process in Matt 23:29–37 and John 9:28.

186. Ricoeur, *Biblical Interpretation*, 75. Ricoeur, however, uses this observation to equate revelation with dictation, and thus neglects the claims to divine discourse in the Bible as well as oversimplifying the concept of divine discourse and revelation, as Wolterstorff points out (*Divine Discourse*, 62–63).

187. Cf. Gilbertson, *God and History*, 162.

188. For a wide-ranging response to this problem, see Bauckham, *Theology of Revelation*, 146–56.

189. Rev 17–18.

190. Pippin, *Death and Desire*, 95.

for the churches. Or maybe the Rome he is prophesying about is still to come, as futurist interpreters of Revelation argue, who see the whore of chapter 17 as representing a future Roman Empire or entity. This approach makes John's prophecy unfalsifiable and contradicts his expressions of imminence (1:1, 3; 22:6, 10).

Or perhaps the whore is not Rome but Jerusalem, which *was* literally destroyed in John's day. This has been argued by a minority of commentators,[191] but it seems to make little sense of John's language: the seven mountains (17:9), "the great city that rules over the kings of the earth" (17:18), the commercial power and luxury described in chapter 18, and even the title Babylon itself, with its connotations of empire, military might, enmity towards Jerusalem, and pretensions to unity like Babel of old.

Perhaps John is describing not the literal city, but its *spirit* or *daimon*. It could be argued that the spirit or religion of pagan Rome was defeated by the witness of the church over several centuries, leading to Constantine's acceptance of Christianity as the new religion of the empire. This would be consistent with John's worldview, but his evocative language in Revelation 18 seems to cry out for a more literal, earthy reading.

We may be on safer ground if we look for parallels with prophets of the Old Testament era. For example, prophetic language in the Old Testament often includes hyperbole. Situations are described[192] and outcomes are predicted in stark language that cannot be taken literally. A prime example is the prophecies of the destruction of the original Babylon (such as in Jer 50:11–16, 29–32, 39–46). Jesus himself, according to Matthew, uses this hyperbolic language when predicting the fall of Jerusalem and its temple, claiming (for example) that "not one stone will be left here upon another" (Matt 24:2). So perhaps John's prediction of the destruction of Rome may be said to be adequately fulfilled in the sack of Rome by the Goths and Vandals,[193] the end of the Western Empire, and the subsequent decline of the city in size and significance.

There is also conditionality in Old Testament prophecy.[194] Bauckham argues that "the predictive element in biblical prophecy is not fatalistic," and in this respect John is closer to classical Hebrew prophecy than to the apoc-

---

191. E.g. Chilton, *Days of Vengeance*; Gentry, *Before Jerusalem Fell*.

192. Heschel writes of the "sweeping allegations, overstatements, and generalizations" of the OT prophets (Heschel, *Prophets*, 1:13, cf. 14–15).

193. Or even the disasters of Nero's day and the convulsions after his death. Stramara (*God's Timetable*, 93–96, 111–15) argues that Nero's mother may be the source of the imagery in Rev 17, if not the sole reference.

194. Cf. Heschel, *Prophets*, 1:16, 194; though Aune (*Prophecy in Early Christianity*, 114) argues that "classical OT prophecy was not as conditional as many have supposed."

alyptic outlook.¹⁹⁵ For instance, we read in Jeremiah that God's warnings of destruction may be averted if the nation concerned "turns from its evil" (Jer 18:8). This principle was dramatically illustrated in the postponement of judgment on Nineveh as a result of their repentance at Jonah's preaching (Jonah 3:4-10; 4:2). Revelation clearly contains cases of conditional prophecy, such as the promises to the conquerors in the seven churches (Rev 2–3; cf. 21:6-7), the threats of punishment to several churches (2:5, 16; 3:3), the offer of Christ to the Laodiceans (3:20), the *lex talionis* warning about violence (13:10), and the warning against tampering with the text (22:18-19). The delayed judgment on Jezebel, giving her space to repent (2:21), reflects a similar pattern of thought. Perhaps, then, John's prophetic stance could be justified by claiming that judgment on Rome was postponed when Constantine and his successors acknowledged God and Christ, stopped persecuting the Christian church, and made other reforms to Roman society.¹⁹⁶

5. Eschatological Vindication

Finally, if John's concept of revelation is to be accepted, there seems to be a need for revelation to eventually become universal and public, to triumph over the skeptics, opponents, and unbelievers, to be unanimously acknowledged. This is what Revelation confidently expects.¹⁹⁷ As previously discussed, John views all human beings, except for a select number, as subject to deception from the devil. However, he does not expect this to last forever; rather the power of the devil to deceive is broken, first for a thousand-year period (20:2-3) and then permanently (20:7-10). This implies that as a result people will become significantly freer to see spiritual reality and understand the revelation of God for themselves.

Ultimately, in the New Jerusalem, revelation of God and the Lamb is all-pervasive (21:22, 23; 22:3, 5), at least to all his servants (22:3, 4). However, according to John, not only Christians will see fully the reality of God and Christ in the end. For example, his description of the final judgment (20:11-15) pictures all people "standing before the throne" (20:12) to be judged by God according to their deeds "as recorded in the books" (20:12). This suggests that everyone will be conscious of God and of the process of judgment; it seems to be a public event where the verdict is based on recorded evidence available (at least in principle) to all. In a similar way,

---

195. Bauckham, *Theology of Revelation*, 149. See discussion on this in chapter 2 above.

196. See also Swinburne, *Metaphor to Analogy*, 194-95.

197. Cf. Pannenberg, "Dogmatic Theses," 132.

John's description of the second coming of Jesus in his prologue stresses its public nature, so that even his enemies will see and wail (1:7).

The witness of the messengers of God, and those who received it, will be vindicated on that day, according to Revelation. Their resurrection and reign with Christ (20:4, 6) seems to imply that the revealed truth they stood for as witnesses, even at the cost of their lives, is now publicly vindicated and acclaimed as the official truth. They are avenged on those who persecuted them for their witness (16:4–6; 18:20; 19:2; 20:9–10) and are justified at the final judgment (20:12, 15).

Thus John is confident that the whole world will know the truth one day. This is implied by the picture of the light of the New Jerusalem shining throughout the earth (21:24), the promise of "the healing of the nations" (22:2), and the final removal of the deceiver (20:7–10; also 22:3). Moreover anyone who refuses to submit to the truth and life witnessed to by the Christians, or who distorts the message, will be "outside" the city and will apparently know that they were wrong (21:27; 22:15, 19). To sum up, John believes that the truth he proclaims will be vindicated at the end of history.

Such an emphasis on the future universal revelation as we find in Revelation first of all relativizes the knowledge we can have now from revelation; "Now I know only in part," as Paul puts it (1 Cor 13:12). Thus Pannenberg suggests that the meaning of the present and of revelation depends on the future—"the revelation of God and his glory is transferred to the end of all events."[198] The "concept of anticipation" implies the need for Christian truth claims to be vindicated in the future.[199]

Prophetic Risk

John makes a number of prophetic claims in Revelation, most of which cannot be verified independently. His claim to be speaking as a prophet and a witness can be tested, but it cannot be proven because, in the nature of the case, the realities of which he speaks are inaccessible to ordinary human investigation and can only be "seen" in the Spirit. Nonetheless, John calls for a radically committed response, as if these realities were self-evident to everyone. This amounts to a call to the hearer to take a considered gamble, somewhat like Pascal's famous wager.[200] The prophet forces you to make a

---

198. Ibid., 132–33. See comments in Fackre, *Doctrine of Revelation*, 217–21.

199. Pannenberg, *Metaphysics and the Idea of God*, 95–96.

200. Pascal argued that people should "bet on" God rather than the opposite, on the grounds that God's existence was at least possible and that the eternal loss faced by unbelievers if God does exist was not worth the risk. As a "standalone" argument for

choice. The stakes are high: John warns that the results of unbelief are far worse and more enduring than the costs of belief, and he promises that the ultimate rewards for believers outweigh the price paid for enduring suffering now (14:9-13). In this way, the prospect of the Last Judgment becomes part of a Christian epistemology as well as a Christian view of salvation.[201]

REVELATION AS A SOURCE OF TRUTH?

The implication suggested by this study of Revelation is that none of the usual alternative models provides the best picture of truth and knowledge, especially when it comes to spiritual realities. Rather the picture of truth and knowledge suggested by Revelation as fundamental or ultimate is revelatory: the One who knows all shares with us a portion of his infinite knowledge, primarily through his chosen witnesses and prophets. As opposed to Descartes' model, for example, God is the source rather than the end of human inquiry.[202] We can have limited objective knowledge because we begin with God rather than the individual human knower. Our role as humans is to listen, rather than just discover—still less construct—being aware of our limitations and proneness to deception. But of course such claims raise all sorts of issues. Is revelation a valid source of truth? Can revelation lead to universal truth claims? These are important issues that arise out of my consideration of the epistemology of Revelation.

Much of the thinking of modernity rules out any possibility of revelation as a source of objective or public truth. Instead, claims to revelation are redescribed as merely "religious" opinions, values, and/or experiences. The Enlightenment thinkers tended to see revelation as part of the Roman Catholic Church's claim to authority, which had actually been enforced with violence in the preceding centuries and which threatened the claims of autonomous reason.[203]

Revelation, it is argued, cannot be a source of universal truth because it is not universally available, but arises out of local or particular situations

---

Christianity, this argument has not been very successful, but it may have some power for those who are seriously considering Christian faith on other grounds. Moreover Pascal did not present this "wager" as the only evidence or argument for faith, but wrote of the reasons of the heart. Cf. Oppy, "On Reschler on Pascal's Wager," 159-68; Coady, *Testimony*, 109-10; Smith, *Thinking in Tongues*, 58.

201. Cf. Pannenberg, "Dogmatic Theses," 131-35, 141.

202. Of course, this oversimplifies Descartes' thinking. His argument depends, for example, on God's faithfulness in not leading us astray.

203. Cf. Niebuhr, *Meaning of Revelation*, 1, 28-30; Jaspers, *Philosophical Faith and Revelation*, 32-49; Strauss, "Jerusalem and Athens," 112.

and is accepted only by a limited body of people.²⁰⁴ As Leo Strauss argues, "philosophy recognizes only such experiences as can be had by all men at all times in broad daylight."²⁰⁵ On this basis, Gellner denies that there is "a substantive, final, world-transcending Revelation"; in fact, he "firmly repudiates the very possibility of *Revelation*."²⁰⁶ It is hard to see, however, how objective scientific knowledge could arise within a specific culture and yet be culture-transcending, as Gellner argues, while the same could not *possibly* happen in revelation. Gellner doesn't seem to answer this point even when he takes up the issue; he merely calls it "morally unacceptable."²⁰⁷ Many Christians would argue that the revelation of Jesus Christ, while arising historically in a specific culture and being historical in essence, is applicable to all people and can be understood and experienced by people everywhere.²⁰⁸ Others have disputed the claims of Enlightenment secularism, arguing (for instance) that some of the scientific progress attributed to modernity owes more than a little to a Christian perspective, explaining why modern science arose in European Christendom.²⁰⁹

It is also said that "any idea of revelation violates the idea of objective truth as measured by the criteria of empirical verification and falsification."²¹⁰ For instance, Jaspers questions whether the "signs" of revelatory language can be said to refer to an actual reality in space and time, or may be better taken as untranslatable "ciphers" of transcendence.²¹¹ Many modernist thinkers followed Feuerbach's thesis that claims to divine revelation (or even experience of God) could be reduced to psychological projections and were thus illusory.²¹² Of course, people could arguably perform a similar critique on Feuerbach himself and similar theories.²¹³

---

204. Jaspers, *Philosophical Faith*, 8.

205. Strauss, "Theology and Philosophy," 229.

206. Gellner, *Postmodernism, Reason and Religion*, 76 (italics original), see also 81.

207. Ibid., 84.

208. Swinburne (*Metaphor to Analogy*, 76) argues that revelation is quite capable of being transmitted from one culture to another, a presumption behind all Christian missionary work.

209. Meynell, *Intelligible Universe*, 110; cf. Prickett, *Narrative, Religion and Science*, 59–61.

210. Ricoeur, *Biblical Interpretation*, 97; cf. Strauss, "Theology and Philosophy," 226–27.

211. Jaspers, *Philosophical Faith*, 108–9, 123. See also his criticism of use of the word "fact" in assertions of revelation (ibid., 115).

212. Cf. Voegelin, "Immortality," 192–93.

213. Cf. ibid., 193.

Furthermore, it is urged that there are many incompatible claims to revelation (as in the Bible and the Koran, for example) and their claims cannot be adjudicated by revelation—the problem of "canon."[214] On the other hand, similar points can be made about other sources of truth. For example, science in itself is unable to adjudicate between different uses to which its discoveries are put, as illustrated mostly starkly in the development of nuclear weapons. Moreover there are scientific disputes that may not be able to be fully settled by the scientific method, particularly arguments about the origins of the cosmos. This does not invalidate scientific knowledge; it merely shows that science has limitations. Similarly, the concept of revelation is not in itself invalidated by conflicting claims, though we will need to establish ways of adjudicating between them.

Then there is the issue of hermeneutics: revelatory texts, even when accepted as representing the words of God, need to be interpreted by human beings, who often disagree about the meaning and application of the texts concerned.[215] One has only to look at current issues debated by Christians or Muslims to see how intractable such disagreements can be.[216] Thus, as Jaspers put it, "We cannot draw a line between what calls for obedience and what calls for critical discussion, between revelation and its understanding."[217] Some modernists argue that this makes revelation practically useless in the quest for truth. However, postmodernists have pointed out that all knowledge is textual and needs interpreting.

Finally, critics of Christianity in particular have argued that its claims to an exclusive revelation inevitably led to dogmatism and authoritarianism, even violence, as was seen especially in the medieval and early modern church; consider such events as the Inquisition and the Thirty Years' War. Even without the political power of those days, churches still impose authority on their followers based on claimed revelation and this "inwardly denies the equal rights of the 'heathen,' the infidel, the heretic."[218] In fact, Jaspers asserts that any belief in a final or absolute truth, whether based on

---

214. Cf. Voegelin, "Letter of April 22, 1951," 80; Jaspers, *Philosophical Faith*, 17.

215. Cf. Strauss, "Theology and Philosophy," 224–25; Voegelin, "Letter of April 22, 1951," 80–81; cf. the extensive discussion of this problem in Swinburne, *Metaphor to Analogy*, 130–44, 177–209. Swinburne stresses the role of the church and its traditions in interpreting the Bible, and the duty of later generations to reinterpret Scripture in the light of developing understanding of, say, science.

216. Cf. Jaspers, *Philosophical Faith*, 20–21.

217. Ibid., 22.

218. Ibid., 47.

revelation or philosophy, leads to closed minds, intolerance, and division between people,[219] a commonly accepted view today.

In response to such objections, some Christians modified their views of revelation.[220] For instance, the pietist or experiential view of revelation saw religious experience as the content of all knowledge of God and all of the different religions. This idea of revelation was particularly systematized by Schleiermacher[221] and is represented today by such theologians as John Hick, who posit a common religious experience understood variously in the different religions.[222]

Others, influenced especially by existentialism, saw revelation as primarily, if not exclusively, God's personal self-revelation or "dialectical presence,"[223] as opposed to propositional truth.[224] And the pan-historical view, which came out of Hegel and nineteenth-century German idealism, saw revelation as the manifestation of God in the whole sweep of world history. Wolfhart Pannenberg proposed instead a *particular-historical* idea of revelation,[225] arguing that God revealed himself clearly in events and developments of history (particularly the resurrection of Jesus) that were in principle open for all to investigate and could thus function as a basis for faith in the triune God.[226] He thus rejected the radical disjunction between revelation and historical fact found in Barth and the existentialists. God's Word was not itself revelation, but rather, "The word relates itself to revelation as foretelling, forthtelling and report."[227]

Postmodernists, on the other hand, do not necessarily rule out revelation as a concept. However, they still reject the possibility of *universal* truth claims coming out of revelation, because of their tendency towards pluralistic and local ideas of truth. They also maintain the modernist wariness of revelation as a claim to authority, especially non-human authority.[228]

---

219. Ibid., 80–86, 115–17, 132–33.

220. For a summary of modern and postmodern Christian views of revelation, see Pannenberg's Introduction to Pannenberg et al., eds., *Revelation as History*, 3–13; Bloesch, *Holy Scripture*, 46–51; and Fackre, *Doctrine of Revelation*, 16–19.

221. Fackre, *Doctrine of Revelation*, 17.

222. Cf. Hick, *Second Christianity*, 82–92; Voegelin, "Immortality," 197.

223. Fackre, *Doctrine of Revelation*, 17.

224. Cf. Pannenberg, "Introduction," 3–5; Niebuhr, *Meaning of Revelation*.

225. Ibid., 13–19. Cf. Wilkens, "Revelation within the History of Primitive Christianity," 110–15) and Pannenberg, "Dogmatic Theses," 125–31, 142–44.

226. As explained in his defining article, "Dogmatic Theses," 125–55.

227. Pannenberg, "Dogmatic Theses," 152.

228. Cf. Smith, "Rorty on Religion and Hope," 79–80.

For example, Paul Ricoeur attacks the idea of revelation as "a body of truths which an institution may boast of or take pride in possessing" and seeks "to overthrow every totalitarian form of authority which might claim to withhold the revealed truth."[229] Rather he argues for "a concept of revelation that is pluralistic, polysemic, and at most analogical in form."[230] Through an emphasis on the differing concepts of revelation implicit in different genres of the Bible[231] and a hermeneutical approach to poetic discourse, Ricoeur constructs his view of revelation as analogous to the way good literature gives us deeper insight into reality by creating its own world,[232] appealing to the imagination rather than reason.[233] On the other hand, Ricoeur does not eliminate any connection between revelation and fact: by use of the concept of testimony, he "introduces the dimension of historical contingency."[234]

Riceour's thinking is very relevant to Revelation, which clearly appeals primarily to our imagination with its imagery and story line, as I will explore in chapter 6. On the other hand, it is in the form of a testimony, as I showed above, and this relates the text to the claimed experience of John as well as to the historical reality of his day.[235] Further, the text makes claims to authority (albeit prophetic, not institutional authority), as noted previously.

Finally, others point out that every religion or church makes its own distinct claims to revelation truth and has its own criteria for testing these. Hence claims to revelation are only testable and valid within the tradition or community in which they arise. There is no way of differentiating and adjudicating between the rival revelation claims of Christianity and Islam, for example. An effective Christian defense of revelation as a valid source of truth must therefore take the claims of other religions into consideration, which I will attempt to do in chapter 7.[236] For example, one view sees revelation as a

---

229. Ricoeur, *Biblical Interpretation*, 95.

230. Ibid., 75.

231. Ibid., 87, 90–91.

232. Ibid., 104. Cf. Smith, *Thinking in Tongues*, 73–75 on the way film coveys meaning.

233. Ibid., 117. Jaspers (*Philosophical Faith*, 57), however, calls this approach a dilution or flattening of the idea of Christian revelation; he would rather just say, "I don't believe in revelation."

234. Ibid., 109.

235. Cf. Wolterstorff, *Divine Discourse*, 241–60 on the relation between biblical narrative and the distinction between history and fiction.

236. Note, however, Swinburne's (*Metaphor to Analogy*, 95–97) claim that Christianity is the *only* religion that grounds its teaching on a supernaturally-validated revelation.

gradual unfolding of the reality of God[237] and thus also accepts the presence of revelation in other religions and pre-Christian traditions.[238]

Perhaps a common factor in nearly all modernist and postmodernist Christian views of revelation is their tendency to dismiss propositional revelation.[239] For example, Ricoeur argues that "the analysis of religious discourse ought not to begin with the level of theological assertions,"[240] and Voegelin argues that doctrinal statements can "be *misunderstood* as propositions referring to things in the manner of propositions concerning objects of sense perception."[241]

However, total rejection of propositional revelation is mistaken. A Christian view of revelation that wants to be faithful to a biblical perspective must include the elements I have identified in this study of Revelation (prophecy, testimony, and eschatological vindication). It should include the concept of God's self-revelation, which is clearly integral to the Bible as a whole and John's experience reported in Revelation, a perspective on history as a whole and on particular events in history,[242] and it should be related in some way to religious experience. It will necessarily include some progressive element, for God does not reveal himself or any truth all at once. But it cannot *exclude* the idea of propositional truth.[243]

For example, Revelation makes explicit propositional claims (such as that the time for its fulfillment is near; 1:3) and some at least of its descriptive passages can be stated in propositional language (for instance, the description of the judgment of the dead in 20:11–15 can easily be restated as a series of propositions, such as "God will judge all people according to their deeds").[244] As Swinburne argues, propositional revelation is necessary since, for example, "events are not self-interpreting" and can only function as revelation if accompanied by a revealed interpretation in propositional form. He contends that belief in propositional revelation was virtually unanimous in the Christian church until the eighteenth century.[245]

---

237. Voegelin, "Gospel and Culture," 164, cf. 159–75.

238. See discussion in chapter 7.

239. But see the recent defense of the notion in Swinburne, *Metaphor to Analogy*, e.g., 3–4.

240. Ricoeur, *Biblical Interpretation*, 90. Cf. Niebuhr, *Meaning of Revelation*, 92–93.

241. Voegelin, "Immortality," 177–79 (italics added).

242. Cf. Bloesch, *Holy Scripture*, 49–50, 73–74.

243. Cf. ibid., 48–55, 62–68.

244. As in Rom 2:6.

245. Swinburne, *Metaphor to Analogy*, 3–4.

Testing Revelation

I am arguing that a Christian response arising out of this study of Revelation would defend the validity of revelation as a source of universal truth, that is, truth that lays claim on all people everywhere and that can be stated at times in propositions. But in order for this claim to be taken seriously, valid, objective, and accessible criteria would have to be available to test claims to revelation. Are there any possible criteria that can be used? Let's briefly examine several.

First, a claim to revelation should be coherent with existing accepted revelation.[246] Thus early Christian apologists, in the New Testament and subsequently, strove to demonstrate that Christianity was not a totally new religion but logically followed on from the Scriptures accepted by the Jews. Others made similar arguments for Christianity as a development of the highest insights of classical philosophy or, more recently, of Hindu or Buddhist thought. Some of these arguments are highly controversial, but they demonstrate an acceptance by the thinkers involved that any claim to revelation must not be totally unprecedented.[247] Similarly, claimed revelation must also not violate our moral sensibilities, even if challenging or extending them at certain points.[248]

Second, claimed revelation ought to show coherence with empirical reality (including the events of history). No claims to revelation can stand that radically contradict people's ordinary knowledge or experience of reality (as opposed to going beyond it). This is the criterion that lies behind the struggles to relate Christian faith to modern science, since true revelation cannot contradict true science;[249] it is also reflected in traditional arguments for and against Christianity or theism generally, such as the argument from design, the argument from fulfilled prophecy, or discussion about the "problem of evil." Pannenberg, for instance, argues that "An understanding that puts revelation into contrast to, or even conflict with, natural knowledge is in danger of distorting the historical revelation into a gnostic knowledge of secrets."[250] At this point, Revelation may have a useful point to offer. As I showed in chapter 2, many of the Jewish apocalypses indulge in somewhat detailed cosmology drawn from ancient knowledge and speculation.[251] The

---

246. Cf. Strauss, "Theology and Philosophy," 226.

247. Similar arguments are mounted by Islamic apologists with respect to the Hebrew and Christian Scriptures.

248. Cf. Swinburne, *Metaphor to Analogy*, 2, 86–88.

249. Cf. Jaspers, *Philosophical Faith*, 53–54.

250. Pannenberg, "Dogmatic Theses," 135.

251. Cf. *1 En.* 34–36; 41:3–7; chs. 72–82; *3 Bar.* 10:9–10; *T. Naph.* 2:8; *2 En.*

absence of such speculation in Revelation contains an important implication: revelation cannot function as the foundation of science, in the sense of deriving scientific facts from prophetic writings. Revelatory knowledge of the fundamental spiritual realities and ordinary human enquiry into natural reality must coexist in their own spheres.[252] Thus while Revelation is open to a kind of gnostic interpretation, it is also rooted in public events like the crucifixion of Jesus (1:5; 5:9; 11:8).[253]

Third, the phenomenology of claimed revelatory experiences must be studied. While studies of the phenomenology of religious experience suggest that there are similarities between experiences of different religions, all religious experiences are not identical in nature. Similarly, Christian critics of claims to revelatory experiences within other religions, and among Christians today, often point to phenomenological factors in their critique; for instance, the degree to which the person involved is "possessed" or out of control.[254]

Fourth, the status of the person making claims to revelatory experiences is a significant criterion for examining their claims. While prophets may often be controversial and eccentric, no religion accepts just *anyone* bringing authoritative revelation to its adherents. The credibility of prophets must be established by previous success in prediction, for example, as well as by their moral practice, spiritual insight, and even supernatural signs.[255] Their institutional position may also be significant, though not often decisive; for instance, even Roman Catholicism takes seriously visions recounted by people without any institutional power in the church.

A fifth criterion for accepting claims to revelation is their internal consistency and ability to be understood. A prophecy that contradicts itself or is incoherent cannot be accepted, though readers of such texts may argue long and hard about whether or not a particular text *is* consistent or coherent.[256] This criterion thus implies that interpretation of texts is not

---

3–22,40; *3 Bar.* 2–11.

252. This seems to have been the thinking behind Francis Bacon's concept of God's "two books," a view that liberated empirical science to go out and find how the creation actually functioned (cf. Lessl, *Rhetorical Darwinism*, 53–57).

253. Cf. Pannenberg, "Dogmatic Theses," 150–51.

254. Cf. 1 Cor 14:32. See the discussion of spiritual discernment, in which phenomenology is critical, in Yong, *Beyond the Impasse*, 129–61. See also discussion of similar ways of assessing a claim that "God spoke" in Wolsterstorff, *Divine Discourse*, 274–80.

255. See above and Newton, "Holding Prophets Accountable," 63–79.

256. See, for example, Jaspers' (*Philosophical Faith*, 112–14) arguments about the misuse of dialectics as a way of avoiding this test.

an impossible task, nor is it impossible for us to speak clearly about God or other spiritual realities. This contradicts the *via negativa* suggested by some neo-Derrideans such as Kevin Hart.[257] As Swinburne argues, "If sentences of human language cannot tell us quite a bit about God, there can be no significant propositional revelation."[258]

Sixth, a claim to revelation needs to have one or more signs of divine origin. For instance, if the content of the supposed revelation does not go beyond what ordinary human experience teaches, its claim to divine origin is very questionable.[259] It may also be confirmed by supernatural events such as miracles.[260] However it happens, there needs to be an element of the extraordinary about the event or content of the claimed revelation, or at least an extraordinary depth of insight, for its claim to be credible.

Finally, revelation is tested by its acceptance by the community of faith over a period of time. In the case of Christianity, this refers to the process of canonization of texts that are accepted as authoritative Scripture. This criterion works only within a particular tradition, but nonetheless serves to eliminate many claims of revelation, perhaps at times prematurely. And as I noted earlier, a strong case can be made for the importance of tradition in all epistemological development.[261]

None of these tests can be shown to have final or infallible validity. They all leave the status of a particular claim to revelation unproved. This, however, does not necessarily destroy the idea of revelation. It only makes it difficult to establish it as a strong foundation for other knowledge.

Revelation, Philosophy, and Foundationalism

I began this chapter by looking at the problems currently faced by various forms of foundationalism in epistemology. It is now appropriate to consider how this discussion of the validity of revelation impacts on that issue.

In my opinion, the view of revelation I have just described is consistent with belief in the possibility of objective universal truth. God's prophets are seen to be able to receive insights about reality from the one Source that stands "outside" the particular human perspectives and *has* an Archimedean point of reference—that is, God. Moreover, at the end of time, all people will have knowledge of the key truths about reality through the processes of

---

257. Cf. Hart, *Trespass of the Sign*.
258. Hart, *Metaphor to Analogy*, 162.
259. Cf. Swinburne, *Metaphor to Analogy*, 89
260. Ibid., 90–93. But see above on John's less than enthusiastic attitude to this.
261. Cf. MacIntyre, *Whose Justice?*; Alston, *Perceiving God*, 191–94.

the Last Judgment and the coming of new heavens and earth envisaged in Revelation 21–22.

However, this view sees limits to the ability of human beings to discover objective truth now. According to Revelation, in this age human beings cannot independently attain to complete objective or absolute knowledge (at least about spiritual reality), due to their limitations as creatures, their bias as sinners, and the deception of the devil. Those who are spiritual can receive limited objective knowledge through God's prophets. However, even *they* are vulnerable to deception, as the messages to the seven churches make abundantly clear. As Yong points out, the spiritual realm is inherently ambiguous and Christians themselves are influenced by more than one kind of spirit.[262]

In conclusion, a Christian worldview derived from study of Revelation supports the view that human enquiry *independent of God* cannot discover the fundamental nature of reality. As Karl Jaspers claimed, "What the world in which we find ourselves is as a whole, whence it comes, where it goes—this we do not know, and never will know."[263] On the other hand, a Christian view displays a confidence that there is an objective physical and spiritual reality and that real knowledge of this reality *is* possible *through (or on the basis of)* revelation, partially and selectively now, but more fully and completely in the eschaton. Paul put it well when he wrote,

> For we know only in part, and we prophesy only in part; *but when the complete comes*, the partial will come to an end. . . . For *now* we see in a mirror, dimly, but *then* we will see face to face. *Now* I know only in part; *then* I will know fully, even as I have been fully known. (1 Cor 13:9–13; emphasis added)

Does confidence in revelation mean that human enquiry and reason are discarded?[264] Early Christian writers debated this at length. Some, like Justin Martyr and Clement of Alexandria, saw Greek philosophy as the precursor to Christian theology, led to some degree at least by the preincarnate Logos. Others, such as Tertullian, rejected philosophy as incompatible with Christian truth.[265] More recently, in dialogue with Eric Voegelin, Leo Strauss argued that revelation and reason are incompatible in their presuppositions, methodologies, and theologies,[266] whereas Voegelin contended that revela-

262. Yong, *Beyond the Impasse*, 166.
263. Jaspers, *Philosophical Faith*, 4–5.
264. For a lengthy discussion, see ibid., 22–28, 54–60.
265. Brown, *Philosophy and the Christian Faith*, 7–8, 13; Charlesworth, *Philosophy and Religion*, 50–52, 86; Tarnas, *Passion of the Western Mind*, 151–53.
266. Strauss, "Jerusalem and Athens," 112, 131–33, 137; "Theology and Philosophy,"

tion gives humans the "pregivens" of perception, and the gospel functions as the climax of a long process of revelation through the ancient Greek philosophers.[267] When I consider the relationship between Revelation and rival worldviews of its day (in chapter 7), I will argue that there are elements of both approaches in this text. But as I argued earlier, there is certainly no rejection of "natural" knowledge in Revelation, and neither should there be in a Christian worldview.

Moreover revelation is not just a function of a Christian community or tradition. In Revelation, revelation always comes from above and outside of the community of believers, challenging, extending, and unsettling their half-formed traditions. This is certainly how this text presents the seven messages to the churches in Revelation 2–3. Moreover John claims to have a revelation from God that stands in judgment on the alternative religious belief systems of his day.[268]

Meanwhile, religious knowledge (in a Christian worldview) rests on a claim to authority. The prophet declares the word of God without attempting to prove it. The witness testifies to what he or she has "seen" or "heard." The revelator speaks in the name of God the Creator and Judge. He or she makes promises and threats in God's name. Hearers must decide for themselves whether or not to accept and follow, having done the kind of checking envisaged above, but without being able to prove the claims involved. In this sense, Ricoeur is right to speak of the nonviolent appeal of revelation.

217–23, 229. See also Wiser, "Search and Response," 237–41. Cf. Jaspers, *Philosophical Faith*, 9–10, 27.

267. Voegelin, "Letter of April 22, 1951," 80–83; idem, "Gospel and Culture," 140–45, 153–55, 160–68, 173–75; idem, "Immortality," 202.

268. These statements will be developed and nuanced in chapter 7 when I examine how John approaches the insights of other traditions.

CHAPTER 5

The Significance of Personhood

ONE OF THE KEY worldview questions everyone has core beliefs about is, "Who am I?" That is, not just who I am as an individual, but who I am as a human being? What is a human being? How are humans different from other creatures or animals? How do humans relate to the rest of the world? How do different kinds of humans (such as male and female, or humans of different cultures) relate to each other? But also, what is the individual self made up of and how does it engage with reality beyond itself?

These are not just theoretical issues. They have significant implications, psychologically (my self-concept drives how I feel about myself and others), sociologically (my concept of humanness drives how I think about and relate to others, including animals), and even politically (what I expect of the political processes I engage in, or disengage from, and what goals I seek to achieve are very much influenced by my view of what a human being is and what humans can achieve). Current issues reflect different worldviews here. Abortion debates are driven by alternative views of what a human being is—when a new life becomes fully human, and the expected roles of male and female adults. Debates about preservation of endangered species, treatment of domestic animals, and protection of the environment generally also reflect basic worldview convictions about humanness and the responsibilities and rights of humans as related to the rest of the natural order. Christianity has been accused of justifying, if not causing, exploitation of the environment because of an arrogant presumption of human superiority derived from Genesis. But, ironically perhaps, environmental responsibility itself implies that humans are unique and have a unique responsibility for the earth, as in the viewpoint of Genesis 1–2.

The "grand narratives" of modernity, though grounded in a humanist worldview that privilege human reason and progress, as opposed to obedience to God, actually led to a lower view of humanity. Not only did modernism tend to a Eurocentric disregard of non-Western cultures and peoples and a masculinist arrogance towards the female gender, but it also tended to produce a generalized "essentialist" theory of human nature that suppressed or dismissed cultural diversity. For example, the Marxist metanarrative imposed a uniform "straitjacket" that would supposedly work in all countries and justified the project of remaking humanity in the communist world into the image proposed by Marxism-Leninism, through propaganda, terror, gulags, forced collectivization, and elimination of traditional values and customs. The worldview that emerges from Darwinian evolution also undermines the idea of human uniqueness and even confidence in human knowledge and reasoning, since humanity is not exempt from the evolutionary process.

This book is considering the implications of a study of Revelation for the construction of a Christian worldview relevant to the shift from modernity to the emerging era of postmodernity. One of the key areas that such a worldview must address, then, is the question of personhood, since postmodernism has set a new agenda regarding the human person. Debates around personhood, or subjectivity, include such areas as the concept of humanity and human nature, the role of the subject (especially in epistemology), the role of gender, and the place of personhood in any notion of cosmology. Postmodernism has a different approach to such questions than the discourses of modernity.

DEVELOPMENTS IN THE CONCEPT OF HUMANITY

As explored in chapter 2, the ancient Mediterranean world, the context of Revelation, was strongly hierarchical, as exemplified in its attitude toward work. For example, in ancient Greek society, "the essence of a notable was that he was a man of leisure, independent and *fully human*,"[1] whereas "to be a merchant, or to work for others, remained by and large anathema."[2] Greek philosophy also disdained ordinary occupations and privileged such

---

1. Veyne, *Bread and Circuses*, 46 (italics added). See also Green, *Alexander to Actium*, 363, 470–71.

2. Green, *Alexander to Actium*, 471; cf. Veyne, *Bread and Circuses*, 52.

activities as contemplation and participation in the *polis*.³ A hierarchical worldview was also reflected in the political systems of the day and in their religious thinking.⁴

Bruce Malina also writes of "the nonindividualistic, strongly group-oriented, collectivistic self-awareness that seems to have been typical of the first-century people in our New Testament."⁵ Conscience functioned mainly as an index of one's reputation in the eyes of others.⁶ A person's identity was primarily drawn from his/her group, and groups were seen largely in terms of what we today would call stereotyping.⁷ Thus, "Individual psychology, individual uniqueness, and individual self-consciousness are simply dismissed as uninteresting and unimportant."⁸

In the Middle Ages, while the dominance of Christianity enhanced a sense of personal accountability to God, people were still locked into a rather rigid social class structure and were expected to behave appropriately to their station in life.⁹ This also had its religious equivalents, with the average Christian near the bottom of a ladder that stretched upwards via priests, monks, bishops, and popes to the saints, the angels, Mary and Jesus. and ultimately to the remote and terrifying God himself. Some readers might remember the Grimms' fairy tale that illustrates this well: a poor peasant catches a flounder that tells him he is really a prince and then grants his grasping wife increasing wealth and power. She becomes king, then emperor, then even pope, but when she asks to be God she returns to the original humble pigsty of a cottage where they had started.¹⁰

The birth of modernity, beginning with the Renaissance, revolutionized the way people thought about themselves. The status of man was enhanced, so that Shakespeare could write,

> What a piece of work is man! How noble in reason! how infinite
> in faculties! in form and moving, how express and admirable! in

---

3. Taylor, *Sources of the Self,* 211–12. Such attitudes persisted well into the modern era.

4. Cf Malina, *New Testament World*, 104–5.

5. Ibid., 60.

6. Ibid., 58–60.

7. Ibid., 63–65.

8. Ibid., 75. However, there could at times be a more individualized emphasis (cf. Green, *Alexander to Actium*, 56–64, 605).

9. Cf. Goudzwaard, *Capitalism and Progress,* 4–6.

10. See "The Fisherman's Wife" at http://www.authorama.com/grimms-fairy-tales-10.html.

action how like an angel! in apprehension, how like a god! the beauty of the world! the paragon of animals![11]

Later, Immanuel Kant contended that "Enlightenment is man's emergence from his self-incurred immaturity."[12] In fact, according to Karl Barth, "the amazing scientific spirit of that time . . . was unquestionably one of the manifestations of *all-conquering, absolute man*."[13]

The place of the individual person was enhanced by the growth of the middle class, by the stances of the Reformation (defying the authority of popes and recovering the "priesthood of all believers"), by the adventures of European explorers, by the gradual breakdown of feudalism, by the emergence of modern science which heroized the individual researcher or discoverer, by the new language of "rights,"[14] by a new valuing of ordinary life associated with a breakdown of hierarchy,[15] and finally by the revolutions that shook the old political order in the late eighteenth and nineteenth centuries.

The new worldview of modernity was focused on the subject, the foundation of knowledge ever since Descartes' "*Cogito ergo sum.*" Charles Taylor's monumental study identifies features such as individualism, disengagement (that is, the self is no longer seen as part of a cosmic order), self-responsibility, and a dualistic emphasis on the inner workings of the mind or soul (as contrasted with the external world of objects) as peculiarly symptomatic of the modern view of self.[16] There is also a tension between an emphasis on a universal and stable human nature, inherited from the ancient world, and a stress on individual differences and change.[17]

To these features, the later Enlightenment (such as Romanticism) added belief in the inherent goodness of humanity and nature,[18] so that

---

11. Shakespeare, *Hamlet*, act 2, scene 2. For other examples, see Goudzwaard, *Capitalism and Progress*, 12; and Taylor, *Sources of the Self*, 199–201.

12. Kant, "What Is Enlightenment?," 51.

13. Barth, *Protestant Theology*, 41 (italics added). Cf. Goudzwaard, *Capitalism and Progress*, 40.

14. Taylor argues that this modern language of rights implied a view of the subject as "disengaged" from a larger world order and hence the idea of individual autonomy (Taylor, *Sources of the Self*, 11–13). See also ibid., 36, 82–83, 395.

15. Cf. ibid., 211–33.

16. Ibid., 12–13, 36, 111–13, 177, 181–82, 185–86, 370–71, 389. Stephen Prickett (*Narrative, Religion, and Science*, 94–114) sees this reflected in the rise of the modern novel.

17. Taylor, *Sources of the Self*, 181–82, 375.

18. Ibid., 317. Though both Rousseau and Kant had also a strong sense of human evil (ibid., 356, 366).

from then on the rival goals of "rational control" and "expressive articulation" dominate modern thought about human life.[19] Romanticism glorified primitive humans, as opposed to civilized humanity,[20] thus privileging feelings,[21] nature,[22] and society. These ideas greatly affected the emerging discipline of modern anthropology and also the rise of socialism in the nineteenth century.

Mark Taylor traces back the "epoch of selfhood" to Augustine[23] and argues,

> When man is represented as the image of God, the self also appears to be self-identical, self-present, and self-conscious. The proper theological subject is the solitary self, whose self-consciousness assumes the form of an individual "I" that defined itself by opposition to and transcendence of other isolated subjects. Such a self is primarily and essentially a unique individual.... In most cases, the locus of indivisible singularity is identified as an absolute private interiority or purely personal inwardness.[24]

Later developments in modernity undermined confidence in individualism. Hegel, for example, criticized liberal individualism, putting forward instead a concept of freedom in which individual fulfillment is attained within society as a whole.[25] Darwinian evolution implied that human beings were within nature, subject to the same processes as every other living being,[26] and not necessarily more valuable than other forms of existence. This kind of thinking has often led to a reductionist view of human nature, especially seen in behaviorism, and tends to make both the origin of personality and the concept of the human person problematic.[27] Similarly, as I explored in chapter 1, Bellah refers to Freud as "the gravedigger of the Enlightenment" because he disclosed the "enormous nonrational forces of

---

19. Ibid., 319, 376, 390.
20. See Taylor's comments on Rousseau in ibid., 355–63.
21. Cf. ibid., 282–84, 291–96, 371–73, including sensual pleasures eventually (328–29, 373).
22. Cf. ibid., 277–81, 296–99, 368.
23. Taylor, *Erring*, 14.
24. Ibid., 130 (italics original). Comp. Taylor, *Sources of the Self*, 111–13.
25. McGowan, *Postmodernism*, 51.
26. Cf. Miller, "Emerging Postmodern World," 9.
27. See the reflections in Jaspers, *Philosophical Faith*, 1–6.

the unconscious" not susceptible to rational analysis[28] and "emphasized the relative weakness and fragility of rational processes."[29]

Existentialism, on the other hand, stressed the human subject against the implications of naturalism, attempting to build a concept of freedom and value apart from science or reason,[30] seeing individuals not as rational observers of reality but as involved players in the drama of life. Heidegger paved the way for postmodernism by rejecting "the transcendental, privileged status of the Cartesian subject," because "Man . . . is always historical, rooted and a product of a particular manifestation of Being."[31] Meanwhile, quantum physics shook the modernist emphasis on the distinction between the observer and the real world, showing that in certain circumstances the act of observation itself affects the object being investigated.[32] And recent developments in neuroscience, genetics, and biotechnology are blurring the distinction between humans and machines and humans and other animal species, and calling into question assumptions about human freewill and the human soul.[33]

According to Cahoone, postmodernists have tended to query even the *existence* of the subject as a unified self.[34] Similarly, Bertens argues, "the autonomous subject of modernity, objectively rational and self-determined, . . . gives way to a postmodern subject which is largely other-determined, that is, determined within and constituted by language."[35] Thinkers like Foucault ask such questions as, "How are we constituted as subjects of our own knowledge? How are we constituted as subjects who exercise or submit to power relations? How are we constituted as moral subjects of our own actions?"[36] Thus the self is seen as fluid and plastic, even able to be reinvented if necessary.

Postmodernist theologian Mark Taylor explores how the attempt by humanists of modernity to assert the human self as a kind of new god

---

28. Bellah, *Beyond Belief*, 239. See also Vanhoozer, *Is There a Meaning?*, 67.
29. Bellah, *Beyond Belief*, 252.
30. Miller, "Emerging Postmodern World," 7.
31. Hekman, *Gender and Knowledge*, 65.
32. Grenz, *Primer on Postmodernism*, 52.
33. For a brief introduction to this, see Green, *Body, Soul, and Human Life*, xv–xvi, 20, 38–46, 73–87.
34. Cahoone, *Modernism to Postmodernism*, 15. Cf. Eagleton, *Against the Grain*, 145; Harvey, *Condition of Postmodernity*, 53–54.
35. Bertens, *Idea of the Postmodern*, 6. See also Gellner, *Postmodernism, Reason and Religion*, 24–26; Taylor, *Sources of the Self*, 34–35.
36. Foucault, "What Is Enlightenment?," 49. Cf. idem, "Truth and Power," 59.

mastering reality and negating "the other" is "finally *self*-defeating."[37] Later he argues, "The recognition of the differential character of predicates further unravels the identity of the subject and makes any notion of the self-in-itself unintelligible";[38] "the subject is always already bound in a self-surpassing linguistic web."[39] Taylor argues instead for self in relation: "Neither completely undifferentiated nor entirely separate, the deconstructed 'subject' is situated in the midst of multiple and constantly changing relations."[40]

The modernist concept of "man" is also being deconstructed, as in Foucault's famous assertion that, "As the archaeology of our thought easily shows, man is an invention of recent date. And one perhaps nearing its end."[41] In place of "the abstract Enlightenment universalism of an undifferentiated human nature,"[42] which thinkers like Foucault tend to historicize,[43] postmodernists emphasize the plurality of human beings of various eras and cultures. Simultaneously, feminism demonstrates the gendered nature of the concept of "man" and calls for its correction or even destruction.

Western males are no longer seen as paradigmatic for a general human nature. Whereas "primitive" people could be seen in the modernist world as somehow less than fully human (sometimes justified by appeals to Darwinian evolution), the death of this view raises new questions about our concept of the human person.[44] And other postmodernists like Griffin criticize not only individualism and patriarchy but also "anthropocentrism."[45] While postmodernists are generally still humanistic[46] in the sense of rejecting a transcendental source of truth or meaning such as God—deriving all meaning, truth, and values instead from human experience, language, and

---

37. Taylor, *Erring*, 13–14.
38. Ibid., 133.
39. Ibid., 135.
40. Ibid., 135.
41. Foucault, *Order of Things*, 387, as quoted in Grenz, *Primer on Postmodernism*, 129. See also Foucault's ("What Is Enlightenment?," 35) challenge to Kant on this point. Cf. Hekman, *Gender and Knowledge*, 19–20.
42. Laclau and Mouffe, as quoted in Bertens, *Idea of the Postmodern*, 190.
43. Rabinow, ed., *Foucault Reader*, 4.
44. Cf. Friesen, *Imperial Cults*, 10.
45. Griffin, ed., *Spirituality and Society*, xi. Cf. Cahoone, *Modernism to Postmodernism*, 12.
46. However, a recent trend has taken the name "posthumanism" (e.g., Nayar, *Posthumanism*). The precise meaning of this term is as confused and debated as "postmodernism." It certainly refers to a challenge to and modification of modernist humanism, but not apparently a return to any form of premodern theism.

ideas—they tend to have a more jaundiced, ironical, or limiting view of what human beings are worth or can achieve.[47]

As Leonard B. Meyer wrote five decades ago,

> Man is no longer to be the measure of all things, the center of the universe. He has been measured and found to be an undistinguished bit of matter different in no essential way from bacteria, stones and trees. His goals and purposes; his egocentric notions of past, present, and future; his faith in his power to predict and, through prediction, to control his destiny—all these are called into question, considered irrelevant, or deemed trivial.[48]

On the other hand, in the era of postmodernity, as Lyotard observes, temporary contracts are "supplanting permanent institutions" in the arenas of industrial, professional, emotional, sexual, family, and political life.[49] This is causing increasing atomization of society.

HUMANS IN REVELATION

Against this background of ferment in discourses concerning the nature and value of humanity, does Revelation have anything to contribute?

A striking feature of Revelation is the range of language used to characterize human beings. They are seen as witnesses, hearers, actors, conquerors, worshippers, servants, world dwellers, members of diverse nations, sinners, saints, traders, creatures, violent, slaves or free, men or women. However, the text of Revelation shows only passing interest in the differences in humanity. Social class is rarely mentioned; for example, 6:15 describes people along class lines and the merchants of Rome come in for special negative attention in chapter 18. Friesen notes that John uses broad brushstrokes and binary contrasts when he does refer to such distinctions.[50] The existence of different nations, languages, and ethnic groups is regularly alluded to (5:9; 7:9; 10:11; 13:7; 14:6; 15:4; 17:15; 21:3, 24, 26; 22:2), but only one is named—the Jews (2:9; 3:9). To the extent that Revelation tries to classify humanity, it divides them into just two groups according to its dualistic mindset: those in the book of life versus those who are not, those who worship the beast and take his mark versus those who are marked with

---

47. See chapter 1.

48. Meyer, "End of the Renaissance?" (1963), 186, as quoted in Bertens, *Idea of the Postmodern*, 24–25.

49. Lyotard, *Postmodern Condition*, 66.

50. Friesen, *Imperial Cults*, 191–92.

the names of God and Christ (7:3; 9:4; 13:8, 16, 17; 14:1, 9, 11, 12; 15:2; 16:2; 20:4, 15).[51]

One of the most frequent ways in which Revelation describes humans is to speak of their being subject to death (2:13, 23; 6:4, 8, 9, 11; 9:5, 6, 15, 18; 11:7–10, 13; 12:11; 13:10; 14:13; 19:21; 20:4, 12–14; 21:4). Death is the lot of all, believers and unbelievers alike, though the latter are especially warned of the "second death" (20:14). Death and Hades are personified in the vision of the pale green horse (6:8) and they are destroyed at the end (20:13, 14). Revelation seems to point to mortality as a limit to human ability, a correction to human hubris.

However, death is not reified to the degree found in some of Heidegger's thought, in which human life finds its meaning in "being towards Death."[52] Revelation embraces the Christian hope of bodily resurrection, both in its affirmation that Jesus is risen from death (1:5, 18; 5:6) and has the keys of Death and Hades (1:18), and its confidence in a universal resurrection at the end (2:10; 20:4–6, 13). This implies a strong value on individual human life and destiny. As Pannenberg asserts,

> Resurrection rescues from mortality unique, individually existing humans who are linked with God, and awards them fellowship with the eternal God without subsuming their creaturely identity into the divine being.[53]

This attitude stands out from the thinking of most ancients.

Humans as Worshippers

In Revelation, it is seen as normal, even central, for humans to worship powers greater than themselves. As Friesen writes, "No other apocalyptic text can be characterized by such a strong emphasis on worship," and "worship time" dominates John's concept of time.[54] In this John is not just following the expectations of ancient Mediterranean cultures, which justified their whole existence by devotion and sacrifice to gods;[55] he sets up worship as a major rhetorical emphasis in the light of his attack on idolatry and imperial cults.[56]

51. See chapter 2.
52. Cf. Pannenberg, *Metaphysics and the Idea of God*, 84–86.
53. Pannenberg, *Idea of God*, 65.
54. Friesen, *Imperial Cults*, 158.
55. Cf. Leithart, *Defending Constantine*, 16–20, 27–28, 192, 340–41.
56. Ruiz, "Praise and Politics," 69–80.

Worship is viewed as a central part of life in heaven, which functions as a kind of model for the church's life (4:8–11). Significantly, worship is also offered to the Lamb (5:8–14).[57] This worship is given by heavenly beings (4:8–10; 5:8–12; 7:11,12; 11:16), by the whole cosmos (5:13), and by the redeemed (7:9–10,15; 15:3). Meanwhile, on earth the saints offer worship and prayer to God (8:4), the temple focuses on worship (11:1) as a kind of model of heaven (11:19), and the nations are summoned to worship the Creator (14:7; 15:4).[58]

Where Revelation diverges from most cultures of its day, which tended to some form of syncretism,[59] is in its concept of forbidden worship: worship of demons and idols (9:20), the dragon and the beast (13:4,8,12), and its image (13:15; 14:11; 16:2; 20:4). If the human drive to worship is misused and misdirected, John implies, particularly towards worship of deified humans,[60] it can become blasphemous, deceptive, and oppressive (13:6, 7, 14, 15); such a politico-religious system can become like a wild beast (13:2).[61] Even John himself has to be twice restrained from worshipping the interpreting angel (19:10; 22:8–9).

Revelation is making a statement in these passages about the nature of humanity. By seeing humans first of all as worshippers, John stresses that they are not autonomous, but dependent and vulnerable. Humans are not in control of their own destiny; they are subject to higher powers, ultimately to God himself, who alone is worthy to be worshipped.[62]

Humans as Language Users

Postmodern thought has placed increasing focus on language, in particular how the use of language constructs reality and identity, as in the use of rhetoric. In this light, several studies have appeared analyzing how John uses rhetoric and language to achieve his purposes in Revelation.[63] But in this section I am more concerned with how John portrays human use of

---

57. Bauckham, *Theology of* Revelation, 58–63.

58. Cf. ibid., 32–35

59. See above, chapter 2; and Hengel, *Judaism and Hellenism*, 1:73, 94, 212–14, 261.

60. The design of Greek temples "traditionally permitted different gods and mortals to share the temple with the main deity" (Price, *Rituals and Power*, 146).

61. Cf. Bauckham, *Theology of Revelation*, 37–38, 45; Ruiz, "Praise and Politics," 71–74.

62. Cf. Friesen, *Imperial Cults*, 195–97; Bauckham, *Theology of Revelation*, 51.

63. E.g. DeSilva, *Seeing Things John's Way*.

language, and the importance of language in John's worldview, than with how he himself uses it.

To begin with, we see a wide range of ways that the humans in Revelation use language. Some of these ways have to do with addressing God in worship and song (4:10, 11; 5:13; 7:10; 11:13,16, 17; 14:3; 15:3,4; 19:6) or prayer (6:10; 8:3, 4; 22:17; for example, saying "Amen" in 5:14; 19:4) or with worship of other forces (13:4) or blaspheming or cursing God (13:5, 6; 16:9, 11, 21). Other language uses express emotions, such as celebrating (11:10; 18:20; 19:3, 7), crying aloud (6:16; 12:2), and lamenting (18:10, 16, 19); the "self-talk" attributed to the prostitute (18:7) is related to this use. Another group of language uses is designed to influence others: teaching (2:14,15), exhorting (13:14), lying (14:5), proclaiming or evangelizing (14:6,7; 21:3), and warning (22:18).

John's thinking is revealed in the way humans are also portrayed as hearers (1:3; 2:7; 3:20; 22:18) and witnesses (1:2; 2:13; 6:9; 11:3; 12:11; 19:10; 22:16). Considerable attention is given to the language of the courtroom: accusing (12:10), confessing and denying (2:5; 3:8), and testifying (1:2; 11:7; 12:11,17; 19:10; 22:20).[64] There is also prophesying, which is one of John's favorite ways of describing what he himself is doing (1:3; 10:7, 11; 11:3, 6; 22:7, 10).[65] Humans are viewed as those who are called to hear from God, either directly or indirectly, and to bear witness to what they see and hear. Thus John rarely portrays language used in dialogue, except where he relates discussions he had with angels (7:13-14; 17:6, 7). As a prophet, he is not interested in discussing his views with other human beings; for instance, his missives to the seven churches are worded as direct fiats from Jesus, in contrast with the style of, say, Paul's letters.

Three aspects of language use referred to in Revelation are portrayed as particularly powerful. The first of these has to do with writing. Apocalypses are essentially written prophecy; thus written texts seem to be particularly important to John, since they can be read aloud (1:3) and "kept" (1:3; 22:7, 9). He regularly reports being commanded to write things down (1:11, 19; 2:1 and parallels; 14:13; 19:9; 21:5),[66] and once being forbidden to do so (10:4). Written texts play an important part in his story: the sealed scroll (5:1)[67] launches the plot; eating the little scroll of 10 is part of John's recommissioning (10:2,8-10); written records form part of the last judgment (20:12); and the presence of a person's name in the Book of Life

64. See chapter 4.
65. See chapter 4.
66. Cf. Beale, *Revelation*, 216.
67. Cf. Aune, *Revelation 1-5*, 338-46.

determines their ultimate destiny (3:5; 13:8; 17:8; 20:12, 15). Finally, in the end it is emphasized that his own written text is trustworthy (22:6), ought to be kept (22:7), should not be sealed up (22:10), and must be preserved intact and unchanged (22:18, 19).[68] It is clear that written language, particularly written prophecy, has special significance and authority in John's thought world.[69]

A second range of language use mentioned frequently, and portrayed as especially significant, is naming.[70] The conquerors among the seven churches are sometimes promised new names, even the names of God and Jesus (2:17; 3:12).[71] On the other hand, the beast is associated with blasphemous names and naming (13:1, 6; 17:3) and the whore has blasphemous names as well as one that reveals her identity (17:3, 5). People's ultimate loyalties are described in terms of the names they bear: the beast's followers are marked with his name (13:17; 14:11),[72] and similarly the followers of the Lamb bear his name and that of his Father (14:1; 22:4). They are differentiated by whether or not their names are in the Book of Life (13:8; 17:8; 20:15).[73] The tale of Christ's appearance for the climactic battle is full of names: he is called Faithful and True, Word of God, and "King of kings and Lord of lords" (19:11, 13, 16), but he also is described as having a name inscribed "that no one knows but himself" (19:12).[74] The holy city is named after both the tribes of Israel and the twelve apostles (21:12–14). And, of course, all the names John uses in his text are loaded with intertextual significance, which John employs in a rhetorical strategy to guide his readers in their responses: people or groups he wants us to reject are given negative names drawn from the Old Testament (Jezebel, Balaam, synagogues of Satan, Sodom, Egypt, Babylon),[75] while, less frequently, positive names are given to those John approves of (New Jerusalem, olive trees, saints).

Finally, we need to consider the symbolism of things proceeding from the mouth. Jesus is pictured with a sword coming out of his mouth (1:16;

---

68. Cf. Aune, *Revelation 17–22*, 1208–15, 1229–32.

69. For parallels in the Jewish and Greco-Roman world, see Aune, *Revelation 1–5*, 85–87.

70. Cf. Resseguie, *Narrative Commentary*, 25–26.

71. Cf. Charles, *Revelation of St. John*, 1:92; Beale, *Revelation*, 254–58, 293–94. As Beale argues, this is not likely to endorse the idea of secret divine names having magical power (ibid., 257).

72. Cf. Beale, *Revelation*, 715–17.

73. Cf. Resseguie, *Narrative Commentary*, 96–97.

74. According to Barr (*Tales of the End*, 246), this may be related to the idea that knowing someone's name may give someone power of them.

75. Cf. Barr, *Tales of the End*, 98, 309, 320; Carey, "Ambiguous Ethos," 178.

2:16; 19:15); with this he is said "to strike down the nations" (19:15). Later John tells of fire coming out of the mouths of the two witnesses to destroy their opponents (11:5). It seems unlikely that he intends us to take this language literally, so what is he trying to say? Probably John is alluding to such places in the Old Testament as Isaiah 49:2, where we read of the Lord's servant that "He made my mouth like a sharp sword";[76] Psalm 64:3, where evildoers "whet their tongues like swords"; and Jeremiah 5:14, where God promises the prophet to make "my words in your mouth a fire" to consume the people (see also Jer 23:29). In other words, John is graphically describing the power of their words when they speak as representatives of God (out of whose mouth comes "devouring fire" in 2 Sam 22:9). God's words have incredible effects, but all language is significant and powerful, and what people say is very important, as I will discuss further below.

Humans as Servants and Conquerors

Many of John's pictures of humanity emphasize human contingency, dependence, and subordination. In the vision of Revelation, humans are not the rulers of the cosmos, nor are they independent; they are servants of God. John calls himself a servant (1:1) who faithfully hears and conveys God's word (1:2). Similarly, Antipas is honored as "my witness, my faithful one" (2:13), and it is God's servants who are sealed (7:3) and thus protected (9:4).

However, in John's vision God's servants are called to conquer. It is the conquerors who are promised eternal rewards in the messages to the churches (2:7, 11, 17, 26; 3:5, 12, 21; 21:7),[77] and these rewards include dominion (2:26–28; 3:21).[78] Jesus envisages his followers as comprising a kingdom and a priesthood (1:6; 5:10). Christians are part of his army (19:14),[79] having been numbered for war (7:4–8; 14:1–4), for they too are conquerors of the dragon and the beast (12:11; 15:2). The martyrs are promised "authority to judge" and a thousand years of reigning (20:4), and the servants of Jesus will reign forever (22:3–5).

This is a militant vision. Clearly the Christians are seen as conquering by witness and death (12:11), but there is no compromise allowed. While being conquered by the beast (13:7, 10), they ultimately conquer him (15:2).

76. Cf. Aune, *Revelation 1–5*, 98–99.
77. Cf. ibid., 151.
78. Ibid., 208–12.
79. According to one reading of this verse, based partly on the parallel with 17:14 (cf. Beale, *Revelation*, 960–61). Others see this army as consisting of angels (e.g., Aune, *Revelation 17–22*, 1059–60).

Friesen is correct when he argues that "John considered the churches to be an alternative sovereignty, a polity resisting the imperialism of his time."[80] Of course, the danger here is that Christians become defined in terms of their enemies—the classic problem of binary thinking criticized by postmodernism. Thus John's dualistic thinking can become a danger if adopted uncritically or taken out of context of his other thought. It can decline into hatred or rejection of people who are different, and it can be used to legitimate domination of one group by another.

However, for John rejection of the beast means rejection of a particular socio-politico-religious structure; the symbolization dehumanizes the struggle, so that it does not focus on individual Romans. It has always proved difficult to identify the symbols in Revelation with any concrete individuals, and this may be deliberate on John's part; he does not want us to take up arms (literally or metaphorically) against a particular emperor, but to resist the ungodly demands of the empire.[81] Although these will always be concretized in particular people and situations, the anti-Christian persecutors may be as much captive to the system as manipulators of it.

Of course, there *are* human enemies in Revelation, those who persecute God's people and the specific individuals and groups that John attacks, such as Jezebel, the "false" Jews, and the Nicolaitans in Revelation 2–3. Moreover, according to John, *God* divides people and throws some into the lake of fire (20:15). However, the real enemies are not people but the spiritual forces represented by the dragon, the beast, and the whore, which seduce, capture, exploit, and oppress people and turn them away from God.

The conquest called for is thus not some kind of military "holy war" against infidels but a spiritual war of liberation that is in principle *for* everyone. John does not call for Christians to conquer (in the sense of taking captive) any *human*, but rather to overcome the devil and change the world for the better. People and nations are to be "conquered" by being set free as converts to Jesus Christ (1:5); in this way, all nations come to faith in Christ and worship of the true God (5:9, 10; 7:9, 10; 15:4; 21:24–26).[82] Moreover nations are not annihilated in the end that John envisages (21:24, 26; 22:2), which implies that John is not against diversity as such, only rejection of God and his laws.

---

80. Friesen, *Imperial Cults*, 181.
81. See also ibid., 177.
82. Cf. Bauckham, *Theology of Revelation*, 98–104.

The Importance of the Individual in Revelation

As I argued in chapter 2, Revelation departs from the general attitude of the ancient world towards the group and the individual in significant ways. For example, traders and craftspeople are condemned as part of the Babylon system in 18:11–24, not because John has a hierarchical view of society, but rather because of their participation in a system of injustice, exploitation, and deception (18:4, 7, 13, 20, 23, 24; cf. 13:16–17).[83] The only distinction made between people has to do with their relationship to God and Christ: the faithful witnesses are described as a kind of future aristocracy (20:4–6), but otherwise everyone is equal before God's judgment (20:12). Moreover there is no hierarchy among those who worship God and Christ, and no mention of leadership structures in the churches. As Thompson argues, they constitute "an egalitarian *communitas*" since "worship is a radical equalizer."[84]

When Revelation describes and passes judgment on the society of its day, it often tends to reflect the group-oriented concept of the self that was common in the worldview of the time. This is found, for example, in its attitude to non-Christian Jews (2:9; 3:9), its characterization of unbelievers generally (6:15–17; 9:20–21; 11:9–10), of specific groups such as merchants (18:11–24), and particularly the subjects of the beast (13:3–4, 8, 14–17; 16:2, 6, 9–11, 21; 17:8; 18:3): they are seen collectively and pictured as acting as one, with their individual personalities not given attention.[85] In a similar way, faithful Christians are grouped together. Each of the seven churches, for example, has its group identity seen as covering all the individual believers in that place (2–3), and group identity is seen in the cry of the martyrs (6:9–11; 12:10–11), the 144,000 saints (7:4–8; 14:1–5), the great multitude who came out of the great ordeal (7:9–14), and the conquerors of the beast (15:2–4). The use of symbolism accentuates this trend in the text; for instance, the characterization of different groups as stereotypical female figures: a prostitute (chs. 17–18), a persecuted mother (ch. 12), and the bride of the Lamb (19:7–8; 21:2, 9), as I will explore in the next section of this chapter.

On the other hand, there is a contrary tendency threaded through the text: an emphasis on individual accountability and a heroizing of

---

83. Contra Royalty, *Streets of Heaven*, 111. Royalty contends that John uses the prevailing contempt for merchants for his own rhetorical purposes, portraying Rome as a commercial power in order to reduce its status in the eyes of his readers.

84. Thompson, *Apocalypse and Empire*, 69–71.

85. Pippin ("Heroine and the Whore," 69) points to a similar stereotyping in the way John views women.

non-conformists who are loyal to God and Jesus rather than their groups. For example, while the churches are addressed largely as groups, they are not completely uniform: there are Balaamites among the Pergamum church (2:14-15), the church in Thyatira is divided into a Jezebel party and "the rest . . . who do not hold this teaching" (2:24), and a few in Sardis are exempt from the charge of spiritual death leveled against the rest (3:1-4). Moreover each member of the churches is addressed as an individual with the promise to those who conquer (2:7, etc.; 21:7), and this is emphasized especially in the address to the Laodiceans, where Jesus invites any (Gk. *ean tis*, "if anyone")[86] who hear to open the door to him (3:20). Repeatedly the text honors those who stand up for Jesus *against* the pressure of the group: Antipas and the Pergamene believers (2:13), the martyrs in general (6:9; 12:11), the two witnesses (11:3-12), those who did not worship the beast or take its mark (13:8-10,15; 14:12-13; 15:2; 20:4-6), and those who come out of Babylon (18:4). And while there is collective judgment on peoples and cities, the final judgment is markedly individual (20:12-15). Even the collective judgments have an individual aspect; thus Christians are not guaranteed salvation if they are not faithful, for instance, if they tamper with John's manuscript (22:18-19). In such ways Revelation, like the New Testament generally, plants the seed of individualism that came to influence strongly the Western worldview.

Individualizing like this can easily be equated with the modernist concept of the self. However, John balances his individualism with the corporate identity mentioned above. His final vision (after the sifting of the final judgment in ch. 20) is a community, a city called a bride (21:2—22:5). A Christian worldview likewise needs to balance an emphasis on individuality and individual responsibility with the equally biblical emphasis on community and the body of Christ.

Gender in Revelation

Revelation seems not to question gender roles in its society; rather it usually follows accepted ideas of its day. For example, it uses female figures in stereotypical ways as metaphors or symbols of Israel (the mother), the empire (the whore), and the church (the bride).[87] In fact, John's use of feminine imagery is similar in striking ways to Roman imperial mythology.[88]

---

86. This is obscured in the NRSV, which (perhaps in the interests of a gender-neutral translation) renders this as "you."
87. Cf. Pippin, "Eros and the End," 200.
88. Friesen, *Imperial Cults*, 177-78.

In passing, Revelation alludes to female experiences such as pregnancy and childbirth (12:2, 4, 5), the need for protection (12:6, 13–16), sex (14:4; 17:2), prostitution (17:1, 4, 5), rape (17:16), widowhood (18:7), and marriage (19:7, 8; 21:2, 9)—but always as metaphors for spiritual truths. The only specific woman mentioned, Jezebel (2:20), is negatively characterized along conventional lines as a temptress ("beguiling" and leading people to commit adultery).

Men, in contrast, are implied by references to war and violence (6:4, 9; 9:15–18; 11:7; 13:7,10; 16:14; 19:11–21; 20:4, 9). Male virgins are described as "these who have not defiled themselves with women" (14:4), and males commit fornication, adultery, and rape (2:22; 17:2, 16; 18:3). The only contemporary man specifically named (other than John himself), Antipas, is a hero and martyr, though he suffers violence rather than committing it (2:13). Violence towards women is described, but not condoned, and is not truly gender based. For example, the real victims of the violence described with sexual imagery in 17:16 would be male and female Romans or Jews.

Postmodernist writers point to the dangers of sexism implicit in the conventions used by John. For instance, Stephen Moore concentrates on the picture of God as the Ultimate Ruler and "Hypermasculine" Hero of the text, reinterpreting the God of Revelation as a projection of the Roman emperor's image into heaven.[89] Moore compares this with the cult of bodybuilding[90] and Revelation is thus read as "a male fantasy."[91]

Many feminist critics have pointed out how John's imagery can tend to reinforce misogynist attitudes and stereotypes. For example, Elisabeth Schüssler Fiorenza points to the use of "dualistic feminine symbolizations" that "perpetuate prejudice and injustice against wo/men."[92] She also seeks to "rehabilitate" the opposing (largely female) prophetic voice in the Asian churches, using "a hermeneutic of historical imagination."[93] Finally, she calls for the "'poison' propagated in the name of G*d"[94] by Revelation and some of its readers to be identified and annulled. This amounts to a program of editing out objectionable features of the text, such as its "pornographic violence"[95] and "misogynist discourses."[96]

89. Moore, "Beatific Vision," 49.
90. Ibid., 32.
91. Ibid., 55.
92. Fiorenza, "Words of Prophecy," 13.
93. Ibid., 16.
94. Ibid., 18.
95. Ibid., 19.
96. Ibid., 18.

More strongly, Tina Pippin accuses John of maintaining a "sexist ideology which is of no use to women."[97] As she reads the text, females are "not allowed to speak their own identity," there are "no real flesh and blood women,"[98] women (both those in the narrative and women readers) are victimized,"[99] and in Revelation's vision of a godly utopia "women are left exactly where they were in Mediterranean society—excluded from the realm of power."[100] Similarly, Alison Jack urges, "for women the text always needs deconstruction rather than reconstruction."[101]

However, John is using imagery from his world, both from Mediterranean culture and from the Israelite heritage, rather than actually defending conventional values about human sexual identity or roles. For example, Pippin asserts, "The New Jerusalem is a woman, but women are not included in the utopian city."[102] But is this really so? I can find no exclusion of women in Revelation 21–22. Elsewhere Pippin explains that she is deducing the exclusion of women from 14:4,[103] but she persists in confusing the image with its meaning when she argues, "The 144,000 represent the whole number of the faithful, and they are men." John is certainly portraying a male group (an army[104]), but if this represents "the whole number of the faithful," then women are included, just as the woman of Revelation 21 includes men.

The most shocking image discussed by Pippin is the whore of Babylon, who is stripped, murdered, and eaten (17:16). It is indeed a violent and horrific scene, and no doubt it particularly filled women readers/hearers with horror and fear. John is employing this description for all the emotional power and shock value he can muster to make his point to readers of both genders. But, as Pippin herself relates, just as horrific an end comes to her male destroyers (19:17–21). Moreover John portrays both the whore and the bride as female, though what they stand for in fact included men. Pippin

---

97. Pippin, *Death and Desire*, 104.

98. Ibid., 103. It must be noted, however, there are few real flesh and blood people of either gender in Revelation!

99. Pippin, "Eros and the End," 194.

100. Pippin, *Death and Desire*, 103. Cf. ibid., 91.

101. Jack, *Texts Reading Texts*, 196. Cf. Jack, "Out of the Wilderness," 149–62.

102. Pippin, "Eros and the End," 195.

103. Pippin, "Heroine and the Whore," 68.

104. A number of commentators have noted that the reference to them not having "defiled themselves with women" (14:4) is probably based on the laws for warfare in the Old Testament; e.g. Bauckham, *Theology of Revelation*, 78; Beale, *Book of Revelation*, 738; Caird, *Revelation of St. John*, 179. For other alternatives, see Aune, *Revelation 6–16*, 810–12.

speaks of men being able to "gaze on the pure Bride of Christ"[105] (presumably sexually), even though she knows that they are part of this bride in John's vision! Thus Pippin seems to ignore or minimize the literary and theological task John is engaged in here.[106]

On the other hand, the fact that John uses gender-based symbolization so centrally is an indication that for him the concept of gender is a central and original part of reality. The roles played by the archetypal mother, prostitute, and wife are central to the plot of Revelation. Matching them are the good and bad male figures: Jesus as the military commander (19:11–16), royal prince (1:5,13–16), and husband (19:7; 21:2; 22:4) on one hand; the violent cannibals and rapists represented by the dragon (12:4, 13) and the beast (17:16) on the other. These are symbols, but they are not chosen solely because of their conventional relevance. John is implying that human sexuality reflects or symbolizes the fundamental spiritual realities that Revelation is concerned to reveal.[107] As I will discuss later, the idea of romance is integral to the narrative structure of Revelation, and this inevitably assumes a rather conventional image of male and female, which John translates into his rhetoric of discipleship.

This implies that, for John, an accurate explanation of reality cannot do without the language of gender. However, it does not necessarily imply that he is happy with the values and practices of gender-based culture as he knew it or that he views the saints in strongly gendered ways. In fact, Friesen contends that "John is remarkably egalitarian in regard to gender among the saints."[108] The implications for building a Christian attitude to gender and sexuality need more exploration than I have space for here, but postmodernist attempts to affirm less traditional views or deconstruct conventional concepts of gender and sexuality would struggle to find support in Revelation. On the other hand, John's use of gender in his narrative to describe bigger realities implies that he has a more personal cosmology than that of modernity, as I will pick up shortly.

Emphasis on Externals

In chapter 3 I argued that the thinking of Revelation is strongly dualistic in two senses: its emphasis on external appearances versus spiritual realities, and its stress on the moral and soteriological good versus evil in the

105. Pippin, "Eros and the End," 202.
106. See also the discussion in Friesen, *Imperial Cults*, 185–87.
107. Cf. Pattemore, *People of God*, 186–88.
108. Friesen, *Imperial Cults*, 189.

spiritual realm. However, when it comes to its approach to human nature, Revelation has little emphasis on a body-soul dualism, nor does it anticipate the stress on the inner workings of the mind or soul, which the modern worldview inherited particularly from Augustine.[109]

There are occasional places in the text that speak of the inner workings of persons (for example, 2:23, where Jesus is said to be "the one who searches minds and hearts") or of "souls" as opposed to bodies (for example, the souls of the martyrs in 6:9) or of the importance of attitudes (such as the accusation against the church in Ephesus that they had "abandoned the love you had at first"; 2:4).

But the overwhelming emphasis in the assessments of the seven churches is on outward behavior: "works" (2:2, 5, 6, 19, 22, 26; 3:1, 2, 8, 15), teachings (2:14, 15, 20, 24), things people say (2:9; 3:9, 17), or other outward actions such as enduring persecution (2:10, 13; 3:10). Even inner attitudes are assessed largely by "works" rather than psychological states (2:5, 23). Similarly, the Last Judgment also focuses on "works" (20:12, 13; 22:12), the sins listed in the text are largely defined externally (9:20, 21; 16:6, 9; 18:4–8; 19:2; 21:8, 22; 22:11, 15), and the seven blessings of the text are given to people largely on the basis of, or in the form of, actions (1:3; 14:13; 16:15; 19:9; 20:6; 22:7, 14).

People's identity and standing before God is frequently described in external imagery even when it may well be related to inward character: for example, in terms of their clothing being clean, dirty, or absent (3:4, 17, 18; 6:11; 7:9, 13, 14; 16:15; 19:8, 14; 22:14), or in terms of names (or other signs) being written on them (3:12; 7:3; 9:4; 13:16–18; 14:1, 9, 11; 15:2; 16:2; 17:5; 19:12, 16, 20; 20:4; 22:4), or in terms of their names being in a book (3:5; 13:8; 20:15; 21:27).

Finally, when Revelation describes people's emotional states—9:6 (longing for death); 11:11, 13; 18:10 (fear); 12:17 (anger); 13:3, 4; 17:6–8 (amazement); 17:16 (hatred); 18:7 (grief)—the emphasis is on the actions that express the emotion. For example, the dragon in anger makes war on the woman (12:17) and the kings stand at a distance in fear of the "torment" of Babylon (18:10). More frequently, we infer emotions from people's actions: for example, wailing (1:7; 18:9), weeping (5:4), mourning (18:8, 15, 19; 21:4), singing or celebration (5:9, 12; 11:10, 17; 19:1, 6), crying out (6:9, 10; 12:2; 16:9, 11, 21), hiding or calling out for protection (6:15–17), or falling down in worship (19:10; 22:8). The focus is largely on actions more than inner states. In this respect, Revelation reflects ancient attitudes rather than anticipating modern ones.

109. Cf. Taylor, *Sources of the Self*, 127–42.

A Christian worldview that draws on Revelation may therefore call into question the introversion that became a strong feature of both Catholic and Protestant spirituality from the sixteenth century onwards. The Bible does call on people to search their hearts; for instance, Jesus speaks of the importance of the inner heart (e.g., Matt 5:28; 12:34; 15:8, 18–20; Rev 2:23). But it is questionable whether or not the New Testament places such a stress on the inner person as emerged in the modern West. Perhaps we may conclude with John that actions and words, which proceed from the heart, are just as significant. Similarly, many theologians are now questioning the body-soul dualism of much traditional Christian anthropology.[110]

Human Sinfulness

The outlook of modernity increasingly tended to view humans as basically good. Evil behavior tended to be ascribed to the influence of forces outside the individual, such as oppressive structures, tradition, superstition, or lack of education. Such ideas persist today.

But John seems to have a different view. While Revelation never states that all people are sinners, as does Paul (Rom 3:23, for instance), it regularly portrays people sinning (Rev 2:14, 20–22; 3:17; 9:20, 21; 11:10,18; 13:5, 14; 17:2, 4; 18:3, 5, 9, 23; 19:2; 21:27; 22:11, 15) and calls for repentance (2:5, 16, 21, 22; 3:3, 19; 9:20, 21; 16:9, 11). On the whole, Revelation is pessimistic about the possibilities of ordinary human beings doing what is good. For example, it does not expect those who suffer God's judgments to repent as a result (9:20;[111] 16:9, 11; the only exception is in 11:13); instead they sometimes curse God (16:9, 11, 21). Except for those whose names are written in the Book of Life, no one resists the attractions of the beast (13:8; 17:8) and most of them support the persecution of Christians (11:9, 10; 16:6). The severity of the calamities that God sends on the world implies that, to John's mind, people are guilty and deserve punishment (16:5, 6). At the end, he seems resigned to the fact that people will not change (22:11).

Even among those who claim to be God-fearers, we read of false Jews who follow Satan (2:9; 3:9), false prophets, teachers and apostles (2:2,15,20), and Christians who are susceptible to falsehood and spiritual decline (2:4, 14, 15, 20–23; 3:1, 2, 4, 15–18). All this suggests a pessimistic view of human nature.

---

110. Space forbids any discussion of these debates. For a summary of key issues and positions see Erickson, *Christian Theology*, 538–57; for an argument against such dualism see Green, *Body, Soul, and Human Life*.

111. Cf. Aune, *Revelation 6–16*, 541.

Of course, Revelation also speaks of those who do successfully resist the devil and his forces (2:3, 10, 13; 3:4, 8, 10; 6:9; 11:18; 12:10, 11; 13:8, 10; 14:1–5, 12, 13; 17:14; 18:4; 20:4; 21:7). Moreover the ultimate outcome of the story is optimistic: all nations will finally worship God (15:4), there will be an innumerable host in heaven (7:9), and the nations will be healed (22:2). But these positive hopes are grounded on God's redeeming work rather than on human perfectibility (5:9; 7:14; 22:2, 14). The overwhelming emphasis of most episodes is on humans behaving badly and suffering God's punishments.

Summary

What conclusions follow from this examination of the text?

First, it is clear that human identity for John is built on the relationship of humanity to God. People find their true identity as humans in faithfully listening and witnessing to God's word, in worship, and in radical and militant service to him. On the other hand, people who refuse to embrace this vision of humanity distort the gifts of creativity and freedom imparted by God and become violent, deceived, and oppressive, to the extent of persecuting the servants of God. To use the language of the text, they become like wild beasts. John's view contrasts with the anthropology of the modern and postmodern era. As Friesen puts it,

> To an age that strives for individual freedom, John would respond that autonomy and self-gratification are not suitable human goals. Humanity, according to John's text, finds satisfaction in obedience and worship.[112]

Second, in Revelation this submission to God's order extends to the area of sexuality and gender. Since the concept of gender is part of God's fundamental creation, it cannot be sidelined or relativized, though this does not mean that John approves of gross male domination or other sexual abuses. Those who are violent towards women (even symbolically) are always evil, for instance. It seems therefore that a Christian worldview should seek to reclaim rather than annul the language of sexuality, in keeping with God's original and final intentions. While this is not a major theme of Revelation, this text may play a part in this work of reclamation, with its vision of final restoration. However, the critiques and insights of feminists will need to be engaged with in this process.

---

112. Friesen, *Imperial Cults*, 215.

Third, Revelation, like the New Testament generally, plants the seed of individualism which came to influence strongly the Western worldview, especially since the Renaissance and Reformation. The sight of, say, Luther standing alone against the might of the Holy Roman Empire and the papacy recalls the courage of Antipas or John himself standing against the tide of Roman oppression.[113] However, Revelation also balances this with an emphasis on corporate solidarity, especially in its address to the seven churches and its vision of the final "New Jerusalem."

Finally, Revelation portrays human beings very much as speakers and actors. John clearly believes that language and actions have power; he is less interested in exploring motives, emotions, and the inner world of the psyche. Here he is dissimilar to some aspects of the thought of modernity, as opposed to ancient perspectives on human nature. Perhaps this also makes his worldview less susceptible to the problems created by Cartesian dualism.[114] It certainly affects his thinking about history.

HUMAN SIGNIFICANCE IN HISTORY

I was working on this passage in the midst of news of a huge earthquake and tsunami in Japan in which thousands died, not long after a tragic earthquake in Christchurch, New Zealand, and devastating floods and a cyclone in Australia. These events have underlined how powerful nature can be and how dependent and vulnerable we all are, even in the modern world. The humanistic confidence born out of the Enlightenment often leads to a hubris that is quite unrealistic and opposed to humble dependence on almighty God.[115]

But the Bible also does not call us to a fatalistic passivity in the face of disaster. Disasters can sometimes be prevented, or at least guarded against, by prudent measures (such as earthquake-resistant buildings) and they often challenge humans to rise up and help each other, thus displaying our best instincts rather than selfish pragmatism. On the other hand, human foolishness, greed, and pride can often cause or exacerbate "natural" disasters; for example, excessive land clearing can lead to massive loss of life through floods and landslides. Worse still are the disasters deliberately inflicted by humans on other humans. While I write, Syrian dictator Assad is attacking his own fellow citizens with bombs and rockets in order to try to

113. Readers can think of many other suitable recent examples: Bonhoeffer, Luther King, Mandela, etc.

114. Cf. Green *Body, Soul, and Human Life*, 48–50.

115. To parody the preface to Australia's federal constitution.

stay in power. The point of these musings is that human actions have special power and significance; we are not just robots or dumb animals under the hands of God. And this is a significant prelude to studying the attitude of Revelation toward the role and place of humanity in God's world.

The Significance of Human Free Will

Revelation does not portray God as acting directly and intervening openly in all situations. More often, in fact, he works through and around the choices and actions of angels, devils, and human beings.[116] While the natural order is totally at his disposal and under his control, he acts in an orderly way and does not constantly interrupt the order he has established.[117] Moreover, while God's sovereignty over human beings is real and emphasized in John's vision, it is more complex than some may imagine. Human beings are not portrayed as puppets of God and are held accountable for their actions.

This is made clear in several aspects of the plot of Revelation. For instance, God's two witnesses have authority, within certain boundaries, "to shut the sky," turn the waters into blood, and "to strike the earth with every kind of plague, *as often as they desire*" (11:6; emphasis added). Moreover people are also seen as able to resist God's commands. The majority of people are unwilling to respond to huge judgments (9:20, 21; 16:9-11, 20). They worship false gods and "beasts" (9:20; 13:3-4, 8, 12; 17:8), celebrate the death of God's prophetic witnesses (11:10), destroy the earth (11:18), and resist calls to return to God in the gospel (14:6-11).

Political life is seen as both independent of God and (paradoxically) under his control. The earth's kings co-operate with the plans of the devil by yielding to the leadership of demons (16:14), submit to the beast in an unholy alliance against the Lamb (17:12-14,17), and destroy the whore of Babylon (17:16) after having "committed fornication with her" (17:2; 18:3, 9). Yet this all serves God's purpose (17:17).[118]

Ungodly cultures arise and come under God's judgment in Revelation. The whore of Babylon is a portrayal of a city with such an ungodly culture, influencing the course of the nations (17:2) as "the mother of whores and of earth's abominations" (17:5). She is utterly opposed to God's representatives,

---

116. Boyd (*God at War*, 200) argues that the Bible as a whole represents spiritual beings as free, not under God's detailed control. This view probably understates the sovereignty of God as presented in Revelation, but recovers the balancing concept of free will.

117. A fact that makes science possible and encouraged the early modern scientists.

118. Cf. Aune, *Revelation 17-22*, 958.

"drunk with the blood of the saints and . . . the witnesses to Jesus" (17:6; see also 18:24; 19:2). Revelation blames her for this and predicts her forthcoming doom as an act of God's judgment executed through the evil attacks of the "ten horns" (17:16; 18:8; 19:2).

In all these instances, people, nations, cities, and spiritual beings act "independently" of, and even antagonistically towards, God—while being subject to his overall control. How these two lines of thought cohere is, of course, a complex and longstanding theological and philosophical problem. But in a Christian worldview, such a tension between human free will and God's sovereignty cannot be eliminated or ignored.

The Demands of Justice

Not only is John committed to the idea of human free will, but God's actions are seen as driven by his justice. This is most vividly seen in the last judgment (20:12–15), where "the dead were judged according to their works, as recorded in the books" (20:12). But there are other, less ultimate instances too.

For instance, in the messages to the seven churches (chs. 2–3), we see that none of the churches are treated exactly the same: their future depends on their response to the voice of the Spirit (2:11), often they are called to repent (2:5,16,22; 3:3,19), and the promises held out to them are conditional (3:20). Depending on their choices, some of these churches may be removed (2:5), imprisoned (2:10), seduced into false beliefs and practices (2:14–15, 20, 24), punished with distress, death, and sickness (2:22–23), or even be "spat out"[119] by Jesus (3:16) as a result of their complacent blindness (3:15–17).

In particular, the false prophet Jezebel (2:20–24) is not being opposed just because she is a woman. Rather John makes her behavior and teaching the issue.[120] Moreover he points out that she has had time to repent of her ways (because God is patient) and may still be spared if she repents (2:21–22). Also, those not associated with her are clearly separated out to a better outcome (2:24–25), followed by a general warning: "I will give to each of you *as your works deserve*" (2:23; emphasis added).

The accusation John makes against the great bulk of people is that they did not repent as a result of God's judgments (9:20–21; 16:9, 11). In contrast, in the city where the two witnesses prophesied, "the rest were terrified

---

119. Gr., εμεσαι, spit out or vomit, from which comes the English "emetic."

120. On the issue of eating food sacrificed to idols, see Aune, *Revelation 1–5*, 192–94.

and gave glory to the God of heaven" (11:13). The strong implication here is that the judgments are measured and may be lessened if people repent.

Revelation 14, with its mixture of warnings (14:6–11) and promises (14:12–13), conveys a similar emphasis on human choice. Moreover the use of the usual Christian words for evangelism[121] in 14:6 suggest that God wants people to respond in repentance and faith and thus receive his salvation. The image of the double harvest in 14:14–20 also implies that God is acting in response to consistent behavior of the people of the earth. The ripeness of the harvest (14:15,18) suggests that their behavior has reached a point where action (judgment) is demanded and can no longer be postponed (in order to see if people will repent, for example).

The discussion that takes place prior to and during the bowl plagues also centers on the justice of God (15:3, 4; 16:5–7). And later John follows Old Testament models in building up a "covenant lawsuit" against Babylon. God's actions against her are not arbitrary, according to Revelation, but are in response to her chosen behavior (18:5–6). This section concludes with an affirmation of the justice of God's actions against her (19:2). John's world is thus a world of ultimate justice, even if the evil one is allowed to oppress the saints for a time. As Heschel writes in another context, "Others have considered history from the point of view of power . . . the prophets look at history from the point of view of justice."[122]

John's concept of justice helps explain the incredible violence of the imagery and narrative descriptions in Revelation, which have bothered many readers of all ages. Tina Pippin, for instance, writes,

> The violence of the book is startling; violence is done to nature and people and supernatural beings. There are swords and slaughter and hunger and martyrs. . . . The war is bloody; there are casualties on both sides. Cannibalism is part of the warfare tactics. . . . There is torture in the lake of fire and sulfur.[123]

Similarly, Brian Yhearm criticizes general twentieth-century scholarship on Revelation for ignoring or "explaining away" its violence and vengefulness:[124] "John presents us with an all-powerful vindictive, cruel, and tyrannical God"[125] and "a powerful, militaristic and vengeful Lamb who

---

121. εὐαγγέλιον and εὐαγγελίζω. Compare Mark 16:15; Rom.1:9.
122. Heschel, *Prophets*, 1:171, see also 174–75.
123. Pippin, *Death and Desire*, 99.
124. Yhearm, *Sitz im Leben*, 1–10.
125. Ibid., 131.

will obliterate the enemies of, and on behalf of, the *pantokrator* God"[126]—a Christology out of step with trends in John's day, let alone now.

On the other hand, Pablo Richard sees this language as expressing "the limit-situation of extreme oppression and anguish that the community is undergoing."[127] He contends that the basic position of the text is for nonviolence[128] as it seeks to inspire us toward building an alternative society.[129] However, W. G. Carey argues that John is caught up in the very authoritarian ethos he is criticizing in Rome[130] and that the modern day "interpretive clash" over Revelation "is rooted in Revelation's own rhetorical ethos: a struggle between resistance and repression."[131]

Our postmodern mind is uncomfortable with violence and suffering (even though we indulge it vicariously in movies, sports, and video games), and the idea of eternal judgment is almost literally unthinkable. This is due to a shift in worldview: according to Charles Taylor, Westerners after the Enlightenment no longer see humans as part of a cosmic order that needs restoring though terrible punishments.[132] John seems to embrace a theology of vengeance, for instance in the prayers of Revelation: prayers for vengeance seem to be included approvingly (6:10), prayers seem to result in violent judgments (8:4–5), and God's people are called to rejoice at destruction (11:16–18; 18:20; 19:3). Olutola Peters is one of many readers who point out the discrepancy between such praying, which in Revelation is "honored with positive answers," and the examples of Jesus (Luke 23:24) and Stephen (Acts 7:60), who prayed for their persecutors to be forgiven.[133]

John's worldview, however, is governed by the idea of justice, and in his mind this paradigm justifies the violence exercised by, or on behalf of, God and Christ.[134] Whether or not the contemporary reader finds this convincing, it has at least one important implication: it supports the traditional Western view of personal accountability. Human beings are not just victims or animals, as far as John is concerned; they are responsible for their actions and will be dealt with accordingly.

126. Ibid., 169.
127. Richard, *People's Commentary*, 4.
128. Ibid., 4. Cf. Friesen, *Imperial Cults*, 189–90.
129. Richard, *People's Commentary*, 5. Cf. Miguez, "Apocalyptic and the Economy," 250–62.
130. Carey, *Attention-Seeking Behavior*, 244. This insight is attributed to Richard Terdiman. Cf. also ibid., 251–52.
131. Ibid., 245.
132. Taylor, *Sources of the Self*, 12–13.
133. Peters, "Politics of Violence," 2–4.
134. Ibid., 7–16.

The Significance of the Actions of God's People

Revelation was written primarily to influence the actions of Christians, especially the members of the seven churches to whom it was addressed (1:1–4), since it could not be taken for granted by John that all believers would see things as he saw them or respond to the situation of that day as he wanted them to. The very fact that John writes this text, and that he uses rhetorical devices to influence Christians, shows that believers were free to choose their course.[135]

John sees the choices they made as important for the future of Christianity and, indeed, for the future of the world, since he believes that believers have a profound influence on the course of history. As Pattemore puts it, "the particular story which is at the center of the universal struggle is one in which the audience of Asian Christians must play a part."[136] As followers of Jesus, they are a kingdom of priests (1:6; 5:10): they represent God's rule and represent the world before God. To the overcomers in Thyatira therefore Jesus promises

> I will give authority over the nations;
> to rule them with an iron rod,
> as when clay pots are shattered—
> even as I also received authority from my Father.
> (2:26–28; cf. 3:21)

These promises suggest that the choices made by these believers will affect the course of political and religious history in their own locality and beyond.

The story of the two prophetic witnesses in chapter 11 illustrates graphically John's view of the importance of Christians to God's purposes in history. While the exact identity of these two witnesses is not clear,[137] they are certainly humans, not angels, since they are able to be killed (11:7–9), and they are Christians, since the crucified one is "their Lord" (11:8). Their authority and power from God resembles that exercised by Old Testament prophets, particularly Moses (Rev 11:6; cf. Exod 7:17–24) and Elijah (Rev 11:5–6; cf. 1 Kgs 17:1; 2 Kgs 1:9–12).[138] Their death at the hands of the

---

135. Cf. McIlraith, *Reciprocal Love*, 30–31; DeSilva, *Seeing Things John's Way*, 49–50, 63, 70, 82–85, 90.

136. Pattemore, *People of God*, 97.

137. Theories as to their identity include Moses and Elijah (sometimes with Enoch replacing Moses), Jesus and John the Baptist, the apostles Peter and Paul, and the church as a whole (cf. Aune, *Revelation 6–16*, 598–603).

138. Hence some commentators see them as symbolizing the witness to Christ of

beast is a major event that causes great celebrations around the world (Rev 11:7–10). Their public resurrection and ascension (11:11–12), attended by an earthquake and considerable loss of life (11:13), has major effects on the people of the day (11:13). In other words, these two are portrayed as playing a central role in the history of the city in which they operate and of the whole earth.

The significance of believers' actions in John's thought is also seen in the power of their witness to overcome the devil. One of the most powerful scenes in Revelation is the struggle in chapter 12 between the dragon and God's people. The heavenly commentary on the dragon's defeat emphasizes that it was not accomplished by angels alone, or even by God and the Messiah (12:10). Rather,

> *they* have conquered him by the blood of the Lamb and by the word of *their* testimony, for *they* did not cling to life even in the face of death. (12:11; emphasis added)

The witness of the faithful followers of Jesus, according to Revelation, changes the course of history, defeats the devil, and brings them the reward of world dominion (2:26; 20:4–5), though in the process many lose their lives, just like their leader Jesus. In fact, the whole story of Revelation may be written as "The Triumph of the Martyrs," who change the course of history.[139]

The prayers of the saints are also seen as significant. They are portrayed as ascending to God like incense (5:8; 8:3–4), followed by "peals of thunder, rumblings, flashes of lightning, and an earthquake" on earth (8:5). While the exact relationship between the saints' prayers and the events that follow is not spelled out, at the very least these passages show that the saints' prayers are heard by God and influence the course of events on earth.

The way Revelation speaks of the deaths of God's people also emphasizes the value God places on their lives. He carefully notes when they are persecuted or killed (2:10, 13) and keeps a count of their deaths (6:11). He holds their persecutors accountable for each death and promises to avenge them (6:10–11; 16:6; 17:6; 18:20, 24). As Pattemore writes, "by that very death, they are . . . linked in the most intimate way to the courts of heaven,

---

the Law and the Prophets (e.g., Corsini, *Apocalypse*, 195).

139. Jesus (Rev 1:5–6; 5:7, 9–10; 6:1, etc.; 6:16; 11:15; 14:1–8, 14–20; 17:14; 19:11–21); his followers (1:18; 2:26–28; 11:12–13; 12:7–12; 17:14; 18:20; 20:4–6). In this way Revelation has parallels with Acts, which is the story in historical form of the witnesses to Jesus (Acts 1:8).

their very existence demanding God's attention."[140] These deaths are not meaningless; they even affect the course of history.

The final destiny of the saints also implies that their lives on earth are significant and influential on the course of history. For example, those who have been beheaded for their Christian stand are seen as coming to life and reigning with Christ a thousand years (20:4, 6). This ascribes a significance to the lives of ordinary Christians of all ethnic backgrounds that would have astonished the upper classes of first-century Rome, Ephesus, and Jerusalem.

A Different View of the Future

John's view of history, and of the role of individuals and groups within history, amounts to a rejection of rival concepts of his day. As I concluded in chapter 2, the Greek cyclical view of history saw history as governed by the movements of the stars, producing repetition of historical events and catastrophes, derived probably from Babylonian astrological thinking.[141] John's thinking differs from both the determinism and the circularity inherent in this concept. His view is Hebrew and linear.

But as I also argued in chapter 2, Revelation also departs significantly from the common Jewish apocalyptic outlook in that John calls his readers to a much more activist role in creating the future and thus he sees the future as more open.[142] The apocalyptic view of history and the future, as reflected in their use of *ex eventu* prophecy,[143] was much more deterministic;[144] the future seems very much set. There is little challenge to the readers of the Jewish apocalypses to involve themselves in creating a new future with God.[145]

---

140. Pattemore, *People of God*, 82, see also 91.

141. Hengel, *Judaism and Hellenism*, 1:191–92.

142. See the discussion in Gilbertson, *God and History*, 168–71, 193–95.

143. Cf. Russell, *Jewish Apocalyptic*, 96–100. Russell argues that the apocalyptists were motivated to clarify and systematize unfulfilled predictions made by the classical prophets, particularly those of the glorious future of Israel, especially in the hazardous times of the Maccabean revolt and later Roman domination.

144. Collins, "Pseudonymity," 335.

145 As discussed in chapter 2, this distinction has been challenged in two directions. Portier-Young (*Apocalypse Against Empire*, 42–44, 246–50) challenges the way apocalypses are characterized as deterministic; for her, the determinism in the apocalypses serves to motivate the faithful to resistance. To the extent that her thesis is upheld—and I think the outcome is driven partly by the choice of apocalypses to analyze—the difference between Revelation and these Jewish apocalypses will be lessened. John Collins urges that Revelation is just as deterministic as the other apocalypses, as shown by 1:1 ("what must soon take place"; Collins, "Pseudonymity, Historical Reviews and Genre," 339), and certainly there *is* a stress in Revelation on the predetermined

In classical Hebrew prophecy, however, long-range predictive prophecy is uncommon: most of the material in, say, Isaiah or Jeremiah, is exhortation, comment on current events, or short-range prediction. This at least gives the impression of a reasonably fluid future, especially in those places where it is clear that the outcomes are dependent on the response of the hearers.[146]

Revelation resembles such classical prophecy whenever it addresses the churches and calls Christians either to repentance or to faithful endurance or to disassociation from the enemy state (2:5; 13:10; 18:4.) As Pattemore argues,

> there is no determinism in John's interaction with the Asian churches. Although he prophesies the future suffering and vindication of the church, he does not describe a definitive future for the particular groups of believers to whom he writes. The martyr church is portrayed as something that exists, with a history and a future, and with which they may or may not choose to identify.[147]

Mathias Rissi goes even farther and sees the same openness in John's thinking about all humanity: "All the visions of judgment, which stand under the divine 'must,' have finally a very evident 'if not' before them."[148] In other words, most of John's predictions are conditional, as I suggested in chapter 4.

Thus all these aspects of the worldview of Revelation are consistent with the way it directly portrays human beings. Human personhood and free will are real and significant. God acts with justice according to human choices and humans create the future with God. In other words, God takes human beings and their decisions seriously and offers them a role in history.

---

direction of history. But elsewhere Collins (*Apocalyptic Imagination*, 213–14) concedes that according to Revelation, because of the victory of Christ over the dragon (Rev 12), Christians too "can defeat the dragon if they are 'washed in the blood of the lamb' and are prepared to lay down their lives . . ."

146. Cf. "Pseudonymity," 336–37. However, Wright (*People of God*, 298) argues that to distinguish between the apocalypses and classic prophecy in this way "is to capitulate to a Josephus-like Hellenization of categories."

147. Pattemore, *People of God*, 115 (italics added).

148. Rissi, *Time and History*, 104, see also 113–15.

A PERSON-CENTERED COSMOLOGY

The Cosmology of Revelation

One of the key elements in the shift from a premodern worldview to that of modernity was the reorientation of cosmology caused by the work of such scientists as Copernicus and Galileo. This made a medieval Christian worldview, in which earth and man are at the center, impossible to sustain. Nonetheless, as Barth argued, for Enlightenment thinkers "man is all the greater for this, man is in the center of all things . . . for he was able to discover this revolutionary truth by his own resources . . ."[149] But recent science makes this concept of a vast universe, in which the earth and solar system are peripheral, even more stark, and Darwinian evolution even removes the presumption that we are unique beings with a central role in the cosmos. The ancient psalmist saw this quandary (Psalm 8) and a contemporary Christian worldview must address it too.

In chapter 3 I argued for a postmodern Christian paradigm that adjusts the mechanistic worldview that arose from modernity and allows for the reality of spiritual beings, including angels and demons, in our universe. But the place of personhood in a Christian cosmology also needs addressing. Bruce Malina claims, "we must recover some adequate ancient model of an earth-centered total system of the universe to be considerate readers of Revelation."[150] Certainly the ancient Mediterranean world held to a geocentric concept of the universe.[151] Ancient Greek thinkers agreed that the κόσμος (world or universe) was characterized by order, unity, beauty, and eternity and was thus an object of praise, even being seen as divine.[152] Moreover they believed that *"human beings are related to the κοσμος as microcosm to macrocosm."*[153]

As discussed in chapter 2, Revelation appears to accept the traditional idea of the universe as "a closed system, closed in by a celestial vault or firmament," which was "outfitted with an opening of sorts that allowed access to the other side."[154] In this "triple-decker" universe,[155] the heavens (including the stars) were above, the earth in the middle, and the underworld

---

149. Barth, *Protestant Theology*, 37. Cf. Küng, *On Being a Christian*, 27.

150. Malina *Genre and Message*, 3.

151. Walbank, *Hellenistic World* , 185–86. Cf. Green, *Alexander to Actium*, 454.

152. Adams, *Constructing the World*, 64–69.

153. Ibid., 66 (italics original).

154. Malina, *Genre and Message*, 19.

155. As opposed to the Hellenistic idea of seven heavens surrounding a spherical earth (cf. Aune, *Revelation 1–5*, 318).

below (5:3; sometimes the sea is seen as a separate realm, as in 5:13 and 14:7).[156] Thus Jesus' second coming will be from *above*,[157] from the realm of the clouds (1:7; cf. 14:14); the New Jerusalem also "comes *down* from my God out of heaven" (3:12; cf. 21:2, 10); John goes *up* to heaven in the spirit (4:1); the "stars of the sky *fell* to the earth" during the sixth seal (6:13; also 8:10; 9:1–2); smoke rises from "the bottomless pit" onto the earth's surface (9:2); angels come "*down* from heaven" (10:1; 20:1–3); a beast "comes *up* from the bottomless pit" to kill the two prophets (11:7; also 17:8), who later are raised to life and go *up* to heaven in a cloud (11:12); the land beast is "making fire come *down* from heaven to earth" (13:13); huge hailstones are thrown *down* from heaven (16:21); and fire comes *down* from heaven to consume the devil's army (20:9; see also 7:2; 10:5; 12:4, 9, 10, 12, 13; 18:5).

This assumes the idea of a geocentric universe. However, Revelation does not indulge in cosmological speculation, unlike the Jewish apocalypses.[158] It makes no specific statements about the relationship of the earth to the heavenly bodies, frequently speaks of them in metaphorical terms, and uses spatial language more to indicate moral and spiritual relationships. Thus heaven is "up" because God and his angels are more powerful than, or superior to, earth-dwellers, and the "bottomless pit" is "down" because it consistently represents forces of chaos and evil. As Thompson puts it, "Divine forces come down from heaven, and evil forces come up from the abyss."[159] John's cosmology is more complex than we might think; hence Minear argues that "we cannot accuse him of holding a naïve three-storied idea of the physical world."[160] Rather his cosmology is at the service of his eschatology and his view of history.[161] Revelation does not contest the geocentric cosmology of its contemporaries but it also shows little interest in defending it.[162] It also views the universe as God's creation rather than divine (4:11; 10:6; 14:7).

Tina Pippin has sought to deconstruct John's cosmology by studying the notion of the abyss or "bottomless pit" in Revelation. The abyss is "measureless" and thus "defers the closure of the text." Its presence is a constant

---

156. Cf. Friesen, *Imperial Cults*, 152–57.

157. Terms denoting spatial movement in this paragraph are italicized for emphasis.

158. Cf. 2 *En.* 3–22, 40; 3 *Bar.* 2–11; 1 *En.* 34–36, 72–82.

159. Thompson, *Apocalypse and Empire*, 76.

160. Minear, "Cosmology of the Apocalypse," 34.

161. See the excellent discussion of the spatial dimension in Gilbertson, *God and History*, 81–108.

162. Consider the distinction made by Swinburne (*Metaphor to Analogy*, 166–67) between what is said in the Bible and "the presuppositions in terms of which it is cast."

threat to the sense of order in the text;[163] it represents the threat of otherness and chaos, which Pippin sees as "the ultimate dangerous female,"[164] "both the Unconscious and unconscious desires,"[165] and "the excess of desire, surplus erotic power."[166] This is one way of interpreting the gendered nature of reality as described in Revelation. John does not see this threat of chaos in female terms, however. For him chaos is the work of the beasts and the dragon, who emerge from the abyss, and they are portrayed in masculine terms. Chaos is also seen as ultimately defeated.[167]

Towards a Person-Centered Cosmology

The implication of the discussion earlier in this chapter is clearly that the relationship between God and human beings, as portrayed by Revelation, is central to the shaping of history and the future of the whole universe. This is most clearly seen in the closing chapters of the text, where God creates a new home for his people. This involves not only a renewed earth, but also heaven (21:1); indeed the present roles of the sun and moon are abolished (21:23; 22:5). While it is difficult to take John's language literally (his description is too impressionistic and contradictory for that, and he uses cosmological language metaphorically elsewhere, as in 12:1,4), he seems at least to be claiming that the end of human history has cosmic, or at least global, consequences. The future of the universe is bound up with the future of humanity.

Revelation thus embraces a cosmology and view of cosmic history that places personhood right at the center. History for John is created by persons: a personal God in personal interaction with both spiritual beings and humanity. The mechanistic picture of the universe as subject to mathematical laws, which underlay the scientific revolution, is foreign to his thinking. This view is also being challenged, or at least modified, in postmodernity.

Personhood is the missing ingredient in the late modern worldview, with its mechanical and evolutionary universe, but it will not be denied; it is simply too fundamental to our intuition and experience of reality.[168] As Charles Taylor argues, such values as "respect for life and integrity" are "uncommonly deep, powerful, and universal" and "seem to involve claims,

---

163. Pippin, "Peering into the Abyss," 253.
164. Ibid., 260.
165. Ibid., 261.
166. Ibid., 264.
167. See chapter 6.
168. Cf. Taylor, *Sources of the Self*, 4–14.

implicit or explicit, about the nature and status of human beings" which need to be explained.[169] Only a worldview that makes space for spirituality and a personal God can give a credible explanation for our intuitive sense as human beings that we possess significance, meaning, and accountability.

So perhaps there is room for Christians to articulate a new worldview that, while not retreating to medievalism, can restore personhood to the center of reality. Taylor argues that modernity lost the sense of "human beings as playing a role in a larger cosmic order or divine history,"[170] but we can only make sense of ourselves through a narrative understanding of life.[171] In the next chapter, then, I shall explore the narrative of Revelation in relation to the Christian worldview I am articulating. But first let us look at some other proposals for a person-centered cosmology. Two thinkers of the twentieth century argued in different ways for a person-centered cosmology similar in some ways to that found in Revelation, albeit in today's different context.

John Macmurray

John Macmurray argues that "the form of the personal" is "the emergent problem of contemporary philosophy."[172] He faults modern philosophy for being "characteristically *egocentric*" in the sense of taking "the [individual] Self as its starting point," as in the Enlightenment subject, the "thinker in search of knowledge."[173] This tends to sideline the role of other persons, becoming "a philosophy which is debarred from thinking the 'You and I,'"[174] failing to provide an adequate conceptual framework for interpersonal knowledge.[175] Macmurray proposes instead that "we should substitute the 'I do' for the 'I think' as our starting point and center of reference,"[176] thus concentrating on humans as agents rather than subjects. Such a shift supports the idea of free will as against determinism,[177] puts agency into central focus

---

169. Ibid., 4–6.
170. Ibid., 13.
171. Ibid., 48–50.
172. Macmurray, *Self as Agent*, 21.
173. Ibid., 31.
174. Ibid., 72.
175. Ibid., 73.
176. Ibid., 84.
177. Ibid., 134–35.

in discussions of the concept of causation,[178] and reintroduces the idea of personal action into our view of the cosmos.[179]

Macmurray thus argues for the necessity of a personal God, because when we look at "the unity of experience as it appears from the standpoint of the Agent," the only way this can be conceived is "by thinking the world as one action."[180] This is illustrated by Macmurray's discussion of history: when we focus on human history, with its emphasis on personal agency and particular events, we cannot help conceiving of "a multitude of individual acts as constituting a single action, in virtue of a community of intention."[181] For Macmurray, conceiving the world as a single process is impossible, but it is quite possible to conceive it as a single action.[182] Thus if reality is ultimately personal, then the origin of reality in a personal God becomes quite logical. Religion characteristically "behaves towards its object in ways that are suitable to personal intercourse; and the conception of a deity is the conception of a personal ground of all that we experience."[183]

Hugo Meynell

In a different way, Hugo Meynell attempts to revive a form of the traditional cosmological argument for the existence of God. After discussing some of epistemological problems of modern philosophy, he concludes that if knowledge of the world is possible, then "the world's capacity to be known entails something about its overall nature and structure";[184] that is, that the universe is such as to be intelligible to persons like ourselves. But this can only be if "there is something analogous to human intelligence in the constitution of the world."[185] And this implies that the universe is the result of the will of a personal Creator:

> The intelligibility of the world . . . is perfectly to be accounted for if the world is due to the fiat of an intelligent will which

---

178. Ibid., 148.
179. Ibid., 159.
180. Ibid., 204.
181. Ibid., 213.
182. Ibid., 220.
183. Ibid., 17.
184. Meynell, *Intelligible Universe*, 118.
185. Ibid., 68.

conceives all possible worlds, and wills the one which we actually inhabit.[186]

However successful Meynell's argument may prove to be, it is also predicated on a view of reality as ultimately personal, because intelligible. Thus it seems to show that such a conception of reality is at least coherent.

Conclusion

The worldview of Revelation is significantly different in many respects from the thinking of modernity and postmodernism about the nature and significance of human persons and the significance of personhood in an overall cosmology. To what extent can it act as a guide for a Christian worldview for the twenty-first century?

Clearly it would be difficult for today's Christians to adopt every aspect of John's thought. A geocentric cosmology, for example, is literally out of the question for anyone aware of developments in science since Copernicus and Galileo. Other aspects are at least controversial, such as John's concept of a gendered universe, his advocacy of militant service of God, and his view of divine justice. These issues will need to be worked through with care by postmodern Christian thinkers, lest John's thought be misused, as has happened in the past.

It is also impossible to return a premodern concept of the person in a cosmic order. The conclusion that Charles Taylor reaches from his study of the modern identity is:

> how all-pervasive it is, how much it envelops us, and how deeply we are implicated in it: in a sense of self defined by the powers of disengaged reason as well as of the creative imagination, in the characteristically modern understandings of freedom and dignity and rights, in the ideals of self-fulfillment and expression, and in the demands of universal benevolence and justice.[187]

In other words, we can't go back to a premodern view of the person. In fact, the modern view owes some of its ideas to Christian theological developments and indeed, as I have argued here, to Revelation. However, this should not mean that Christians cannot propose modifications to the modern concept, as Taylor himself does, for instance in his critique of the cult of self-fulfillment[188] and in his modest advocacy of a Dostoyevskian

186. Ibid., 70.
187. Taylor, *Sources of the Self*, 503.
188. Ibid., 507.

theistic perspective.[189] Hopefully this discussion of Revelation suggests some other ways this may be done.

Study of Revelation may lead to other useful and relevant lines of thought for Christians to develop further in the postmodern setting. John's emphasis on the significance of individual persons and their actions could help function as the basis for Christian ethics and political involvement, for example. His emphasis on the dependency and limitations of human beings may make a useful contribution to postmodern debates, for instance about ecology. And his God-centered perspective on human identity and cosmology as a whole could suggest Christian approaches that challenge both the impersonal "Newtonian" mechanistic view of the universe and some of the postmodern proposals such as the Gaia view of the universe as a single organism. Certainly the concept of a personal universe must be "on the table" for consideration again.

Here then are some suggested lines of thought from this chapter.

First, Christians should not be afraid to affirm and build on a biblical view of humanity as created in God's image with a unique nature and a unique charter and responsibility for caring for God's creation and each other.

Second, Christians should be at the forefront of ecological responsibility, reminding others who share this concern that it is most successfully grounded in a biblical worldview.

Third, Christian ethics must always affirm the value of human beings. They are never objects to be used or discarded, animals to be studied or manipulated, or machines to be programmed. This implies a negative attitude to abortion (though not to women facing difficult challenges, often through no choice of their own), a resistance to eugenics and other attempts to manipulate human nature, and a determination to maintain the dignity of the handicapped, poor, and dying. The late Mother Teresa was a good model of such values in practice.

Fourth, Christians affirm the sovereignty of God (which needs reaffirming in this day and age) but do not embrace a hard determinism that eliminates human free will. Rather a Christian worldview affirms human agency as a key factor in history and a mirror of God's agency as Creator.

Fifth, affirmation of human agency, freedom, and responsibility is the grounds for a Christian reaffirmation of justice which has implications for a Christian view of law and even punishment. It is also the grounds for a Christian theory of politics that is not dependent on modernist metanarratives such as Marxism, liberal democracy, or capitalism.

189. Ibid., 518–21.

Finally, Christians should confidently affirm that the earth is God's creation, without getting sidetracked into unprofitable debates about the mechanism or method used by God. All Christians are "creationists," whether or not they deny evolution as a scientific theory or accept a literal view of Genesis 1–11.

CHAPTER 6

The Centrality of the Biblical Story

Postmodernism and History

WHAT IS THE MEANING of history and what part, if any, can I as an individual human being play in it? Is history going anywhere in particular? How meaningful is the personal narrative I construct to make sense of my own life and to what extent does such a narrative reflect more than my own biased perspective colored by nostalgia or tragedy?

So far this book has identified some fundamental presuppositions for Christian thought, elements of a Christian worldview that are relevant in the light of the issues being raised by postmodernism. This has involved considering the reality of the spirit world, the validity of revelation as a form of knowledge, and the priority of personhood in terms of how we think about humanity and cosmology. Many of the issues come together in debates about metanarrative, which has implications for consideration of the meaning of history.

Questioning Progress and Meaning

In the West, modernity successfully replaced medieval thinking about history (governed largely by the story of the Bible) with its own story of human progress towards some kind of paradise, whether envisaged as "humanity's passage to its adult status"[1] (as in Kant's thought), the emergence of the liberal bourgeois nation state, the triumph of spirit (Hegel), or the classless society of Marx. History had meaning because progress could be traced in such a direction.[2] To repeat the iconic statement of John Dewey, "The future rather than the past dominates the imagination. The Golden Age lies ahead of us not behind us."[3]

Similarly, Lyotard argues that whereas traditional societies sought legitimation in local myths and the past origins or glories of the specific group, "the great discourses of modernity"[4] focused on the future: "they look for legitimacy not in an original founding act but in a future to be accomplished, that is, in an Idea to be realized."[5] On the other hand, they also created their own myths of the past, such as the story of the American Revolution validating the idea of democracy and creating a unity around it.[6]

However, the tragedies of the twentieth century have undermined these kinds of hopes[7] since postmoderns have lost faith in such modern models. As Don Cupitt writes,

> History has "ended," in the sense that we suddenly find that we no longer have any form of the old belief in progress or in linear eschatological time. That is, we are no longer gripped by any of the old stories about a better hereafter.[8]

Many question whether history as a whole has *any* meaning. Indeed Darwin's theory of evolution would suggest that there is no special meaning in human history, unless we can somehow invest it with an existential significance.[9] As Nietzsche wrote, "We wished to awaken the feeling of man's sovereignty by showing his divine birth: this path is now forbidden,

---

1. Foucault, "What Is Enlightenment?," 38.
2. Cf. Prickett, *Narrative, Religion and Science*, 103.
3. Dewey, *Reconstruction in Philosophy*, as quoted in Middleton and Walsh, *Truth Is Stranger*, 14. This statement may be traced back to the epitaph on the tomb of French socialist Saint-Simon (d. 1825) (Goudzwaard, *Capitalism and Progress*, 47).
4. Lyotard, "Sign of History," 394.
5. Lyotard, "Apostil on narratives," 29. See also Lyotard, "Memorandum on Legitimacy," 55–69.
6. Cf. Prickett, *Narrative*, 15, 18. The form of these modern stories arguably owed something to the structure of the modern novel with its omniscient narrators and neat plot conclusions (ibid., 26).
7. Strauss, "Jerusalem and Athens," 133.
8. Cupitt, "Post-Christianity," 218. Cf. Tracy, *Blessed Rage*, 11.
9. Cf. Jaspers, *Philosophical Faith*, 105–8.

since a monkey stands at the entrance."[10] Human beings have emerged in a similar way to other forms of reality and are likely to become extinct (or superseded) in the future.[11]

Influentially, Michel Foucault argued,

> History has no "meaning," though this is not to say that it is absurd or incoherent. On the contrary, it is intelligible and should be susceptible to analysis down to the smallest detail—but this in accordance with the intelligibility of struggles, of strategies and tactics.[12]

What Foucault appears to be saying is that any attempt to find an *overall* meaning in history is futile, though one can still analyze aspects of history meaningfully. As he puts it elsewhere, "The forces operating in history are not controlled by destiny or regulative mechanisms, but respond to haphazard conflicts."[13] Furthermore, Foucault is famous for showing how human discourse (such as the study of history) can be used by power-holders to suppress knowledge that does not suit their interests and exclude other groups of human beings on the basis of gender, race, or other differences.[14]

Thus, as John Webster puts it,

> The severe postmodern vision involves dismantling the idea that there is any essence to history. "History" is both mutable and multiple, without direction or form, literally inconsequential . . . to attempt to give history some sort of plot, to see it as in some sense more than erratic, is mere fiction . . .[15]

Postmodernist Theologies of History

Twentieth-century theologians have engaged in a lengthy debate about the methodology and meaning of history, and its relation to Christian faith. Michael Gilbertson's study surveys these developments, beginning with Troeltsch's unsuccessful attempt to derive "a universal principle lying

---

10. Nietzsche, *Dawn of Day*, as quoted in Foucault, "Nietzsche, Genealogy, History," 79.
11. Cf. Miller, "Emerging Postmodern World," 1–19.
12. Foucault, "Truth and Power," 56.
13. Foucault, "Nietzsche," 88.
14. Cf. Hekman, *Gender and Knowledge*, 17–21, 68–73; Grenz, *Primer on Postmodernism*, 137.
15. Webster, "Barth and Postmodern Theology," 29.

behind historical events" from normal historical method,[16] in contrast with Bultmann's dualistic view in which "meaning in history is to be found in momentary existential encounter."[17] Pannenberg's reaction against Bultmann, which sought to rehabilitate historical investigation as a ground of faith (provided that "transcendent reality" was not ruled out), reaffirmed the unity of history while rejecting attempts to "impose a pattern on historical development."[18] Finally, Moltmann's emphasis on the future, on Christian hope, and on the priority of action to transform history[19] flows from a postmodern perspective in which no human observer can attain a vantage point to see a universal flow to history, which is multiple, "not merely one process."[20]

Postmodernist theologians have repudiated traditional Christian as well as modernist visions of history. For instance, Mark Taylor resists any order, beginning, or ending in history, attributing such views to a psychological need: "Unhappy/lacerated consciousness seeks to cure its ills by assuming a central role in a lawful plot."[21] The original blessing pictured in Genesis 1–2 is dismissed as "'an illusion' created to explain and repress the tensions that forever inhere in everything that is actual."[22] The ideas of a "pure origin" and a final resolution contained in the traditional Christian salvation story are unsustainable;[23] in fact, for Taylor such concepts are totalizing. Rather we need to affirm what is incomplete and insufficient.

More systematic discussion is found in Peter Hodgson's attempt to articulate a postmodern Christian view of history.[24] According to Hodgson, traditional salvation history cannot be sustained under the cultural shift to postmodernism.[25] He writes of

> the crisis of *history* brought on by the collapse not only of traditional theological views but also of their post-Enlightenment substitutes, namely, liberal-bourgeois ideas of progress and

---

16. I.e., within a modernist worldview that ruled out positing supernatural influences in history (Gilbertson, *God and History*, 5).
17. Ibid., 10.
18. Ibid., 12–13, see also 156–66.
19. Ibid., 17–19.
20. Ibid., 167–68.
21. Taylor, *Erring*, 153.
22. Ibid., 155.
23. Ibid.
24. Hodgson, *God in History*.
25. Ibid., 11–31, 39, 42–43.

Marxist-Leninist theories of dialectical advance toward a classless society.[26]

Instead history must be seen as an "imaginative construct" from the "traces" of the past.[27] And any theology of history needs to be rethought as "noninterventionist, nonmiraculous, and noncausal in its understanding of divine providence, nonlinear in its teleology, and nonsuprahistorical in its eschatology";[28] "a plurality of partial, fragmentary, always ambiguous histories of freedom," as opposed to, say, Hegel's more unified story.[29]

The Issue of Metanarratives

Many of the values and ideas of postmodernism, especially regarding history, come together in the rejection of "metanarratives," a term particularly associated with the work of Lyotard, who famously wrote, "Simplifying to the extreme, I define *postmodern* as incredulity towards 'metanarratives.'"[30]

Lyotard primarily sees metanarratives as large-scale stories ("grands récits") that function in the modern era as a means of legitimating social arrangements, universities, or political programs by appeal to the universal progress of all mankind.[31] These metanarratives of modernity drew their power particularly *from* the prestige of modern science (which seemed to provide a uniquely objective, culture-transcendent, universal road to truth) even as they also functioned as a legitimation *of* science.[32] However, as Lyotard argues, "Scientific knowledge cannot know and make known that it is the true knowledge without resorting to the other, narrative, kind of knowledge, which from its point of view is no knowledge at all."[33]

---

26. Ibid., 30.
27. Ibid., 170–72, 166–67.
28. Ibid., 42–43.
29. Ibid., 47, comp. 110, 233.
30. Lyotard, *Postmodern Condition*, xiv.
31. Cf. Grenz, *Primer on Postmodernism*, 4; Goudzwaard, *Capitalism and Progress*, 39–41. This contrasted with the actual progress that made modernism dominant, which was strongly associated with European imperialism, the slave trade, and the exploitation of landless peasants in the new factories of the Industrial Revolution (cf. Barth, *Protestant Theology*, 38).
32. Lyotard, *Postmodern Condition*, 31–32.
33. Ibid., 29. Similarly, Prickett (*Narrative*, 23–26) shows how science involves telling stories.

There were competing metanarratives, of course. Lyotard identifies several:[34] the dialectics of the Spirit or "speculation,"[35] the hermeneutics of meaning, the emancipation of the rational subject, the emancipation of the working subject, and the creation of wealth. Christianity too (at least since Augustine) can be included as a metanarrative of modernity in that it criticized the classical thinking of antiquity[36] and became "the oldest and most all-encompassing Western grand narrative."[37] All these metanarratives are philosophical and universal, seeking to bring order into the events of history.[38]

What deficiencies does Lyotard find in such metanarratives? First, they have lost credibility alongside the declining confidence in traditional thinking about truth and reality[39] and the "exploding of language into families of heteronomous language-games."[40]

Second, the effectiveness of modern metanarratives depended on the concept of a universal subject, as in "We, the people" or "humanity as the hero of liberty";[41] but in practice "we" are singular, contingent, and local—not everyone is included.[42] Hence the followers of the Enlightenment, who saw themselves as the voice of "the people," were active in "destroying the traditional knowledge of peoples, perceived from that point forward as minorities or potential separatist movements destined only to spread obscurantism."[43] Thus the failure of modernity may be due to the "insurmountable diversity of cultures"[44] or local narratives with their emphasis on origins.[45]

---

34. Lyotard, *Postmodern Condition*, xxiii. Subsequently he refers to them mainly in two categories: "the life of the spirit" and "the emancipation of humanity" (e.g., ibid., 51). Comp. Lyotard, "Apostil on Narratives," 29.

35. Lyotard, *Postmodern Condition*, 33.

36. Lyotard, "Apostil on Narratives," 29. Comp. idem, "Name of Algeria," 169; idem, "Universal History and Cultural Differences," 315.

37. Lyotard, "Wall, the Gulf, and the Sun," 114.

38. Lyotard, "Universal History," 314–15.

39. Lyotard, *Postmodern Condition*, xxiv.

40. Lyotard, "Sign of History," 410. Cf. idem, *Postmodern Condition*, 41–43.

41. Lyotard, *Postmodern Condition*, 31.

42. Lyotard, "Universal History," 316.

43. Lyotard, *Postmodern Condition*, 30.

44. Lyotard, "Universal History," 319.

45. Cf. Lyotard, "Universal History," 322. Cf. Boer, "Slacker's Guide," 65. Prickett (*Narrative*, 51–53) discerns this conflict in the resistance of German romanticism to the French Enlightenment metanarrative.

Third, the credibility of the "great narratives of emancipation" has been undercut by events such as Auschwitz and the Soviet oppression of workers.[46] Thus modernist confidence in universal progress towards a single idea (such as emancipation) is no longer sustainable. Such a project can only be carried forward by terror, as demonstrated in these events of the twentieth century.[47]

In place of these "grand narratives," according to Lyotard, the one unifying or common feature driving history forward is "the impostor-subject and blindly calculating rationality called Capital" and its "criterion of performativity,"[48] which is increasingly dominating scientific research through the need for funds—"No money, no proof—and that means no verification of statements and no truth."[49] Lyotard is not optimistic here; as a former socialist, he can no longer believe either that capitalism may be liberating or that it will be overthrown in the name of liberation. All that seems possible to withstand the omnipresent power of capital is to emphasize heterogeneity.[50] Thus, in the sphere of science or truth, Lyotard calls for a new model of legitimation based on "difference understood as paralogy."[51]

One result of this is the loss of a sense of history, in the sense of a beginning or eschatological hope. In Lyotard's own attempts to retell the story of the cosmos, drawing from various postmodern scientific researches, "the hero is no longer Man"; the driving forces are chance, system, energy, evolution, and language; and liberal democracy is favored simply because of its ability to improve the "system," which is also working to survive the inevitable collapse of the sun by making ways for the brain to survive in a different, unforeseeable future elsewhere in space.[52] Lyotard is trying to be true to the theory of evolution, in which concepts like progress and purpose are illegitimate, though they are often smuggled in to tell an attractive story,[53] but even he has slipped into purposive language and introduced a note of hope.

46. Lyotard, "Universal History," 318. See also idem, "Sign of History," 393. Cf. Best and Kellner, *Postmodern Theory*, 23–26; Eagleton, *Literary Theory*, 123.

47. Lyotard, "Sign of History," 409. Comp. Voegelin, "Immortality," 195.

48. Lyotard, "Sign of History," 410.

49. Lyotard, *Postmodern Condition*, 45, see also 46–53. See comments in Prickett, *Narrative*, 18–19.

50. See the conclusion in Lyotard, "Sign of History," 410.

51. Lyotard, *Postmodern Condition*, 60. Lyotard consciously opposes Habermas' view of universal consensus here (ibid., 60–66). Cf. Prickett, *Narrative*, 21–23.

52. Lyotard, "Wall, the Gulf, and the Sun," 120–23.

53. Cf. Prickett, *Narrative*, 27–30, 32–33.

Others argue that metanarratives are overambitious and attempt to do the impossible. There is simply no story that explains or includes everything; moreover no one can predict the future with any certainty, and yet all the competing modern metanarratives are predicated on what Derrida calls "progressivism": a discourse of the end, a secular eschatology reminiscent of the language found in Revelation, as in Marx's prediction of the ultimate end of the class struggle.[54]

Others stress that metanarratives are oppressive and exclusionary. By taking the story of one particular group (such as Western Europe or the proletariat) and presenting it as the overarching story of human history, for example, they must exclude (or assimilate) the stories of other groups.[55] Thus minorities are oppressed, marginalized, and excluded by the dominant metanarrative, as in the case of Australia's Aboriginal people, whose own narratives were dismissed as primitive and subjugated to the neo-modern narrative of the march of British civilization, even as the representatives of British civilization frequently tried to literally wipe them out.[56]

Are all metanarratives comprehensive in scope? Marxism attempts to explain all of human history in all cultures by its central idea of dialectical materialism, and makes predictions that ultimately cover every human society. This is metanarrative at its most grand! On the other hand, there are narratives of, say, an ethnic group, which may be just as totalizing in respect to the individuals in that group, but make no claims to universality. In that sense, according to J. M. Bernstein, everyone has a metanarrative,[57] and Best and Kellner propose that it might be helpful to distinguish different levels of grandness in "grand narratives."[58] On the other hand, ethnic stories are not only particularist, but rooted in the past, like the stories that animated the fighting in the former Yugoslavia in the 1990s, and unlike future-oriented modern metanarratives like Marxism.[59]

Others have argued that some forms of postmodernism look suspiciously like a new metanarrative, especially when they divide history into premodern, modern, and postmodern periods and provide a comprehensive,

---

54. Derrida, "Apocalyptic Tone," 80. Cf. Abrams, "Theme and Romantic Variations," 14–19; Hodgson, *God in History*, 12.

55. Cf. Hodgson, *God in History*, 233–34, where Hodgson criticizes "overarching linear teleology" for its tendency to a "totalitarian vision."

56. Cf. Reynolds, *Indelible Stain?*

57. Bernstein, "Grand Narratives," 122.

58. Best and Kellner, *Postmodern Theory*, 172.

59. Nazi ideology was a mix of both: grounded in past racial glories but looking towards a great future for the Aryan race.

explanation of reality, language, politics, and rival worldviews.[60] On the other hand, Foucault prefers to speak of modernity "rather as an attitude than as a period of history," an attitude characterized by such features as breaking with tradition and an "ironic heroization of the present."[61]

A Christian Metanarrative?

What kind of response should Christians make to the postmodern critique of metanarratives? Is Christianity itself vulnerable to the same critique?

According to Prickett, "Christianity was the original grand narrative" that presented "the final and coherent Theory of Everything."[62] By the Middle Ages, this metanarrative tried to incorporate all branches of knowledge—even that of classical antiquity—into its vision. It was used to justify the existence of the institutional church just as later the Marxist metanarrative justified the role of the Communist Party or the Soviet Union. But it suffered the fate of all metanarratives,[63] splintering into competing versions: Catholic, Orthodox, Protestant, Anabaptist, and so on. It struggled to cope with the re-emergence of other religions onto the world stage, being unable to successfully explain them in Christ-centered terms.[64] It proved insufficient to explain many features of the cosmos, especially in the light of modern science. And related to this, its sense of progress towards a future realization of Christian ideals has declined in credibility due to the violence and crises of the twentieth century.

Further, Christianity often became oppressive and exclusionary when in a position of power, even leading to violence against minorities that could not (or would not) be assimilated into the Christian worldview or culture. Hodgson, for example, refers to "the sad history of Christian persecution of the Jews," which he attributes to Christianity's "often powerful tendency toward christocentrism."[65]

Finally, such Christian metanarratives have been accused of imposing a structure on history that is not really there. As Thornhill puts it, "historical interpretations, including Christian ones, have too readily claimed what was really a time-conditioned cultural or theological construct to be

---

60. Cf. Rée, "Narrative and Philosophical Experience," 78; Prickett, *Narrative*, 20–21.

61. Foucault, "What Is Enlightenment?," 39–42.

62. Prickett, *Narrative*, 128.

63. Ibid., 128–35.

64. Cf. Hodgson, *God in History*, 30.

65. Ibid., 106.

an 'over-arching divine plan.'"[66] On the other hand, it can be argued that at least the broad outlines of a Christian Story have been held in common by almost all Christians, regardless of their theological positions, from the beginning of Christianity until at least the Enlightenment.

Christian responses to these criticisms have varied, but may be divided into three main categories. Some theologians have sought to reinterpret the Christian faith using postmodernist categories, thus delivering it from the predicament of being an oppressive, exclusive, or overambitious metanarrative. This can be carried out by creating Christian theologies that disavow metanarratives or absolute claims[67] (for instance, John Hick's "complementary pluralism," in which Christianity makes its contribution to theology and spirituality alongside other partners such as Hinduism),[68] or by looking at the Bible's story from the perspective of those frequently excluded from traditional interpretations, such as women or blacks.

Another defensive approach is to differentiate sharply between Christian "salvation history" as found in Scripture and a natural realm more subject to the "laws" of nature, including secular history.[69] As Hodgson observes, this approach in liberalism after Schleiermacher meant that theology became oriented "not to the knowledge of God or truth claims of any sort about objective reality, but to the practical life and piety of the church."[70] In other words, various forms of modern Christianity tended to accept the sacred-secular divide implied by Kant, and thus abandoned most areas of knowledge to modernity.[71]

Certainly many recent Christian thinkers agree that any Christian metanarrative must be disavowed. So, for example, John Thornhill accepts "the judgment that doctrinal systems claiming to explain the totality of our life-world cannot be sustained."[72] John Webster, following Barth, contends that "what Christian faith says about history is properly not a 'grand narrative,' not a 'world picture.'"[73] He decries any attempt to simplify the processes of history into a neat conceptual schema or worldview (even a Christian one), even while (paradoxically) asserting a covenant-centered

---

66. Thornhill, *Modernity*, 222.
67. Cf. Hodgson, *God in History*, 107.
68. Cf. Hick, *Second Christianity*, 76–92.
69. Cf. Hodgson, *God in History*, 16–28.
70. Ibid., 25.
71. Something like this seems to motivate the postliberal approach to theology; see analysis in chapter 1.
72. Thornhill, *Modernity*, 127–28, cf. 222.
73. Webster, "Barth and Postmodern Theology," 31.

christocentric view of human history.[74] Some of these responses imply that metanarratives are inherently humanistic in their attempt to construct a scheme that incorporates or explains all history; this resembles the effort to build the tower of Babel, and God's judgment on that can be seen as privileging local stories.[75]

However, some evangelical scholars take almost the opposite approach. Middleton and Walsh, for example, assert that biblical Christianity "is undeniably rooted in a metanarrative that claims to tell the true story of the world."[76] While they concede that this has sometimes been used "as a weapon, legitimating prejudice and perpetuating violence against those perceived as the enemy,"[77] they argue that the Bible as a metanarrative "works ultimately *against* totalization" due to its "*radical sensitivity to suffering*" and its rootedness in "*God's overarching creational intent* that delegitimates any narrow, partisan use of the story."[78]

It seems to me that there is a good case to be made that Christianity inherently presupposes an overarching Big Story that claims to explain, or at least frame, the stories of humanity within its parameters. This is suggested, first, by the parallels between the Christian Story and metanarratives of modernity such as Marxism: the positing of a central driving force of history, the confident expectation of a final triumph of justice,[79] the sense of struggle between the forces of light (liberation) and darkness (oppression), and the existence of a vanguard of liberation consisting of an enlightened group of believers. In fact, it has been argued that all these Western metanarratives may be seen as alternative versions of the salvation history of Christianity.[80]

Second, the priority of this Story seems to be implied by the claims made in the Old and New Testaments for the Judeo-Christian faith; for example, their growing monotheism (Exod 20:3–6; Isa 40:25–26; 43:10; 44:6–8), the exclusive claims made on behalf of Jesus (John 14:6; Acts 4:12), and the way the biblical authors respond to the other narratives of their day, beginning with the Genesis creation story itself, which is structured in

---

74. Ibid., 32–42. Cf. Heschel, *Prophets*, 1:176.

75. Cf. Gen 11:1–9. See comments in Hart, *Trespass of the Sign*, 109; Middleton and Walsh, *Truth Is Stranger*, 187–89.

76. Middleton and Walsh, *Truth Is Stranger*, 83.

77. Ibid., 84.

78. Ibid., 87 (italics original); cf. 179; Grenz, *Primer on Postmodernism*, 164; Groothuis, *Truth Decay*, 135–38, 194–95.

79. Though the Christian Story is also rooted in the past, in the creation stories of Genesis, for instance, far more than the metanarratives of modernity.

80. Hodgson, *God in History*, 12. Cf. Webster, "Barth and Postmodern Theology," 31; Küng, *On Being a Christian*, 31.

a kind of polemical parallel to creation stories of other ancient cultures,[81] though it is far from being a seamless narrative.[82]

Of course, if one is inclined to accept the priority of this Story as a fundamental explanation of history and reality, one will have to ask if such a stance is inherently intolerant, even violent, and if it even does justice to such a multi-generic and wide-ranging book as the Bible. But first I want to explore what Revelation has to contribute to these questions.

HISTORY AND REVELATION

Hope for the Future in Revelation

According to Abraham Heschel, the Hebrew prophets have a unique take on history: "It is an act of evil to accept the state of evil as either inevitable or final. Others may be satisfied with improvement, the prophets insist on redemption";[83] and, "History is not a meaningless conglomeration of neutral facts, but a drama unfolding the relationship between God and man."[84] A similar set of perspectives may be discerned in the mind of the author of Revelation.

According to the postmodernists referred to earlier in the chapter, history is not really going anywhere, or at least anywhere humans can ever know. This perception can lead to hopelessness or pessimism. But John's view is more optimistic, in spite of the violence of the judgments he foresees and the complexity, even opaqueness, of the story he tells. This is because, as he sees it, not only does God's sovereignty guarantee that history is going somewhere, but human beings have a part to play, led by Jesus.

Jesus as Messianic Governor of History

As I argued in chapter 2, the ancient Jewish apocalypses nearly all place the messianic hope at the center of their predictions. Similarly, Revelation sees Jesus as the ultimate ruler of history under God, the governor and savior of the world, in spite of all claims to the contrary by Caesar and others.[85]

81. Cf. Boyd, *God at War*, 100–112; Houston, *I Believe in the Creator*, 64–66; Dumbrell, *End of the Beginning*, 169–74.

82. Cf. Prickett, *Narrative*, 33–34.

83. Heschel, *Prophets*, 1:181 (italics original).

84. Ibid., 1:190.

85. Particularly the language used about Augustus (cf. Friesen, *Imperial Cults*, 32–34, 201). John turns the mythology of the Roman imperial cult on its head, as will

John presents Jesus as God's Messiah (Christ) right from the start (1:1) and proclaims him "the ruler of the kings of the earth" (1:5).[86] John's appeal to Psalm 2, one of the most significant psalms for the early Christians,[87] is characteristic of his perspective.

Psalm 2 presents the rule of Lord's "anointed" ("Messiah") being resisted by the nations, peoples, kings, and rulers (vv. 1–3), but to no avail, since God has determined to set his king on Zion (vv. 4–6) as his son (v. 7), and to make him ruler over the nations, even "the ends of the earth" (v. 8), with "a rod of iron" (v. 9). Therefore the rulers are warned (v. 10) to submit to his rule, "for his wrath is quickly kindled" (v. 12). On the other hand, he blesses those who "take refuge in him" (that is, as savior) (v. 12). John makes repeated references to the text of this psalm (Rev 2:26–27; 12:5; 19:15; 6:16; 14:1)[88] so as to lead readers to the conclusion that Jesus is Lord, installed as king (Messiah) by God, and that all resistance to him is ultimately futile.

The claims John makes about the effects of Jesus' death and resurrection have the same implications. Jesus' blood makes his followers a kingdom (1:6; cf. 5:10). He "ransomed for God saints from every tribe and language and people and nation" and is therefore worthy to open the sealed up scroll (5:9; cf. 7:9, 14) and receive the full panoply of a world emperor (5:12). John claims that Jesus' violent death (and subsequent resurrection) has won for him an international kingdom that must ultimately defeat that of the dragon (12:11).

The symbolic portraits of Jesus contained in Revelation also emphasize his messianic lordship. He is portrayed as "one like the Son of Man" (1:13), clearly referring to Daniel, but the picture and the effect of this vision on John suggests he is more like Daniel's "ancient of days," that is, God.[89] He also holds "seven stars" in his hand, which Malina sees as implying that "Jesus is *Polokrator*, controller of the pole of the universe."[90] References to

---

be discussed in the next chapter. Cf. Friesen, "Myth and Symbolic Resistance," 309.

86. An allusion to Ps 89:27, part of a passage expressing God's covenant with David, probably with messianic overtones. Cf. Malina, *Genre and Message*, 262. Comp. Fekkes, *Isaiah and Prophetic Traditions*, 74–77. Other messianic references are found in Rev 1:5–7 (conflating Dan 7:13 and Zech 12:10, both passages which at least *some* Jews took to be messianic); Rev 3:7 (comp. Isa 22:22); Rev 5:5 (referring to Gen 49 and Isa 11:1, 10); Rev 11:15; 12:5 (comp. Isa 9:6–7); 12:10; and 22:16.

87. See Acts 4:25–28; 13:33; Heb 1:5; Matt 3:17.

88. Cf. Moyise, "Psalms in Revelation," 231, 233–34; Beale, *Revelation*, 190–91, 266–68.

89. Pattemore (*People of God*, 122–23) refers to an Old Greek version of Dan 7 in which "the son of man comes 'as the Ancient of Days.'"

90. Malina, *Genre and Message*, 72, 262.

his return (such as 1:7;[91] 3:3; 16:15; 19:11-21;[92] 22:7, 12, 20) also highlight the centrality of Christ to the meaning and direction of history as seen by John.

Clearly, too, the Lamb is the central protagonist of Revelation and his dominant role in its plot speaks loudly of John's faith in Jesus' lordship in and over history. In fact, as Friesen writes, "the significance of the slaughter of the Lamb goes beyond the bounds of history. The victim has been slaughtered from the foundation of the world; this act *constitutes history itself.*"[93] John clearly has a christocentric view of history somewhat like that decried by Hodgson.[94]

The End of History

According to Revelation, history is moving inexorably towards the goals God has set for it, as described in chapters 20–22: the reign of the saints, the defeat of the devil, the final judgment, the new heavens and earth, and the New Jerusalem. John foresees a dramatic climax that finally resolves the struggle between good and evil and issues in a new age of peace based on the unchallengeable victory of God, Christ, and the saints.

All through the book, there are pointers to the end: warnings of Jesus' final return (16:15; 22:7, 12, 20), the escalating severity of the judgments recorded in the story, statements declaring God's assumption of kingly rule (11:15, 17; 12:10) and the fulfillment of his plans (10:6-7), warnings of the final destruction of the devil (12:12; 20:2-3, 7-10), the fall of Babylon and/or the kingdom of the beast (14:8; 16:19; 17:8, 11, 14, 16; 18:2, 5, 8, 10, 16-17, 19, 21; 19:19-21), the final judgment (11:18; 14:7, 10-11; 20:12-15; 21:8; 22:15), and promises of final salvation to the overcoming Christians (2:7, 11, 17, 26-18; 3:5, 12, 21; 5:10; 7:15-17; 19:7-8; 21:3-4, 7; 22:3-5, 14, 19). John's thinking about the future is thus similar to that of the Jewish apocalypses, virtually all of which look forward to a final consummation of world history,[95] as I discussed in chapter 2.

However, there are two objections to this interpretation of Revelation. First, many commentators take many of the statements referred to above

---

91. Cf. Beale, *Revelation*, 197-99; Aune, *Revelation 1-5*, 50-54.
92. Aune, *Revelation 17-22*, 1046.
93. Friesen, *Imperial Cults*, 176.
94. See above, 239-240.
95. Cf. Collins, "Morphology of a Genre," 9; and idem, *Apocalyptic Imagination*, 205. Comp. Aune, *Prophecy in Early Christianity*, 110-12; Hengel, *Judaism and Hellenism*, 1:194-95.

to refer to the end of an era in history rather than to the end of history as such. Thus, for example, John is referring to the downfall of Rome, the triumph of Christianity over Roman paganism, or even the future triumph of Christianity as a missionary force throughout the world. This is a difficult argument to address in a short space. It is quite possible that many of the statements referred to above do indeed refer to events prior to the final end of history; for example, the predicted fall of Babylon is described in language similar to that used in the Old Testament for the downfall of many ancient empires.[96]

However, the language of Revelation 20–22 is much more final and sweeping than this. It speaks of a *final* end to the devil *after* a more temporary defeat (20:2–3, 7, 10). It speaks of a *final* and *universal* resurrection *after* a more limited one (20:4–6, 12–13). It speaks of a *final* judgment that encompasses *all* the dead, and indeed Death and Hades too (20:12–15). It speaks of a time when Death (and sorrow and pain) will be no more (21:4; cf. 7:16–17). It speaks of the present heaven[97] and earth being replaced and the sea being eliminated (21:1), of a new order (21:1–2) that is radically different and permanent, as signaled by the Greek *kainos*.[98] It speaks of a city where the present order of nature is radically altered (21:23, 25; 22:2, 5). Even though this is figurative language, it points to something unimaginably glorious and different to the present order of things. As Dumbrell argues, in Revelation, "Neither the renewal of the existing order nor its purification is sought, but rather its replacement."[99]

The second objection argues that, even at the end of Revelation, evil has not been eliminated, only defeated, and hence history is not ended. The evildoers are "outside" the city (22:15) and cannot enter it (21:27), but they still exist and there is still a world outside the city that interacts with it (21:24–26),[100] hence the possibility that the nations will again be corrupted and that war will break out again between good and evil. This argument is consistent with a postmodern resistance to closure and the thought that good needs evil for its definition. Pippin, for example, sees that closure is rendered impossible by the existence of the "bottomless pit" (abyss).[101]

---

96. Comp. Rev 18 with passages such as Jer 46–51; Ezek 27–32; Obad; Nah 3; and Zeph.

97. Cf. Raber, "Revelation 21:1–8," 296; Minear, "Cosmology of the Apocalypse," 25–33.

98. Cf. Minear, "Cosmology of the Apocalypse," 27.

99. Dumbrell, *End of the Beginning*, 167.

100. Pippin, "Peering into the Abyss," 251–53.

101. Ibid., 262.

Certainly there is dissonance in John's pictures: on the one hand, those outside the city are in the lake of fire and forbidden to enter (21:8, 27; 22:15); on the other hand, there are others outside the city but free to enter it on pilgrimage (21:24-26). There have been various attempts to overcome this dissonance, and Gilbertson argues that "It is surely wiser to acknowledge the ambiguities of the text" than try to tidy it up.[102] However, it seems to me that we can resolve the difficulty satisfactorily if we recognize that, following the prophets (from whom this imagery is drawn), John does not envisage a city that literally encompasses the world, but rather a world capital.[103] Thus there will be two classes of people "outside" the city: evildoers in the lake of fire, and "the nations" of the righteous, whose names are in the Lamb's Book of Life and who are healed by the leaves of the Tree of Life and come to the city bearing "the glory and honor of the nations" (21:24-27; 22:2; cf. Isa 2:2; 56:6-8; 60:1-11).[104]

In other words, this apparent ambiguity does not undermine the *finality* of John's language about the defeat of evil. The division of humanity into two classes of people with radically different ends seems irreversible. The sinners are not just "outside" the city; they are "inside" the lake of fire suffering the "second death" (20:15; 21:8), helpless to mount any kind of further rebellion against God, as is the devil (20:10). Revelation uses the language of permanence here: the devil and his cohorts are tormented "forever and ever" (20:10); the gates of the city "will never be shut" (21:25); "nothing accursed will be found there any more" (22:3); the servants of God and the Lamb "will reign forever and ever" (22:5). And, as Gilbertson observes, the abyss is not mentioned after 20:3, implying that "the forces that were associated with the abyss have been finally overcome."[105]

Hence it seems clear that John *is* trying to describe the end of history, at least in the sense of conflict, in his last few chapters. Evil has been finally defeated; the goal of history has been reached; a new permanent world order has been established; Sabbath rest has been regained for creation as a whole.[106] Following Gilbertson again, "The message could not be clearer: with the descent of the New Jerusalem we have moved from the description

102. Gilbertson, *God and History*, 107 n. 81.

103. See further discussion of Jerusalem in the next chapter.

104. Cf. Pattemore, *People of God*, 202. For the opposite view (that the New Jerusalem literally extends throughout the world), see Beale, *Revelation*, 1098-99, 1109-11. A third view, that the people outside are exclusively the unrighteous, who gradually are able to leave the lake of fire and enter the city, is expressed by Rissi (*Time and History*, 132-33).

105. Gilbertson, *God and History*, 97 n.51.

106. Cf. Dumbrell, *End of the Beginning*, 41, 47, 52, 99, 135, 178-79, 192.

of the penultimate future to description of the ultimate future."[107] In other words, John brings closure to his story. On the other hand, as Gilbertson also points out, it is not the end of history in the sense that *nothing more happens*: future events are suggested by the depictions of future pilgrimage and healing.[108]

Hopeful Anticipation

As I explained in chapter 2, the worldview of most people in the first century looked backward rather than forward, with a tendency to idealize a past golden age[109] and to value stability in the face of potential chaos[110]—a chaos that most ancient societies had regularly experienced in some form. Revelation graphically reflects the fear of chaos and instability that formed part of the ancient Mediterranean worldview, even though the final outcome is a stable world order (22:1–5). On the other hand, we also noticed that in Revelation it is largely *God's* hand that unleashes chaos (as in the woes unleashed in chs. 6–9) and Revelation is largely hostile to the the Pax Romana, viewing it as a false stability destined to be destroyed by the judgment of God.

Revelation does not primarily look back to the past. There is a note of "paradise regained" in the promises to the overcomers (2:7) and in the ultimate new world order (22:1–2, 14), but the ultimate perspective is progressive, looking *forward* to paradise, which moreover is pictured as a city, not a garden (21:2, 10–22:2, 14, 19).[111] Here we see some of the roots of the modern belief in progress.

However, John's hope is grounded in God and Christ, not in human effort or ideals, even though he sees human participation in the process.[112] In fact, in Revelation God seems determined to destroy human civilization in order to build a new world order. This sets John's hope apart from the humanist faith in progress born in the Enlightenment, with its eye on reason,

---

107. Gilbertson, *God and History*, 137.

108. Ibid., 192.

109. Cf. Green, *Alexander to Actium*, 392, 470; Price, *Rituals and Power*, 99. Goudzwaard (*Capitalism and Progress*, 45–46) explains how this idea dominated particularly Stoic thought.

110. Ibid., 363; see also, 458–459, 472. Cf. Malina, *New Testament World*, 90.

111. Cf. Gilbertson, *God and History*, 190.

112. See chapter 5 above.

material wealth, and political freedom, for which Christian hope was an obstacle to be overcome.[113]

In fact, John vigorously opposes materialism in his prophetic critique of "Babylon" (chs. 17–18).[114] His "utopia" is not primarily focused on human prosperity, freedom, or equality, even though such elements may be implied by some of his imagery, such as the Tree of Life "producing its fruit each month" (22:2). Rather his hope is for a new world order characterized by satisfaction of the deepest human longings (21:6), exclusion of destructive immoral behavior (21:8, 27), unrestricted access to the presence of God (21:22–23; 22:3–5), and peace among the nations, who are healed of their national "sicknesses" (21:24–26; 22:2).

Such a hope is central to a Christian worldview and helps equip Christians with what Elisabeth Schüssler Fiorenza calls "a vision of a just world."[115] On the other hand, this new order is the result of destruction and violence and John seems at times to be a very imperialistic anti-imperialist, telling a potentially oppressive metanarrative.[116] We must therefore give consideration to John's narrative world, the plot he constructs to convey his worldview.

REVELATION AS STORY AND THE BIG STORY OF SCRIPTURE

Revelation as a War Story

That the book of Revelation has a definite and complex storyline with plot and characters is now well recognized. Some have seen it as resembling a Greek play, for example.[117] Classic plot features of a drama or novel may be identified in the text, such as the problem (ch. 5) and the climax (ch. 19). I want to explore this by looking at Revelation first as a war story, highlighting the tension John sees between Christianity and other forces in his world.

Revelation as a war epic traces the battle between good and evil. In the final episodes of the story, the conflicts that moved the story forward are

---

113. Cf. Goudzwaard, *Capitalism and Progress*, 19–23, 42–48.

114. Strong critiques of modern capitalism have been derived from Revelation by many recent commentators (e.g., Howard-Brook and Gwyther, *Unveiling Empire*, 236–77).

115. Cf. Fiorenza, *Vision of a Just World*.

116. Cf. Yhearm, *Sitz im Leben*, ch. 5.

117. Cf. Smalley, *Thunder and Love*, 103–10; Barr, "Oral Enactment," 243–56; Barr, "Symbolic Transformation," 45.

resolved in a final battle, and ultimately "they all live happily ever after," or as John puts it, "they will reign forever and ever"; 22:5). This is seen in the descriptions of the defeat and destruction of the devil in chapters 19 and 20, which takes several stages: the defeat and capture of the beast and false prophet and the violent destruction of their earthly followers (19:17-21), the imprisonment of the dragon himself for a thousand years (20:1-3), the dragon's final challenge (20:7-9),[118] the dragon's final defeat and confinement to the lake of fire (20:9-10), and the final judgment of his followers, who join him in the lake of fire with his agents "Death and Hades"[119] (20:13-15; 21:8).

Parallel to this, the victory and vindication of the Lamb and his followers is also in several stages: the victory of the rider on the white horse (19:19-21), the resurrection and thousand-year reign of the martyrs (20:4-6), their deliverance from the final siege (20:9),[120] the vindication of those written in the Book of Life in the final judgment (20:12, 15; 21:27), and the final reward for the Lamb's followers (21:1—22:5).

Not only the storyline itself, but also other literary features of the final chapters (19:11—22:5), mark out the ending of this particular narrative; for example, allusions to earlier parts of the story (such as the description of the rider on the white horse in 19:11-13),[121] the reappearance of the beast and the "false prophet" at the climax (cf. 19:20; 16:13; 13:11-17), and the resurrection of those who had not worshiped the beast or received its mark (20:4, reflecting 13:4, 8, 15-17; 14:9-12). Finally, there are indications of closure in the ending of the story, as identified previously, and the text ends by applying the "moral" of the story to the readers in terms of warnings and assurances (22:10-19).

There are other indications, apart from the plot structure, that this cosmic conflict, expressive of the dualism identified in chapter 2, is at the heart of Revelation. Richard Bauckham, for instance, has argued that Revelation could be seen as a Christian "war scroll," resembling in its theme the *War*

---

118. Cf. McIlraith, *Reciprocal Love*, 112-22.

119. Death and Hades may be seen in Revelation equally as agents of God's judgment and as representing the devil's temporary sovereignty over sinners. The risen, victorious Christ speaks of having "the keys of Death and of Hades" (Rev 1:18) and they are cast with the devil into the lake of fire (20:10, 14). Cf. Rissi, *Time and History*, 104-6.

120. Ironically contrasting with the fate of Jerusalem in A.D. 70.

121. E.g., the name "faithful and true" (Rev 19:11, reflecting 1:5 and 3:14); his eyes "like a flame of fire" (19:12, reflecting 1:14); the "sharp sword" coming out of his mouth (19:15, reflecting 1:16 and 2:12); and the statement that he will rule the nations "with a rod of iron" (19:15, reflecting 2:27 and 12:5).

Scroll of Qumran and other Jewish literature,[122] which focus on the theme of holy war and "the final victory of the divine Warrior over his people's and his own enemies."[123] Both texts emphasize the role of God's people in the final war, though in Revelation the holy war traditions are reinterpreted metaphorically.[124]

The evidence brought forward by Bauckham includes the promises to the "conquerors" in the seven churches[125] and the descriptions of the 144,000; for example, the census of Rev 7:2-24, in the light of Old Testament background, implies that they are an army, and their ritual purity in Rev 14:4 is also grounded in Old Testament rules of war (Deut 23:9-14; 1 Sam 21:5; 2 Sam 11:9-13).[126] A very similar reference occurs in the Qumran literature, where "the only explicit reference to the separation of the sexes . . . appears in a context of ritual cleanness" in connection with a holy war in the document 1 QM 7.3-6.[127]

Clearly the situation of the seven churches is portrayed as one of both internal conflict (such as the struggles with the Nicolaitans; Rev 2:6, 15) and external threat (such as the "synagogues of Satan"; Rev 2:9; 3:9). Jesus is pictured as threatening to engage in war with recalcitrant elements in the churches (2:16 explicitly, but implicitly in 2:5, 22-23; 3:3). Rewards are promised to those who conquer (2:7, 11, 17, 26; 3:5, 12, 21) and this conquest is celebrated in heaven (12:11; 15:2).

Meanwhile the story is full of the language of war, starting with the four horsemen (6:2, 4, 8) and continuing with two huge armies in chapter 9. There is war between the beast and the two witnesses (11:7), between two angelic armies (12:7-9), between the dragon and the rest of the Christians (12:17), and between the beast and the saints (13:7, 10). The gathering of the earth's vintage amounts to a huge bloodbath attributable to war (14:19-20; cf. 8:7; 11:6; 16:3-6). Supernatural events make way for the great battle to take place at Harmagedon (16:12-16). Ten kings form an alliance against the Lamb (17:13-14); having lost that battle, they turn instead on the whore (17:16). The climax of the plot is another great battle (19:11-21); in a ghoulish scene, the birds feast on the slain (19:17, 18, 21). Finally, after the thousand years of respite, there is war again between Gog and Magog and the saints (20:7-9). This is truly an epic war story.

---

122. Bauckham, *Climax*, 210-37.
123. Ibid., 210.
124. Ibid., 212-13; cf. Pattemore, *People of God*, 192-93.
125. Bauckham, *Climax*, 213.
126. Ibid., 215-32.
127. Vermes, *World of Judaism*, 123.

The Ending of Revelation in Relation to the Narrative of the Bible

Revelation is not just an isolated war story, however. There are clear signs that the author of Revelation has identified a central story running through the Bible (viewed as a single text) and consciously written an ending for this story[128] that began in Genesis. He seems to support the idea that "the entire Bible is moving, growing according to a common purpose and towards a common goal,"[129] to judge by other features of Revelation.

Revelation concludes by returning to the imagery and themes of Genesis 1–3. This implies that, for John, Genesis tells the beginning and Revelation the ending of a single story. Thus we read of the defeat of the "ancient serpent" (Rev 20:2; cf. Gen. 3:1–4); the creation of a new heaven and earth (Rev 21:1; cf. Gen 1:1); the de-creation of the sea (Rev 21:1; cf. Gen 1:2, 10); God dwelling with mortals (Rev 21:3; cf. Gen 3:8); the end of death (Rev 21:4; cf. Gen 2:17; 3:19) and of "mourning and crying and pain" (Rev 21:4; cf. Gen 3:16); "the river of the water of life" (Rev 22:1; cf. Gen 2:10–14); the Tree of Life with its abundant fruit (Rev 22:2; cf. Gen 2:9; 3:22–24); the lifting of curses (Rev 22:3; cf. Gen 3:17); the end of night (Rev 22:5; cf. Gen 1:2–5); and "they need no light of lamp or sun, for the Lord God will be their light" (Rev 22:5; Gen 1:3–5, 14–18).

The common thrust of these references is the restoration of paradise, the lifting of the effects of the fall of Adam and Eve, and the final removal of the serpent, but in a new world order different to that created in Genesis 1–2. This suggests that the conflicts of the story of Genesis 1–3 have been resolved; but the story does not just return to the beginning, it goes on to a new stage, a new creation.[130] For example, John does not depict his saints back in the garden, but in a large city that retains evidence of the history of God's people since Genesis: the tribes of Israel (21:12) and the apostles of Jesus (21:14).

The defeat of the dragon and his beasts in Revelation is thus meant to be the end of the story that began in Genesis. John had a vision of the final resolution of the underlying struggle that drives human history.

He therefore makes continual references to the struggle between God and the devil. Probably the clearest case of this is found in Revelation 12, where a battle in heaven is described, clearly rooted in Old Testament

---

128. This does not require us to take a position on the date of writing of Revelation, which is commonly set in the late A.D. 60s (around the fall of Nero) or the late 90s (during the reign of Domitian). Revelation need not be the last book of the Bible written to be its fitting conclusion.

129. Dumbrell, *End of the Beginning*, Introduction.

130. Ibid., 166; Pattemore, *People of God*, 204.

narratives.[131] The woman at the center of this story, who is persecuted and pursued by the dragon, reminds us of the original woman and the original story of the Fall. Eve was deceived by the serpent (Gen 3:1-6, 13), identified here as the dragon (Rev 12:9; 20:2), and became its permanent enemy (Gen 3:15). Her son, who is to "rule all the nations with a rod of iron" (Rev 12:5) and narrowly escapes being devoured by the dragon at birth (Rev 12:4-5), is probably meant to remind us of the other part of God's promise in Genesis 3:15: "I will put enmity . . . between your offspring and hers; he will strike your head, and you will strike his heel." No wonder the dragon wants to eliminate him![132]

The woman also represents Israel (as shown by the symbolism in Rev 12:1; cf. Gen 37:9), who is always in conflict with her enemies (throughout the Old Testament), and who brings forth the Messiah who will save her from her enemies and "rule all the nations with a rod of iron" (Rev 12:5, referring to Ps 2:8-9). The angelic battle (Rev 12:7-9) clearly alludes to the passages in Daniel where Michael contends with the princes of Persia and Greece, as Israel's patron (Dan 10:13, 20, 21; 12:1), about the future of Israel (Dan 10:14; 12:7; 9:24-27). Similarly, the protection of the woman in the wilderness for "a time, and times, and half a time" (Rev 12:14) alludes not only to Daniel 12:7, but to the wilderness experience of Israel after the exodus and to the promise of a similar encounter with God repeated several times in Isaiah (Isa 35:1-10; 40:3-5; 41:17-20; 43:19-21; 44:3-4), including the promise of protection from floods (Isa 43:2; 12:15-16). Significantly, the woman is saved from the flood that the dragon unleashes by the earth (Rev 12:16), which had been placed under a curse in Genesis 3:17. This implies that the downfall of the serpent/dragon begins to reverse the curses that followed the original Fall of humankind.

The declaration of the victory of the Messiah and his followers over the accuser (Rev 12:10) probably alludes to Zechariah 3, in which Satan accuses the high priest Joshua but is vindicated by God, followed by a promise to "remove the guilt of this land in a single day" (Zech 3:9). The birth of a son to Zion, signifying the people of God who are nursed at Jerusalem's breasts, is also proclaimed in Isaiah 66:7-11.

John appears to be declaring that the decisive battle of the age-old war, which has roots in the Fall of Adam and Eve and was expressed particularly in the history of Israel, has now taken place (or is shortly to take place). As a result the devil has lost his place in heaven (Rev 12:8-9), the Messiah and

---

131. As noted in Fekkes, *Isaiah and Prophetic Traditions*, 60-61 n. 5. Other roots of this episode will be considered in the next chapter.

132. Perhaps there is also an allusion to the story of Herod's attempt to eliminate Jesus in Matt 2:13-18.

his followers have conquered him (Rev 12:10-11), and "his time is short" (Rev 12:12), though in the short term this means that the battle on earth will get hotter (Rev 12:12) as the devil raises a new form of resistance to God through the beasts, including (ironically) the healing of the beast's mortal head wound in defiance of Genesis 3:15. In other words, the ancient war is drawing towards its close.

The Fulfillment of God's Promises and Warnings

Another line of evidence that supports the view that Revelation is consciously completing the main biblical storyline lies in statements made in Revelation indicating that particular promises and warnings of God (from the Hebrew Scriptures) have now been (or are about to be) fulfilled, particularly those that are part of the messianic hope of Israel.

The promises include that of a coming messianic king, which I discussed earlier in this chapter, and of a new and glorious Jerusalem.[133] Promises of eschatological salvation are also seen as fulfilled in Revelation;[134] for example, Rev 7:17 speaks of the Lamb guiding his people to "springs of the water of life" (alluding to Isa 49:10 and possibly Ps 23:1-2),[135] and Rev 22:1-2 describes the river of life, alluding to Ezekiel 47:1-12 (note the healing properties of the leaves in Ezek 47:12; 22:2; and also Zech 14:8).[136] Finally, the promise of new heavens and a new earth (Isa 65:17 and 66:22; 21:1)[137] and the promise of universal worship (Ps 86:8-10; 15:3-4)[138] are both fulfilled in the story told in Revelation.

This attempt to write an ending to history that fulfills God's promises was particularly timely in John's day. The Jews were living in the pain of unfulfilled expectations and dashed hopes of liberation as they languished

---

133. Cf. Rev 3:12; 21:2, 10-27 (alluding to Isa 54:11-17 and 60:17); Rev 21:24-26 (alluding to Isa 60:3, 5, 11); Rev 21:27 (alluding to Joel 3:17); and Rev 22:5; 21:23 (alluding to Isa 60:19 and Zech 14:7). See further discussion in the next chapter, and compare Fekkes, *Isaiah and Prophetic Traditions*, 95-101; Dumbrell, *End of the Beginning*, 1-32.

134. Cf. Fekkes, *Isaiah and Prophetic Traditions*, 91-95.

135. Cf. Moyise, "Psalms in Revelation," 243; Beale, *Revelation*, 442. Comp. Rev 21:6 (alluding to Isa 55:1; cf. Beale, *Revelation*, 1056).

136. Cf. Beale, *Revelation*, 1103-8. Other salvation passages speak of relief from sorrow (Rev 21:4; 7:17, alluding to Isa 35:10 and 65:19), restored presence of God (Rev 21:3, alluding to Ezek 37:27; 43:7; 48:35), the end of death (Rev 21:4, alluding to Isa 25:8), and sonship of God (Rev 21:7, alluding to 2 Sam 7:14). Cf. Beale, *Revelation*, 1049-50, 1046-48, 443, 1057.

137. Cf. Beale, *Revelation*, 1041.

138. Cf. Moyise, "Psalms in Revelation," 235-36; Beale, *Revelation*, 797.

under Roman rule and their rebellion (A.D. 66–70) came to nothing. The Jewish apocalypses put forward their own prophetic theories about the fulfillment of these promises.[139] Meanwhile Christians had made big claims about Jesus, but the unjust anti-God world order persisted and Jesus' second coming was failing to eventuate. Christians were in danger of losing hope. John countered this problem by reinterpreting the messianic hope (spiritualizing it), by declaring the imminence of change (Rev 22:7, 20; 1:3), but also (paradoxically) by predicting a postponed end. Probably the "thousand years" of chapter 20 functions as his attempt to balance the hope of forthcoming victory with the realism of delay in the final goal of history, as seen in the other two biblical locations using this phrase (Ps 90:4; 2 Pet 3:8).[140]

Further, many eschatological warnings in the Old Testament (that is those associated with the "last days" or "Day of the LORD") are seen as fulfilled in the judgments and plagues described in Revelation. The sheer size and scope of these judgments seem to imply that they indicate the approaching end of history.

One key source of such allusions in Revelation is the prophecy of Joel. For instance, the eschatological prophecy in Joel 2:30–31 states, "I will show portents in the heavens and on the earth, blood and fire and columns of smoke. The sun shall be turned into darkness, and the moon to blood, before the great and terrible day of the LORD comes." The next verse talks of escapees and survivors from the terrors of that time (cf. also Joel 3:15; Obad 17). Revelation 6:12 seems to allude to this passage when it says "the sun became black as sackcloth, the full moon became like blood," and 6:15 describes a group of refugees from the imminent wrath of the Lamb[141]; similarly 8:7–9 describes plagues of blood and fire.[142]

Ezekiel is another fruitful source for John's imagery, in which he seems to be inviting the reader to see a fulfillment of prophecy. For example, Ezekiel follows his vision of a restored, resurrected Israel (Ezek 37) with its invasion by "Gog, of the land of Magog" (Ezek 38:3), with a mighty army that is visited with "torrential rains and hailstones, fire and sulfur" (Ezek

---

139. See, for example, *2 Baruch* and *4 Ezra*.

140. Similar balance may be seen in Jesus' words about the end; e.g., comp. Matt 24:32–34 with 24:36, 42, 44, 48, 50; 25:5, 13, 19. See comments in Beale, *Revelation*, 1018; and Newton, "Time Language," 147–68.

141. Cf. Beale, *Revelation*, 396–97. Beale points out that many OT passages are in view here, especially Isa 34:4.

142. Also comp. Joel 3:11–12 with Zech 14:2, 3, 12, 13; and Rev 16:14; 19:19–20; 20:8–9; Joel 2:1–27 with Rev 9. Eschatological judgments are sometimes compared to harvests, especially vintages where the grapes are trodden and pressed (Joel 3:13; Isa 63:3–6), reflected in Rev 14:14–20. Cf. Beale, *Revelation*, 774–79.

38:22), and becomes a feast for birds of prey (Ezek 39:4, 17–20.) John picks up Ezekiel's language in the call to the birds of prey in Revelation 19:17–18, 21 and then in his reference to "Gog and Magog" (Rev 20:8).[143] Both Ezekiel (Ezek 28:11–19) and Isaiah (Isa 14:1–21, esp. v. 12) prophesy the doom of a Satan-like figure in language resembling John's pronouncement of doom on the dragon in Revelation 12:9. In all three cases, a satanic empire is involved: Babylon (Isa 14), Tyre (Ezek 28), and most likely Rome (Rev 13). In these cases and others, we see Revelation describing the fulfillment, and super-fulfillment, of the Old Testament's warnings of judgment, once again implying that the end of the story is here.[144]

These features of Revelation thus point towards the recognition that it is indeed written as the final chapter in a truly epic struggle between light and darkness. It is at least arguable that the Bible opens up just such a story to its readers;[145] certainly John seems to have thought so, based on the evidence from Revelation identified in this chapter so far. Revelation thus seeks to represent the final stage of that story, where the plot's threads are drawn together and its conflicts brought to a head and resolved, accompanied by the most spectacular effects.

This conclusion is not new, though the emphasis on the prolonged tale of conflict is not so pronounced in all versions of Christian salvation history. In fact, it has been argued that this story was "the christianization of an essentially pagan view of salvation history" originally created by Tertullian in the second century.[146] But the issue I want to focus on is what this aspect of Revelation implies for its worldview. For example, the universalism of John's language suggests that this story embraces all nations and peoples. As Pannenberg puts it, "The destiny of mankind, from creation onward, is seen to be unfolding according to a plan of God. The apocalyptic thought conceives of a universal history."[147] This suggests that John is proposing a metanarrative. But before we draw this conclusion too firmly, we need to look at his story another way.

---

143. McIlraith, *Reciprocal Love*, 114. Cf. Rissi, *Time and History*, 116–18; Beale, *Revelation*, 967, 1022–23.

144. Comp. Fekkes, *Isaiah and Prophetic Traditions*, 78–91.

145. See the outlines of this biblical story in Newbigin, *Pluralist Society*, 15; Bartholomew and Goheen, *Drama of Scripture*, 27; VanGemeren, *Progress of Redemption*, 33. Wright (*People of God*, 140–43) suggests it could be outlined in a structure similar to a Shakespearean play in five acts.

146. Hodgson, *God in History*, 15.

147. Pannenberg, "Dogmatic Theses," 132. Pannenberg is talking of apocalyptic thought in general rather than Revelation in particular, but the point is still valid.

Revelation as a Love Story[148]

Few commentators on Revelation have given much attention to the romantic element in the text.[149] As far as I know, only Donal McIlraith has systematically and comprehensively studied its love terminology and love imagery. He concludes that "the major use of the verbs ἀγαπᾶν and φιλεῖν is to describe the link between Jesus and the church"[150] and "the nuptial imagery . . . is the point of arrival of the entire work."[151] My interest is in seeing how this is represented in the *plot* of Revelation.

Interwoven into the story of the struggle between the Lamb and the dragon is a love story: the story of the relationship between the Lamb and his future bride. As McIlraith argues, "The love terminology is used to describe this relationship from beginning to end."[152] One way to set out this plot would look like this:[153]

- Prologue: The excellencies of the Lamb as lover (1:10–18), savior (1:5–6), king (1:5), and ultimate victor (1:7) are displayed in word and visually (ch. 1).

- Introduction: Jesus speaks to his bride in the seven churches, calling her to faithful love and reproving those whose loyalties are lukewarm or divided (chs. 2–3).[154]

- Rising action, part 1: The Lamb is revealed as worthy of adoration as the son of the Great King who sacrificed his life for his bride (chs. 4–5).[155]

- Rising action, part 2: Against a background of rising tension (due to the war against the dragon, which is later to be revealed), the Lamb chooses his bride and "promises her the world" (almost literally) (chs. 6–10, esp. ch. 7).

---

148. A version of this section was first published as Newton, "Reading Revelation Romantically," 194–215.

149. McIlraith, *Reciprocal Love*, 3.

150. Ibid., 17, see also 172.

151. Ibid., 74, see also 143–45.

152. Ibid., 200.

153. Roughly following the dramatic structure first proposed by Gustav Freytag in 1863 for five-act dramas.

154. Cf. McIlraith, *Reciprocal Love*, 35–73, for an analysis of the messages to the seven churches from this perspective.

155. According to McIlraith (ibid., 196), "The Lamb, when first seen in 5, 6 is already the bridegroom fully prepared for the wedding."

- Rising action, part 3: During the time of intense struggle between the Lamb and the dragon, the beloved goes through her own struggles as she is pressured to abandon her love-loyalty to the Lamb in favor of the beast and suffers for her resistance to these pressures (chs. 11–14).
- Rising action, part 4: The Lamb takes action against those who assaulted his future bride (chs. 15–16).
- Rising action, part 5: A contrasting story of false love between the prostitute and the beast, which ends in rape and murder (17:1—19:5). This is a warning to the true bride not to be seduced by the beast and thus become part of the prostitute,[156] sharing her fate (18:4).
- Climax: As the marriage banns for the Lamb and his bride are published, the wedding gown is purchased, and the wedding invitations are sent out, there is a final battle between the Lamb (represented by the rider on the white horse)[157] and the beasts (19:6–21).
- Falling action: The true bride, who has proved loyal to the Lamb even under intense pressure, is vindicated and participates in his rule (ch. 20)—but not without an exciting rescue from impending disaster (20:7–9).
- Epilogue: The marriage finally takes place and is consummated (21:1—22:5).

Conclusion: Moral application of the story—the call to faithful love is matched by the longing call of the bride (22:6–21).[158]

The Love Story Ending

The final episodes of the story may be said to bring this plot to its conclusion in the same stages as the war story, though slightly after, in that the marriage cannot take place until the victory of the Lamb is completed. The conflict in this story is resolved by the vindication of the faithfulness of the true bride. As in the war plot, there is a happy ending (22:5.)

Literary features of the final chapters (19:6—22:5) mark the ending of this particular narrative. First, promises (or warnings) given to the seven

---

156. Cf. ibid., 48.

157. Interestingly, the Lamb's armies are dressed in the same clothing as the bride (Rev 19:8, 14). This suggests that both pictures refer to the same people, that is, Christians. Cf. McIlraith, *Reciprocal Love*, 84; Beale, *Revelation*, 960; Aune, *Revelation 17-22*, 1059. On the relation between the battle and the wedding, see McIlraith, *Reciprocal Love*, 87–88, which sees an allusion to Ps 45.

158. Cf. McIlraith, *Reciprocal Love*, 164.

churches, many of which can be read as lover's promises, are described as fulfilled by the end of the story. For example, the Book of Life (20:12, 15; 21:27, reflecting 3:5), the Tree of Life (22:2, reflecting 2:7), the secret name (19:12, reflecting 2:17), the promise of reigning with Christ (20:4, 6, reflecting 2:26–28), white robes (19:8,14, reflecting 3:4–5, 18), the New Jerusalem coming down from heaven (21:2, 10, reflecting 3:12), and the name of the Lamb on the foreheads of his servants (22:4, reflecting 3:12; 14:1).

There are also allusions to earlier stages of the narrative, as far back as the first chapter. Examples relevant to this love theme include the blessing on those invited to the marriage supper (19:9, reflecting 1:3), the promise of "the water of life" (21:6; 22:1, reflecting 7:17), "he will wipe every tear from their eyes" (21:4, reflecting 7:17), and the names of the twelve tribes on the gates of the New Jerusalem (21:12, reflecting 7:4).

The announcement of the impending marriage (19:7–9), which comes just after the disastrous love affair between the great whore and the beast, particularly indicates that the true, virtuous, loyal bride of the Lamb will now be rewarded for her faithfulness. She has resisted the pressures and enticements of the beast (13:8, 13–17; 14:4, 9–13) and the whore (14:8; 18:4). She has now prepared herself[159] and she has been granted clothing of "fine linen, bright and clear." The climax of the love relationship between the Lamb and his bride is drawing near.

The love story closes with the description of the New Jerusalem "prepared as a bride adorned for her husband" (21:2),[160] carefully placed after the passing away of "the first heaven and the first earth" (21:1).[161] The description is fleshed out in 21:9-21, where the glories of the bride/city are celebrated: "It has the glory of God and a radiance like a very rare jewel, like jasper, clear as crystal" (21:11), and "a high wall with twelve gates" and "twelve foundations" (21:12, 14). While these phrases mainly serve to illuminate the features and roots of the *city*, they also imply that the *bride* is well protected, unlike the whore in chapters 17–18, who trusted in her false security (18:7-8).[162] This city/bride is also well proportioned (21:15-17), with a wall "built of jasper, while the city is pure gold, clear as glass" (21:18).

---

159. Compare the process described for a royal bride's preparation in Esth 2:3, 12. McIlraith (ibid., 96–98, 109–111, 185–200) places all this against the background of Hebrew marriage customs.

160. McIlraith (ibid., 123, 131–41, 164) draws attention to the two stages of the descent of the New Jerusalem: a tent (Gk. σκηνὴ, 21:3), followed by a city (Gk. πόλιν, 21:10, etc.). This of course parallels the dwelling of God in the OT, first in a tent then in a city temple.

161. Cf. the amusing account in Raber, "Revelation 21:1–8," 296.

162. Comp. Song 8:8–10.

"The foundations of the wall of the city are adorned with every jewel" (21:19) and "the twelve gates are twelve pearls . . . and the street of the city is pure gold, transparent as glass" (21:21).

Finally, we read the description of her final rapturous state as the wife of the Lamb (21:22—22:5). She lives in the constant presence of the Lamb and his Father (21:22). Her husband is never absent and always visible (22:3-4), and God personally "will wipe every tear from their eyes" (21:4), evidencing an unprecedented intimacy.[163] She basks in his warmth and light (21:23; 22:5), inherits all the glory of the nations (21:24, 26; unlike the whore, who loses all her glories), lives in perpetual daylight totally secure from all evil (21:25, 27; 22:5), and enjoys the waters of life (22:1-2) and the Tree of Life (22:2). She bears the name of her bridegroom (22:4)[164] and she reigns with him as queen forever (22:5). Rudolph Raber sums it up well: "*The* Church Wedding is coming off! Here comes the Bride and the Bride is us, consort and housekeeper, lover and homemaker, God's residence on earth and with *tōn anthrōpōn*."[165]

Moreover this reading of Revelation's ending is enhanced by the many allusions in these passages to the love poem Song of Solomon, which erotically[166] describes the developing relationship between Solomon and the Shulammite,[167] and has often been interpreted as a kind of allegory (or type) of God's love for Israel.[168] The language in Song of Solomon about the male (Song 1:3; 2:8-9; 5:9-16) and the female lover (Song 1:5-6, 9-11, 15; 4:1-15; 6:4-10; 7:1-8) apparently lies behind some of John's imagery. For example, the girl in the poem is adorned with jewels (Song 1:10-11; 4:9; 7:1; cf. Rev 21:18-21) and often described in terms of a building (Song 4:4; 7:4; 8:10; cf. Rev 21:12-14, 17-18), the city of Jerusalem (Song 6:4; cf. Rev 21:2, 10), an army (Song 6:4,10; cf. Rev 14:15; 19:14), a mountain (Song 7:5; cf. Rev 21:10), or a garden with water (Song 4:12, 15; cf. Rev 22:1-2).

Actions in the Song are also alluded to in Revelation. For example, John, as a representative of the bride, faints with awe at the glorious appearance of the royal Lover (Rev 1:17; cf. Song 5:8), and the description of Jesus

---

163. Cf. Raber, "Revelation 21:1-8," 299–300.

164. Compare Rev 3:12; 7:3; 13:16-18; 14:1, 9. Taking the name on the forehead speaks in this book of covenant loyalty, of being "married" either to the beast or the Lamb. Beale (*Revelation*, 1114) takes it to refer to God's protecting presence, which to me is a consequence of covenant.

165. Raber, "Revelation 21:1-8," 301.

166. See Boer, *Knockin' on Heaven's Door*, 56–58, for a very erotic reading of the language of the Song of Solomon.

167. Carr, *Song of Solomon*, 34–41.

168. Cf. ibid., 21–32.

knocking at the door of the Laodicean church is highly reminiscent of Song 5:2–8, where the girl fails to respond to the urgent knock of her lover and is shaken up by a beating from the sentinels of the city as she goes in search of him (cf. Rev 3:19).[169] The promised return of Christ, matched by the bride's longing, also reflects the language of the Song (see, for example, Song 2:8; 8:14; Rev 22:17, 20b).

Love Stories in the Ancient World

This romantic reading of Revelation is supported by a comparison with love stories in the ancient world. Scholars debate whether or not there was a recognized *genre* of love stories in the ancient world.[170] However, what is not debatable is the existence of love stories.

First, there were the Greek romantic novels, such as Longus' *Daphnis and Chloe* (late second century), Xenophon's *Ephesian Romance* (second century), and Chariton's *Chaereas and Callirhoe* (first century, roughly contemporary with Revelation).[171] B. P. Reardon summarizes such prose romance stories as follows:

> a handsome youth and a beautiful girl meet by chance and fall in love, but unexpected obstacles obstruct their union; they are separated, and each is launched on a series of journeys and dangerous adventures; through all their tribulations, however, they remain faithful to each other and to the benevolent deities who at critical junctures guide their steps; and eventually they are reunited and live happily ever after.[172]

The romantic novel can be traced back possibly to the late Hellenistic period, and disappeared after the third century,[173] but love stories form part of larger narratives also, such as ancient epics[174] and various works of his-

---

169. Cf. McIlraith, *Reciprocal Love*, 63–64.

170. To follow this debate see Reardon, *Greek Romance*, 7,10, 46–50, 57, 84–91; Konstan, "Invention of Fiction," 3; Hock, "Ancient Novels," 122; and Anderson, *Ancient Fiction*, 25–26.

171. Cf. Reardon, *Greek Romance*, 4; Konstan, "Invention of Fiction," 13; Hock, "New Testament Scholars," 124; Thomas, "Stories without Texts," 274; and Tolbert, *Sowing the Gospel*, 62–65, for discussion of the dates and other examples of this genre.

172. Reardon, *Greek Romance*, 5, see also 25, 100. Cf. Anderson, *Ancient Fiction*, 2. For a summary that emphasizes more the social dimension of the novels, see Hock, "Greek Novel," 134.

173. Reardon, *Greek Romance*, 7.

174. Cf. ibid., 15–16, 128–29.

toriography and biography,[175] as well as drama (especially comedy)[176] and poetry.[177] Moreover there is evidence that the Greek romantic novel actually has roots in the ancient tales of the Sumerian, Babylonian, and Egyptian civilizations.[178]

There are also love stories in Jewish literature. One early example is Jacob's loving quest for Rachel, summed up in the poignant words, "So Jacob served seven years for Rachel, and they seemed to him but a few days because of the love he had for her" (Gen 29:20). Later the Book of Ruth tells the story not only of Ruth's faithfulness to her mother-in-law, but also of her successful courting of the middle-aged Boaz within the mores of the Israelite culture of the Judges period. Later, the Book of Tobit recounts, among other things, the courtship and marriage of Tobit's son with a young woman named Sarah, telling us that "he fell so deeply in love with her that he could no longer call his heart his own" (Tob 6:18 JB). The book of *Joseph and Aseneth* attempts to tell the story behind Joseph's marriage to Aseneth daughter of an Egyptian priest (Gen 41:45, 50).

Features of Ancient Love Stories

According to Reardon, each Greek romance contained four "essential structural elements"[179] adapted from drama: problem, conflict, development, and solution.[180] While there is a lot of variation in both ancient romance novels and other manifestations of the love story in antiquity, certain features may be said to be generic to them all:

a) *Two persons, male and female*—usually young[181]—whose relationship is central to the plot.

b) *The romantic and sexual attraction* between them, based on their beauty.[182] For example, in *Chaereas and Callirhoe*, she is "an astonishingly

---

175. Ibid., 5–6, 147–49.

176. Ibid., 6, 50–52, 130–31. See also Anderson, *Ancient Fiction*, 38.

177. Reardon, *Greek Romance*, 135–37.

178. Anderson, *Ancient Fiction*, 13, 19, 38, 217–19. Hock ("Greek Novel," 130), however, casts some doubt on Anderson's thesis. See also Konstan, "Invention of Fiction," 4.

179. Reardon, *Greek Romance*, 102.

180. Ibid., 102–3.

181. An exception is the story of Ruth and Boaz, where particular emphasis is placed on her loyalty to family as opposed to romantic love and youth (Ruth 3:9–10).

182. Shea, "Setting the Stage," 68; Reardon, *Greek Romance*, 26, 138–40. This is seen as the problem in New Comedy and romance novels (Reardon, *Greek Romance*, 103).

beautiful young maiden" whose beauty "was not human but divine," while he "surpassed all the others in his physique."[183]

c) *Problems and misunderstandings* in the relationship. In *Joseph and Aseneth*, for instance, Aseneth's first reaction to the thought of being married to Joseph is one of fury, based on her prejudice and misinformation about him.[184] Such problems are often related to a period of physical separation.[185]

d) *Other characters who assist or impede the progress* of the love relationship. For example, Tobias' proposal to marry Sarah is prompted and facilitated by the angel Raphael disguised as a relative (Tob 6:10–7:10). In contrast, Rachel's father tricks Jacob into taking her uglier sister Leah first (Gen 29:21–26).[186] Often complications are caused by the presence of a femme fatale.[187]

e) *A range of literary devices* designed to keep the reader's attention and interest,[188] especially frequent use of speeches.[189]

f) *Background of ancient Mediterranean society*, especially in the period from classical Greece to the early Roman Empire, and its conflicts and customs.[190] The novels reveal the society of their time "by writing *in* it and unconsciously reflecting it, its assumptions, its aspirations."[191]

g) *The role of gods*. The role of Fate and Fortune, seen as gods, is particularly prominent in Greek novels, and the heroes also successfully call on the help of various deities in tight situations.[192] In the Jewish stories, the blessing of God is sought and sometimes angels assist the love story.

---

183. *Chaer.*, 1.1.1–3, as quoted in Hock, "Greek Novel," 134–35.

184. *Jos. Asen.* 4:11–16.

185. Seen as the conflict (Reardon, *Greek Romance*, 104). Separation is a key motif of the Song of Solomon (1:7; 3:1–4; 5:1—6:3), though it is more intermittent than in some of the Greek novels.

186. Compare Anderson, *Ancient Fiction*, 66–68.

187. Reardon, *Greek Romance*, 26, 82.

188. Ibid., 27.

189. Hock, "Greek Novel," 133. Compare the long and emotional speeches in the Song of Solomon and the lament of Sarah (who has lost seven husbands before consummating her marriages) in Tob 3:11–17.

190. Hock, "Ancient Novels," 124–25; idem "Greek Novel," 138–44.

191. Reardon, *Greek Romance*, 13.

192. Anderson, *Ancient Fiction*, 75–78; Tolbert, *Sowing the Gospel*, 64.

h) *Conflicts, dangers and rivalry*;[193] for example, pressure from others to betray or break up the relationship, or dangerous encounters (even apparent death) for either or both of the couple.[194]

i) *A developing plot*[195] that includes adventures, dangers, reverses, crises, fortunate turns, parallel narratives, and other features, and in most cases a lot of travel,[196] which all builds towards the ultimate climax.

j) *A climax* where the conflicts and problems come to a head and are resolved. This often includes a final "recognition scene" (or scenes) that allows the lovers to be reunited.[197]

k) *A happy ending* in which the lovers are united and their love vindicated.[198] Romances thus followed comedy rather than tragedy; the negative events in the plot heighten suspense but are not fatal.[199] Also the happy ending was justified theologically: the gods could be relied on to see that true love won out in the end.[200]

Parallels in the Developing Plot of Revelation

The above elements of the ancient love story are all arguably represented in some way in the story of Revelation:

a) *Two persons, male and female.* Jesus takes the part of the male lover in the story, initiating the love relationship and creating the basis for it to come about (1:5; 5:9). He is portrayed as the royal prince, "the ruler of the kings of the earth" (1:5), unimaginably glorious and fearsome (1:10–17), and the all-conquering warrior (19:11–16). The female role

---

193. On handling rivals, see Anderson, *Ancient Fiction*, 65.

194. E.g., the threat of death for Tobias when he goes in to his newly wedded wife Sarah (Tob 6:14–15; 7:10–11), such that his father-in-law even starts digging a grave for him "just in case" (Tob 8:9–14).

195. Cf. Anderson, *Ancient Fiction*, 122–27.

196. Reardon, *Greek Romance*, 5, 104–105,141.

197. Cf. Tolbert, *Sowing the Gospel*, 75–76, which finds parallels in Mark's Gospel concerning the recognition of the identity of Jesus.

198. "Every incursion only leads inexorably to the final chapter, the reunion of those who have been separated," writes Douglas Edwards ("Pleasurable Reading," 41) about *Chaereas and Callirhoe*.

199. Reardon, *Greek Romance*, 81.

200. Ibid., 5, 81. Compare the endings of the Song of Solomon and *Joseph and Aseneth*. On the other hand, the story of Jacob and Rachel has a more ambiguous ending, and Rachel dies prematurely in giving birth (Gen 35:16–20), just as Jacob is coming into his inheritance.

(the bride) is taken by the church or Christians. She gains value primarily from the grace of her Lover (1:5; 5:9–10). While she vacillates in her response to him, she ultimately proves herself worthy of his love (19:7–8) and is described also in highly imaginative language as the bride (21:9—22:5).

b) *The romantic and "sexual" attraction* between them. The relationship portrayed in Revelation between Christ and his bride is portrayed in romantic, even sexual terms. The Lover (Christ) initiates the love relationship (1:5), but Jesus demands nothing less than abandoned passion for himself from his church (2:4–5; 3:15–16), and its best representatives respond accordingly (such as the 144,000 in 14:1–5; their status as virgins may represent their exclusive devotion to the Lamb).[201]

c) *Problems and misunderstandings* in the relationship. There are many problems in the relationship, all on the side of the bride,[202] because this Lover is always faithful. In the messages to the churches, John identifies such problems as abandonment of their first love (2:4–5),[203] flirtation with other lovers (2:14–16, 20–22), unconscious death of their love (3:1–3), lukewarmness in their attitude (3:15–16), and failure to welcome or respond to the Lover (3:20). There is also an emphasis on the physical separation between the bride and the Lover as they overcome the difficulties and problems their relationship faces and await the time of final union. The Lamb's visible return is delayed (1:7); though he is accessible in the Spirit (1:10; 2:7 and parallels; 4:2) and his people can have communion with him (3:20), there is still the implication of absence in his promises and threats to "come" (2:5, 16, 25; 3:3, 11; 16:15; 22:7, 12, 20) and in his hovering just out of range (14:1,14; 19:11–16,19). His absence increases the danger for the bride: she is vulnerable to be slaughtered (6:9–11; 13:15), conquered by the beast (13:7), and threatened with captivity (13:10) and economic deprivation (13:17). However, she is to some degree protected by him even in his absence, provided that she remains faithful (3:10; 7:3–4; 13:8; 18:4).

d) *Other characters who assist or impede the progress* of the love relationship (often including a femme fatale). The femme fatale in Revelation is represented by the "great whore" who makes the inhabitants of the earth drunk with the wine of her fornication (17:2; 18:3). She clearly

---

201. Comp. McIlraith, *Reciprocal Love*, 82–83.
202. This also parallels the Song of Solomon.
203. Cf. McIlraith, *Reciprocal Love*, 39–45.

has a powerful attraction for which sexual terms[204] are appropriate and to which members of the true bride are vulnerable (18:4).[205] Other characters in our story include the beast (the rival of the Lamb for the loyalty of the bride) and the dragon (his evil controller), who persecute the true bride and wage war on the Lamb, and (on the other side) the two witnesses and the woman who gives birth to the male child, both of whom in some way symbolize, represent, or assist the true bride; and a cast of angels. Each side of the conflict also has its local representatives in the seven churches: the false Jews, the Nicolaitans, and Jezebel (another femme fatale who successfully seduces some believers)[206] on one side, Antipas and the conquerors among the churches on the other.

e) *A range of literary devices* designed to keep the reader's attention and interest. Some of the devices specifically related to the love story are the vision of the Lamb-Lover (1:10-20), John's bitter weeping over the sealed scroll, which introduces the Lamb (5:3-5), the majestic hymns, especially in honor of the Lamb (5:9-10, 12, 13; 7:10; 12:10-12), the passages where the bride is in danger (12; 13:7-8, 15-17), the lurid description of the "great whore" (17:3-6), and the tantalizing promises of Christ's coming (1:7; 16:15; 22:7, 20). These also heighten suspense, which is never fully relieved; at the end of the story, we still haven't seen the coming actually happen.[207] There are also speeches, including the bride's cry at the end to the Lover (22:17, 20b), Jesus' seven speeches to the specific churches in Asia (chs. 2-3), and the numerous speeches by heavenly beings, praising the Lamb-Lover (5:9, 10, 12, 13), encouraging the bride (7:14-17; 13:10; 14:13; 18:4; 19:6-9), heralding the end of the story (10:5-7; 11:15-18; 12:10-12; 15:3-4;

---

204. As well as economic terms (Rev 18:3, 11-19, 23).

205. McIlraith (McIlraith, *Reciprocal Love*, 21-23, 28) argues that Christ's loving redemptive work takes believers out of Babylon and brings them into relationship with himself (comp. Rev 1:5 and 18:4-5, linked by the plural "sins," which occurs only in these places in the text). Thus Christ's love is actually offered to the harlot with a view to redemption. This places the harlot in a different structural role than I am suggesting. The emphasis on Rev 18 is clearly on the coming judgment of the harlot and the need for Christians to dissociate themselves from her, rather than on the possibilities of the harlot being redeemed.

206. Rev 2:20-24.

207. Most commentators take Rev 19:11-21 (the passage about the rider on the white horse) as referring to the second coming of Christ. If this is so, it doesn't mention common features associated with this coming elsewhere (1:7) and the next character mentioned is an angel, not Christ (20:1). At the end of the book, the Spirit and the bride are still crying out for the coming to happen (22:17, 20).

21:3-4), and pronouncing doom on the enemies of God and of the lovers (14:8-11; 16:5-7; 17:7-18; 18:2-8, 21-24; 19:2-3; 22:10-11).

f) *Background of ancient Mediterranean society* and its conflicts and customs. Both persons in the relationship have their place in the wider society, which affects each of them and their relationship. In this case, the Lover is also the heavenly royal prince (1:5)[208] with many governmental responsibilities (as shown in his opening of the seven seals in 6) and constant military campaigns (as in 19:11-21). The girl is also a subject of the Roman Empire (ch. 13). The bride is frequently caught up in the cause of the Lover (19:14; 20:4) and suffers from her association with him (6:9-11; 13-14; 16:6; 17:6; 18:24; 19:2). Moreover the story is clearly set in the ancient Mediterranean Greco-Roman world with the constant threat of war (16:12), a society built on slavery (6:15; 18:13), trade (6:15; 18:11-19), and violence (6:4,9,15), and held together by the rule of Rome (13:7; 17:9-18), which at times came close to breaking down (13:3; 17:16). There is also the Jewish background: synagogues (2:9; 3:9), the twelve tribes (7:4-8; 21:12), the temple (11:1-2), Jerusalem (11:2, 8) and so on.

g) *The role of deity.* As in both Greek and Jewish romances, the whole plot is supervised by deity, who can also be called on when the lovers are in trouble. We noted previously[209] the strong sense of God's sovereign direction in the story (1:1; 22:10). God also intervenes at some dangerous moments on behalf of the lovers; for example, restraining the winds and angels while the 144,000 are sealed (7:1-4), snatching the infant Christ away from his would-be killer (12:4-6), protecting the infant's mother from the dragon (12:6,13-16), and sending down fire when the bride is besieged (20:9). However, as in the romance novels, this intervention is selective; both the lover and the bride still suffer: he sheds his blood for her (5:9; 12:11) and she suffers persecution on his behalf (13:7-10). Moreover God takes a particular personal interest in this love relationship as the Father of the Groom (1:6; 2:18, 28; 3:5) and (paradoxically) the one who "gives away the bride" (3:12; 21:2, 10). He issues the invitations to the wedding (19:9) and he will dwell with the married couple after their wedding as a paternal protector (21:3-4, 22; 22:3, 5).

h) *Conflicts and rivalry.* This is at the heart of the plot of Revelation. All the way through the book, the bride is being pressured to be unfaithful

---

208. Comp. Song 3:6-9.
209. In chapter 5.

to her Lover. For example, John writes of the allurement of false teaching that produces spiritual, if not literal, fornication (2:6, 14, 15, 20, 21), which is a betrayal of the Lover (2:14, 20). The bride suffers persecution by the enemies of the Lover; the call in such occasions is for faithfulness[210] (2:10, 13; 13:10) or endurance (13:10; 14:12), as she is tempted to betray or abandon her Lover under such pressure, in which her very life is under threat (2:10; 6:9–11; 12:11; 13:10, 15). There is a combination of seduction and persecution organized by the Lamb's archenemy Satan (the dragon), through his agents the beasts, designed to bring all people into allegiance to himself (ch. 13) and so effective that only the true members of the bride will be able to withstand it (13:8). Allied to this is the pressure to be part of the "great whore" of Babylon, the mistress of the beast and an intoxicating lover (17:1–6; 18:3–4). The true bride is called on to "come out of her" (18:4) and remain faithful to her Lover (17:14), since ultimately the relationship between the whore and the beast breaks down with extreme sexual violence (17:16). The threat of death (real or apparent) affects the bride (6:9–11; 11:7–10; 12:13–16; 13:15; 16:6) and the Lover (5:9; 12:4–5; 19:13), but it is unable to defeat their love (11:11–12; 12:11; 14:13; 15:2; 19:7–8; 20:4).

i) *A developing plot* that builds towards the ultimate climax. Some of the stock plot features similar to those in the ancient romances include conflicts with enemies (2:2–3), slanderous accusations against the lovers (2:9), imprisonment (2:10), captivity (13:10), death (2:b13; 6:9; 13:10; 17:6), warfare (6:4; 13:7; 14:20; 19:11–14), sieges (20:9), invasions (9:14–19; 16:12), famines (6:6, 8), attacks by wild animals (6:8), earthquakes (6:12; 16:18–19), people hiding in caves and mountains (6:15), volcanic eruptions (8:7–9), eclipses (8:12), locust plagues (9:3–11), escapes from death (11:7–12; 13:3), fleeing from dangerous enemies (12:6, 14), floods (12:15), signs from heaven (11:5–6; 13:13–14), fierce heat waves (16:8–9), political machinations (13:1–18; 17:8–18), and destruction of cities (14:8; 16:19; 18:2, 8, 21–23). Travel is rarely mentioned (except perhaps in 14:4). However, just as in the Greek novels, the whole Greco-Roman world is the stage for the adventures (5:9; 7:9; 9:14; 11:9; 13:7–8; 14:6; 20:8). Special attention is given to specific locations: Jerusalem (11:8; 21:10), Babylon (14:8; 16:19; 17:5, 18; 18:2, 10, 21), the Euphrates River (9:14; 16:12), and the seven cities of Asia (1:11, chs. 2–3). There are also many references to geographical

---

210. Or faith. The Greek is the same.

movement (6:2, 15; 9:14–15; 12:6, 13–14; 13:1; 14:4, 20; 16:12–16; 18:17–19; 19:11–14,17–19; 20:7–9; 21:24–26).

j) *A climax* where the conflicts and problems come to a head and are resolved. Most commentators agree that the story climaxes in chapter 19 with the penultimate battle that makes way for the marriage of the Lamb and his bride.[211] Moreover the unveiling of the rider on the white horse (19:11–16) may be seen to function somewhat like a "recognition scene" in Homer or the romance novels.

k) *A happy ending* in which the lovers are united and their love vindicated. This has also been discussed above.

The above evidence shows that the storyline of Revelation has many parallels to ancient romances, both Greek and Jewish. Moreover there are similarities in the style and language used, in particular the repetitive use of sentences beginning with *kai* ("and"), also found in Mark's Gospel.[212] Whether or not John was acquainted with the ancient Greek romance novels or their forebears in Sumerian or Babylonian mythical stories, he must have been acquainted with at least some Jewish romantic stories. Moreover it seems evident that this "popular prose genre . . . produced and distributed throughout the eastern Mediterranean" would have been familiar to the *audience* of a text like Revelation with their Hellenistic background.[213] Thus John was writing popular literature designed to be accessible to a wide audience, not just an esoteric apocalypse.[214] What conclusions flow from this?

I am not suggesting that Revelation falls into the genre of ancient romance novels or that John consciously wrote a romance novel in disguise: in spite of the similarities, the purpose is different. Moreover it is obvious that John's focus is much broader than a simple story: he is writing on an epic scale. He is telling a "mega-romance," where everything is larger than life, as is indicated by his propensity for the use of the word "mega" (Gk. μέγα, large, great), which in some form or other he uses seventy-two times in the book.[215]

---

211. Cf. Newton "Time Language"; Beale, *Revelation*, 949.

212. Cf. Tolbert, *Sowing the Gospel*, 42, 68. Tolbert points out that such literary devices are part of Greek rhetorical theory, related to the fact that texts were written to be read aloud (ibid., 43–44). Other stylistic similarities between Mark and the ancient novel (ibid., 65–69, 74–78) apply also to Revelation.

213. Ibid., 63, see also 66, 69. As Tolbert points out, later Christian literature such as the *Acts of Paul and Thecla* follow similar plot patterns to the romance novels, almost to the point of becoming "an antitype of the erotic novel" (ibid., 69 n. 74).

214. Cf. ibid., 70–72.

215. Including twenty uses with φωνὴν (voice or sound), thus "with a loud voice"; not including uses as a prefix describing "great" people.

So what might John have been trying to achieve by including this love theme in his prophetic-apocalyptic mega-epic? Most likely he was seeking to encourage his readers and hearers in the seven churches to embrace a radical commitment to Jesus, motivated by (spiritual) love and expressed in faith, endurance, service, and witness,[216] that would withstand both the opposition and the seduction of the Greco-Roman culture around them (as symbolized by the beast and the whore).

But he was doing this in the context of his sense of a bigger narrative through the whole Bible. This bigger story has already been touched on with respect to the war story side of Revelation. Can the main plot of the biblical narrative also be interpreted as a love story?

Revelation as the Final Chapter of a Love Story

I have already argued, with respect to its war theme, that Revelation positions itself as the final chapter of a much larger narrative contained in the Christian Scriptures as a whole. I now want to explore reading the same Big Story as a romance, with a view to relating this to the question of metanarrative.

The evidence in this case is less abundant, but the picture of God as a Lover and his people Israel as his (often unfaithful) wife is found intermittently through the Old Testament, especially in the prophets.[217] For instance, Hosea is based on the parallel between the prophet's failed marriage and the unfaithfulness of Israel to their husband God. Ezekiel 23 is the story of two daughters who, though "they became mine" (Ezek 23:4), behaved like prostitutes with the young men of Assyria and Babylon, by whom they are eventually destroyed (language reminiscent of Rev 17:15–16).[218]

This theme is also found in Jesus' parables, especially the wedding feast to which the invited guests refused to come (Matt 22:1–14; Luke 14:15–24; cf. Rev 19:9) and the ten bridesmaids (Matt 25:1–12). It is also reflected in Jesus' relationship with his disciples, male (John 13:23; 20:2; 21:15–19) and female (Matt 26:6–13; Luke 7:36–50; 10:39–42; John 12:1–8), his demands for radical loyalty to himself (Luke 14:25; 18:22, 28), and in his lament over Jerusalem (Matt 23:37; Luke 19:41–42).

---

216. McIlraith (*Reciprocal Love*, 182) maintains that, "Together these works constitute the core of Christ's works given to individuals... and keeping or maintaining them constitutes overcoming, νικῶν."

217. Cf. ibid., 95–96.

218. See also Isa 5:1–7; Jer 2:1; 31:31. Cf. Dumbrell, *End of the Beginning*, 90.

Finally, Paul in several places views the church or the individual believer as betrothed or married to Christ (Rom 7:1-4; 2 Cor 11:2; Eph 5:23-32), and he follows the lead of Hosea in declaring God's patience and faithfulness to Israel in spite of Israel's unfaithfulness to God (Rom 3:3; 9:25-26; 10:21; 11:25-29).

So it seems reasonable to retell the Bible story as a tale of God reaching out in love to a resistant world, an unfaithful Israel, and an inconsistent church. Even his wrath may be seen as the anger of a jealous husband. And if this is so, then it follows that Revelation can be read as the final chapter in that love story, since it contains allusions to these themes in other parts of Scripture. As McIlraith claims, John transfers an existing tradition of the love between God and Israel to the Lamb.[219] Consider, for example, the allusions to the Song of Solomon (referred to above), the theme of the wedding banquet (Rev 19:8; cf. Isa 25:6), and the allusions to the fate of unfaithful Israel/Judah in the story of the whore of Babylon (Rev 17:1, 2, 16).

As McIlraith concludes (writing particularly about Rev 10:7),

> This is the μυστήριον, God's great plan of salvation. In the Apocalypse its final shape is seen to be nuptial. This prophetic symbol of the covenant is the one chosen to express the final, eschatological fulfillment of all the covenant promises and hopes.[220]

Now if Revelation is written in part as a mega-romance, and as the conclusion to a larger love story in the Bible as a whole, what implications does this have for the idea that Revelation implies the existence of an overarching Christian metanarrative?

It may be argued that this love story is not presented as The Story of the whole human family. Rather, both in Revelation and elsewhere in the Bible, and in keeping with the whole idea of romance, this is a story of election: it portrays the love relationship between God/Christ and a section of humanity (Israel/church,) excluding the rest. Thus, for example, the elect are to "come of her, my people" (18:4): John is insistent on believers having no truck with the wider society and its values. So perhaps this dtory is a particular narrative (one among many) rather than a metanarrative.

On the other hand, we must note the inclusive language of Revelation, which tends to balance its more particularist language[221] and implies that any person could be a member of the bride of the Lamb; certainly it is an

---

219. McIlraith, *Reciprocal Love*, 96.

220. Ibid., 184.

221. See the comments in Bauckham, *Climax*, 238–337, where Bauckham presses the universalist language as far as it will go. Cf. Rissi, *Time and History*, 124–34.

international company (5:9; 7:9; 15:4; 21:24–26).[222] This story does therefore include everyone (at least in principle): everyone is either part of the bride or part of the whore or the beast, that is, either a lover of Christ or his enemy, in keeping with John's dualism, as the language of the final judgment seems to demand (20:11–15), and in keeping with the gendered nature of reality in John's worldview.

Thus the love story in Revelation is vulnerable to criticism by feminists in particular. Certainly the partners in the romance are far from equal, and it is the male who is idealized, the female who is weak and at times inconsistent. Feminist critics also point to the threats of the Lover, especially in his addresses to the seven churches, some of which involve violence, even perhaps sexual violence (2:5, 16, 22, 23; 3:3, 19), as well as John's other "misogynist" imagery, such as the cannibal rape in 17:16. John follows the conventions of his day, of the romance genre, and of the earlier parts of the Christian Scriptures here; as Tina Pippin says, "The ideology of the female in the Apocalypse remains true to the dominant ideology of its culture."[223]

A twenty-first-century author might choose different imagery to make her point, though it must be insisted that the theology of Revelation demands a portrayal of Jesus in transcendent, authoritative, and romantic (loving) terms. He and his bride cannot be equal; rather, as McIlraith puts it, "The Church is a dependent reality, drawing its existence moment by moment from the ἀγαπῶν, the foundational constant loving activity of Christ."[224] The romance language is covenant language and there is no equality between God and his people.[225]

METANARRATIVE, THEN?

I have been arguing that John's war romance epic is presented as the concluding chapter of a much larger Story threaded through the Bible. Further, there are suggestions in both Revelation and other Bible texts that this is meant to include the stories of all peoples, at least in a sense of a frame or a main plot. In other words, this Story is given priority among the narratives of humanity from a God-centered perspective. Moreover this Story clearly is used throughout the Bible (including Revelation) to explain and justify

---

222. See comments in McIlraith, *Reciprocal Love*, 188.
223. Pippin, "Heroine and Whore," 77.
224. McIlraith, *Reciprocal Love*, 41.
225. McIlraith (ibid., 131) sees the covenant inequality as "overcome in the marriage image," but this is to import a modern concept of equality between sexes into an ancient context. More appropriate is his use of "parity" or "reciprocal" love.

the existence of Israel and the Christian church in terms of their role in the plot. And it is a Story going somewhere: history, according to this perspective, has a goal and destination.

Perhaps the love story found in Revelation qualifies this line of thought. The Story has little in common with a philosophy of history as found in, say, Hegel, so it might be argued. It is told for the purpose of dramatically drawing its readers into a relationship with God and Christ rather than imparting the meaning of history. Similarly, Gilbertson criticizes the idea that New Testament writers like John were making a "conscious attempt . . . to set out an account of the progression of salvation history." He argues, rather, that in Revelation "the stress . . . is heavily upon the *imminence* of the end time events . . . rather than upon a sense of historical *development*."[226]

But this is surely a false antithesis. John's sense of history is represented by his desire to tell the end of the Story, which he sees as imminent. McIlraith is more on track when he suggests that Revelation "presents the Church with a set of prophetic symbols by which it can . . . understand and evaluate the Christian meaning of history."[227]

If we broaden our perspective to the whole of the Bible, we must concede that it is a book of many plots and perspectives, not all of them logically consistent, and it never attempts to explain everything.[228] Even the readings I have just proposed of the plot of Revelation require a measure of simplification and do not explain every aspect of that text. Nonetheless this way of interpreting the Bible offers a solid intellectual grounding for Christian hope.

Hodgson, who is "highly critical of overarching, linear teleologies,"[229] agrees that "a Christian theology of history must take up the quest for a way beyond tragedy" since "its mode of historical emplotment is comic, not romantic, satirical, or tragic," and because otherwise "hope is stifled."[230] However, Hodgson's postmodernist emancipatory vision may be "utterly aborted by nuclear or environmental devastation,"[231] "the 'plot' of God's saving presence in history is much more complex than once we thought," the story is "labyrinthine and unfinished,"[232] "the future is open and the

---

226. Gilbertson, *God and History*, 51 (italics original).
227. McIlraith, *Reciprocal Love*, 74. Cf. Gilbertson, *God and History*, 49.
228. See discussion of foundationalism in chapter 3.
229. Hodgson, *God in History*, 184.
230. Ibid., 114, see also 158, 238–40.
231. Ibid., 127.
232. Ibid., 161.

outcome of the process is uncertain,"²³³ and finally, "the threat of nihilism [remains] ever-present in our time."²³⁴ So we can hope only in the weaker sense of that term. But John, writing in a period that also experienced overwhelming violence and tragedy, recalls a narrative that could face the evil, explain it, and still see a love story at work through history, thus providing a solid basis for confidence towards the future, especially in the light of redemptive meaning of the death/resurrection of Jesus.²³⁵

However, there are clear dangers in using Revelation, or the Bible as a whole, to construct a metanarrative. The biblical Story can be overstated, without sufficient attention being given to its nuances, unresolved tensions, and alternatives. For example, some interpreters of Revelation have too confidently tried to use the text to predict the future, particularly those following a historicist or futurist interpretive paradigm. Others have misused the dualisms in the text to define enemies of Christianity and justify persecuting them; the use of the criticisms of false Jews is a case in point. Still others have used Revelation to justify the actions of the church in history, even when she was not playing the romantic role assigned to her by John, but acting more like the whore of Babylon. And then others have used this very critique to promote anti-Catholic prejudice. Whenever interpretive communities try to *take control of* the text and use it to justify *their* position, the Big Story is being abused!

This is perhaps the strongest contribution the love story theme can make to this debate. It reminds the reader that love, not war, is the ultimate purpose of God, the ultimate objective of the Story. The quest now is to see how John positions his Story and worldview in relation to the alternative narratives of his day.

---

233. Ibid., 175, see also 182, 243–44, 250.
234. Ibid., 168, see also 183.
235. Morris, *Apocalyptic*, 93.

CHAPTER 7

Rival Narratives

WE LIVE IN A period in history where it seems everything is changing. Old certainties are being eroded or challenged. Our identities as peoples are changing. Non-Christian religions that were quaint and distant to the average Westerner have arrived in our backyards. New Atheists, radical green groups, militant Muslims, and many others are disputing Christianity or putting up alternative metanarratives. Christians are more aware than ever of rival worldviews and often struggle with an appropriate response.

This book has been exploring the way in which an ancient but authoritative Christian text, the Book of Revelation, can assist in the quest of constructing a recognizably Christian worldview that is nonetheless credible, meaningful, or at least relevant in a postmodern world. So far this has meant identifying both areas of promise for Christianity in postmodernist thought and areas where Christians may want to differ from postmodernism.

The last chapter focused on the question of metanarratives, a core issue in the postmodernist critique of modernity, and specifically the question, "Is a Christian metanarrative implied throughout the Bible, and in particular in Revelation?" I concluded that Revelation consciously attempts to write the ending of a Big Story of God's dealings with the world beginning with Genesis, implying perhaps that Revelation might lead its believing readers to construct a Christian metanarrative, in the form of a war epic. On the other hand, such a hypothesis is open to many objections and may need qualifying in the light of the use of features of romance genre in the text and in the light of recent criticism of metanarratives in general. This is a vital question, one that focuses issues such as the possibility of universal or absolute truth and the interpretation of human history.

In order to reach a conclusion, we must discuss how a Christian narrative or worldview responds to alternative narratives. This will mean taking up the question of pluralism and then exploring how Revelation responds to the rival narratives of first-century Christianity.

POSTMODERN PLURALISM

If postmodernism can be summed up as "incredulity towards metanarratives," perhaps even more succinctly it can be said that postmodernists are resistant to *closure*, the attempt to articulate the singular final answer to a question or issue, since the attempt to bring such closure inevitably means that some of the relevant data or perspectives are "privileged" because they support the answer being argued for, and data inconsistent with it are explained away, de-emphasized, or even suppressed.

In a similar way, the meaning of a text is seen as dynamic and plural.[1] According to Steve Moyise, the concept of deconstruction warns us that "determining *the* meaning of a text always involves privileging some aspects of it at the expense of others."[2] Hence postmodern critics of Revelation place emphasis on the many conflicting interpretations offered of this text over the centuries, concluding that a single correct interpretation is an impossible and perhaps undesirable goal. As Rowland argues, Revelation "resists our attempts at neatness and order."[3]

The issue is pluralism. Today's world of shifting populations has led to the presence of racial and religious minorities in many formerly more homogeneous societies. Thus many different cultures, religions, and worldviews live side by side in full awareness of each other's existence and difference (*factual pluralism*), and hopefully in a state of more or less mutual toleration and respect (*political pluralism*). But some contemporary thinkers also embrace a *philosophical* or *religious pluralism* which suggests that all the truth claims made by those different groups are of more or less equal value, veracity, or (in)coherence; hence the idea that any religious (or ideological) claim is better or truer than others cannot be accepted.[4]

However, this trend can cause dilemmas for some. As Don Cupitt expresses it,

---

1. Cf. McKnight, *Post-Modern Use*, 160–61.
2. Moyise, "Does the Lion?" 184.
3. Foreword to Moyise, ed., *Studies*, xi.
4. Cf. Carson, *Gagging of God*, 13–22, 495.

> How can we each hold fast to our own particular set of moral and religious beliefs while at the same time professing to accept and even welcome the fact that in our society such issues are regarded as inherently disputable and unsettleable? Must not a pluralistic society drift towards relativism or subjectivism?[5]

All contemporary societies and their citizens wrestle with this dilemma.

According to Cupitt, most people resolve the dilemma in practical life by accepting the conclusions of science as in some way binding on all, but "regarding matters of religion, morality, and the like as matters of free private judgment."[6] This is the solution of modernity, based on the Kantian fact/value distinction. According to Ernest Gellner, the scientific method is thus a means of gaining objective, transcultural truth.[7] But as Cupitt points out, science, by excluding moral ideas and "final causes," becomes less useful as a guide to life.[8]

Another potential response to plurality of religions or worldviews is the suppression of rival worldviews, amounting to an attempt to return to a premodern world. For example, Muslim movements like Al-Qaeda seem to be calling for such a return to absolute truth enforced on all, at least in Muslim societies. Some Christian groups may have similar aspirations.

A third possibility is the gradual permeation through the society of a postmodernist mindset that accepts plurality of truth in all areas of life, even at the cost of a measure of relativism, putting all claims to objective truth on the defensive (as explored in chapter 4).[9] But is a fully pluralistic society ultimately sustainable? Without some kind of central ideology, is it not in danger of breaking up into a multi-individual (or multi-group) non-society? Or is a new ideology of "compulsory pluralism," one in which all claims to absolute truth (especially in religion) will be penalized, inevitable? Such issues are being wrestled with in postmodern multicultural nations like Australia, where successive recent governments have wrestled with the minimum core values and beliefs needed to hold the nation together.[10]

Such questions are not new. They have been faced by all multi-ethnic or multi-religious societies since the beginning of history, including the Roman Empire of John's day. How then should Christians respond? How

---

5. Cupitt, *Leap of Reason*, 3.
6. Ibid., 4.
7. Gellner, *Postmodernism, Reaso,n and Religion*, 82.
8. Cupitt, *Leap of Reason*, 7.
9. Cf. Hollinger, "Church as Apologetic," 185.
10. Cf. Newton, "Worldview Wars," 193–94.

can a Christian worldview survive, and even flourish, in a pluralist and post-Christian setting such as the Western world now presents? What do Christians do about the more offensive claims of traditional Christian theology and the Bible itself, which seem to relegate non-Christians to a terrible hell, a position that hardly seems tolerant, and is perhaps not tolerable, in a pluralistic society?

Pluralism and Christianity

Terrence Tilley, in the final chapter of his *Postmodern Theologies*, summarizes the main theories that have arisen amongst Christians seeking to account for the diversity of religions in the world, particularly from a soteriological perspective:[11]

1. Exclusivism: only those who consciously believe in Christ can be saved.

2. Inclusivism: others who do not consciously accept Jesus may still be saved on the basis of his redeeming work.

3. Pluralism: there are many paths to the same One God: either reductive pluralism (all religion reduces to "one basic or hidden truth") or phenomenal pluralism (all religion finally refers to the same "transcendent reality" conceived in different ways).

4. Particularism: takes the differences in religions seriously without pretending to know the final answer to the big soteriological questions.

Pluralist Theologies

The fact of religious plurality has shaped much postmodern theology. Many Christian theologians have taken as given the need to reinterpret the "claim to finality" of the major monotheisms in order to "allow for desirability of nonproselytizing interreligious dialogue and cooperation, and for the possibility of salvation, however defined, outside the one true faith, if there is such a thing."[12]

David Tracy, for instance, advocates a "revisionist model" for contemporary theology[13] that will help it function as a public discourse, especially

---

11. Tilley, *Postmodern Theologies*, 158–59. Cf. Yong, "'Not Knowing Where,'" 82; Carson, *Gagging of God*, 26–27, 142–50.

12. Lindbeck, *Nature of Doctrine*, 46.

13. Tracy, *Blessed Rage*, 32.

in a society that "claims to affirm a pluralism of religious options."[14] Tracy argues that religions speak about Ultimate Reality,[15] and he uses the category of the religious classic (whether texts, rituals, symbols, or myths) to show how this can be communicated in a pluralist society, because such a work combines "a curious datedness with an excess and permanence of meaning which yield fruitful reflection for later interpreters"[16] and "resists a 'definitive' interpretation."[17]

For Tracy, "religion is an intrinsically pluralistic and ambiguous phenomenon of otherness,"[18] and inter-religious dialogue[19] is a central demand that has the capacity to gradually transform Christian theology.[20] This means not only affirming such religions as Buddhism (one of Tracy's favorite discussion partners) but also primal religious practices and beliefs long dismissed as paganism.[21] While looking for points of similarity or commonality between seemingly opposing views,[22] Tracy is guarded about too premature a closure in interreligious dialogue. The challenge is to balance the need for new answers to the situation of religious pluralism with the preservation of genuine Christian identity.[23] This is quite a challenge!

Another response, articulated by John Hick,[24] sees religious pluralism as becoming a problem in the light of the conviction that religion responds to a divine reality of some kind,[25] and especially that the multiple claims of particular religions are "a valid response to the divine . . . embodying true beliefs."[26] They cannot all be true; that is, the gods believed in by all the religions (especially the monotheistic ones) literally cannot all exist as proposed.[27]

14. Tilley, *Postmodern Theologies*, 32.
15. Tracy, *Dialogue*, 93.
16. Ibid., 40.
17. Ibid., 62.
18. Ibid., 59.
19. Tilley, *Postmodern Theologies*, 38, 54–55.
20. Tracy, *Dialogue*, xi, see also 4–5, 30, 39–40, 49, 95, 98.
21. Ibid., 48–67.
22. Ibid., 30, 41–42.
23. Ibid., 96.
24. Hick, "Religious Pluralism," 99–116.
25. Ibid., 99.
26. Ibid.
27. Ibid., 103.

However, Hick, believing that "the same sort of thing is going on" in the worship of each of the great religions,[28] calls for a "Copernican revolution" in religious thinking. In other words, Christians should abandon a Christ-centered view of religion in favor of one in which all religions are seen as bearing witness more or less accurately to a transcendent reality,[29] or "filtering out the infinite divine reality and reducing it to forms with which we can cope."[30]

Hick clearly believes in such a transcendent reality, but he explains different religious beliefs in terms of linguistic and cultural constructs governed by history[31]—a kind of "religious ethnicity."[32] At this point, however, his thinking runs into unbearable tensions. How can we accept such a transcendent reality when the religions conceive of it in such incompatible ways? For example, he claims,

> God is neither a person nor a thing, but is the transcendent reality which is conceived and experienced by different human mentalities in both personal and non-personal ways.[33]

This concept of God as neither personal nor non-personal is either self-contradictory or vacuous.[34]

Approaches Critical of Pluralism

A very different approach to Hicks' is taken by Lesslie Newbigin.[35] Newbigin attributes the development of pluralism to the success of the Enlightenment humanist worldview, especially the division of facts from values, which essentially privatized religion and disallowed it from making universal truth claims.[36] Newbigin affirms the universal truth of the Christian gospel, rejected by Enlightenment thinkers because of its supposed irrationality

---

28. Ibid., 100.
29. Cf. Hick, *Second Christianity*, 76–82.
30. Hick, "Religious Pluralism," 115.
31. Ibid., 104, 110, 112, 115.
32. Hick, *Second Christianity*, 90. Similarly, in Lindbeck's (*Nature of Doctrine*, 18) "cultural-linguistic" model the propositions and values of each religion are like the rules of the road in different countries.
33. Hick, "Religious Pluralism," 101.
34. See also the critique of Hick in Carson, *Gagging of God*, 146–48; and in Plantinga, *Warranted Christian Belief*, ch. 2, pt. 2.
35. Newbigin, *Pluralist Society*.
36. Ibid., 1–7.

and "the scandal of particularity."[37] He describes this truth as essentially a story that is witnessed to and "indwelt" by the Christian church over the centuries,[38] which challenges the reigning "plausibility structures" of our culture and furnishes believers with a new plausibility structure[39] that discloses "the truth about the human story."[40]

Newbigin thus rejects religious pluralism, including the drift towards a new form of polytheism implicit in some recent pluralist thinkers,[41] in favor of acknowledging "Jesus Christ as the unique and decisive revelation of God for the salvation of the world."[42] He thus affirms the place of absolute truth, though warning against the presumption that we possess it,[43] and presents Christianity as "a whole worldview, a way of understanding the whole of human experience."[44]

More stridently, D. A. Carson argues against all forms of religious or philosophical pluralism from a more exclusivist soteriology, based on his view that universalism[45] and pluralism are closely linked.[46] He challenges pluralists like Hick to justify their claims about God and truth,[47] and contends that the implication of postmodernist pluralism is to make all beliefs and practices acceptable, which is clearly unthinkable: we are nearly all agreed that Nazism, cannibalism, and widow burning (for example) are evil.[48] He strongly attacks the way religious pluralists use biblical texts, arguing, "Too often their readings appear compromised by the philosophical commitment to pluralism."[49]

For Carson, pluralism amounts to a return to idolatry when it "allows other gods to be raised to the status of the one true God";[50] thus what is at stake is monotheism as such. Religious or philosophical pluralism is thus

---

37. Ibid., 72.
38. Ibid., 97.
39. Ibid., 99.
40. Ibid., 126.
41. Ibid., 156–61.
42. Ibid., 171.
43. Ibid., 162–64.
44. Ibid., 172.
45. The teaching that all will ultimately be saved, which actually goes back to ancient Christian theology in some forms, e.g., Origen.
46. Carson, *Gagging of God*, 142
47. Ibid., 176.
48. Ibid., 147–48, 177.
49. Ibid., 177–81.
50. Ibid., 233–234, see also 238, 497.

incompatible with Christianity;[51] hence, for example, the current emphasis on interreligious dialogue must not cause Christians to forsake proclamation of the gospel,[52] though Carson is keen to point out that this does not mean Christians should seek to impose their perspective on everyone else.[53] Carson stresses the centrality of the Bible's storyline in constructing a Christian response to postmodernist pluralism,[54] urging that "the Bible provides us with a metanarrative, a comprehensive 'story' that provides the framework for a comprehensive explanation, a comprehensive worldview."[55]

Theology of Religions

On the other hand, some thinkers have proposed an approach in which the soteriological question is put to one side in favor of asking, more generally, what is the nature of the religions of the world and what should a Christian stance towards them be? For example, Pentecostal theologian Amos Yong argues that the debate about a Christian perspective of religions has tended to bog down over questions such as "Can a person be saved without explicitly trusting in Jesus Christ?"[56] He proposes instead beginning with the work of the Holy Spirit and the concept of spirit in general. This approach is strongly Trinitarian[57] and rejects the subordination of pneumatology to Christology, affirming that the Holy Spirit can work outside the bounds of the Christian faith, such as in non-Christian religions.[58]

Such an affirmation raises the question of discernment: how can we decide whether a particular teaching, experience, or practice (whether in a non-Christian or Christian setting) comes from the Holy Spirit, a demonic force, or a purely human source?[59] While traditionally this question was answered christologically (that is, in terms of how much the teaching confessed Jesus Christ),[60] Yong identifies several difficulties with this; for example, he criticizes formulas derived from taking christological proposi-

51. Ibid., 238, 277–78.
52. Ibid., 508–9, see also 349.
53. Ibid., 422.
54. Ibid., 193–314.
55. Ibid., 191.
56. Yong, *Beyond the Impasse*, 22–29. However, he indicates his sympathy for the "inclusivist" approach identified above (ibid., 27, 107).
57. Ibid., 42–44, 50.
58. Cf. ibid., 36–48, 54, 79.
59. Cf. ibid., 72, 166.
60. Cf. ibid., 86.

tions in the Bible out of context.⁶¹ He wants to explore other possibilities, particularly involving empirical study of religions that examine the spirit(s) at work through the phenomena produced.⁶² However, this does not lead to a final answer, since any criteria offered are human constructions,⁶³ and there is ambiguity and mixture in the spiritual world.⁶⁴

Yong affirms that "a Christian theology of religions needs to emerge out of a genuine dialogue with the religions."⁶⁵ However, he struggles to provide an adequate definition of religion,⁶⁶ which makes it very difficult to compare religions and apply relevant biblical material to the question. For example, Yong affirms as an axiom that *"The religions of the world, like everything else that exists, are providentially sustained by the Spirit of God for divine purposes."*⁶⁷ Does this mean that the Spirit endorses the doctrines, practices, ethics, and rituals of all religious groups?

Yong is sympathetic towards "an authentic pluralism" that "enables emphasis to be laid on the particularity and difference of all non-Christian others."⁶⁸ However, he still comes from a definite Christian commitment. For example, he writes, "pneumatologists of religion may be able to affirm the place of the religions in the divine providence even as they affirm the absolute centrality of Jesus Christ's life, death and resurrection for salvation."⁶⁹

Obviously, responses to postmodernist pluralism are radically varied. Can Christians draw any ideas from Revelation to help think through the issues? For example, how legitimate is Yong's appeal to Revelation to affirm "the universal presence and efficacious activity of the Spirit?"⁷⁰ More to the point, how does Revelation handle the debate between its Big Story and the alternative stories and worldviews of the first century, and does this give us any kind of model for dialogues and debate between worldviews today?

---

61. Ibid., 169–170.
62. Ibid., 107, 138–39, 144, 150–54.
63. Ibid., 159.
64. Ibid., 166.
65. Ibid., 19. See also 54, 172–83.
66. E.g. ibid., 16–17, 93, 165. Cf. Friesen, *Imperial Cults*, 5–15.
67. Yong, *Beyond the Impasse*, 46 (italics original).
68. Ibid., 55, see also 73.
69. Ibid., 50.
70. Ibid., 40.

REVELATION AND THE HOPES OF THE ANCIENT WORLD

Revelation and the Hopes of the Jews

As this book has been arguing, Revelation seeks to present the "true" interpretation and conclusion of the story of the Old Testament. Revelation thus shares the storyline of the Hebrew Scriptures, as seen for example in the reappearance of themes from the early chapters of Genesis. Indeed Wright claims, "first-century Judaism and Christianity have a central worldview-feature in common: the sense of a story now reaching its climax. And, most importantly, *it is the same story*."[71] However, Revelation presents this ending from a Christian perspective rejected by most Jews of his day (and since).

As I argued in chapter 2, John has an intimate knowledge of, and sympathetic respect for, the distinctive features of Jewish faith and practice, as shown by his frequent references to heaven using the language of the temple (5:8; 6:9; 8:4–5; 11:19; 15:5; 16:7) and his positive references to the tribes of Israel (7:4–8; 21:12), the temple and altar (11:1–2), the holy city (11:2; 20:9; 21:2, 10), the commandments (12:17; 14:12), Mount Zion (14:1), ritual purity (14:4), and Moses "the servant of God" (15:3). Revelation supports the frequent Jewish expectation of a world-ruling Messiah (11:15) of the tribe of Judah and line of David (5:5), defeating and subduing the nations (19:15). However, I also argued that Revelation is hostile to at least some Jews (2:9; 3:9), calling them a "synagogue of Satan." They are seen as false Jews who "slander" the followers of Jesus (2:9), perhaps inciting persecution against them (Rev 2:10; 3:8; cf. Acts 18:12–13).

Moreover John's concept of the Messiah and his victories differs strongly from the concept shaped by the Maccabean wars. John supports only passive resistance to Rome at best, in spite of his war story language.[72] For example, the climactic battle of Revelation 19 has messianic overtones (19:15) and a violent, ghoulish outcome (19:17–18, 21), but the only weapon is the sword coming out of the Messiah's mouth (19:15, 21), and no real fighting is described, even though there are captives and victims (19:20–21).[73] In addition, the basis of the Messiah's rule in Revelation is his own violent death (5:5–10).[74]

---

71. Wright, *People of God*, 150 (italics original).
72. Cf. Caird, *The Revelation*, 75.
73. Cf. Friesen, *Imperial Cults*, 177; Caird, *Revelation*, 245–48.
74. Cf. Friesen, *Imperial Cults*, 176.

The Messiah's thousand-year reign, as told by John, does not entirely satisfy Jewish expectations either. Certainly it has its headquarters in "the beloved city" (20:9) and power is shared with the faithful martyrs (20:4, 6), but there is no mention of the prophetic promises associated with the Messianic Age, such as the return of the ten tribes of northern Israel. In fact, most of the glorious promises made by the Old Testament prophets are not taken up until John writes of the New Jerusalem (chs. 21–22).[75]

Revelation and the Future of Jerusalem

Jerusalem was central to the Jewish worldview and the Jewish faith.[76] It was seen as the center of the earth[77] and, according to Wright, most Jews "looked to Jerusalem, and its Temple, as the center of their homeland, and as their very *raison d'être* as a people."[78] Restoration of Jerusalem and the temple in all its glory and original purity was part of the hope of all Jewish streams.

Jerusalem had become central to Israel in the days of David, who made it his capital (2 Sam 5:6–9; 1 Chr 11:4–8). The city was clearly part of the heart of the psalmists,[79] and the prophets continue this focus, even as they begin to predict her downfall and destruction.[80] It was seen as the place of worship and pilgrimage for Israelites,[81] the dwelling place of God's presence and name,[82] the center of the hope of Israel for restoration after being ravaged and exiled from their land,[83] as well as the ultimate capital of the world in the days of the Messiah,[84] to which all nations would make

---

75. Cf. Koester, *End of All Things*, 183–84.

76. Hengel, *Judaism and Hellenism*, 1:60.

77. Cf. Pss 122; 132; Malina, *New Testament World*, 184–85; Wright, *People of God*, 247.

78. Wright, *People of God*, 157; cf. Collins, *Between Athens and Jerusalem*, 111; Mendels, *Jewish Nationalism*, 135, 148, 150–51.

79. Ps 51:18–19; 79:1; 102:13, 21; 116:18, 19; 122:1–6; 135:21; 137:5–6.

80. E.g., 2 Kgs 19:21–28; 21:13; Isa 4:3–6; 24:23; Jer 15:5; 26:4–6, 11; Mic 3:9–12

81. Ps 9:14; 116:18–19; 122:1–4; 2 Chr 20:5–6, 28; 30:1–5, 13–14; Ezra 1:2–4; 3; Ezek 36:38; Dan 5:2–3; 6:10; Mic 3:11.

82. Ps 9:11; 135:21; 2 Kgs 19:21, 34; 2 Chr 20:8–9; Isa 31:9; Dan 9:16, 19; Joel 3:16–17; Zech 3:2.

83. Ps 51:18–19; 79:1; 102:13; Isa 4:3–6; Ezra 2:1; Neh 1:2–3; Isa 27:13; 40:2, 9; 44:26, 28; 52:1–2, 9; 62:6–7; 65:18–19; 66:20; Jer 33:15–16; Dan 9:2, 24–25; Joel 2:32; 3:1, 17, 20; Mic 4:7–8; Zeph 3:14–20; Zech 1:14–17; 2:4, 12; 8:3–8; 9:9; 12:2–10; 13:1; 14:2–4, 8, 10–14.

84. Ps 2; 68:29; Isa 24:23; Jer 3:17; Mic 4:1–3; Zech 2:10–12; 8:22; 9:9–10; 14:9–10.

pilgrimage, bringing in their wealth,[85] and from which God's governing law would go out.[86]

The Jewish apocalypses also bear witness to the importance of Jerusalem.[87] For example, in 2 Baruch, we find this anguished cry:

> if you destroy Your city, and deliver up Your land to those that hate us, how shall the name of Israel be again remembered? Or how shall one speak of Your praises? or to whom shall that which is in Your law be explained? Or shall the world return to its nature of aforetime, and the age revert to primeval silence? (2 Bar. 3:5-6)[88]

However, 2 Baruch spiritualizes Jerusalem,[89] identifies its restoration with the messianic hope,[90] and predicts only a partial restoration.[91]

John adheres to the Jewish understanding of Jerusalem's place in God's plans to some degree; for instance, when he describes the Lamb standing on Mount Zion with his army of 144,000 virgins (Rev 14:1, 4; cf. Ps 2:6) and describes Jerusalem as the "holy city" (Rev 21:10; 11:2). His description of the "new" Jerusalem reflects the hope of the prophets (cf. Isa 54:11-12 and Tob 13:21, 17 with Rev 21:11, 19-21), and the identity of Jerusalem as capital of Israel (Rev 21:12) and the world, and center of pilgrimage (Rev 21:24-26).

However, in chapter 11 especially, John takes a prophetic stance towards Jerusalem somewhat reminiscent of some Old Testament prophets and Jesus' "Olivet Discourse" (Matt 24; Mark 13; Luke 21). He sees Jerusalem as under judgment, occupied by the Gentiles (Rev 11:2), as "prophetically called Sodom and Egypt, where also their Lord was crucified" (Rev 11:8), thus emphasizing both her subjugation to Rome and her resistance to prophets of God (especially Jesus), recalling earlier prophetic denunciations of Jerusalem (Isa 1:9-10; Jer 23:14), and reminding the reader that God's judgments on Sodom and Egypt were also extended to Jerusalem when she turned against her God (Ezek 16:46-58). In the light of the similarities

---

85. Cf. Acts 11:27-30; 24:17; Rom 15:26, 27; 1 Cor 16:1-4. Cf. Dumbrell, *End of the Beginning*, 29.

86. Isa 2:2-4, 60:1-11; Mic 4:1-3; Zech 8:22-23; 14:16-19. Cf. Dumbrell, *End of the Beginning*, 5-27.

87. *T. Dan* 5:7; *Sib. Or.* 5:339; 4 *Ezra* 3, 10. Similar sentiments are found in the apocryphal books; e.g., Tob 1:4; 13:9-12, 21-23; 14:5; Jdt 4; 1 Macc 1:21-41; 4:36-61; 7:36-37; 2 Macc 1:12, 18-36; 2:16-18, 22; 3:6-40; 5:15-17; 14:31; 15:17.

88. Cf. also 2 *Bar.* 10:7; 31:4; 35:1-5; 2; 61; 67.

89. 2 *Bar.* 4:1-7

90. 2 *Bar.* 40:1.

91. 2 *Bar.* 68:5, 6.

between some of the disasters described in Revelation and those that befell those two places,[92] this is a significant implication.

John portrays the inhabitants of Jerusalem as joining in the general jubilation at the murder of God's two witnesses (Rev 11:7–10). Not only does Jerusalem resist the prophets, she also allies herself with the beast in persecuting them.[93] He portrays a partial destruction of Jerusalem by an earthquake (11:11–13, resulting in at least some repentance), and a far greater destruction (if "the city" in 14:20 is indeed Jerusalem), resembling Josephus' descriptions of the fall of Jerusalem in A.D. 70. Thus John cautions the Jews and Jewish Christians against hoping for God to defend and save Jerusalem in his day. As McIlraith puts it, "For the Apocalypse the earthly Jerusalem was where the 'Lord was crucified' and thus shares in the reality of the 'great city' (11,8). The earthly Jerusalem is no longer the Holy City."[94]

However, John portrays the New Jerusalem in glowing terms that partly reflect the Old Testament prophets.[95] It is transcendental in scope and origin (21:2, 10, 16), the center of a totally new order of things (21:1; 22:5). It is also international, not just as the messianic world capital, but also being open to all ethnic groups, embracing all cultures (21:24–26), and bringing blessing to all nations (22:2). It involves a substantial return to the Edenic order before the Fall (21:4; 22:1–2), a pre-Israelite order.

But it is also a Christian city. It has its roots in Israel (21:12), but its foundations are named with the names of Jesus' twelve apostles (21:14). It is the city of the Lamb (21:9, 14, 22, 23, 27; 22:1, 3), and its citizens are "those who are written in the Lamb's book of life" (21:27). It has no physical temple, for "its temple is the Lord God the Almighty and the Lamb" (21:22).[96] The implications are clear: this is no longer just the Jewish capi-

---

92. Comp. Gen 19:24–28 (Sodom) and Rev 8:7–11; 9:17–18; 19:3; 20:9–10. Among the plagues on Egypt were water to blood (Exod 7:17–24; comp. Rev 16:4; 11:6); boils on humans and animals (Exod 9:8–12; comp. Rev 16:2); destructive hail storm with thunder and lightning (Exod 9:17–35; comp. Rev 16:21; 11:19); plague of locusts (Exod 10:3–20; comp. Rev 9:3); thick darkness (Exod 10:21–29; comp. Rev 16:10); and death of all the firstborn (Exod 11:4–10; 12:29–32; comp. Rev 11:13; 14:20). John also alludes to the Red Sea miracle and judgment (Exod 13–14; comp. Rev 15:2, 3; 12:13–16).

93. This is similar to the story presented in the four Gospels and Acts about the execution of Jesus and the subsequent persecution of the early Christians (for example, Acts 4:21–30).

94. McIlraith, *Reciprocal Love*, 127.

95. Cf. Dumbrell, *End of the Beginning*, 1–5, 31–32; Pattemore, *People of God*, 199–200.

96. Contrast the prophecy of Ezekiel, to which John clearly alludes in Rev 20–22, and which contains a very detailed description of an ideal temple (Ezek 40–48).

tal founded by David; in fact, Jews may not be welcome there unless they embrace the Lamb. Thus John refines the hopes of many Jews for restoration of Jerusalem.[97]

In summary, we could say that Revelation's position with respect to the hopes of the Jews is one of completion and fulfillment, but also reinterpretation.[98] Their narrative is included in his Big Story, but not without some adjustment to make it fit, a position rejected by most Jews of his day. John's desire to claim the Hebrew narrative for his Christian Story can only be accepted by those who believe that Jesus is the long-awaited Messiah, which has always been a minority position within Judaism. For most Jews today, John is constructing a metanarrative with all the worst features of such an enterprise. On the other hand, John himself sees this Story as a Hebrew-Christian story that draws heavily on the imagery and themes of the Hebrew Scriptures and hence affirms those writings.

Revelation and the Combat Myth

Studies over the past few decades have demonstrated significant similarities between Revelation and ancient Mediterranean genres of literature that express worldviews very different to that identified in Revelation; for example, Adela Yarbro Collins' examination of the allusions to the ancient combat myth.[99] What are the implications? To what extent has John's thinking been influenced by that of non-Jewish, non-Christian religions and philosophies? And what position does Revelation take toward the myths, hopes, and ideals of the non-Jewish world?

Does John import alien worldviews into his own thought, as claimed by those who made "an early attempt to explain the similarities between Babylonian texts and the Old Testament" by claiming "that all religious and cultic symbolism derives from the Babylonian worldview?"[100] How could such a worldview cohere with the declared worldview of Revelation, with its core elements of monotheism and Christianity, and its hostility to idolatry and syncretism?[101] Or is John deliberately using features of these genres to make his own response to the worldviews, religions, and myths (narratives) they represent, either undermining them, radically reinterpreting them, or transforming them to serve an apologetic strategy?

97. Cf. Friesen, *Imperial Cults*, 183.
98. Cf. ibid., 174–76.
99. Collins, *Combat Myth*.
100. Ibid., 207.
101. Cf. Rev 2:14, 20, 24; 9:20, 21; 13:5, 6, 13–15; 14:11; 18:4; 21:8, 27; 22:15.

Let's examine, first, the case of the combat myth. Adela Yarbro Collins has argued,

> The underlying pattern of Revelation and much of its imagery have strong affinities with a mythic pattern of combat which was widespread in the ancient Near East and the classical world. . . . One of the combatants is usually a monster, very often a dragon. This monster represents chaos and sterility, while his opponent is associated with order and fertility. Thus their conflict is a cosmic battle whose outcome will constitute or abolish order in society and fertility in nature.[102]

Taking Revelation 12 as the center point of the text (which she supports by a sophisticated structural analysis,)[103] she demonstrates the similarities between the literary features of that chapter and various forms of the combat myth, and then extends her thesis to the story of Revelation as a whole, using chapter 12 as a "paradigm."[104]

Collins argues that the redacted text we now have closely follows the pattern of Canaanite and Greek forms of the combat myth,[105] and that John's mind was full of "traditional images with a long history and a rich variety of connotations and associations."[106] John was influenced especially by the combat myth of Leto and Apollo and the traditions concerning Isis.[107] On the other hand, she remarks, "It would seem that the author of Revelation was consciously . . . incorporating and fusing traditional elements from a variety of cultures,"[108] asserts that John uses the combat myth to "interpret a situation of persecution,"[109] and sees John following the Old Testament practice of "*adapting* the ancient Near Eastern combat myths to *interpret* the conflicts in which Yahweh and his people had been engaged."[110]

Thus the use of such myths by John and his Jewish sources does not imply "a leveling sort of syncretism";[111] rather the author(s) borrow from pagan sources to make their own Jewish or Christian points.[112] This explains

---

102. Collins, *Combat Myth*, 57.
103. Ibid., 5–44, esp. 16–32.
104. Ibid., 231–33. See also Newton, "Story-Lines," 67–68.
105. Collins, *Combat Myth*, 142–43.
106. Ibid., 57.
107. Ibid., 67, 70, 75, 83–84, 101–14, 128–45, 161.
108. Ibid., 58; cf. 187.
109. Ibid., 3, cf. 186; also Bauckham, *Climax*, 196–98.
110. Ibid., 2 (italics added).
111. Ibid., 129.
112. Ibid.

how "Revelation does not simply reflect the pattern of the combat myth as found in any particular mythic text."[113] Moreover John reinterprets his Jewish source in a way that has the effect of "shifting the emphasis from a nationalistic conflict between the Jewish people and Rome to a universal, cosmic conflict."[114] Collins agrees with Caird that "the myth reflected in Revelation 12 was deliberately adopted and rewritten to contradict its current political application" by the supporters of the emperor, especially Nero.[115] Such comments suggest that John was engaged in rhetorical strategy.

Various passages of the Old Testament have already picked up the combat myth and used it for their own purposes, and John has drawn on these,[116] using the combat myth as a useful heuristic device that would allow him to communicate meaningfully with his contemporaries in the Greco-Roman world.[117] Far from adopting the *ideologies* associated with the combat myth, John adapted and reinterpreted the combat myth as part of a Christian apologetic strategy, and in a sense turned the myth on its head.

Bauckham thinks that John is exploiting the ambivalence of pagan religion at this point: the serpent could be both divinized, as in the cults of Asklepios and Isis, and demonized, as in the combat myths.[118] But John shows no such ambivalence himself: the serpent/dragon is always the enemy; in that sense he is privileging the perspective of the combat myth, which posited a war between God and evil, over that of other pagan cults.

But 12:1–5 also seems to be recalling the primeval story of the Hebrew Scriptures. The description of the woman alludes to the tribes of Israel with her "crown of twelve stars" (Rev 12:1; cf. Gen 37:9). More fundamentally, her pregnancy and her male child seem to be a very clear allusion to the promise of Genesis 3:15, where the offspring of the original woman is said to strike the head of the serpent—a very strong reason for the hostility of the dragon towards both the child and his mother. John may be implying that these passages represent the original or paradigmatic version of the combat myth, of which the other versions are variations, and that his story amounts to the return to and completion of that original story.

---

113. Ibid., 215.

114. Ibid., 144.

115. Ibid., 188–90.

116. Ibid., 76, 117–18, 120, 134, 140, 162–65, 172–73, 211, 227–30. Cf. Bauckham, *Climax*, 194–95; Boyd, *God at War*, 74–113; Friesen, *Imperial Cults*, 172.

117. Collins, *Combat Myth*, 217. Cf. Friesen, *Imperial Cults*, 172.

118. Bauckham, *Climax*, 195–98.

Furthermore, I suggest that John believed that his Christian Story provided a better solution to the problems addressed by such myths. These myths expressed the desire of ancient Mediterranean peoples for stability and prosperity, and their fear of chaos. John shows his sympathy with such aspirations, but his text provides a radically different version of the myth in order to offer a different response to their hopes. Stability, order, and prosperity are all features of the New Jerusalem, which has been made possible by Jesus fulfilling the true meaning of the Mediterranean combat myths (Rev 12:10–11), and it is available to those who follow him (Rev 21:7, 9, 27; 22:3–5, 14). According to Friesen, both imperial propaganda and Revelation "connected mythology and historical figures through established paradigms from the past," seeing myths as fulfilled in some way through "specific human beings," whether Caesar or Jesus.[119]

In the same way, John strategically incorporates the combat myth, in a twice-amended version, into his Christian narrative.

Revelation and Hellenistic Thought

As I have pointed out,[120] the Hellenistic world had its own special hopes, including the priority of stability; in fact, Green points out that economic progress was retarded because of their worldview that prized stability and the "divinely established order on which the world's harmony depended."[121] Moreover their ideal society was expressed in the Greek city or *polis*, seen as "the ultimate framework of social life."[122]

On the other hand, in the later Hellenistic period, there seemed to be a growing attention of philosophers to questions of peace of mind.[123] Partly due to the loss of political freedom, "men were driven, more and more, if they could not be masters of their fate, at least to remain captains of their souls."[124] The dominant philosophical schools of the Hellenistic and Roman eras were all individualistic and inward focused.[125]

Revelation shows some sympathy for these aspirations, but seeks to adjust them and address them from a Christian standpoint. For example,

119. Friesen, *Imperial Cults*, 173.

120. In chapter 2.

121. Green, *Alexander to Actium*, 469, 605.

122. Veyne, *Bread and Circuses*, 39.

123. Walbank, *Hellenistic World*, 196. Cf. Green, *Alexander to Actium*, 53, see also 58, 603.

124. Green, *Alexander to Actium*, 605. See also Tolbert, *Sowing the Gospel*, 39–40.

125. Green, *Alexander to Actium*, 56–64, 605.

as noted in chapter 2, the final paradise in Revelation takes the form of a Greek-like city, a *polis* (3:20; 21; 22:2, 14, 19) with walls, gates, a river, a street and trees (21:12–22:2), and a king's throne (22:3), albeit with some significant differences to any actual Greek city; for example, no temple (21:22) and a much stricter moral code: "dogs and sorcerers and fornicators and murderers and idolaters, and everyone who loves and practices falsehood" (22:15) were excluded. John is responding to and adjusting (Christianizing) the ideal Greek *polis*.

Revelation also speaks strongly to the Hellenistic longing for inner peace and spiritual freedom in a world "out of control," but in its own unique way. Revelation is hardly a peaceful text to read. It is full of conflict, oppression, danger, death, and the threat of martyrdom. Its story evokes the ancient world at its most dislocated, as in the year of the four emperors (A.D. 69), or the Jewish-Roman War of A.D. 66–70. But in the middle of these conflicts there are promises of inner refreshing in Christ (3:20; 22:17), protection in the midst of at least some trials (3:10; 7:3; 9:4), rest for those who are killed for Christ (6:9–11; 14:13), and above all eschatological salvation and blessing (2:7, 11, 17; 3:12, 21; 7:15–17; 19:9; 20:4–6; 21:1–7; 22:1–5). There is also comfort to be found in the realities of the sovereignty of God, the enthronement and lordship of Jesus, and the steady reality of heaven. John is speaking to the legitimate aspirations of the Greeks but pointing them to Christ as the only true fulfillment of their hopes.

Revelation and the Stars

Most of the ancient cultures of the Mediterranean and ancient Near Eastern world sought meaning in history from their ancient myths, various "prophetic" sources (oracles, oral or written), and the movements of the heavenly bodies.[126] What does John think about the role of the stars? Certainly the cosmology of Revelation is not dominated by an impersonal Fate. Rather its view of history is centered on the sovereignty of God and Jesus; that is, it is a personal rule, grounded in justice and open to influence by prayer.[127] The stars are not alive, nor are they ruling, nor symbolic of gods. Rather they are totally under the sovereign rule of the one true God and their movements have predictive significance only as portents displayed by him. However, with those provisos, it is clear that John accepts the significance of the heavenly bodies as indicators of God's plans.

---

126. See chapter 2.
127. See chapter 4.

Bruce Malina proposes that John's visions are the result of an "altered state of consciousness" while John is contemplating the night sky.[128] What he sees are constellations, comets, planets and the like, which he then interprets in terms of his Hebrew background to bring understanding of what is going on in his day (consequential on the recent and distant past), under the guidance of "sky beings" (such as angels) with whom he interacts. Thus, "the book of Revelation and works like it are really a subset of the astronomical and astrological literature of antiquity."[129] For example, the Lamb in Revelation is actually the constellation Aries (the Ram), which was pictured somewhat like a lamb "slaughtered" and yet standing,[130] and the pictures seen when the seven seals are opened (Rev 6) are comets that "invariably bode ill for the inhabitants of the land over which they appear,"[131] in this case Israel.

However, John is not uncritically adopting the worldview of the general Mediterranean world, according to Malina; rather he is amending it in terms of his Jewish-Christian heritage. For instance, "cosmic beings designated as deities by John's contemporaries are regarded simply as sky beings in God's entourage" and Jesus "transcends the role of Messiah of Israel," being seen as "cosmic lord" with "preeminence and primacy over all celestial beings."[132] Malina shows clearly that John reinterprets astrological knowledge of his day in the service of his Christian worldview.

But Malina has not totally explained why John does this. He explains John's strategy mainly in terms of encouraging the seven churches to persevere in their faith and not be deceived by the prevailing idolatry of the Greco-Roman world.[133] But while he sees the influence of the biblical story on John's writing, such as the lessons from the antediluvian and postdiluvian world,[134] he tends to downplay Israel's history, hopes, and Scriptures as a factor in Revelation, in favor of a more universalistic perspective.[135] Thus he virtually ignores the plot structure of Revelation discussed in the previous chapter of this book.

Malina's structure of Revelation is based on sectors of the sky and the likely position of the stars at various points of history, especially in the very distant past. This leads him to read Revelation 12 as primeval antediluvian

128. Malina, *Genre and Message*, 1–2.
129. Ibid., 12.
130. Ibid., 53, 79, 101–2. This is still a picture of Jesus, however.
131. Ibid., 54, see also 112–18.
132. Ibid., 261–62.
133. Ibid., 259–60, 264, 267.
134. E.g., ibid., 177, 232–33, 253.
135. E.g., ibid., 191.

history (which is probably partly true) and chapters 17–18 as referring to Babel and Jerusalem, which is more problematic. But in either case the sense of narrative structure in the text is minimized. I think it more likely that John's use of astrology would serve the narrative he is writing, and the larger Story he is presuming, than the reverse. Moreover the allusions to astrology in Revelation actually support the mega-narrative of war and romance identified in the previous chapter.

For example, Malina's interpretation of Revelation 12 as a primeval series of events rests on three main lines of thought: parallels with Genesis (the woman and the serpent),[136] ancient myths (similar to those identified by Yarbro Collins),[137] and the way John describes the woman as giving birth:

> it is significant that John sees this constellation [Virgo] as a Pregnant Woman, while traditional lore has it as Mother and Child. What this means is that John views the constellation when it still formed a single entity, before the birth of the Child, hence as a cosmic Pregnant Woman. This vision places us in prehistoric times. As previously noted, since the Dragon is still in the sky, the scenario here considers the sky as it was early on at the time of creation.[138]

This argument is then supported with reference to *1 Enoch*. The only reference to John's present time is the "other seed" of the woman mentioned in Revelation 12:17, who "derive somehow from that ancient period."[139]

There is considerable strength in this reading, however, it seems one-sided to me. For example, Malina ignores the time period of 1,260 days (12:6, 14), which links this episode with the narrative plot (11:3; 13:5), and all likely references to the historical Jesus (12:5,11), except for 12:17. Thus he fails to explain how the throwing down of the dragon is related to the death of Jesus and the witness of his followers (12:11). A convincing reading of Revelation 12 must explain how it relates to *both* ancient events *and* John's day. Malina hardly begins this process, but it must include consideration of how this episode fits into John's overall story and that of the Bible as a whole.

The key to this would seem to lie in Genesis 3:15, which starts off the conflict between the woman and the serpent, pronounces his ultimate

---

136. Ibid., 154, 171.
137. Ibid., 156–60.
138. Ibid., 160.
139. Ibid., 172.

doom, and explains it by the suffering of her "seed" (both the Messiah and his followers):[140]

> I will put enmity between you and the woman,
> and between your offspring and hers;
> he will strike your head,
> and you will strike his heel.

Malina only mentions this briefly at the end, but it implies that Revelation presupposes a salvation history.[141]

Revelation clearly does employ astrological knowledge and ideas, and cannot be interpreted successfully without consideration of this,[142] but the text invests these with a Christian significance and puts them at the service of the Big Story. John is trying to give what he sees as the true meaning behind the constellations in the light of the ancient stories and the events of his day surrounding the birth of Christianity.

John's Purpose

These examples show that John's approach to many of the alternative narratives of his day involves amplifying, adjusting, and Christianizing, rather than simply rejecting or excluding them. While he is putting forward a Big Story that seeks to be the last word on history and reality, this is not intended to be exclusive or unsympathetic to the other myths and dreams of the Jewish or Greco-Roman world.

His purpose, even when undermining rival views, is to promote Christianity and the new worldview it represents as more satisfying and comprehensive than the alternatives. As Elisabeth Schüssler Fiorenza proposed some time ago, "the early Christian movement and its literature should be viewed as rooted in the attempt to attract and convince the persons of the Hellenistic world, be they already Christians, Jews, or pagans."[143] Revelation is no exception to this.

---

140. Cf. Newton, "Story-Lines," 68.

141. See chapter 6.

142. E.g., Rev 1:16, 20; 6:12–14; 8:10–12; 9:1; and 12:1–4 make no sense without the astrological background, and many other passages make better sense with this knowledge.

143. Fiorenza, "Miracles, Missions, and Apologetics," 1–2.

REVELATION AND THE NARRATIVES OF IMPERIAL ROME

So far I have been examining the narratives that John has some sympathy with and chooses to include, reinterpret, revise, or transform in keeping with his Christian Story. Here he seems to have a clear apologetic purpose: to show how the legitimate aspirations and traditions of all peoples can be transformed and fulfilled in a Christian worldview. Like much apologetic writing, this was probably addressed to the Jewish and Greek members of the seven churches of Asia, who had not abandoned wholly their hopes as Jews or Greeks, but needed to reinterpret them from their new Christian standpoint.

However, there were some worldviews, religions, philosophies, or ideologies that were simply incompatible with Christianity, even in an amended form, and needed to be refuted rather than adopted by a Christian worldview. Such rejected ideas in Revelation include polytheism, since John advocates an uncompromising stance to all forms of polytheistic idolatry (2:14, 20, 24; 9:20; 21:8; 22:15), sorcery (9:21; 21:8; 22:15), and sexual immorality (2:14, 20–23; 9:21; 21:8; 22:15). John absolutely rejects most of the religious practices and beliefs of the non-Jewish world,[144] even though he sympathizes with their aspirations.

His attitude to Roman myths is even more hostile.[145] As Howard-Brook and Gwyther argue, for John, "Rome was not an order with which one could cooperate. It was, instead, an incarnation of 'Satan.'"[146] This is first made clear in the beast episodes of Revelation 12–14. It is expressed not only in religious terms but also political and economic language, most strikingly in the chapters on Babylon. The whore incorporates all the negative aspects of pagan religion: sexual immorality (17:2, 4, 5; 18:3, 9; 19:2), sorcery (18:23), and blasphemy (17:3), though no specific mention is made of idolatry. But John's condemnation of her is based on her persecution of Jesus' followers (17:6; 18:24; 19:2), her pride based on her prosperity and apparent security (18:7), her "abominations" (17:4, 5), and her negative influence on the world of the day, which is described in terms such as "fornication" (17:2, 4; 18:3, 9; 19:2), "corruption" (19:2), deception (18:23), and drunkenness (17:2; 18:3).

She is seen as the stronghold of abominations and deception (17:5), which seems to point towards pagan idolatry in particular. This may be one

---

144. See Howard-Brook and Gwyther, *Unveiling Empire*, 111–13, on how Revelation parodies aspects of local religious cults. Comp. Carson, *Gagging of God*, 270–73.

145. Cf. Newton, "Story-Lines," 69–70.

146. Howard-Brook and Gwyther, *Unveiling Empire*, 116.

reason for calling her Babylon, which functioned as the "capital city" of false religion for the prophets of the Old Testament (as in Isa 47). But other common factors between Babylon and Rome are their roles in the history of the Jews (especially the destruction of Jerusalem and her temple), their dominant political position, and their emperor cults (particularly mentioned in Daniel).[147]

Revelation allows the voice of the empire to be heard reflectively and indirectly as well as in direct statements. Thus its dominance is the result of conquest (6:2, if this refers to Roman conquest); it rebounds from dire situations that threaten its existence (13:3); and is seemingly invincible (13:4; 18:7). It is universal in scope (13:7), bringing all of life into a single system with its own ruler cult that serves to unite the populace under a common loyalty—a traditional role of religion (13:13-18). The various political entities have yielded power to the empire and profited thereby (17:12-13; 18:3); in fact, the system thus created has brought incredible wealth to those who participate in it (18:3, 11-19).

This amounts to a fair description of the Greco-Roman world under the principate (which brought stability and peace after the tumultuous years of the later republic), similar to the propaganda of Rome itself.[148] But John's perspective is founded on the conviction that the seemingly stable and prosperous world he describes is actually in opposition to God and Christ and doomed to destruction. How does he go about undermining the claims of the empire?

First of all, he reminds his readers of the flaws in the system. For example, the conquest of the world by Rome, represented by the white horse (6:2), is followed not simply by peace and prosperity, but by war (6:4), food shortages,[149] and inflation (6:5-6), disasters caused by war, famine, and pestilence (6:8), and persecution (6:9-11). He also probes the question of who benefits from this system. The economic prosperity of the empire provides luxury and wealth for some—the merchants and ship owners (18:3, 11, 15, 17, 23), the subordinate kings (18:3, 9), and the upper classes of Rome who "lived luxuriously" (18:7)—but not everyone is included (13:16-17) and the system is maintained by the slave trade (18:13).[150]

He points out the moral and religious bankruptcy of this prosperous world (9:20-21; 13:5-6) and calls Christians to "come out" of it (13:8,

---

147. Cf. Friesen, *Imperial Cults*, 138–140.

148. Cf. Howard-Brook and Gwyther, *Unveiling Empire*, 88–89; Friesen, *Imperial Cults*, 19, 204.

149. Cf. ibid., 97–99.

150. Cf. ibid., 98–101.

17; 14:9–13; 18:4–5; 20:4). He gives voice to those "others" left out of the system: those slaughtered for the word of God (6:9–10; 12:10–11, 17; 13:7, 10; 14:13; 16:5–6; 18:24), the Jews (11:2), and the followers of the Lamb (14:1–4). In fact, his whole book takes the martyrs' perspective against that of the dominant powers in the empire. These "others" rejoice in the demise of Rome because they were excluded from and oppressed by the system (18:20; 19:1–3).

Finally, he reminds the empire of its vulnerability to civil war (8:7–11?; 14:18–20; 16:3–6; 17:16), invasion from the East (one of the major threats to the order of the Greco-Roman world, 9:14–19; 16:12–16), and natural disasters (6:12–17; 8:12; 9:1–11; 11:13; 16:8–11, 18–21). And in the midst of its stability and prosperity, he warns of its coming destruction: "fallen is Babylon" (14:8; 16:19; 17:8; 18:2–8, 10, 21).[151] In other words, the empire is under God's judgment.

Thus he undercuts the empire's main claim—to permanency. This is incisively captured in 18:7–8:

> Since in her heart she says,
> "I rule as queen;
> I am no widow,
> and I will never see grief,"
> therefore her plagues will come in a single day—
> pestilence and mourning and famine—
> and she will be burned with fire;
> for mighty is the Lord God
> who judges her.

Howard-Brook and Gwyther show how Revelation exposes and opposes the key myths of Rome (Empire, the Roman Pax, Victoria, Faith, Eternity) with its own claims.[152]

John refuses to accept the claims to total truth or control represented by the Roman political, social, and economic system. This system claims authority over "*every* tribe and people and language and nation," a claim accepted by "*all* the inhabitants of the earth" (13:7, 8 [italics added]; see also 17:8, 15; 18:3). John, however, sees three contrary points: first, Rome can only exercise such power by divine permission (13:7; 17:17); second, *not everyone* accepts the control of the system (12:11, 17; 13:8, 10; 14:4, 12, 13; 18:4; 20:4); third, there is a competing kingdom that will ultimately prevail over the Greco-Roman system (1:5, 6, 9; 2:26–28; 3:21; 5:9–10; 11:15–18; 12:5, 11; 15:3–4; 19:6–9, 15, 16; 20:4). He thus de-totalizes the Roman world

---

151. Cf. Friesen, *Imperial Cults*, 141.
152. Howard-Brook and Gwyther, *Unveiling Empire*, 223–35.

as a system, though in the name of what is apparently a rival totalization, the kingdom of God.

He disassembles the Greco-Roman worldview and system into its constituent features (idolatry, sexual impurity, sorcery), getting behind the rhetoric to the reality it conceals. For instance, many cities in the empire built idols to the emperor and to the goddess Roma. But in John's vision, Roma becomes a prostitute.[153] She is "clothed in purple and scarlet, and adorned with gold and jewels and pearls" but is holding "a golden cup full of abominations and the impurities of her fornication" (17:4). She is "the mother of whores" (17:5) and drunk on Christians' blood (17:6), and "the wine of the wrath of her fornication" (18:3). Moreover she is destined to be stripped and burned (17:16) by her erstwhile allies—one of John's more striking and controversial metaphors, though not original to him (see Ezek 16:35-42). As Richard Bauckham argues,

> To those who associate with her she offers the supposed benefits of the Pax Romana, much lauded in the Roman propaganda of this period. Rome offered the Mediterranean world unity, security, stability, the conditions of prosperity. But in John's view these benefits are not what they seem: they are the favours of a prostitute, purchased at a high price. The Pax Romana is really a system of economic exploitation of the empire.[154]

The Emperor Cult

How did ancient Rome function as God's enemy in the first century? Its persecution of Christians was only sporadic then, and its destruction of Jerusalem and the temple would probably have been seen by Christians as the work of God's judgment.[155] But Rome was already starting to function as the champion of traditional Greco-Roman polytheism as against new "superstitions." Wilken points out that the Romans saw themselves as more religious than other peoples, strongly believing in divine providence as the basis for the prosperity of their empire, distinguishing between true

---

153. Drawing on prophetic imagery from the Old Testament used to attack various nations (see Friesen, *Imperial Cults*, 205-7) and possibly the story of the actual empress/imperial mother Julia Agrippina (Stramara, *God's Timetable*, 93-96, 111-15).

154. Bauckham, *Climax of Prophecy*, 347.

155. Following the lead of Jesus as quoted in Matt 23:34—24:2; Mark 13:1-2; Luke 21:5-6; see also John 2:19-20; Matt 26:61; Mark 14:58; Acts 6:13-14.

religion and groundless superstition[156] and "suspicious of innovations and mistrustful of new religious ideas and practices."[157]

However, there was a growing emperor cult outside Rome, especially strong in the territory of Asia Minor (the location of the seven churches of Revelation), which had three provincial cults by A.D. 100.[158] Here cults of Roman power (for example, the goddess Roma) began as early as the second century B.C.,[159] but specific imperial cults came with the rule of Augustus Caesar, in recognition of the stability and prosperity he had brought:[160] he was called a god, son of god, and savior, and his birth was considered as "the beginning of the breath of life"[161] or "the beginning of all things"[162] for his citizens. As Howard-Brook and Gwyther point out, "the foundational myth of the Roman Empire . . . was the myth of *Augustus*," linked in turn to the myth of the past "golden age."[163]

According to Price, "The imperial cult . . . was probably the most important cult in the province of Asia."[164] Nearly all cities were involved,[165] with the initiative coming from the citizens in most cases.[166] Cities competed with other cities for the honor of having an imperial temple or festival and being able to claim the title of *neokoros* ("temple warden").[167] The cult was represented visually by statues of the emperor, temples dedicated to him,[168] and various images of him which functioned as "an expression of imperial ideology."[169]

"The honors, temples, priests, festivals and sacrifices, were curiously close to the honors given to the traditional gods,"[170] and sometimes explicitly called the emperor a god,[171] though the deified emperor was still carefully

156. Wilken, *Christians*, 57–63.
157. Ibid., 62.
158. Friesen, *Imperial Cults*, 54.
159. Price, *Rituals and Power*, 224; Friesen, *Imperial Cults*, 28–29.
160. Price, *Rituals and Power*, 54–56, 106; Friesen, *Imperial Cults*, 25–32.
161. Price, *Rituals and Power*, 55, quoting a document of the assembly of the province of Asia. Cf. Friesen, *Imperial Cults*, 32–34.
162. Price, *Rituals and Power*, 245; Friesen, *Imperial Cults*, 33.
163. Howard-Brook and Gwyther, *Unveiling Empire*, 114, see also 226–27.
164. Price, *Rituals and Power*, 130.
165. Ibid., 83; Friesen, *Imperial Cults*, 56.
166. Price, *Rituals and Power*, 36, 56. Cf. Friesen, *Imperial Cults*, 36–38.
167. Price, *Rituals and Power*, 64; Friesen, *Imperial Cults*, 37, 47, 55.
168. Price, *Rituals and Power*, 3, 134–36, 169.
169. Ibid., 171.
170. Ibid., 3. Cf. Friesen, *Imperial Cults*, 120.
171. Price, *Rituals and Power*, 3, 244. For example, one dedication called Tiberius

subordinated to the traditional gods[172] and usually the sacrifices of the cult were offered *for* him (to the gods) rather than *to* him.[173] However, there *were* times when sacrifice was made *to* the emperor or to the *Sebastoi* (the emperors as a group), or where cult was demanded, as by Gaius (Caligula).[174]

Cults were established with a view to being permanent and obligatory, with severe penalties for acting against the regulations involved.[175] The imperial cult was seen primarily as a force for order and loyalty[176] and helped unite the peoples of the empire.[177] As Steven Friesen argues, "A whole new aspect of religious discourse was evolving in the empire, one with potential for symbolic coherence at several levels of community life."[178] The imperial cult was shaping the worldview of the populace, including how they thought about time[179] and history, space (with Rome as the center of the world), gender, death, and the future (the cults looked for the permanent continuance of the Roman empire).[180]

The early Christians were troubled by the imperial cult and did not participate in it. This caused considerable outcry, and many were martyred during imperial festivals, though mainly for their opposition to traditional cults in general rather than specifically that of the emperors.[181] When Christians refused to offer sacrifice to the image of the emperor, it was partly because this meant sacrificing to a man and partly because it meant sacrificing to the pagan gods.[182] They probably had a similar perspective to that of Friesen, who sees the emperor cults as "an imperialist elaboration within Greco-Roman polytheism."[183]

There are apparent allusions to most of the features of the emperor cult in Revelation. For example, the famous beast passages in Revelation

---

Caesar "the greatest of the gods" (ibid., 63).

172. Ibid., 232.

173. Ibid., 209-15, 233. Cf. Friesen, *Imperial Cults*, 124-25.

174. Price, *Rituals and Power*, 209, 212, 215-18; Friesen, *Imperial Cults*, 39-41.

175. Price, *Rituals and Power*, 61, 112, 121, 184, 204-5; Friesen, *Imperial Cults*, 131.

176. Price, *Rituals and Power*, 132.

177. Howard-Brook and Gwyther, *Unveiling Empire*, 102.

178. Friesen, *Imperial Cults*, 95, see also 126-27.

179. As expressed in the calendar and festivals (cf. Friesen, *Imperial Cults*, 125-26, 158).

180. Friesen, *Imperial Cults*, 122-31.

181. Price, *Rituals and Power*, 123-25, 221-22. Comp. the famous tests ordered by Pliny in the early second century (see Wilken, *Christians*, 25-28).

182. Price, *Rituals and Power*, 221.

183. Friesen, *Imperial Cults*, 4.

13-14[184] allude to its institutionalization (13:11-18), its importance in people's lives (13:4,16), its universality (13:7,11-15), its popular origins (13:3-4,11-12),[185] the involvement of the emperor (13:5-8), the pressure to establish such cults (13:12-15), the penalties imposed on non-conformists (13:15-17),[186] the willingness of the Greeks to explicitly call the reigning emperor a god and offer cult to him (13:3-8) including explicit worship (13:4, 15; 14:11), the representation of the cult by statues and images of the emperor (13:14-15), and portents associated with these (13:13-14).

Revelation agrees that the imperial cult was a force for order and loyalty, and expressed the ideals and conflicts of the world of that day (13:3-4; 17:13, 17; 18:9-10). There are probable allusions to the centrality of the city of Pergamum (which was permitted to construct the first provincial temple dedicated to Augustus)[187] in the cult (2:13). Revelation seems to allude to the earlier cults of Roman power and the goddess Roma (17:1-6, 18),[188] the honors given to Augustus Caesar (1:6, 10, 17-18; 2:8, 18; 3:14; 5:9, 12; 7:10; 12:10; 17:9-10; 22:13), and the decision of early Christians not to participate in it, even at the cost of persecution and death (13:7-10; 14:6-13; 20:4).

Many early Christians were eager not to seem disloyal or to portray Jesus as a threat or rival to the emperor, in spite of claims that this was the case.[189] However, the claim that Jesus was Lord[190] inevitably meant that conflict would arise. John makes this more explicit when he portrays Jesus as divine world ruler and savior, both in the titles he ascribes to him (1:5, 17; 2:8, 18; 3:14; 17:14; 22:12), and in his symbolic imagery of Jesus as a glorious majestic imperial figure (1:13-16; 3:21), a source of salvation to his followers (5:9; 7:10), an invincible general (19:11-16), and head of a thousand-year reign (20:6)—especially in the "coronation scene," where Jesus is recognized in heaven as the rightful Messiah and world ruler, worthy of acclamation and worship (Rev 5). Even John's phrase "the Lord's day" (1:10) amounts to an assault on the empire's pretensions to control time.[191]

John does not mention the emperor cult by name or specifically argue against it. His approach, in some ways similar to that of the other

184. Cf. Price, *Rituals and Power*, 146, 201-4.
185. Cf. ibid., 202-3.
186. Cf. Howard-Brook and Gwyther, *Unveiling Empire*, 104.
187. Friesen, *Imperial Cults*, 25-27.
188. Cf. ibid., 26-28, 38.
189. See Acts 17:7; 25:8,11; Rom.13:1-7; 1 Pet.2:13-14.
190. E.g., Matt 28:18; Acts 2:34-36; Rom 10:9; 1 Cor 8:5-6; Eph 1:20-22; Phil 2:9-11; Col 1:15-18; 2:10.
191. Cf. Friesen, *Imperial Cults*, 157-61.

apocalypses, is to use symbolic language to reinterpret and undermine what the cult stands for, as in Revelation 13. He describes the emperor or empire by using the symbolic picture of two wild beasts, one from the sea (representing the emperor or empire, 13:1) and one from the land (13:11, representing those who promote and enforce the cult). This devalues the emperors: they are not only not divine or even heroic, they are not even truly human, and as wild beasts they are not champions of order but threats to it. John here draws on apocalyptic traditions that represented ungodly kingdoms as wild beasts,[192] and the earlier myths of Leviathan and Behemoth, to "label Rome as the ghastly embodiment of all of history's oppressors, one of the greatest sources of chaos in the world, and a mythic opponent of Israel's God."[193]

He attributes the origin of the beast to the dragon (13:2, 4), the devil or Satan, "the deceiver of the whole world" (12:9), who has lost his position in heaven (12:8–10) and is engaged in a hopeless "last stand" because "he knows that his time is short!" (12:12).[194] Thus the emperor is seen as the tool of the evil one rather than the favored one of the gods or a god himself, and worship of him is really worship of the dragon (13:4). Three angels warn of the consequences of worshipping the beast (14:6–11).

In these ways, John turns his audience against the emperor cult, and indeed against the imperial narrative as such, by reinterpreting the whole system as a deceptive and deadly plot.[195] And yet he does this by describing features of the emperor cult and system that everyone would recognize, using symbolic apocalyptic language that his Jewish and Christian readers could immediately relate to. He has taken a position *outside* the system (as a Christian) to critique it in terms of its unstated assumptions and implications (blasphemous claims, oppression, persecution of dissidents) as against its own (quite credible) claims to provide order and promote prosperity in the ancient world. In a sense, then, John has deconstructed the cult and the propaganda of the empire as such.

CONCLUSION

The evidence and arguments of this chapter support the idea, framed in the previous chapter, that Revelation points to and presupposes the existence of a Christian Story and a worldview that attempts to give a framing explanation of human history, including the experiences and aspirations of all

---

192. Cf. Daniel 7.
193. Friesen, *Imperial Cults*, 175.
194. Ibid., 202.
195. Ibid., 147.

cultures and peoples, in terms of the salvation history of the Bible, viewed as both a war epic and a mega-romance. Revelation does this largely by visualizing the end of history in the context of its Old Testament origins, predicting how the different experiences and struggles of humanity will turn out.

This Story makes universal claims and rejects such claims by its rivals. As Steven Friesen rightly argues, "The two great cities claiming dominion over John's congregations were Jerusalem and Rome, and John attempted to strip both of their claims."[196] In other words, he refuses to subordinate his story to the metanarratives of the Jews or the Romans.

However, John's attitude to the other narratives is not just hostile; he is quite ready to take up the narratives of many different cultures if they can serve his Christian purpose in some way. Thus the narrative of Judaism is included, reinterpreted, but fulfilled by the Christian message, according to Revelation. Many of the narratives of the non-Jewish world (such as the combat myth or astrological knowledge) are more radically transformed, but can still be included, or explained sympathetically, as part of this Christian perspective. The aspirations and hopes of both Jews and Gentiles are taken up into John's Big Story, as we see especially in the description of the New Jerusalem, which is a Jewish-Christian-Greek *polis* in a setting of order and stability.

On the other hand, some rival narratives (most notably those of imperial Rome) and polytheistic practices must be refuted and rejected completely, because their claims are ultimately "blasphemous."

Thus John shows us a possible strategy for Christians today in their response to other worldviews and ideologies of our time. While postmodern Christians perhaps may be wary of the term "metanarrative," with its loaded implications, they should not be afraid of claims that involve seeing the Christian Story as framing and explaining the narratives of different cultures and providing them with a hope of fulfillment of their highest aspirations in Christ, albeit with alterations and adjustments. Only the most blasphemous (that is, syncretistic or imperialistic)[197] claims need to be rejected utterly. In making these responses, Christians are giving priority to the Big Story traced in the Bible.

Thus if by "pluralism" is meant that all narratives are valid, or valid only within specific cultures, an authentic Christian worldview would disagree, because the Jesus of the New Testament (including Revelation) makes claims to uniqueness and universal lordship,[198] claims not found in most

---

196. Ibid., 162.

197. In the sense of exalting human rule above worship of God.

198. As discussed in chapter 5.

other major world religions and ideologies. The spiritual and soteriological dualism explored in chapter 3 of this book, and the ideas of universal truth discussed in chapter 4, undergird the priority of the Big Story identified in chapter 6. This Story does have similarities to a metanarrative in its claims. Moreover the last judgment scene in Revelation 20 seems to imply some form of soteriological exclusivism.

However, if by "exclusiveness" is meant that all other human stories and aspirations must be totally rejected, this goes too far in the other direction. The Big Story implied by Revelation leads us to search for ways in which all stories (other than those that are blasphemous) find their true fulfillment in the Story of Christ,[199] which is itself to be seen primarily as a love story, not something to be imposed on non-Christians by any form of human power.

For, contrary to what is sometimes believed, this Story does not end in a bland uniformity. The nations are not abolished with the establishment of the New Jerusalem. They are healed (22:2), they walk by the light of the city of God (22:24), and they bring their glory into the city (21:24, 26), but their "glory and honor" (21:26) are preserved. In other words, the new world order envisaged by John does not imply a uniform culture, but a variety of reformed Christian cultures (21:27). Absolute truth coexists with diversity of expression.

---

199. Cf. Carson, *Gagging of God*, 299.

CONCLUSION

Towards a Christian Worldview for the Twenty-First Century

Recapitulating the Study

THE GOAL OF THIS study has been to explore and construct a biblical Christian response to the issues raised by the growing dominance of postmodernist thought in Western culture, by studying a book of the Christian Scriptures that seemed to interact with its contemporary rival worldviews in a way that might prove relevant and suggestive today.

In chapter 1, I began by arguing that the gradual shift to postmodernism involves a change in the modern Western worldview, perhaps even the creation of a new worldview that is literally "post-modern" in that it is supplanting the Enlightenment worldview of modernity. Christian responses to this shift have been varied, contradictory, and confused, but this study has demonstrated that there is a tension between postmodernism (and modernity) and some understandings of the Christian worldview, and that there are battles going on concerning the interpretation of the Christian Scriptures themselves. Postmodernist approaches to Revelation illustrated the tensions uncovered in a particular textual situation, confirming these conclusions.

In the Introduction, I argued that the text of Revelation may be profitably explored for possible Christian responses to important worldview questions raised by the postmodernist debate. Chapters 3–6 sought to show how this might work by examining specific issues where modernity, postmodernism, and Christianity are interacting and asking what light could be shed on these by studying the text of Revelation. Specifically, I have been trying to identify some of the essential features of a Christian worldview through this process.

Before examining such contemporary issues, in chapter 2 I examined the relationship between Revelation and the worldviews of its own day, both the broad ancient Mediterranean and Near Eastern worldview and the more specific Hellenistic and Jewish forms. I argued that Revelation, though it embodies ancient thinking, strikes out in new directions compared with its contemporary worldviews, thus implying that it may yet help us construct a Christian worldview for today.

I then argued that a Christian worldview ought to reaffirm the reality of the spirit world and that Christians should also maintain a spiritual dualism that differentiates between good and evil, true and false, spirituality. This will be in tension with most forms of postmodernism (chapter 3).

Turning to questions of epistemology, focused especially around the question of foundationalism, I then argued for the validity of revelation (supported by testimony and prophecy) as a genuine source of knowledge, even as a paradigm of a Christian epistemology. This raises many issues to do with truth, and again there will be tensions with some postmodernisms, but revelation seems to be an essential concept for a Christian worldview (chapter 4).

Next, in the light of postmodernist criticism of the "subject" of modernity and modern concepts of the human person, my examination of Revelation led to a multifaceted picture of the human person, particularly centered on relationship to God. This was followed by an exploration of personhood as a central concept to a Christian cosmology in the light of the Christian views of God and creation (chapter 5).

The last two chapters have explored the concept of metanarrative, one of the distinctive ideas contributed by postmodernism to current discourse, and asked whether or not there is (or should be) a Christian metanarrative. This discussion necessitated looking at the traditional Christian salvation history, as reflected in Revelation, and interacting with postmodernist forms of pluralism. I have argued that there is a Christian Story that can be told somewhat like a metanarrative in the sense that it offers a framework for all the stories of humanity, seeking to fulfill the true aspirations of varying cultures, but sifting out their false elements and providing hope of a final end to history. Structured as a war epic, with the implication that it decisively rejects rival stories, this Story encapsulates the dualism referred to before. On the other hand, this Big Story does not answer all questions and should not be used to exclude all other stories from sympathetic consideration, provided that they are not "blasphemous." Rather this Story should be told primarily as a romance, demonstrating that it is not meant to be used oppressively (chapters 6–7).

RELEVANCE OF REVELATION

This book has shown that John, in the Book of Revelation, has successfully created a sense of a Christian Story within which Christians can interact with alternative worldviews and narratives, both those of his day and, by implication, those of our day. Hence Revelation has something relevant and valuable to contribute to Christian thinking in the twenty-first century. While its worldview and emphases must be examined critically in the light of two thousand years of history, developments in human knowledge in the modern era, and the particular issues of postmodernism, this text is able to help define a Christian worldview appropriate for a postmodern world.

This is an important conclusion since Revelation has notoriously been misused over the centuries since it was written.[1] It has certainly been put into service to justify a Christian metanarrative in the worst sense of the term. For example, its hostility to syncretism has been used to justify persecution of non-Christian minorities in the world of Christendom, especially in the Middle Ages and the age of European empires. It has also been used to try to predict the future directions of history, sometimes with initial success, but often with the result of producing narrow sects and even cults.

Today this text is being pressed into service for all kinds of agendas, from liberation theology to fundamentalist dispensationalism; others are rejecting it because it will not serve their agendas. In this book, I have described one way of responsibly using this text that is not just of antiquarian interest, demonstrating how Revelation can become a conversation partner and guide for postmodern Christians.

DEFINING A CHRISTIAN WORLDVIEW

Revelation, together with the whole Bible, can help us identify a Christian worldview relevant to this era. Clearly such a claim is open to challenge, and of course there is more than one possible way of articulating such a worldview. Inevitably, and rightly, a Christian worldview will take on the coloring (cultural forms and nuances) of its location, just as it did in John's case, with his sympathy to both Jewish and Greek ideas.

---

1. I develop this point further in Newton, *Revelation Reclaimed*.

However, I still maintain that there can be a *distinctively Christian* worldview that is able to be extrapolated from its contexts in time and space. Moreover the worldview features identified in this book will prove to be an essential part of such a Christian worldview. That is, a truly Christian worldview will always need to affirm the reality of the spirit world (with dualistic features), the validity of revelation (however defined) as a form of real knowledge, the fundamental nature of personhood, and the priority of the biblical Story of creation, redemption, and consummation as an overarching explanation of human history.

CHRISTIAN POSITIONS AND OTHER VIEWS IN TODAY'S WORLD

We live in a time when rival worldviews—not just those of modernity and postmodernity, but also a resurgent Islam and Westernized Hinduism—are competing for space and dominance in the world. What responses can Christians make to this?

One possibility would be for Christians to align themselves with one of the non-Christian alternatives. To some degree this is what happened in the West in the modern era: many Christian theologians and biblical scholars accepted the worldview of Enlightenment modernity and tailored their faith to either suit this position (theological liberalism) or fight it on its terms (fundamentalism). But the rationalistic worldview of Enlightenment modernity was fundamentally incompatible with Christianity, hence it became a straightjacket that hindered the full expression of a biblical viewpoint, for example, on the supernatural.

It seems to me that a simple alignment with postmodernism would be just as contradictory and unworkable. If Christians are going to take their own Scriptures seriously as revelation of truth, they will have to take the worldview of the Scriptures seriously, and its claims to final truth are too strong to be glossed over, as this study of Revelation makes plain.

But the opposite strategy is equally faulty. Christians cannot simply return to the premodern worldview of the ancient and medieval eras. The insights generated within modernity, especially the scientific outlook and the liberal democratic aspirations of the Enlightenment, cannot easily be jettisoned, and neither should they be. The same point applies to the insights produced by postmodernism about the perspectival nature of truth and the effect of political considerations on our enquiries and interpretations of reality and texts. It must also be said that the aspirations of postmodernity are not only here to stay, but are often compatible with (even demanded by) a

Christian position in areas such as justice, tolerance, multicultural sensitivity, and restoration of forgotten or suppressed perspectives (such as those of indigenous peoples).

A Christian Story must therefore be told romantically, not oppressively; not "riding roughshod" over other people's aspirations, beliefs, and traditions, but looking for ways in which these can be fulfilled in the Story. However, many of the legitimate and defensible perspectives of premodern Christianity also need to be recovered and re-examined. Christians need to defend the reality of the spiritual and supernatural, the viability of revelation as a starting point for enquiry, the centrality of personhood, and the credibility and relevance of the Christian Story. They also need to resist postmodern ideas such as that all spirituality is good or that no absolute truth can be found. This study of Revelation brings these issues to the forefront for serious consideration.

Christians in the twenty-first century thus need to perform a balancing act to remain both true to Scripture and in touch with the cultures and worldviews around them.

Bibliography

Abraham, Joseph. "Feminist Hermeneutics and Pentecostal Spirituality: The Creation Narrative of Genesis as a Paradigm." *AJPS* 6/1 (2003) 3–21.
Abrams, M. H. "Apocalypse: Theme and Romantic Variations." In *The Revelation of St. John the Divine*, edited by Harold Bloom, 7–34. New York: Chelsea House, 1988.
Adams, Edward. *Constructing the World: A Study in Paul's Cosmological Language*. Edinburgh: T. & T. Clark, 2000.
Allen, Diogenes. "Christian Values in a Post-Christian Context." In *Postmodern Theology: Christian Faith in a Pluralist World*, edited by Fredric Burnham, 20–55. San Francisco: Harper and Row, 1989.
Alston, William P. *Perceiving God: The Epistemology of Religious Experience*. Ithaca, NY: Cornell University Press, 1991.
———. "Religious Experience as a Ground of Religious Belief." In *Religious Experience and Religious Belief: Essays in the Epistemology of Religion*, edited by Joseph Runzo and Craig K. Ihara, 31–51. Lanham, MD: University Press of America, 1986.
Anderson, Allan. *An Introduction to Pentecostalism*. Cambridge: Cambridge University Press, 2004.
———. "Stretching the Definitions: Pneumatology and 'Syncretism' in African Pentecostalism." *JPT* 10 (2001) 98–119.
Anderson, Graham. *Ancient Fiction: The Novel in the Graeco-Roman World*. London: Croom Helm, 1984.
Anderson, Janice Capel, and Stephen D. Moore, editors. *Mark and Method: New Approaches in Biblical Studies*. Minneapolis: Fortress, 1992.
Archer, Kenneth J. "Pentecostal Hermeneutics: Retrospect and Prospect." *JPT* 8 (1996) 63–81.
Aune, David E. "The Apocalypse of John and the Problem of Genre." *Semeia* 36 (1986) 65–96.
——— (ed). *Greco-Roman Literature and the New Testament: Selected Forms and Genres*. Atlanta: Scholars Press, 1988.
———. *The New Testament in Its Literary Environment*. Philadelphia: Westminster, 1987.
———. *Prophecy in Early Christianity and the Ancient Mediterranean World*. Grand Rapids: Eerdmans, 1983.
———. *Revelation 1–5*. Word Biblical Commentary 52A. Dallas: Word, 1997.
———. *Revelation 6–16*. Word Biblical Commentary 52B. Nashville: Thomas Nelson, 1998.

———. *Revelation 17–22*. Word Biblical Commentary 52C. Nashville: Thomas Nelson, 1998.
Barr, David L. "The Apocalypse as a Symbolic Transformation of the World: A Literary Analysis." *Interpretation* 38 (1984) 39–50.
———. "The Apocalypse of John as Oral Enactment." *Interpretation* 40 (1986) 243–56.
———. *Tales of the End: A Narrative Commentary on the Book of Revelation*. Salem, OR: Polebridge, 2012.
———. "Towards an Ethical Reading of the Apocalypse: Reflections on John's Use of Power, Violence, and Misogyny." In *SBL 1997 Seminar Papers*, 358–73. Atlanta: Scholars Press, 1997.
Barth, Karl. *Protestant Theology in the Nineteenth Century*. London: SCM, 1972.
Bartholomew, Craig G., and Michael W. Goheen. *The Drama of Scripture: Finding Our Place in the Biblical Story*. Grand Rapids: Baker Academic, 2004.
Bauckham, Richard. *Bible and Mission: Christian Witness in a Postmodern World*. Milton Keynes: Paternoster, 2003.
———. *The Climax of Prophecy: Studies on the Book of Revelation*. Edinburgh: T. & T. Clark, 1993.
———. *The Theology of the Book of Revelation*. Cambridge: Cambridge University Press, 1993.
Beale, G.K. *The Book of Revelation*. The New International Greek Testament Commentary. Grand Rapids: Eerdmans, 1999.
———. *John's Use of the Old Testament in Revelation*. JSNTSS. Sheffield: Sheffield Academic, 1998.
———. *The Use of Daniel in Jewish Apocalyptic Literature and in the Revelation of St John*. Lanham, MD: University Press of America, 1984.
Beasley-Murray, G. R. *The Book of Revelation*. New Century Bible. London: Oliphants, 1974.
Bellah, Robert N. *Beyond Belief*. New York: Harper & Row, 1970.
Benjamin, Andrew, editor. *The Lyotard Reader*. Oxford: Basil Blackwell, 1989.
Berger, Peter L. *Invitation to Sociology*. Harmondsworth: Penguin, 1966.
———. *A Rumour of Angels*. Harmondsworth: Penguin, 1970.
———. *The Sacred Canopy*. New York: Anchor, 1969.
Bertens, Hans. *The Idea of the Postmodern: A History*. London: Routledge, 1995.
Bernstein, J.M. "Grand Narratives." In *On Paul Ricoeur: Narrative and Interpretation*, edited by David Wood, 102–23. London: Routledge, 1991.
Best, Steven, and Douglas Kellner. *Postmodern Theory: Critical Interrogations*. London: Macmillan, 1991.
Bible and Culture Collective (Aichele, George, et al.). *The Postmodern Bible*. New Haven, CT: Yale University Press, 1995.
Biguzzi, Giancarlo. "Ephesus, Its Artemision, Its Temple to the Flavian Emperors, and Idolatry in Revelation." *NovT* 40 (1998) 276–90.
Blanning, Tim. *The Pursuit of Glory*. London: Penguin, 2007.
Bloesch, Donald G. *Holy Scripture: Revelation, Inspiration, and Interpretation*. Downers Grove, IL: InterVarsity, 1994.
Blomberg, Craig L. "New Testament Genre Criticism for the 1990s." *Themelios* 15 (1990) 40–48.
Blond, Phillip. *Post-Secular Philosophy: Between Philosophy and Theology*. London: Routledge, 1998.

Bloom, Harold, editor. *The Revelation of St. John the Divine*. New York: Chelsea House, 1988.
Blount, Brian K. "Reading Revelation Today: Witness as Active Resistance." *Interpretation* 54 (2000) 398–412.
Boer, Roland. *Knockin' on Heaven's Door: The Bible and Popular Culture*. London: Routledge, 1999.
———. "A Slacker's Guide to Postmodernism." *APS* 2/3 (2000) 63–71.
Borgen, Peder and Soren Giversen, editors. *The New Testament and Hellenistic Judaism*. Peabody, MA: Hendrickson, 1997.
Boring, M. Eugene. "The Apocalypse as Christian Prophecy: A Discussion of the Issues Raised by the Book of Revelation for the Study of Early Christian Prophecy." In *SBL 1974 Seminar Papers*, vol. 2, edited by George MacRae, 43–62. Cambridge: Society of Biblical Literature, 1974.
———. *Revelation*. Interpretation Series. Louisville: John Knox, 1989.
Botha, P. J. J. "God, Emperor Worship and Society: Contemporary Experiences and the Book of Revelation." *Neotestamentica* 22 (1988) 87–102.
Bowman, John Wick. *The Drama of the Book of Revelation*. Philadelphia: Westminster, 1955.
———. "The Revelation to John: Its Dramatic Structure and Message." *Interpretation* 9 (1955) 436–53.
Boyd, Gregory A. *God at War: The Bible and Spiritual Conflict*. Downers Grove, IL: InterVarsity, 1997.
Brighton, Louis A. *Revelation*. Concordia Popular Commentary. St. Louis: Concordia, 2009.
Brooten, Bernadette J. "Early Christian Women and Their Cultural Context: Issues of Method in Historical Reconstruction." In *Feminist Perspectives on Biblical Scholarship*, edited by Adela Yarbro Collins, 65–91. Atlanta: Scholars Press, 1985.
Brown, Colin. *Philosophy and the Christian Faith: A Historical Sketch from the Middle Ages to the Present Day*. London: InterVarsity, 1969.
Bruce, Steve. "Cathedrals to Cults." In *Religion, Modernity and Postmodernity*, edited by Paul Heelas, 19–35. Oxford: Blackwell, 1998.
Burnett, David. *Clash of Worlds*. Crowborough, UK: MARC, 1990.
Burnham, Frederic, editor. *Postmodern Theology: Christian Faith in a Pluralist World*. San Francisco: Harper & Row, 1989.
Byrd, Joseph. "Paul Ricoeur's Hermeneutical Theory and Pentecostal Proclamation." *Pneuma* 15/2 (1993) 203–14.
Cahoone, Lawrence, editor. *From Modernism to Postmodernism: An Anthology*. Cambridge, MA: Blackwell, 1996.
Caird, G. B. *The Revelation of St. John the Divine*. London: A & C Black, 1984.
Caputo, John, editor. *Deconstruction in a Nutshell: A Conversation with Jacques Derrida*. New York: Fordham University Press, 1997.
———. *The Prayers and Tears of Jacques Derrida: Religion without Religion*. Bloomington: Indiana University Press, 1997.
Carey, William G. "Attention-Seeking Behavior: Rhetoric, Resistance, and Authority in the Book of Revelation." PhD diss., Vanderbilt University, 1996.
Carey, Greg. "The Apocalypse and Its Ambiguous Ethos." In *Studies in the Book of Revelation*, edited by Steve Moyise, 163–80. Edinburgh: T. & T. Clark, 2001.

Cargal, Timothy B. "Beyond the Fundamentalist-Modernist Controversy: Pentecostals and Hermeneutics in a Postmodern Age." *Pneuma* 15/2 (1993) 163–87.
Carr, G. Lloyd. *The Song of Solomon*. Tyndale Old Testament Commentaries. Leicester: InterVarsity, 1984.
Carrell, Peter R. *Jesus and the Angels: Angelology and the Christology of the Apocalypse of John*. Cambridge: Cambridge University Press, 1997.
Carson, D. A. *The Gagging of God: Christianity Confronts Pluralism*. Grand Rapids: Zondervan, 1996.
Cartledge, Mark J. *Practical Theology: Charismatic and Empirical Perspectives*. Carlisle: Paternoster, 2003.
Cavanaugh, William T. "The City: Beyond Secular Parodies." In *Radical Orthodoxy*, edited by John Milbank, Catherine Pickstock, and Graham Ward, 182–200. London: Routledge, 1999.
Chadwick, Henry. *The Early Church*. Harmondsworth: Penguin, 1967.
Charles, R. H. *A Critical and Exegetical Commentary on the Revelation of St. John*. 2 vols. Edinburgh: T. & T. Clark, 1920.
———, editor. *The Apocrypha and Pseudepigrapha of the Old Testament in English*. Oxford: Clarendon, 1913.
Charlesworth, J. H. "From Jewish Messianology to Christian Christology: Some Caveats and Perspectives." In *Judaisms and Their Messiahs at the Turn of the Christian Era*, edited by Jacob Neusner, William Scott Green, and Ernest S. Frerichs, 225–64. Cambridge: Cambridge University Press, 1987.
Charlesworth, Max. *Philosophy and Religion: From Plato to Postmodernism*. Oxford: Oneworld, 2002.
Chevalier, Jacques M. *A Postmodern Revelation: Signs of Astrology and the Apocalypse*. Toronto: University of Toronto Press, 1997.
Chilton, David. *The Days of Vengeance: An Exposition of the Book of Revelation*. Tyler, TX: Dominion, 1987.
Clines, David J. A. "The Postmodern Adventure in Biblical Studies." *APS* 1 (March 1998) 41–54.
Coady, C. A. J. *Testimony: A Philosophical Study*. Oxford: Clarendon, 1992.
Collins, Adela Yarbro. *The Combat Myth in the Book of Revelation*. Missoula, MT: Scholars Press, 1976.
———. *Crisis and Catharsis*. Philadelphia: Westminster, 1984.
———. "The Early Christian Apocalypses." *Semeia* 14 (1979) 61–122.
———, editor. *Feminist Perspectives on Biblical Scholarship*. Atlanta: Scholars Press, 1985.
———. "Feminine Symbolism in the Book of Revelation." *Biblical Interpretation* 1 (1993) 20–33.
———. "Reading the Book of Revelation in the Twentieth Century." *Interpretation* 40 (1986) 229–42.
Collins, John J. *The Apocalyptic Imagination*. New York: Crossroad, 1984.
———. *Between Athens and Jerusalem*. New York: Crossroad, 1983.
———. "Genre, Ideology, and Social Movements." In *Mysteries and Revelations*, edited by John J. Collins and James H. Charlesworth, 14–25. Sheffield: JSOT Press, 1991.
———. "Jewish Apocalypses." *Semeia* 14 (1979) 21–59.
———. "Pseudonymity, Historical Reviews and the Genre of the Revelation of John." *CBQ* 39 (1997) 329–43.

———. "Towards the Morphology of a Genre." *Semeia* 14 (1979) 1–20.
Collins, John J., and James H. Charlesworth, editors. *Mysteries and Revelations*. Sheffield: JSOT Press, 1991.
Corsini, Eugenio. *The Apocalypse: The Perennial Revelation of Jesus Christ*. Translated by Francis J. Moloney. Wilmington, DE: M. Glazier, 1983.
Court, John M. *Revelation*. Sheffield: Sheffield Academic, 1994.
Cox, Harvey. *Fire from Heaven*. Reading, MA: Addison-Wesley, 1995.
Craffert, Pieter F. "Altered States of Consciousness." In *Understanding the Social World of the New Testament*, edited by Dietmar Naufeld and Richard E. De Maris, 126–46. Oxford: Routledge, 2010.
Cukrowski, Kenneth. "The Influence of the Emperor Cult on the Book of Revelation." *Restoration Quarterly* 45 (2003) 51–64.
Cunningham, Conor. "Language: Wittgenstein after Theology." In *Radical Orthodoxy*, edited by John Milbank, Catherine Pickstock, and Graham Ward, 64–90. London: Routledge, 1999.
Cupitt, Don. *The Leap of Reason*. Philadelphia: Westminster, 1976.
———. "Post-Christianity." In *Religion, Modernity, and Postmodernity*, edited by Paul Heelas, 218–32. Oxford: Blackwell, 1998.
Davis, Steven J. "Introducing an Arabic Commentary on the Apocalypse: Ibn Katib Qaysar on Revelation." *HTR* 101/1 (2008) 77–96.
Dawkins, Richard. *The God Delusion*. London: Bantam, 2006.
Del Colle, Ralph. "Postmodernism and the Pentecostal-Charismatic Experience." *JPT* 17 (2000) 97–116.
Dempster, Murray W., Byron D. Klaus, and Douglas Petersen, editors. *The Globalization of Pentecostalism: A Religion Made to Travel*. Oxford: Regnum, 1999.
Derrida, Jacques. ———. "Of an Apocalyptic Tone Recently Adopted in Philosophy." Translated by John P. Leavey Jr. *Semeia* 23 (1982) 63–97.
Derrida, Jacques, and Gianni Vattimo, editors. *Religion*. Stanford, CA: Stanford University Press, 1998
DeSilva, David A. "Final Topics: The Rhetorical Functions of Intertexture in Revelation 14:14—16:21." In *The Intertexture of Apocalyptic Discourse in the New Testament*, edited by Duane Watson, 215–41. Atlanta: Society of Biblical Literature, 2002.
———. *Seeing Things John's Way*. Louisville: Westminster John Knox, 2009.
Desrosiers, Gilbert. *An Introduction to Revelation: A Pathway to Interpretation*. New York: Continuum, 2000.
Dewitt, Richard. *Worldviews: An Introduction to the History and Philosophy of Science*. Malden, MA: Blackwell, 2004.
Dockery, David S. editor. *The Challenge of Postmodernism: An Evangelical Engagement*. Grand Rapids: Baker, 1997.
Dodds, E. R. *Pagan and Christian in an Age of Anxiety*. Cambridge: Cambridge University Press, 1968.
Dumbrell, William J. *The End of the Beginning: Revelation 21–22 and the Old Testament*. Homebush West, NSW: Lancer, 1985.
Eagleton, Terry. *Against the Grain*. London: Verso, 1986.
———. *Ideology: An Introduction*. London: Verso, 1991.
———. *Literary Theory: An Introduction*. Oxford: Blackwell, 1996.
Edwards, Douglas R. "Pleasurable Reading or Symbols of Power?: Religious Themes and Social Context in Chariton." In *Ancient Fiction and Early Christian Narrative*,

edited by Ronald F. Hock, J. Bradley Chance, and Judith Perkins, 31–46. Atlanta: Scholars Press, 1998.

Ellington, Scott A. "History, Story and Testimony: Locating Truth in a Pentecostal Hermeneutic." *Pneuma* 23/2 (2001) 245–63.

———. "Pentecostalism and the Authority of Scripture." *JPT* 9 (1996) 16–38.

Emberley, Peter, and Barry Cooper, editors. *Faith and Political Philosophy: The Correspondence Between Leo Strauss and Eric Voegelin, 1934–1964*. Translated by Peter Emberley and Barry Cooper. University Park: Pennsylvania State University Press, 1993.

Erickson, Millard J. *Christian Theology*. Grand Rapids: Baker, 1998.

———. *Postmodernizing the Faith: Evangelical Responses to the Challenge of Postmodernism*. Grand Rapids: Baker, 1998.

Ervin, Howard M. "Hermeneutics: A Pentecostal Option." *Pneuma* (1981) 11–25.

Fackre, Gabriel. *The Doctrine of Revelation: A Narrative Interpretation*. Edinburgh: Edinburgh University Press, 1997.

Fairlamb, Horace L. *Critical Conditions: Postmodernity and the Question of Foundations*. Cambridge: Cambridge University Press, 1994.

Farrer, Austin. *The Revelation of St. John the Divine*. Oxford: Clarendon, 1964.

Fee, Gordon D. *Revelation*. New Covenant Commentary Series. Eugene, OR: Cascade Books, 2011.

Filho, Jose Adriano. "The Apocalypse of John as an Account of a Visionary Experience: Notes on the Book's Structure." *JSNT* 25/2 (2002) 213–34.

Fiorenza, Elisabeth Schüssler. *The Book of Revelation: Justice and Judgment*. Minneapolis: Fortress, 1998.

———. "Composition and Structure of the Book of Revelation." *CBQ* 39 (1977) 344–66.

———. "The Followers of the Lamb: Visionary Rhetoric and Social-Political Situation." *Semeia* 36 (1986) 123–46.

———. "Miracles, Mission, and Apologetics: An Introduction." In *Aspects of Religious Propaganda in Judaism and Early Christianity*, edited by Elisabeth Schüssler Fiorenza, 1–25. Notre Dame: University of Notre Dame Press, 1976.

———. "Remembering the Past in Creating the Future: Historical-Critical Scholarship and Feminist Biblical Interpretation." In *Feminist Perspectives on Biblical Scholarship*, edited by Adela Yarbro Collins, 43–63. Atlanta: Scholars Press, 1985.

———. "Revelation." In *The New Testament and its Modern Interpreters*, edited by E. J. Epp and G. W. MacRae, 407–27. Philadelphia: Fortress, 1989.

———. *Revelation: Vision of a Just World*. Minneapolis: Fortress, 1991.

———. "The Words of Prophecy: Reading the Apocalypse Theologically." In *Studies in the Book of Revelation*, edited by Steve Moyise, 1–20. Edinburgh: T. & T. Clark, 2001.

Fish, Stanley. *Is There a Text in This Class?* Cambridge, MA: Harvard University Press, 1980.

Foucault, Michel. "Truth and Power." In *The Foucault Reader*, edited by Paul Rabinow, 51–75. London: Penguin, 1991.

———. "What Is Enlightenment?" In *The Foucault Reader*, edited by Paul Rabinow, 32–50. London: Penguin, 1991.

Fowler, Robert M. "Postmodern Biblical Criticism." *Forum* 5 (1989) 3–30.

Fox, Robin Lane. *The Classical World*. London: Penguin, 2006.

Franke, John R. "Reforming Theology: Toward a Postmodern Reformed Dogmatics." *WTJ* 65 (2003) 1–26.
Friesen, Steven J. *Imperial Cults and the Apocalypse of John*. Oxford: Oxford University Press, 2005.
———. "Myth and Symbolic Resistance in Revelation 13." *JBL* 123 (2004) 281–313.
Garrow, A. J. P. *Revelation*. London: Routledge, 1997.
Gellner, Ernest. *Postmodernism, Reason, and Religion*. London: Routledge, 1992.
Georgi, Dieter. "Socioeconomic Reasons for the 'Divine Man' as a Propagandistic Pattern." In *Aspects of Religious Propaganda in Judaism and Early Christianity*, edited by Elisabeth Schüssler Fiorenza, 27–42. Notre Dame, IN: University of Notre Dame Press, 1976.
Giblin, Charles Homer. "Recapitulation and the Literary Coherence of John's Apocalypse." *CBQ* 56 (1994) 81–95.
Gilbertson, Michael. *God and History in the Book of Revelation*; Cambridge: Cambridge University Press, 2003.
Glass, James J. "Eschatology: A Clear and Present Danger—A Sure and Certain Hope." In *Pentecostal Perspectives*, edited by Keith Warrington, Keith, 121–46. Carlisle: Paternoster, 1998.
Glasson, T. Francis. "What Is Apocalyptic?" *NTS* 27 (1980) 98–105.
Goldin, Judah. "The Magic of Magic and Superstition." In *Aspects of Religious Propaganda in Judaism and Early Christianity*, edited by Elisabeth Schüssler Fiorenza, 115–47. Notre Dame, IN: University of Notre Dame Press, 1976.
Goldstein, Jonathan A. "How the Authors of 1 and 2 Maccabees Treated the 'Messianic' Promises." In *Judaisms and Their Messiahs at the Turn of the Christian Era*, edited by Jacob Neusner, William Scott Green, and Ernest S. Frerichs, 69–96. Cambridge: Cambridge University Press, 1987.
Goudzwaard, Bob. *Capitalism and Progress: A Diagnosis of Western Society*. Carlisle: Paternoster, 1997.
Green, Joel B. *Body, Soul, and Human Life: The Nature of Humanity in the Bible*. Milton Keynes: Paternoster, 2008.
Green, Peter. *Alexander to Actium: The Hellenistic Age*. London: Thames and Hudson, 1990.
Gregersen, Niels Henrik, and J. Wentzel van Huyssteen, editors. *Rethinking Theology and Science: Six Models for the Current Dialogue*. Grand Rapids: Eerdmans, 1998.
Gregg, Steve, editor. *Revelation: Four Views*. Nashville: T. Nelson, 1997.
Grenz, Stanley J. *A Primer on Postmodernism*. Grand Rapids: Eerdmans, 1996.
Grenz, Stanley J., and Franke, John R. *Beyond Foundationalism: Shaping Theology in a Postmodern Context*. Louisville: Westminster John Knox, 2001.
Griffin, David Ray. "Introduction: Postmodern Spirituality and Society." In *Spirituality and Society: Postmodern Visions*, edited by David Ray Griffin, 1–32. Albany: State University of New York Press, 1988.
———. "Introduction: Varieties of Postmodern Theology." In *Varieties of Postmodern Theology*, edited by David Ray Griffin, William A. Beardslee, and Joe Holland, 1–8. Albany: State University of New York Press, 1989.
———. "Liberation Theology and Postmodern Philosophy." In *Varieties of Postmodern Theology*, edited by David Ray Griffin, William A. Beardslee, and Joe Holland, 129–48. Albany: State University of New York Press, 1989.

———. "Peace and the Postmodern Paradigm." In *Spirituality and Society: Postmodern Visions*, edited by David Ray Griffin, 143–54. Albany: State University of New York Press, 1988.

———. "Postmodern Theology and A/theology: A Response to Mark C. Taylor." In *Varieties of Postmodern Theology*, edited by David Ray Griffin, William A. Beardslee, and Joe Holland, 29–62. Albany: State University of New York Press, 1989.

Grigg, Viv. "Urban Theology as Transformational Conversation: Hermeneutics for Post-Modern Critics." *PCBC Journal*, November 2000, 7–12.

Groothuis, Douglas. *Truth Decay: Defending Christianity against the Challenges of Postmodernism*. Downers Grove, IL: InterVarsity, 2000.

Hampshire, Stuart. "Fallacies in Moral Philosophy." In *Revisions: Changing Perspectives in Moral Philosophy*, edited by Stanley Hauerwas and Alasdair MacIntyre, 51–67. Notre Dame, IN: University of Notre Dame Press, 1983.

Hannah, Darrell D. "The Throne of His Glory: The Divine Throne and Heavenly Mediators in Revelation and the Similitudes of Enoch." *ZNW* 94 (2003) 68–96.

Hanson, Paul D., editor. *Visionaries and Their Apocalypses*. Philadelphia: Fortress, 1983.

Harrington, Hannah K., and Rebecca Patten. "Pentecostal Hermeneutics and Postmodern Literary Theory." *Pneuma* 16/1 (1994) 109–14.

Hart, Kevin. *Postmodernism: A Beginner's Guide*. Oxford: Oneworld, 2004.

———. *The Trespass of the Sign*. Cambridge: Cambridge University Press, 1989.

Harvey, David. *The Condition of Postmodernity*. Oxford: Blackwell, 1989.

Hatina, Thomas R. "Intertextuality and Historical Criticism in New Testament Studies: Is There a Relationship?" *BibInt* 7 (1999) 28–43.

Hauerwas, Stanley, and Alasdair MacIntyre, editors. *Revisions: Changing Perspectives in Moral Philosophy*. Notre Dame, IN: University of Notre Dame Press, 1983.

Heelas, Paul, editor. *Religion, Modernity, and Postmodernity*. Oxford: Blackwell, 1998.

Hekman, Susan J. *Gender and Knowledge: Elements of a Postmodern Feminism*. Cambridge: Polity, 1990.

Hellholm, David, editor. *Apocalypticism in the Mediterranean World and the Near East*. Tubingen: J.C.B. Mohr, 1983.

———. "The Problem of Apocalyptic Genre and the Apocalypse of John." *Semeia* 36 (1986) 13–64.

Helms, Charles Robert. "The Apocalypse in the Early Church." PhD diss., Oxford University, 1991.

Hengel, Martin. *Judaism and Hellenism*. 2 vols. Philadelphia: Fortress, 1974.

Heschel, Abraham J. *The Prophets: An Introduction*. 2 vols. New York: Harper & Row, 1962.

Hey, Sam. "Contemporary Developments in Pentecostal Hermeneutics." *PCBC Journal*, August 2001, 1–6.

Hick, John. *The Second Christianity*. London: SCM, 1983.

———. "Towards a Philosophy of Religious Pluralism." In *Religious Experience and Religious Belief*, edited by Joseph Runzo and Craig K. Ihara, 99–116. Lanham, MD: University Press of America, 1986.

Hill, David. "Prophecy and Prophets in the Revelation of St. John." *NTS* 18 (1972) 401–18.

Hock, Ronald F., J. Bradley Chance, and Judith Perkins, editors. *Ancient Fiction and Early Christian Narrative*. Atlanta: Scholars Press, 1998.

Hock, Ronald F. "The Greek Novel." In *Greco-Roman Literature and the New Testament: Selected Forms and Genres*, edited by David E. Aune, 127–46. Atlanta: Scholars Press, 1988.

———. "Why New Testament Scholars Should Read Ancient Novels." In *Ancient Fiction and Early Christian Narrative*, edited by Ronald F. Hock, J. Bradley Chance, and Judith Perkins, 121–38. Atlanta: Scholars Press, 1998.

Hodgson, Peter C. *God in History: Shapes of Freedom*. Nashville: Abingdon, 1989.

Hollinger, Dennis. "The Church as Apologetic: A Sociology of Knowledge Perspective." In *Christian Apologetics in the Postmodern World*, edited by Timothy R. Phillips and Dennis L. Okholm, 182–93. Downers Grove, IL: InterVarsity, 1995.

Houston, James M. *I Believe in the Creator*. Grand Rapids: Eerdmans, 1980.

Howard-Brook, Wes, and Anthony Gwyther. *Unveiling Empire: Reading Revelation Then and Now*. Maryknoll, NY: Orbis, 1999.

Howson, Barry. "Eschatology in Sixteenth and Seventeenth Century England." *EQ* 70 (1998) 325–50.

Humphrey, Edith M. "The Sweet and the Sour: Epics of Wrath and Return in the Apocalypse." In *Society of Biblical Literature 1991 Seminar Papers*, edited by Eugene H. Lovering, 451–60. Atlanta: Scholars Press, 1991.

Hurtgen, John E. *Anti-Language in the Apocalypse of John*. Lewiston, NY: Mellen Biblical, 1993.

Husserl, Edmund. "The Crisis of European Sciences." In *From Modernism to Postmodernism: An Anthology*, edited by Lawrence Cahoone, 226–42. Cambridge, MA: Blackwell, 1996.

Ihde, Don. "Text and the New Hermeneutics." In *On Paul Ricoeur: Narrative and Interpretation*, edited by David Wood, 124–39. London: Routledge, 1991.

Ingleby, Jonathan. "Two Cheers for Postmodernism." *Third Way* 15/4 (1992) 24–27.

Jack, Alison M. "Out of the Wilderness: Feminist Perspectives on the Book of Revelation." In *Studies in the Book of Revelation*, edited by Steve Moyise, 149–62. Edinburgh: T. & T. Clark, 2001.

———. *Texts Reading Texts: Sacred and Secular*. JSNTSS 179. Sheffield: Sheffield Academic, 1999.

Jaichandran, Rebecca, and B. D. Madhav. "Pentecostal Spirituality in a Postmodern World." *AJPS* 6/1 (2003) 39–61.

Jameson, Frederic. *Postmodernism, or, The Cultural Logic of Late Capitalism*. London: Verso, 1991.

Jang, Young. "Narrative Function of the Apocalypse." *Scriptura* 80 (2002) 186–96.

Jaspers, Karl. *Philosophical Faith and Revelation*. Translated by E. B. Ashton. London: Collins, 1967.

Jeffrey, David Lyle, and C. Stephen Evans, editors. *The Bible and the University*. Milton Keynes: Paternoster, 2007.

Johns, Jackie David. "Pentecostalism and the Postmodern Worldview." *JPT* 7 (1995) 73–96.

Johns, Jackie David, and Cheryl Bridges Johns. "Yielding to the Spirit: A Pentecostal Approach to Group Bible Study." *JPT* 1 (1992) 109–34.

Johnson, William Stacy. "Rethinking Theology: A Postmodern, Post-Holocaust, Post-Christendom Endeavour." *Interpretation* 55/1 (2001) 5–18.

Jones, Bruce. "More About the Apocalypse as Apocalyptic." *JBL* 87 (1968) 325–27.

Jones, Serene. "Bounded Openness: Postmodernism, Feminism, and the Church Today." *Interpretation* 55/1 (2001) 49–59.
Juergensmeyer, Mark. *Terror in the Mind of God: The Global Rise of Religious Violence.* Berkeley: University of California Press, 2000.
Kallas, James. "The Apocalypse—An Apocalyptic Book?" *JBL* 86 (1967) 69–80.
Kant, Immanuel. "An Answer to the Question: 'What Is Enlightenment?'" In *From Modernism to Postmodernism: An Anthology*, edited by Lawrence Cahoone, 51–57. Cambridge, MA: Blackwell, 1996.
Karkkainen, Veli-Matti. "Pentecostal Hermeneutics in the Making: On the Way from Fundamentalism to Postmodernism." *JEPTA* 28 (1998) 76–109.
Kearney, Richard. "Between Tradition and Utopia: The Hermeneutical Problem of Myth." In *On Paul Ricoeur: Narrative and Interpretation*, edited by David Wood, 55–73. London: Routledge, 1991.
Keener, Craig S. *Miracles.* 2 vols. Grand Rapids: Baker Academic, 2011.
Kenneson, Philip D. "There's No Such Thing as Objective Truth and It's a Good Thing Too." In *Christian Apologetics in the Postmodern World*, edited by Timothy R. Phillips and Dennis L. Okholm, 155–72. Downers Grove, IL: InterVarsity, 1995.
Kermode, Frank. *The Genesis of Secrecy.* Cambridge, MA: Harvard University Press, 1979.
Kirk, J. Andrew. "The Confusion of Epistemology in the West and Christian Mission." *TynBul* 55/1 (2004) 131–56.
Koch, Klaus. *The Rediscovery of Apocalyptic.* Translated by Margaret Kohl. London: SCM, 1972.
Koester, Craig R. "The Message to Laodicea and the Problem of Its Local Context: A Study of the Imagery in Rev. 3:14–22." *NTS* 49 (2003) 407–24.
———. *Revelation and the End of All Things.* Grand Rapids: Eerdmans, 2001.
Konstan, David. "The Invention of Fiction. In *Ancient Fiction and Early Christian Narrative*, edited by Ronald F. Hock, J. Bradley Chance, and Judith Perkins, 3–18. Atlanta: Scholars Press, 1998.
Kraft, Charles H. *Christianity in Culture: A Study in Dynamic Biblical Theologizing in Cross-Cultural Perspective.* Maryknoll, NY: Orbis, 1994.
Krodel, Gerhard A. *Revelation.* Augsburg Commentaries. Minneapolis: Augsburg, 1989.
Kuhn, Thomas. "The Nature and Necessity of Scientific Revolutions." In *From Modernism to Postmodernism: An Anthology*, edited by Lawrence Cahoone, 309–11. Cambridge, MA: Blackwell, 1996.
Küng, Hans. *On Being a Christian.* Translated by Edward Quinn. London: Collins, 1978.
Laclau, Ernesto, and Chantal Mouffe. *Hegemony and Socialist Strategy: Towards a Radical Democratic Politics.* Translated by Winston Moore and Paul Cammack. London: Verso, 1985.
Lakeland, Paul. *Postmodernity: Christian Identity in a Fragmented Age.* Minneapolis: Fortress, 1997.
Land, Steven J. *Pentecostal Spirituality: A Passion for the Kingdom.* Sheffield: Sheffield Academic, 1993.
Lee, Michelle V. "A Call to Martyrdom: Function as Method and Message in Revelation." *NovT* 40/2 (1998) 164–94.
Leithart, Peter J. *Defending Constantine.* Downers Grove, IL: IVP Academic, 2010.
Lessl, Thomas L. *Rhetorical Darwinism.* Waco, TX: Baylor University Press, 2012.

Levinas, Emmanuel. "On the Jewish Reading of Scriptures." In *Levinas and Biblical Studies*, edited by T. C. Eskenazi, G. A. Phillips, and D. Joblind, D., 17–31. Semeia Studies 43. Atlanta: Society of Biblical Literature, 2003.
Lewis, Gordon R. "Is Propositional Revelation Essential to Evangelical Spiritual Formation?" *JETS* 46/2 (2003) 269–98.
Lindbeck, George A. *The Nature of Doctrine: Religion and Theology in a Postliberal Age*. Louisville: Westminster John Knox, 1984.
Linton, Gregory Leroy. "Intertextuality in the Revelation of John." PhD diss., Duke University, 1993.
———. "Reading the Apocalypse as an Apocalypse." In *Society of Biblical Literature 1991 Seminar Papers*, edited by Eugene H. Lovering, 161–86. Atlanta: Scholars Press, 1991.
Long, Tim. "A Real Reader Reading Revelation." *Semeia* 73 (1996) 79–107.
Lord, Andy. "Principles for a Charismatic Approach to Other Faiths." *AJPS* 6/2 (2003) 235–46.
Lyotard, Jean-François. "Answer to the Question: What is the Postmodern?" In *The Postmodern Explained to Children: Correspondence 1982–1985*, translations edited by Julian Pefanis and Morgan Thomas, 11–25. Sydney: Power Publications, 1992.
———. "Apostil on Narratives." In *The Postmodern Explained to Children: Correspondence 1982–1985*, translated and edited by Julian Pefanis and Morgan Thomas, 29–32. Sydney: Power Publications, 1992.
———. "Memorandum on Legitimacy." In *The Postmodern Explained to Children: Correspondence 1982–1985*, translated and edited by Julian Pefanis and Morgan Thomas, 51–69. Sydney: Power Publications, 1992.
———. "The Name of Algeria." In *Political Writings*, translated by Bill Readings and Kevin Paul 168–69. Minneapolis: University of Minnesota Press, 1993.
———. *Political Writings*. Translated by Bill Readings and Kevin Paul. Minneapolis: University of Minnesota Press, 1993.
———. *The Postmodern Condition: A Report in Knowledge*. Translated by Geoff Bennington and Brian Massumi. Manchester: Manchester University Press, 1984.
———. *The Postmodern Explained to Children: Correspondence 1982–1985*. Translated and edited by Julian Pefanis and Morgan Thomas. Sydney: Power Publications, 1992.
———. "The Sign of History." In *The Lyotard Reader*, edited by Andrew Benjamin, 393–411. Oxford: Blackwell, 1989.
———. "A Svelte Appendix to the Postmodern Question." In *Political Writings*, translated by Bill Readings and Kevin Paul, 25–29. Minneapolis: University of Minnesota Press, 1993.
———. "Universal History and Cultural Differences." In *The Lyotard Reader*, edited by Andrew Benjamin, 314–23. Oxford: Blackwell, 1989.
———. "The Wall, the Gulf, and the Sun." In *Political Writings*, translated by Bill Readings and Kevin Paul, 112–23. Minneapolis: University of Minnesota Press, 1993.
Ma, Julie. "A Comparison of Two Worldviews: Kankana-ey and Pentecostal." In *Pentecostalism in Context: Essays in Honor of William W. Menzies*, edited by Wonsuk Ma and Robert P. Menzies, 265–90. Sheffield: Sheffield Academic, 1997.

Ma, Wonsuk. "Biblical Studies in the Pentecostal Tradition." In *The Globalization of Pentecostalism: A Religion Made to Travel*, edited by Murray W. Dempster, Byron D. Klaus, and Douglas Petersen, 52–69. Oxford: Regnum, 1999.

MacIntyre, Alasdair. *Difficulties in Christian Belief*. London: SCM, 1959.

———. "Moral Philosophy: What Next?" In *Revisions: Changing Perspectives in Moral Philosophy*, edited by Stanley Hauerwas and Alasdair MacIntyre, 1–15. Notre Dame, IN: University of Notre Dame Press, 1983.

———. *Whose Justice? Which Rationality?* London: Duckworth, 1988.

MacMullen, Ramsay. *Enemies of the Roman Order*. Cambridge, MA: Harvard University Press, 1966.

Macmurray, John. *The Self as Agent*. Atlantic Highlands, NJ: Humanities Press, 1991.

Malina, Bruce J. "How a Cosmic Lamb Marries: The Image of the Wedding of the Lamb (Rev. 19:7ff.)." *BTB* 28 (1998) 75–82.

———. *The New Testament World*. Louisville: Westminster John Knox, 2001.

———. *On the Genre and Message of Revelation: Star Visions and Sky Journeys*. Peabody, MA: Hendrickson, 1995.

Mathewson, David. "Assessing Old Testament Allusions in the Book of Revelation." *EQ* 75 (2003) 311–25.

McGowan, John. *Postmodernism and Its Critics*. Ithaca, NY: Cornell University Press, 1991.

McGrath, Alister E. *Darwinism and the Divine*. Chichester, UK: Wiley-Blackwell, 2011.

———. *A Passion for Truth*. Leicester: Apollos, 1996.

McIlraith, Donal. *The Reciprocal Love between Christ and the Church in the Apocalypse*. Rome: Columban Fathers, 1989.

McKnight, Edgar V. *Jesus Christ in History and Scripture: A Poetic and Sectarian Perspective*. Macon, GA: Mercer University Press, 1999.

———. *Post-Modern Use of the Bible*. Nashville: Abingdon, 1988.

Mendels, Doron. *The Rise and Fall of Jewish Nationalism*. Grand Rapids: Eerdmans, 1997.

Menzies, Robert P. "Jumping Off the Postmodern Bandwagon." *Pneuma* 16/1 (1994) 115–20.

Menzies, William W. "Frontiers in Theology: Issues at the Close of the First Pentecostal Century." *APS* 2/3 (2000) 29–42.

Metzger, Bruce M. *Breaking the Code: Understanding the Book of Revelation*. Nashville: Abingdon, 1993.

Meynell, Hugo A. *The Intelligible Universe: A Cosmological Argument*. London: Macmillan, 1982.

Middleton, J. Richard, and Brian J. Walsh. *Truth Is Stranger than It Used to Be: Biblical Faith in a Postmodern Age*. Downers Grove, IL: InterVarsity, 1995.

Miguez, Nestor. "Apocalyptic and the Economy: A Reading of Revelation 18 from the Experience of Economic Exclusion." In *Reading from This Place*, edited by Fernando F. Segovia and Mary Ann Tolbert, Vol. 2, 250–62. Minneapolis: Fortress, 1995.

Milbank, John. *Theology and Social Theory: Beyond Secular Reason*. Oxford: Blackwell, 1990.

Millar, Fergus. *The Emperor in the Roman World (31 BC–AD 337)*. Ithaca, NY: Cornell University Press, 1977.

Miller, James B. "The Emerging Postmodern World." In *Postmodern Theology: Christian Faith in a Pluralist World* edited by Frederic Burnham, 1–19. San Francisco: Harper & Row, 1989.

Minear, Paul S. "The Cosmology of the Apocalypse." In *Current Issues in New Testament Interpretation*, edited by William Klassen and Graydon F. Snyder, 23–37. London: SCM, 1962.

———. *New Testament Apocalyptic*. Nashville: Abingdon, 1981.

———. "Ontology and Ecclesiology in the Apocalypse." *NTS* 12 (1965) 89–105.

Moberly, R. W. L. *Prophecy and Discernment*. Cambridge: Cambridge University Press, 2006.

Moore, Stephen D. "The Beatific Vision as a Posing Exhibition: Revelation's Hypermasculine Deity." *JSNT* 60 (1995) 27–55.

———. "Deconstructive Criticism: The Gospel of the Mark." In *Mark and Method: New Approaches in Biblical Studies*, edited by Janice Capel 84–102. Minneapolis: Fortress, 1992.

Morris, Leon. *Apocalyptic*. Grand Rapids: Eerdmans, 1972.

Moyise, Steve. "Does the Lion Lie Down with the Lamb?" In *Studies in the Book of Revelation*, edited by Steve Moyise, 181–94. Edinburgh: T. & T. Clark, 2001.

———. "Intertextuality and the Study of the Old Testament in the New." In *The Old Testament in the New: Essays in Honour of J. L. North*, edited by Steve Moyise, 14–52. JSNTSS 189. Sheffield: Sheffield Academic, 2000.

———. *The Old Testament in the Book of Revelation*. JSNTSS 115. Sheffield: Sheffield Academic, 1995.

———. "The Psalms in the Book of Revelation." In *The Psalms in the New Testament*, edited by Steve Moyise and Maarten J. J. Menken, 231–46. London: T. & T. Clark, 2004.

———, editor. *Studies in the Book of Revelation*. Edinburgh: T. & T. Clark, 2001.

Murphy, Frederick J. *Fallen Is Babylon: The Revelation to John*. Harrisburg, PA: Trinity, 1998.

Nash, Ronald H. *Faith and Reason: Searching for a Rational Faith*. Grand Rapids: Zondervan, 1988.

Natoli, Joseph. *A Primer to Postmodernism*. Malden, MA: Blackwell, 1997.

Naugle, David K. *Worldview: The History of a Concept*. Grand Rapids: Eerdmans, 2002.

Nayar, Pramod K. *Posthumanism*. Cambridge, MA: Polity, 2014.

Neusner, Jacob, William Scott Green, and Ernest S. Frerichs, editors. *Judaisms and Their Messiahs at the Turn of the Christian Era*. Cambridge: Cambridge University Press, 1987.

Newbigin, Lesslie. *The Gospel in a Pluralist Society*. Grand Rapids: Eerdmans, 1989.

Newton, Jon K. "The Epistemology of the Book of Revelation." *HeyJ*, 2014, forthcoming.

———. "Holding Prophets Accountable." *JEPTA* 30/1 (2010) 63–79.

———. "Reading Revelation Romantically." *JPT* 18/2 (2009) 194–215.

———. *Revelation Reclaimed: The Use and Misuse of the Apocalypse*. Milton Keynes: Paternoster, 2009.

———. "Story-Lines in the Book of Revelation." *ABR* 61 (2013) 61–78.

———. "Time Language and the Purpose of the Millennium." *Colloquium* 43/2 (2011) 147–68.

———. "Worldview Wars." In *New Frontiers: Redefining Christian Ministry for 21st Century Contexts*, edited by Jon K. Newton, 189–208. Melbourne: Mosaic, 2013.

Nickelsburg, George W.E. "Salvation without and with a Messiah: Developing Beliefs in Writings Ascribed to Enoch." In *Judaisms and Their Messiahs at the Turn of the Christian Era*, edited by Jacob Neusner, William Scott Green, and Ernest S. Frerichs, 49–68. Cambridge: Cambridge University Press, 1987.

Niebuhr, H. Richard. *The Meaning of Revelation*. New York: Macmillan, 1941.

Niekerk, Kees van Kooten. "A Critical Realist Perspective on the Dialogue between Theology and Science." In *Rethinking Theology and Science: Six Models for the Current Dialogue*, edited by Niels Henrik Gregersenand and J. Wentzel van Huyssteen, 51–86. Grand Rapids: Eerdmans, 1998.

Nielsen, Kai. "Religion and Groundless Believing." In *Religious Experience and Religious Belief*, edited by Joseph Runzo and Craig K. Ihara, 19–29. Lanham, MD: University Press of America, 1986.

Nietzsche, Friedrich. "The Natural History of Morals." In *From Modernism to Postmodernism: An Anthology*, edited by Lawrence Cahoone, #186, 104–5. Cambridge, MA: Blackwell, 1996.

Nikkel, David H. "The Postmodern Spirit and the Status of God." *Sophia* 33/3 (1994) 46–61.

Novello, Henry L. "The Nature of Evil in Jewish Apocalyptic: The Need for 'Integral' Salvation." *Colloquium* 35/1 (2003) 47–63.

O'Grady, John F. "Postmodernism and the Interpretation of Biblical Texts for Behavior." *BTB* 33/3 (2003) 95–103.

Oppy, Graham. "On Reschler on Pascal's Wager." *IJPR* 30 (1990) 159–68.

Osiek, Carolyn. "The Feminist and the Bible: Hermeneutical Alternatives." In *Feminist Perspectives on Biblical Scholarship*, edited by Adela Yarbro Collins, 93–105. Atlanta: Scholars Press, 1985.

Pannenberg, Wolfhart. "Dogmatic Theses on the Doctrine of Revelation." In *Revelation as History*, edited by Wolfhart Pannenberg et al., translated by David Granskou, 125–55. London: Collier-Macmillan, 1968.

———. *Metaphysics and the Idea of God*. Grand Rapids: Eerdmans, 1990.

Parker, F. O., Jr. "'Our Lord and God' in Rev. 4,11: Evidence for the Late Date of Revelation?" *Biblica* 82 (2001) 207–31.

Pate, C. Marvin. *Communities of the Last Days: The Dead Sea Scrolls, the New Testament and the Story of Israel*. Leicester: Apollos, 2000.

———, editor. *Four Views on the Book of Revelation*. Grand Rapids: Zondervan, 1998.

Pattemore, Stephen. *The People of God in the Apocalypse*. Cambridge: Cambridge University Press, 2004.

Penner, Myron Bradley. *The End of Apologetics*. Grand Rapids: Baker Academic, 2013.

Peters, Olutola K. "Politics of Violence in the Apocalypse of John: Moral Dilemma and Justification." SBL Seminar Papers 2004, S23–10. Online: http://ntweblog.blogspot.com.au/2004/09/sbl-seminar-papers-on-line.html (downloaded 26/05/05).

Phillips, Timothy R., and Dennis L. Okholm, editors. *Christian Apologetics in the Postmodern World*. Downers Grove, IL: InterVarsity, 1995.

Pippin, Tina. *Death and Desire: The Rhetoric of Gender in the Apocalypse of John*. Louisville: Westminster John Knox, 1992.

———. "Eros and the End: Reading for Gender in the Apocalypse of John." *Semeia* 59 (1992) 193–210.

———. "The Heroine and the Whore: Fantasy and the Female in the Apocalypse of John." *Semeia* 60 (1992) 67–82.

———. "Peering into the Abyss: A Postmodern reading of the Biblical Bottomless Pit." In *The New Literary Criticism and the New Testament*, edited by Elizabeth Struthers Malbon and Edgar V. McKnight, 251–67. JSNTSS 109. Sheffield: Sheffield Academic, 1994.

Plantinga, Alvin. "On Taking Belief in God as Basic." In *Religious Experience and Religious Belief*, edited by Joseph Runzo and Craig K. Ihara, 1–17. Lanham, MD: University Press of America, 1986.

———. *Warrant and Proper Function*. Oxford: Oxford University Press, 1993.

———. *Warranted Christian Belief*. Oxford: Oxford University Press, 2000.

———. *Where the Conflict Really Lies: Science, Religion, and Naturalism*. Oxford: Oxford University Press, 2011.

Poloma, Margaret M. *The Assemblies of God at the Crossroads*. Knoxville: University of Tennessee Press, 1989.

———. "The 'Toronto Blessing' in Postmodern Society." In *The Globalization of Pentecostalism: A Religion Made to Travel*, edited by Murray W. Dempster, Byron D. Klaus, and Douglas Petersen, 363–85. Oxford: Regnum, 1999.

Porter, Roy. *Enlightenment: Britain and the Creation of the Modern World*. London: Penguin, 2001.

Portier-Young, Anthea E. *Apocalypse Against Empire: Theologies of Resistance in Early Judaism*. Grand Rapids: Eerdmans, 2011.

Poythress, Vern Sheridan. "Genre and Hermeneutics in Rev. 20:1–6." *JETS* 36/1 (1993) 41–54.

Pratt, Thomas D. "The Need to Dialogue: A Review of the Debate on the Controversy of Signs, Wonders, Miracles, and Spiritual Warfare Raised in the Literature of the Third Wave Movement." *Pneuma* 13/1 (1991) 7–32.

Price, S. R. F. *Rituals and Power: The Roman Imperial Cult in Asia Minor*. Cambridge: Cambridge University Press, 1984.

Prickett, Stephen. *Narrative, Religion, and Science: Fundamentalism versus Irony, 1700–1999*. Cambridge: Cambridge University Press, 2002.

Raber, Rudolph W. "Revelation 21:1–8." *Interpretation* 40/3 (1986) 296–301.

Rabinow, Paul, editor. *The Foucault Reader*. London: Penguin, 1991.

Reardon, Bryan P. *The Form of Greek Romance*. Princeton, NJ: Princeton University Press, 1991.

Rée, Jonathan. "Narrative and Philosophical Experience." In *On Paul Ricoeur: Narrative and Interpretation*, edited by David Wood, 74–83. London: Routledge, 1991.

Resseguie, James L. *The Revelation of John: A Narrative Commentary*. Grand Rapids: Baker Academic, 2009.

Reynolds, Henry. *An Indelible Stain?: The Question of Genocide in Australia's History*. Ringwood: Viking, 2001.

Rhoads, David, editor. *From Every People and Nation: The Book of Revelation in Intercultural Perspective*. Minneapolis: Fortress, 2005.

———. "Social Criticism: Crossing Boundaries." In *Mark and Method: New Approaches in Biblical Studies*, edited by Janice Capel Anderson and Stephen D. Moore, 135–60. Minneapolis: Fortress, 1992.

Richard, Pablo. *Apocalypse: A People's Commentary*. Maryknoll, NY: Orbis, 1995.

Ricoeur, Paul. "The Hermeneutics of Testimony." In *Essays on Biblical Interpretation*, edited by Lewis S. Mudge, 119–54. Philadelphia: Fortress, 1980.

———. "Life in Quest of Narrative." In *On Paul Ricoeur: Narrative and Interpretation*, edited by David Wood, 20–33. London: Routledge, 1991.

Rienecker, Fritz, and Cleon Rogers. *Linguistic Key to the Greek New Testament*. Regency Reference Library. Grand Rapids: Zondervan, 1980.

Rissi, Mathias. *Time and History: A Study on the Revelation*. Translated by Gordon C. Winsor. Richmond: John Knox, 1965.

Robbins, Vernon K. "The Intertexture of Apocalyptic Discourse in the Gospel of Mark." In *The Intertexture of Apocalyptic Discourse in the New Testament*, edited by Duane Watson, 11–144. Atlanta: Society of Biblical Literature, 2002.

Robeck, Cecil M. "Signs, Wonders, Warfare, and Witness." *Pneuma* 13/1 (1991) 1–5.

Roberts, Alexander, James Donaldson, and A. Cleveland Coxe, editors. *The Anti-Nicene Fathers: The Writings of the Fathers down to A.D. 325*. 10 vols. Peabody, MA: Hendrickson, 2004.

Rorty, Richard. *Consequences of Pragmatism*. Minneapolis: University of Minnesota Press, 1982.

Rowland, Christopher. *The Open Heaven: A Study of the Apocalyptic in Judaism and Early Christianity*. London: SPCK, 1982.

———. *Revelation*. London: Epworth, 1993.

Royalty, Robert M., Jr. *The Streets of Heaven: The Ideology of Wealth in the Apocalypse of John*. Macon, GA: Mercer University Press, 1998.

Ruiz, Jean-Pierre. "Betwixt and Between on the Lord's Day: Liturgy and the Apocalypse." In *SBL 1992 Seminar Papers*, edited by Eugene H. Lovering Jr., 654–72. Atlanta: Scholars Press, 1992.

———. "Praise and Politics in Revelation 19:1–10." In *Studies in the Book of Revelation*, edited by Steve Moyise, 69–84. Edinburgh: T. & T. Clark, 2001.

Runzo, Joseph, and Craig K. Ihara, editors. *Religious Experience and Religious Belief: Essays in the Epistemology of Religion*. Lanham, MD: University Press of America, 1986.

Russell, D. S. *The Method and Message of Jewish Apocalyptic*. London: SCM, 1964.

Sanders, E.P. "The Genre of Palestinian Jewish Apocalypses." In *Apocalypticism in the Mediterranean World and the Near East*, edited by David Hellholm, 447–57. Tubingen: Mohr, 1983.

———. *Jesus and Judaism*. London: SCM, 1985.

———. *Paul and Palestinian Judaism: A Comparison of Patterns of Religion*. London: SCM, 1977.

Sarup, Madan. *An Introductory Guide to Post-Structuralism and Postmodernism*. Athens: University of Georgia Press, 1993.

Satterthwaite, Philip E., Richard S. Hess, and Gordon J. Wenham, editors. *The Lord's Anointed: Interpretation of Old Testament Messianic Texts*. Carlisle: Paternoster, 1995.

Scherrer, Steven J. "Signs and Wonders in the Imperial Cult: A New Look at a Roman Religious Institution in the Light of Rev. 13:13–15." *JBL* 103/4 (1984) 599–610.

Schneiders, Sandra M. "Does the Bible Have a Postmodern Message?" In *Postmodern Theology: Christian Faith in a Pluralist World*, edited by Frederic Burnham, 56–71. San Francisco: Harper & Row, 1989.

Setel, T. Drorah. "Feminist Insights and the Question of Method." In *Feminist Perspectives on Biblical Scholarship*, edited by Adela Yarbro Collins, 35–42. Atlanta: Scholars Press, 1985.

Shea, Chris. "Setting the Stage for Romances: Xenophon of Ephesus and the Ecphrasis." In *Ancient Fiction and Early Christian Narrative*, edited by Ronald F. Hock, J. Bradley Chance, and Judith Perkins, 61–76. Atlanta: Scholars Press, 1998.

Sheppard, Gerald T. "Biblical Interpretation after Gadamer." *Pneuma* 16/1 (1994) 121–41.

———. "Pentecostals, Globalization, and Postmodern Hermeneutics: Implications for the Politics of Scriptural Interpretation." In *The Globalization of Pentecostalism: A Religion Made to Travel*, edited by Murray W. Dempster, Byron D. Klaus, and Douglas Petersen, 289–312. Oxford: Regnum, 1999.

Sims, James H. *A Comparative Literary Study of Daniel and Revelation*. Lewiston, NY: Mellen Biblical Press, 1995.

Smalley, Stephen S. *Thunder and Love: John's Revelation and John's Community*. Milton Keynes: Word, 1994.

Smart, Ninian. *Worldviews: Crosscultural Explorations of Human Beliefs*. Englewood Cliffs, NJ: Prentice Hall, 1995.

Smidt, Kobus de. "Hermeneutical Perspectives on the Spirit in the Book of Revelation." *JPT* 14 (1999) 27–47.

Smith, James K. A. "Advice to Pentecostal Philosophers." *JPT* 11/2 (2003) 235–47.

———. *The Fall of Interpretation: Philosophical Foundations for a Creational Hermeneutic*. Downers Grove, IL: InterVarsity, 2000.

———. *Thinking in Tongues: Pentecostal Contributions to Christian Philosophy*. Grand Rapids: Eerdmans, 2010.

———. "What Hath Cambridge to Do with Azusa Street?: Radical Orthodoxy and Pentecostal Theology in Conversation." *Pneuma* 25/1 (2003) 97–114.

———. *Who's Afraid of Postmodernism?: Taking Derrida, Lyotard, and Foucault to Church*. Grand Rapids: Baker Academic, 2006.

Smith, Nicholas H. "Rorty on Religion and Hope." *Inquiry* 48/1 (2005) 76–98.

Snyder, Barbara Wootten. "Triple-Form and Space/Time Transitions: Literary Structuring Devices in the Apocalypse." In *Society of Biblical Literature 1991 Seminar Papers*, edited by Eugene H. Lovering, 440–60. Atlanta: Scholars Press, 1991.

Spilsbury, Paul. "Flavius Josephus on the Rise and Fall of the Roman Empire." *JTS* 54 (2003) 1–24.

Staniforth, Maxwell, editor and translator. *Early Christian Writings: The Apostolic Fathers*. Harmondsworth, UK: Penguin, 1968.

Stefanovic, Ranko. "The Meaning and Significance of the ἐπὶ τὴν δεξιάν for the Location of the Sealed Scroll (Revelation 5:1) and Understanding the Scene of Revelation 5." *Zeitschrift: Biblical Research* 46 (2001) 42–54.

Stone, Michael E. "Lists of Revealed Things in the Apocalyptic Literature." In *Magnalia Dei, the Mighty Acts of God: Essays on the Bible and Archaeology in Memory of G. Ernest Wright*, edited by F. M. Cross, W. E. Lemke, and P. D. Miller, 414–52. Garden City, NY: Doubleday, 1976.

———. "The Question of the Messiah in 4 Ezra." In *Judaisms and Their Messiahs at the Turn of the Christian Era*, edited by Jacob Neusner, William Scott Green, and Ernest S. Frerichs, 209–24. Cambridge: Cambridge University Press, 1987.

Stramara, Daniel F., Jr. *God's Timetable: The Book of Revelation and the Feast of Seven Weeks*. Eugene, OR: Pickwick Publications, 2011.

Strauss, Leo. "Jerusalem and Athens: Some Preliminary Reflections." In *Faith and Political Philosophy: The Correspondence between Leo Strauss and Eric Voegelin, 1934-1964*, edited and translated by Peter Emberley and Barry Cooper, 109-38. University Park: Pennsylvania State University Press, 1993.

———. "The Mutual Influence of Theology and Philosophy." In *Faith and Political Philosophy: The Correspondence between Leo Strauss and Eric Voegelin, 1934-1964*, edited and translated by by Peter Emberley and Barry Cooper, 217-34. University Park: Pennsylvania State University Press, 1993.

Stronstad, Roger. "Pentecostal Hermeneutics." *Pneuma* 15/2 (1993) 215-22.

Stuckenbuck, Loren T. *Angel Veneration and Christology: A Study in Early Judaism and in the Christology of the Apocalypse of John*. Tubingen: Mohr, 1995.

Sugirtharajah, R. S. *Postcolonial Reconfigurations: An Alternative Way of Reading the Bible and Doing Theology*. London: SCM, 2003.

Sullivan, Lawrence E. *Icanthu's Drum: An Orientation to Meaning in South American Religions*. New York: Macmillan, 1988.

Sutcliffe, Peter A. *Is There an Author in This Text?: Discovering the Otherness of the Text*. Eugene, OR: Wipf and Stock, 2014.

Sweet, John. *Revelation*. TPI New Testament Commentaries. London: SCM, 1990.

Swinburne, Richard. *Revelation: From Metaphor to Analogy*. Oxford: Oxford University Press, 2007.

Talmon, Shemaryahu. "Waiting for the Messiah: The Spiritual Universe of the Qumran Covenanters. In *Judaisms and Their Messiahs at the Turn of the Christian Era*, edited by Jacob Neusner, William Scott Green, and Ernest S. Frerichs, 111-38. Cambridge: Cambridge University Press, 1987.

Tarnas, Richard. *The Passion of the Western Mind*. London: Pimlico, 1996.

Taussig, Michael. *Mimesis and Alterity: A Particular History of the Senses*. New York: Routledge, 1993.

Taylor, Charles. *Sources of the Self: The Making of the Modern Identity*. Cambridge: Cambridge University Press, 1989.

Taylor, Mark C. *Erring: A Postmodern A/theology*. Chicago: University of Chicago Press, 1984.

Thayer, Joseph Henry. *The New Thayer's Greek-English Lexicon of the New Testament*. Peabody, MA: Hendrickson, 1981.

Thiselton, Anthony C. *The Two Horizons: New Testament Hermeneutics and Philosophical Description*. Carlisle: Paternoster, 1980.

Thomas, Christine M. "Stories Without Texts and Without Authors: The Problem of Fluidity in Ancient Novelistic Texts and Early Christian Literature." In *Ancient Fiction and Early Christian Narrative*, edited by Ronald F. Hock, J. Bradley Chance, and Judith Perkins, 273-92. Atlanta: Scholars Press, 1998.

Thomas, John Christopher. *The Apocalypse: A Literary and Theological Commentary*. Cleveland: CPT Press, 2012.

Thomas, Robert L. *Revelation 1-7: An Exegetical Commentary*. Chicago: Moody, 1992.

Thompson, Geoff, and Christiaan Mostert, editors. *Karl Barth: A Future for Postmodern Theology?* Hindmarsh: Australian Theological Forum, 2000.

Thompson, Leonard L. *The Book of Revelation: Apocalypse and Empire*. Oxford: Oxford University Press, 1990.

Thornhill, John. *Modernity: Christianity's Estranged Child Reconstructed*. Grand Rapids: Eerdmans, 2000.
Thrower, James. *Religion: The Classical Theories*. Washington, DC: Georgetown University Press, 1999.
Tilley, Terrence W., et al. *Postmodern Theologies: The Challenge of Religious Diversity*. Maryknoll, NY: Orbis, 1995.
Tolbert, Mary Ann. *Sowing the Gospel: Mark's World in Literary-Historical Perspective*. Minneapolis: Fortress, 1989.
Tracy, David. *Blessed Rage for Order: The New Pluralism in Theology*. San Francisco: Harper & Row, 1988.
———. *Dialogue with the Other: The Inter-Religious Dialogue*. Louvain: Peeters, 1990.
Travis, Stephen H. *Christian Hope and the Future*. Downers Grove, IL: InterVarsity, 1980.
Trites, Allison A. *The New Testament Concept of Witness*. Cambridge: Cambridge University Press, 1977.
Turner, Bryan S., editor. *Theories of Modernity and Postmodernity*. London: SAGE, 1990.
Van Gelder, Craig. "Postmodernism as an Emerging Worldview." *CTJ* 26 (1991) 412–17.
--
VanGemeren, Willem. *The Progress of Redemption: From Creation to the New Jerusalem*. Carlisle: Paternoster, 1995.

Vanhoozer, Kevin J. *Is There a Meaning in This Text?: The Bible, the Reader, and the Morality of Literary Knowledge*. Downers Grove, IL: InterVarsity, 1998.
———. "Philosophical Antecedents to Ricoeur's *Time and Narrative*." In *On Paul Ricoeur: Narrative and Interpretation*, edited by David Wood, 34–54. London: Routledge, 1991.

Vermes, Geza. *Jesus and the World of Judaism*. London: SCM, 1983.
Veyne, Paul. *Bread and Circuses: Historical Sociology and Political Pluralism*. Translated by Brian Pearce. London: Allen Lane, Penguin, 1990.
Voegelin, Eric. "The Gospel and Culture." In *Faith and Political Philosophy: The Correspondence Between Leo Strauss and Eric Voegelin, 1934–1964*, edited and translated by Peter Emberley and Barry Cooper, 139–76. University Park: Pennsylvania State University Press, 1993.
———. "Immortality: Experience and Symbol." In *Faith and Political Philosophy: The Correspondence Between Leo Strauss and Eric Voegelin, 1934–1964*, edited and translated by Peter Emberley and Barry Cooper, 177–216. University Park: Pennsylvania State University Press, 1993.
———. "Letter of April 22, 1951." In *Faith and Political Philosophy: The Correspondence between Leo Strauss and Eric Voegelin, 1934–1964*, edited and translated by Peter Emberley and Barry Cooper, Letter 38, 79–87. University Park: Pennsylvania State University Press, 1993.
Vorster, W. S. "'Genre' and the Revelation of John: A Study in Text, Context, and Intertext." *Neotestamentica* 22 (1988) 103–23.
Wainwright, Arthur W. *Mysterious Apocalypse: Interpreting the Book of Revelation*. Nashville: Abingdon, 1993.
Walbank, F. W. *The Hellenistic World*. Sussex: Harvester, 1981.

Wall, Robert W. *Revelation*. New International Biblical Commentary. Peabody, MA: Hendrickson, 1991.
Walvoord, John F. *The Revelation of Jesus Christ*. Chicago: Moody, 1966.
Watson, Duane F., editor. *The Intertexture of Apocalyptic Discourse in the New Testament*. Atlanta: Society of Biblical Literature, 2002.
Webber, Randall C. "The Apocalypse as Utopia: Ancient and Modern Subjectivity." In *SBL 1993 Seminar Papers*, edited by Eugene Lovering Jr., 104–18. Atlanta: Scholar Press, 1993.
Weber, Max. *Economy and Society: An Outline of Interpretive Sociology*. Vol. 1. Edited by Guenther Roth and Claus Wittich. Berkeley: University of California Press, 1978.
Webster, John. "Barth and Postmodern Theology: A Fruitful Confrontation?" In *Karl Barth: A Future for Postmodern Theology*, edited by Geoff Thompson and Christiaan Mostert, 1–69. Hindmarsh: Australian Theological Forum, 2000.
Weiler, Peter T. "Pentecostal Postmodernity?: An Unexpected Application of Grenz's Primer on Postmodernism." *APS* 2/3 (2000) 51–61.
Wennemyr, Susan E. "Dancing in the Dark: Deconstructive A/theology Leaps with Faith." *JAAR* 66/3 (1998) 571–87.
Westphal, Merold. *Whose Community? Which Interpretation?* Grand Rapids: Baker Academic, 2009.
White, Hayden. "The Metaphysics of Narrativity." In *On Paul Ricoeur: Narrative and Interpretation*, edited by David Wood, 140–59. London: Routledge, 1991.
Wilken, Robert L. *The Christians as the Romans Saw Them*. New Haven, CT: Yale University Press, 1984.
Wilkens, Ulrich. "The Understanding of Revelation within the History of Primitive Christianity." In *Revelation as History*, edited by Wolfhart Pannenberg et al., translated by David Granskou, 72–115. London: Collier-Macmillan, 1968.
Williams, Stephen N. *The Shadow of the Antichrist: Nietzsche's Critique of Christianity*. Grand Rapids: Baker, 2006.
Wink, Walter. "Demons and DMins: The Church's Response to the Demonic." *Review and Expositor* 89 (1992) 503–13.
———. *Unmasking the Powers: The Invisible Forces That Determine Human Existence*. Philadelphia: Fortress, 1986.
Wiser, "Reason and Revelation as Search and Response: A Comparison of Eric Voegelin and Leo Strauss." In *Faith and Political Philosophy: The Correspondence between Leo Strauss and Eric Voegelin, 1934–1964*, edited and translated by Peter Emberley and Barry Cooper, 237–48. University Park: Pennsylvania State University Press, 1993.
Witherington, Ben, III. *Revelation*. New Cambridge Bible Commentary. Cambridge: Cambridge University Press, 2003.
Wolterstorff, Nicholas. *Divine Discourse: Philosophical Reflections on the Claim that God Speaks*. Cambridge: Cambridge University Press, 1995.
———. *Reason within the Bounds of Religion*. Grand Rapids: Eerdmans, 1984.
Wong, David K. K. "The Beast from the Sea in Revelation 13." *BibSac* 160 (2003) 337–48.
Wood, David, editor. *On Paul Ricoeur: Narrative and Interpretation*. London: Routledge, 1991.
Wright, N. T. *The New Testament and the People of God*. Minneapolis: Fortress, 1992.

Yhearm, Brian. "The Sitz im Leben of Revelation; An Examination of the Literary and Social Environment of the Apocalypse of John." PhD diss., University of Newcastle upon Tyne, 1995.

Yong, Amos. *Beyond the Impasse: Toward a Pneumatological Theology of Religions*. Grand Rapids: Baker Academic, 2003.

———. *Discerning the Spirit(s): A Pentecostal-Charismatic Contribution to Christian Theology of Religions*. Sheffield: Sheffield Academic, 2000.

———. "'Not Knowing Where the Wind Blows': On Envisioning a Pentecostal-Charismatic Theology of Religions." *JPT* 14 (1999) 81–112.

———. *The Spirit of Creation: Modern Science and Divine Action in the Pentecostal-Charismatic Imagination*. Grand Rapids: Eerdmans, 2011.

———. " 'Tongues of Fire' in the Pentecostal Imagination: The Truth of Glossolalia in Light of R.C. Neville's Theory of Religious Symbolism." *JPT* 12 (1998) 39–65.

Index of Subjects

(not including footnotes)

Abortion, 1–2, 7, 16, 197, 234
Abyss, 77, 229–30, 250, 251
Accountability, 133, 199, 211, 220, 223, 225, 231, 234
Action(s), works, 73, 75, 198, 216, 217, 219, 221, 223, 224–26, 231, 232, 239
Adam and Eve, 101, 104, 109, 256, 257, 294
Affections: see feelings
Africa, 5, 11, 149
Agency, 231–32, 234
Alexander the Great, 63, 65, 66, 67, 81
America, 16, 17, 18, 58, 120, 237
Angels, 7, 59, 60, 77, 78, 87, 95, 99, 102–3, 104, 105, 110, 112–15, 119, 122, 123–26, 127, 130, 131, 132, 133, 141, 145, 146, 148, 164, 166, 169–70, 174, 199, 200, 206, 207, 220, 224, 225, 228, 229, 255, 257, 267, 270, 271, 297
Animism, 4, 10, 137, 143, 147, 148
Anthropocentrism, 44, 203
Anthropology, 3, 4, 6, 28, 39, 122, 159, 160, 201, 217, 218
Antipas, 172, 173, 209, 212, 213, 219, 270
Apocalypses, apocalyptic, 13, 59, 77, 82, 84, 85, 87, 98–118, 122, 123, 130, 131, 132, 135–36, 146, 148, 165, 167, 168, 170, 174, 183–84, 192, 205, 207, 226, 229, 247, 249, 259, 260, 273, 274, 290, 306–7

Apologetics, 3, 26, 46, 47–48, 118, 192, 292, 294, 299, 300
Apostles, 58, 129, 137, 142, 164, 174, 179, 180, 182, 208, 217, 256, 291
Archaeology, 14, 32
Aristotle, 17, 70
Asia, 57, 132, 133, 141, 182, 224, 227, 272, 300, 304
Astrology, 67–71, 76, 80, 83, 102, 106, 120, 122, 226, 296–99, 308
Atheism, 43, 151, 158, 161, 279
Augustus, 64, 66, 304, 306
Augustine, St., 34, 201, 216, 241
Author, 38, 50, 51, 55, 56–57, 58, 84, 95, 98, 102, 105, 111, 112, 114, 115, 123, 125, 131, 141, 167, 168, 170, 182, 246, 247, 276, 293
Authoritarian, 23, 58, 142, 143, 161, 163, 188, 223
Authority, 18, 19, 20, 22, 26, 35, 43, 54, 58, 61, 75, 97, 116, 130, 142, 144, 152, 153, 163, 168, 172, 173, 175, 177, 178, 179, 180, 181–82, 186, 188, 189, 190, 193, 194, 196, 200, 208, 209, 220, 224, 276, 279, 302
Australia, 1, 6, 17, 219, 243, 281

Babel, 79, 139, 183, 246, 298
Babylon, 67, 70, 78, 79, 94, 113, 123, 129, 132, 135, 138–39, 141, 164, 178, 183, 208, 211, 212, 214, 216, 220, 222, 226, 249, 250, 253, 260, 266, 272, 273, 274, 275, 278, 292, 300, 301, 302

337

Index of Subjects

Bacon, Francis, 21, 22
Balaam, 59, 142
Beast(s), 59, 76, 78, 128, 130, 132, 133, 134, 137, 138, 144, 172, 206, 208, 209, 210, 211, 212, 215, 217, 218, 220, 225, 229, 230, 249, 254, 255, 256, 258, 262, 263, 269, 270, 272, 274, 291, 300, 305, 307
Beliefs, 1-5, 6, 11, 17, 23, 24, 25, 28, 76, 84, 100, 116, 121, 128, 143, 144, 146, 151, 152, 158, 160, 161, 162, 163, 175, 180, 186, 194, 196, 221, 252, 281, 283, 284, 285, 300, 314
  Control beliefs, 161
Bible: see Scripture
Biblical criticism, 49-54, 168
Binary thinking, 35, 131-41, 204, 210, 251
Blood, 96, 97, 110, 114, 125, 138, 172, 178, 221, 225, 248, 255, 259, 303
Book of life, 96, 133-34, 139, 204, 207, 208, 217, 251, 254, 263, 291
Bride: see romance
Buddhism, 5, 161, 192, 283

Canaan: see Land, promised
Capital, capitalism, 18, 34, 234, 241, 242
Caesar, emperor, 64, 80, 81, 129, 210, 247, 294, 295, 296, 303, 304, 305, 306, 307
Change, 8, 10, 16, 21, 259
Chaos, 73-74, 77, 78, 79, 150, 229-30, 252, 293, 295
Christ: see Jesus, Messiah
Christocentric view, 244, 246, 249, 284
Christology, 97, 111, 112, 223, 244, 249, 252, 286
Church (es), 3, 11, 12, 17, 18, 20, 22, 23, 40, 58, 115-16, 125, 132, 133, 134, 136, 138, 139, 140, 142, 149, 153, 164, 166, 172, 174, 178, 180, 183, 184, 188, 190, 191, 193, 196, 206, 208, 209, 210, 211, 216, 227, 244, 245, 261, 264, 265, 269, 270, 274, 275, 276, 277, 278, 285, 308

Seven churches of Revelation, 58, 59, 64, 78, 113, 114, 124, 126, 128, 129, 132, 135, 141, 164, 167, 170, 179, 181, 182, 184, 195, 207, 211, 212, 213, 219, 221, 224, 255, 261, 262-63, 269, 270, 275, 297, 300, 304
City, 74, 79, 80, 83, 91, 94, 95, 96, 103, 116, 128, 133, 134, 142, 178, 182, 183, 185, 199, 208, 212, 214, 220, 221, 225, 250, 251, 252, 256, 263-64, 272, 289, 290, 291, 295, 296, 304, 306, 308, 309
Climax, 106, 249, 253, 255, 260, 268, 272, 273, 288
Closure, 35, 38, 229, 250, 252, 254, 280, 283
Combat myth, 292-95
Conflict: see War
Conquer, conqueror, conquest, 77, 79, 96, 125, 133, 184, 204, 208, 209, 210, 211, 212, 224, 225, 249, 252, 255, 262, 270, 301
Consciousness, 65, 126, 156, 167, 184, 199, 201, 230, 239, 297
  Altered state of consciousness, 297
Constantine, 183, 184
Copernicus, 228, 233, 284
Cosmic order, 200, 206, 223, 233, 293, 297
Cosmogony, 14
Cosmological argument, 232-33.
Cosmology, 6, 14, 22, 39, 77, 79, 92, 105, 112, 115, 123, 127, 145, 146, 149, 192, 198, 215, 228-33, 234, 296, 311
Cosmos, universe, 5, 6, 17, 20, 42, 47, 70, 76, 77, 86, 102, 112, 113, 114, 123, 127, 136, 177, 188, 204, 209, 228-30, 231, 234, 242, 244, 248, 254, 294, 298
Covenant, 82, 84, 86, 88, 89, 95, 110, 116, 222, 245-46, 275, 276
Creation, Creator, 1, 20, 26, 43, 76, 80, 86, 95, 103, 127, 131, 148, 196, 204, 205, 206, 218, 229, 230, 232, 234, 235, 246-47, 251, 256, 260, 298, 311, 313

Creationism, 1, 235
Criticism, 18, 50, 51, 52–53, 54, 55, 58, 60, 75, 76, 87, 144, 151–52, 153, 159, 161, 169, 178, 188, 193, 210, 279, 307, 312
Culture, 4, 6, 7, 8, 9, 12, 18, 25, 26, 28, 30, 32, 33, 35, 36, 37, 39, 40, 41, 49, 50, 52, 53, 57, 63, 65, 68, 72, 73, 78, 80, 82, 83, 84, 87, 92, 122, 134, 135, 138, 145, 148, 151, 153, 154, 160, 187, 197, 203, 205, 206, 214, 215, 220, 240, 241, 243, 244, 266, 276, 280, 281, 284, 285, 291, 293, 308, 309, 310, 311, 312, 314

David, 93, 94, 96, 288, 289, 292
Darwin, Charles, 22, 26, 27, 28, 29, 40, 228, 237
Death, 5, 7, 8, 14, 17, 30, 40, 64, 71, 76, 77, 93, 106, 114, 120, 126, 127, 128, 129, 131, 133, 134, 164, 173, 174, 175, 176, 205, 209, 212, 216, 221, 224, 225–26, 250, 251, 254, 256, 268, 269, 272, 296, 305, 306
  Death of Jesus, 114, 115, 117, 131, 133, 193, 205, 224, 248, 249, 261, 271, 278, 287, 288, 290, 298
Deception, 59, 78, 104, 106, 137, 164, 172, 179, 181, 184, 185, 186, 195, 206, 211, 218, 300, 307
Deconstruction, 39, 43, 44, 49, 52, 56, 58, 121–22, 203, 214, 215, 280, 307
Deism, 158
Democracy x, 7, 18, 24, 72, 73, 237, 242, 313
Demons, evil spirits, devil (see also Satan), 7, 60, 64, 76, 87, 104, 106, 110, 113, 114, 120, 123, 125, 127, 130, 132, 133, 135, 136, 137, 140, 141, 143, 144, 145–46, 148, 150, 164, 169, 178, 181, 183, 184, 195, 206, 210, 218, 220, 222, 225, 228, 229, 249, 250, 251, 253, 256, 257, 258, 286, 294, 307
Descartes, René, 10, 20, 21, 22, 154, 156, 158, 186, 200, 202, 219

Determinism, 27, 108–10, 114, 115, 130, 132, 135–36, 226, 227, 231, 234
Dialogue, 1, 2, 3, 9, 59, 61, 207, 282, 283, 286, 287
Diaspora (Jewish), 89, 90, 91
Disaster, 8, 14, 18, 70, 74, 76, 79, 103, 119, 123, 128, 181, 217, 219, 223, 225, 252, 259, 262, 272, 277, 291, 301, 302
Discourse, 37, 145, 158, 190, 237, 238, 311
Diversity, 25, 39, 59, 84, 141, 198, 204, 210, 241, 242, 309
Doctrine, 5, 43, 44, 46, 148, 155, 158, 159
Dragon, 78, 79, 80, 114, 128, 132, 133, 134, 135, 137, 172, 206, 209, 210, 215, 216, 225, 230, 248, 254, 255, 256, 257, 260, 261, 262, 270, 271, 272, 293, 294, 298, 307
Drama, 59, 123, 124, 141, 169, 202, 225, 247, 249, 253, 266
Dualism, 10, 44, 45, 48, 71, 80, 104, 109, 130–41, 143, 144, 146, 148, 149, 200, 204, 210, 213, 215–16, 217, 219, 239, 251, 254, 276, 278, 309, 311, 313

Ecology, 16, 30, 44–45, 47, 146, 197, 219, 220, 234, 277
Economic, 21, 26, 27, 28, 33, 41, 68, 73, 74–75, 79, 81, 128, 269, 295, 300, 301, 302, 303
Egypt, 67, 75, 81, 208, 266, 290
Elect, election, 88, 95, 111, 135, 275
Elijah, 128, 224
Emotions: see feelings
Empirical, 1, 6, 18, 22, 25, 159, 164, 165, 187, 192, 287
Empiricism, 121, 156, 164
Enlightenment, 7, 11, 14, 17, 18–41, 42, 48, 49, 54, 120–21, 126, 152, 153, 154, 155, 157, 158, 161, 163, 171, 186, 187, 200, 201, 203, 219, 223, 228, 231, 239, 241, 245, 252, 284, 310, 313
Enoch, 83, 100, 102, 105

Index of Subjects

Environment: see ecology
Ephesus, 129, 142, 178, 182, 216, 226
Epistemology, 6, 15, 17, 22, 25, 29, 39, 54, 78, 148, 151–96, 198, 232, 311
Eschatology, 14, 77, 99, 101, 103–4, 106, 107, 110, 148, 163, 184–85, 191, 194, 195, 205, 229, 237, 239, 240, 242, 243, 249–52, 254, 256, 258, 259, 275, 277, 296, 311
Essenes, 84, 87
Ethics, 5, 19, 38, 47, 54, 59, 60, 61, 75, 109, 132, 136, 143, 153, 177, 181, 234
Europe, European, 5, 16, 17, 22, 30, 46, 187, 200, 243
Evolution, 1, 22, 23, 26–28, 29, 198, 201, 203, 228, 230, 235, 237, 242
Exile, 89, 93, 289
Existentialism, 189, 202, 239
Exodus (event), 88, 93, 96, 257
Experience, 4, 8, 23, 25, 32, 46, 52, 59, 100, 140, 146, 151, 157, 158, 161, 162, 164, 165, 173, 174, 175, 187, 192, 194, 203, 232, 285, 307
    spiritual or religious, 1, 46, 59, 60, 76, 95, 124, 126, 137, 143, 145, 147, 148, 149, 150, 157, 159, 160, 166, 167, 168–69, 170, 171, 174, 175, 186, 187, 189, 190, 191, 193, 284
Ezra, 100

Faith, 1, 2, 5, 10, 20, 22, 23–24, 26, 31, 46, 48, 64, 76, 87, 91, 93, 95, 100, 115, 117, 138, 159, 162, 163, 172, 186, 189, 192, 194, 204, 210, 222, 239, 246, 249, 274, 286, 288, 297
Fall of humanity, 26, 101, 113, 165, 256, 257, 291
False beliefs, groups or teachings, 78, 80, 128, 129, 132, 133, 136, 137, 138–39, 141, 142, 144, 164, 168, 178, 179, 210, 217, 221, 254, 270, 272, 278, 288, 296, 301, 311
Falsification, 156, 159, 183, 187
Fate, fatalism, 60, 69–70, 73, 76, 80, 108, 116, 133, 183, 219, 267, 295, 296

Feelings, 23–24, 25, 29, 148, 156, 159, 201, 207, 214, 216, 219
Feminism, 47, 51, 52, 53, 58, 140, 203, 213–14, 218, 230, 276
Foundations, 5, 26, 30, 34, 38, 39, 41, 42, 152, 157, 158–59, 160, 163, 194
Foundationalism, 34, 152–53, 154, 156–57, 160, 161, 162, 193, 194–96, 311
Free will, 109, 110, 132, 202, 220–221, 222, 224, 227, 231, 234
Freud, Sigmund, 27–28, 29, 40, 52
Fundamentalism x, 2, 3, 11–12, 23, 54, 144, 150, 159, 312, 313
Future, 8, 20, 27, 30, 31, 42, 45, 59, 99, 105, 107, 108–9, 112, 114, 115, 123, 135, 146, 163, 166, 170, 177, 183, 185, 204, 211, 221, 224, 226–27, 230, 237, 239, 242, 243, 244, 247, 249, 252, 277, 278, 305, 312

Galileo, 31, 228, 233
Gender, 2, 23, 29, 31, 35, 38, 52, 53, 58, 135, 136, 140, 154, 197, 198, 203, 211, 212–15, 218, 230, 233, 238, 255, 276, 305
Geocentric worldview, 70, 76, 77, 116, 228–29, 233
Gnosticism, 192–93
Gog and Magog, 255, 259, 260
Golden Age, 20, 73, 103, 237, 252, 304
Gospel, 23, 116, 128, 176, 196, 220, 284, 286
Greco-Roman world/culture, 18, 64, 81, 272, 274, 294, 297, 299, 301, 302, 303, 305
Greek (language), 63, 79–80, 81, 83, 117
Group orientation, 24, 71–72, 76, 78, 140, 199, 211, 212, 243

Hades: see Hell
Hasmoneans, 85, 90
Healing, 2–3, 10, 12, 47, 64, 126, 128, 133, 139, 148, 185, 218, 251, 252, 253, 258, 309

Index of Subjects   341

Hearing, hearers, 108, 168, 176, 180, 181, 182, 196, 204, 207, 214, 218, 227, 274, 307
Heaven, 59, 69, 70, 77, 95, 99, 102, 104, 105–6, 113, 116, 120, 122, 123, 125, 127, 131, 135, 163, 164, 165, 166, 167, 169, 177, 206, 213, 218, 222, 225, 228, 229, 230, 249, 250, 255, 256, 257, 258, 259, 263, 271, 272, 288, 296, 306, 307
Hebrew Scriptures: see Old Testament
Hegel, 27, 29, 189, 201, 237, 240, 277
Hell, Hades, 102, 205, 250, 254, 282
Hellenism, Hellenization, 58, 63–84, 87, 90, 105, 108, 109, 110, 115–17, 118, 131, 165, 198, 265, 273, 295–96, 299, 311
Hermeneutics; see also interpretation, 38, 39, 48–49, 50–56, 58, 160, 176, 188, 190, 213, 241
Hinduism, 5, 192, 245, 313
History, 3, 7, 13, 14, 15, 19, 27, 29, 31, 35, 36, 39, 43, 46–47, 50, 51, 58, 68, 70, 80, 84, 85, 87, 99, 100, 102, 103, 104, 106, 108, 109, 112, 114, 115, 116, 117, 128, 130, 132, 133, 140, 141–42, 155, 158, 172, 176, 177, 178, 179, 185, 187, 189, 190, 191, 192, 202, 213, 219–20, 222, 224–26, 227, 229, 230, 231, 232, 234, 236–53, 256, 258, 259, 265–66, 277–78, 279, 281, 284, 293, 296, 297, 298, 299, 301, 305, 307, 308, 311, 312, 313
  End of history, 14, 106, 107–8, 249–53, 258–59, 260, 288, 313
Holiness, 90–92, 97, 134, 208
Homer, 71, 75, 78, 81, 116, 273
Hope, 8, 14, 20, 50, 58, 77, 92–94, 96, 107, 112, 114, 116, 205, 237, 239, 242, 246, 247, 252–53, 259, 275, 277–78, 288–89, 290, 291, 292, 295, 296, 297, 300, 308, 311
Human rights, 16, 18, 20, 200, 233
Humanism ix, 3, 17, 20, 24–25, 29, 32, 34, 43, 47, 68, 80, 153, 161, 198, 202, 203, 219, 228, 237, 246, 284

Humanity, human beings, 2, 5, 7, 14, 15, 18, 19, 20–21, 22, 23, 24, 25, 26, 27, 28, 29, 30, 31, 32, 34, 35, 37, 39, 41, 42, 43, 44, 45, 46, 47, 48, 49, 64, 65, 68, 71, 73, 99, 103, 104, 109, 110, 114, 115, 116, 120, 121, 122, 123, 124, 125, 126, 130, 131, 132, 136, 140, 143, 145, 146, 153, 156, 157, 163, 164, 165, 166, 177, 178, 184, 185, 186, 188, 193, 194, 195, 197–221, 223, 227, 230–231, 232, 234, 236, 237–38, 239, 240, 241, 246, 247, 251, 252, 253, 256, 257, 275, 276, 284, 285, 286, 287, 295, 308, 309, 311, 312
Identity, 84, 97, 134, 199, 206, 208, 214, 216, 218, 234, 279, 283
Ideology, 5, 7, 8, 25, 32, 38–39, 49, 50, 52–53, 60, 81, 117, 159, 214, 237, 276, 280, 281, 294, 300, 304, 308, 309
Imagery, 99, 128, 190, 212–14, 216, 222, 250, 251, 253, 256, 261, 264, 276, 292, 293, 304, 306
Imagination, 43, 50, 190, 233, 269
Imperial (or ruler) cult, 14, 67–68, 80, 81, 137, 205, 301, 303–7
Imperialism, 30, 58, 67, 109–10, 183, 210, 212, 248, 253, 260, 294, 295, 300–307, 308, 312
Inclusive, inclusivism, 39, 275, 282
Individual, individualism, 18, 22, 25, 28, 30, 37, 44, 45, 48, 53, 71–72, 73, 78, 79, 81, 140, 146, 153, 186, 197, 199, 200, 201, 202, 203, 205, 211–12, 217, 218, 219, 226, 231, 234, 236, 295
Interpretation; see also hermeneutics x, 1, 13, 15, 17, 22, 35, 36, 38, 39, 41, 43, 44, 48–54, 55, 56, 57, 58, 60, 125, 142, 145, 150, 156, 160, 164, 166, 176, 177, 178, 182, 188, 191, 193, 206, 245, 249, 278, 279, 282, 283, 288, 292, 293, 294, 297, 299, 300, 307, 308, 310, 313
Intertextuality, 53, 56–57, 142, 208
Intratextual theology, 45–46

Islam, 3, 8–9, 190, 279, 281, 313
Israel, 86, 88, 89, 93, 94, 95–96, 103, 107, 112, 129, 139, 146, 208, 212, 214, 256, 257, 258, 259, 263, 264, 266, 274, 275, 277, 288, 289, 290, 291, 294, 297, 307

Jerusalem, New Jerusalem, 82, 91, 94, 95, 96, 98, 103, 106, 113, 116, 135, 136, 142, 180, 183, 184, 185, 208, 214, 219, 226, 229, 249, 251, 257, 258, 263, 264, 271, 272, 289–92, 295, 298, 301, 303, 308, 309
Jesus, 3, 11, 17, 60, 64, 69, 77, 78, 79, 80, 96, 97–98, 109, 112, 115, 116, 117, 126, 128, 129, 132, 133, 134, 136, 138, 142, 143, 167, 169, 171, 172, 174, 178, 182, 183, 185, 187, 189, 193, 199, 205, 207, 208, 209, 210, 212, 215, 216, 217, 221, 223, 224, 225, 246, 247, 255, 256, 259, 261, 264, 268, 269, 274, 276, 278, 282, 285, 286, 287, 288, 290, 292, 295, 296, 297, 298, 306, 308
  Second coming of, 185, 229, 249, 259, 265, 269, 270
  As messianic ruler and governor of history, 111, 117, 129, 247–49, 296, 306
Jezebel, 59, 76, 78, 136, 141, 142, 164, 169, 180, 181, 184, 208, 210, 212, 213, 221, 270
Josephus, 86, 91, 109, 291
Judaism, 63, 64, 65, 69, 76, 78, 80, 81–110, 112, 115–16, 117, 127, 134, 192, 266, 271, 288–92, 299, 308
Judgment, 77, 78, 79, 100, 106, 110, 113, 133, 134, 135, 138, 163, 164, 166, 172, 177, 178, 179, 184, 185, 186, 191, 195, 196, 207, 209, 211, 212, 216, 217, 220, 221, 222, 223, 227, 245, 247, 249, 250, 252, 254, 259, 260, 276, 290, 302, 303, 309
Justice, 20, 30, 39, 58, 61, 79, 80, 119, 140, 148, 178, 211, 213, 221–23, 227, 233, 234, 246, 253, 296, 314
Justification, 158, 159–63, 184, 185
Justin Martyr, 195

Kant, Immanuel, 18–20, 25, 41, 153, 200, 237, 245, 281
Kingdom of God, 93, 94, 97, 132, 248, 249, 268, 302, 303
Knowledge, 9, 18, 19, 20, 21, 23, 25, 27, 28, 29, 31, 34, 35, 36, 37, 38, 40, 41, 42, 47, 81, 102, 105, 106, 121, 125, 131, 140, 147, 151, 152–64, 165, 176, 185, 186, 188, 189, 192, 193, 194, 195, 196, 198, 200, 202, 231, 232, 236, 238, 240, 241, 244, 245, 247, 297, 311, 312, 313
Koran, 12, 188

Lake of fire, 134, 210, 222, 251, 254
Land, Promised, 84, 89, 90, 94, 96, 142, ??, 290
Language, 4, 18, 29, 35, 36, 37, 44, 49, 54, 66, 77, 79, 99, 101, 105, 109, 117, 121, 123, 124, 135, 137, 142, 148, 153–54, 169, 170, 174, 183, 187, 194, 200, 202, 203, 204, 206–9, 215, 216, 217, 218, 219, 223, 241, 242, 243, 244, 248, 250, 251, 255, 260, 264, 269, 273, 274, 275, 284, 288, 302
Language games, 37, 46, 158, 160, 241
Laodicea, 184, 212, 265
Law (Mosaic), 84, 85, 87, 88–89, 94, 107, 112, 116, 290
Letter, 59, 80, 101, 166, 207
Liberalism x, 5, 11, 23, 24, 25, 26, 27, 46, 48, 50, 60, 158, 201, 234, 237, 242, 245, 313
Liberation, liberation theology and criticism, 27, 46–47, 53, 58, 93, 94, 210, 242, 246, 258, 277, 312
Logical Positivism, 6, 121, 159
Love: see romance

Maccabees, 82–83, 84, 93, 94, 288
Marriage: see romance
Martyrdom, martyrs, 77, 96, 98, 112, 115, 126, 129, 133, 171–72, 174, 176, 209, 211, 212, 213, 216, 222, 225, 226, 227, ??, 289, 296, 302, 305, 306

Index of Subjects   343

Marx, Marxism, 5, 18, 26–27, 28, 29, 34, 40, 198, 234, 237, 240, 243, 244, 246

Materialism, 6, 7, 26–27, 28, 45, 138, 145, 243, 253

Man (see also humanity), 24, 32, 199–201, 202, 203, 204, 228, 237, 242

Mega, 273–74, 275, 298, 308

Medieval, 1, 17, 19, 20, 30, 32, 40, 42, 153, 161, 163, 171, 188, 199, 228, 231, 236, 244, 312, 313

Messiah, messianic, 92–94, 96, 97, 103, 106, 107, 109, 110, 111–12, 115, 117, 225, 247–48, 257, 258, 259, 288–89, 290, 291, 292, 297, 299, 306

Metanarrative, 25, 27, 35, 41, 198, 234, 236, 240–247, 253, 260, 273, 274, 279, 280, 308, 311

   Christian metanarrative or Big Story, 241, **244-47**, 260, **274-78**, 279, 286, 292, 295, 298, 299, 307–8, 309, 311, 312

Michael, 125, 133

Middle Ages: see medieval

Millennium (thousand years), 96, 113, 130, 180, 184, 209, 226, 254, 255, 259, 289, 306

Minorities, 31, 243, 244

Miracles, 2, 7, 10–11, 65, 87, 95, 126, 164, 179, 194

Missionaries, 4, 9

Modern, modernism, modernity x, 1, 3, 5, 6–7, 9, 10, 11–12, 13, 14, 15, 17–40, 41, 42, 43, 44, 45, 47, 49, 50, 51, 54, 55, 57, 60, 61, 62, 68, 74, 75, 79, 120, 121, 122, 123, 141, 143, 145, 147, 149, 150, 152–53, 155, 156, 158, 159, 163, 164, 174, 178, 181, 186, 187, 188, 189, 191, 198, 199, 200–201, 202–3, 212, 215, 216, 217, 218, 219, 228, 230, 231, 233, 234, 237, 239, 240–242, 243, 244, 245, 246, 252, 279, 281, 310–311, 312, 313

Monotheism, 23, 76, 80, 86–88, 95, 97–98, 115, 117, 120, 127–28, 131, 134, 136, 137, 143, 180, 246, 282, 283, 285, 292

Moral, morality, 16, 23, 24, 36, 41, 42, 71, 75, 77, 80, 81, 92, 128, 129, 136, 138, 143, 165, 187, 192, 193, 202, 215, 229, 262, 281, 287, 296

Moses, 83, 89, 95, 100, 128, 224, 288

Myth, 6, 7, 8, 14, 43, 59, 66, 71, 75, 80–81, 83, 104, 146, 212, 237, 273, 283, 292–95, 296, 298, 299, 300, 302, 304, 307, 308

Name(s), naming, 98, 134, 204–5, 207, 208, 216, 217, 251, 263, 264, 289

Narrative, 6, 31, 44, 52, 53, 58, 99, 148, 169, 170, 174, 175, 190, 198, 218, 220, 222, 224, 231, 236, 238, 239, 240, 241, 242, 243, 246, 249, 253–80, 285, 288, 292, 300, 307, 308, 309, 311

   Rival narratives, 243, 246–47, 253, 276, 278, 279–80, 287, 295, 299, 300–307, 308, 309, 310, 311, 312, 313, 314

   Narrative and plot of Revelation, 79, 99, 117, 125, 128, 130, 134, 137, 207, 215, 247, 249, **253-76**, 277, 287, 288, 292, 293, 294, 295, 297-98

   Narrative of the Bible, 13, 52, 83, 88, 96, 101, 107, 109, 165, 247, 256–58, 260, 274–78, 286, 288, 292, 294, 295, 297, 298, 299, 300, 307, 308, 309, 311, 312, 313, 314

Nationalism, 5, 18, 25, 112, 14

Nations, 5, 64, 88, 93, 94, 95, 96, 97, 103, 106, 107, 115, 117, 127, 139, 184, 185, 204, 206, 209, 210, 218, 220, 224, 237, 248, 250, 251, 253, 257, 260, 264, 276, 288, 289, 291, 302, 309

Naturalism, 26, 121, 122, 158, 159, 192, 196, 202

Nature, 18, 20, 21, 24, 26, 27, 29, 30, 44, 45, 63, 64, 74, 76, 122, 123, 132, 144, 146, 156, 159, 164, 196, 197, 200, 201, 219, 220, 222, 230, 245

Index of Subjects

Negative theology, 121–22, 194
Neopragmatism x, 33
New Testament, 57, 58, 71, 79, 86, 109, 112, 125, 145, 179, 192, 199, 212, 217, 219, 246, 277, 308
New world order, 18, 21, 58, 79, 100, 132, 134, 135, 249, 250, 251, 252–53, 256, 291, 309
Nicolaitans, 129, 181, 210, 255, 270
Nietzsche, Friedrich, 40, 41

Objective (e.g. objective truth), 24, 26, 29, 30, 35, 41, 48, 50, 55, 153, 154, 155–56, 162, 177, 179, 186, 187, 192, 194–95, 202, 240, 245, 281
Observation, 69, 74, 154, 155, 156, 164, 173, 174, 175, 202
Old Testament (Hebrew Scriptures), 56, 58, 74, 78, 85, 87, 92, 95, 96, 101, 105, 107, 110, 111, 113, 114, 116, 124, 129, 135, 142, 166, 177, 179, 183, 208, 209, 222, 246, 250, 255, 256–57, 258, 259, 260, 274, 288, 292, 293, 294, 297, 301, 308
Ontology, 14, 39, 119, 136, 158, 231–33.
Oracles, 65–66, 166
Otherness, 35, 46, 182, 203, 230, 283, 287, 302, 314
Overcoming: see conquest

Paganism, 250, 283, 293, 294, 299, 300, 304, 305
Panentheism, 44–45, 47
Pantheism, 70, 147
Papacy, 199, 200, 219
Papua New Guinea, 4, 9, 64
Paradise, 20, 79, 80, 95, 96, 100, 102, 106, 236, 252, 256, 291, 296
Particularist, particularity, 36, 40, 46, 117, 186–87, 275, 282, 285, 287
Patmos, 132, 141, 172
Patriarchal, 51, 52, 58
Paul (apostle), 57, 97, 133, 180, 181, 185, 195, 207, 217, 275
Peace, 130, 253, 296, 301
Pentecostalism x, 6, 11–12, 144, 147–50, 286

Pergamum, 64, 129, 212, 306
Persecution, 57, 78, 98, 129, 133, 134, 135, 172–73, 178, 184, 185, 210, 216, 217, 218, 223, 225, 244, 262, 269, 270, 271, 272, 278, 288, 291, 293, 300, 301, 302, 303, 306, 307, 312
Person, concept of, human, 14, 71, 72, 120, 146, 161, 197–235, 236, 284, 311, 313, 314
Personal cosmology, 64, 127–28, 161, 230–233, 234, 236, 311, 313, 314
Perspective, perspectivalism, 35–36, 47, 51, 142, 147, 154–55, 156, 164, 174, 177, 178, 236, 276, 286, 294, 301, 302, 308, 313–14
Pharisees, 84, 87
Phenomena, Phenomenology, 7, 168, 193, 282, 283, 287
Philadelphia, 135
Philo, 85
Philosophy ix, x, 4, 5–6, 7, 8, 15, 21, 25, 26, 41, 42, 43, 44, 50, 68–69, 71, 72, 73, 119, 121, 148, 151, 156, 164, 175, 187, 189, 192, 195–96, 198–99, 221, 231–32, 241, 277, 280, 285, 292, 295, 300
Plato, Platonic, 68, 70, 80, 131, 165
Plausibility, 2, 3, 4, 7, 12, 285
Pluralism, 36–37, 38, 39, 52, 53, 56–57, 60, 143, 160, 162, 189, 190, 203, 240, 245, 280–286, 287, 308, 311
Politics, political ix, 2, 3, 7, 14, 16, 21, 33, 37–39, 41, 46, 50, 53, 54, 58, 60, 65, 68, 73, 75, 79, 81, 90, 116, 123, 128–29, 132, 134, 140, 144, 174, 178, 188, 197, 199, 200, 204, 206, 220, 224, 234, 240, 244, 253, 272, 280, 294, 295, 300, 301, 302, 313
Polytheism, 64, 76, 78, 129, 146, 285, 300, 303, 304, 305, 307, 308
Positivism, 21, 29
Postcolonial readings, 58
Postliberalism, 45–46, 160
Postmodern/-ism ix–x, 1, 8–13, 15, 16, 24–61, 62, 117, 118, 119, 121–22, 139–47, 148, 150, 151, 152,

153–57, 159, 162, 163, 164, 168, 171, 174, 175, 176, 177, 178, 181, 188, 189, 191, 198, 202, 203, 204, 206, 210, 213, 215, 218, 219, 223, 228, 230, 233, 234, 236–40, 242, 243, 245, 247, 250, 277, 279, 280, 281, 285, 286, 287, 308, 310–311, 312, 313, 314
Postmodernist theology, 11, 42–49, 122, 239–40, 282–84, 313
Poststructuralism x, 33, 44, 121
Power, 7, 27, 38, 41, 44, 47, 51, 57, 58, 69, 73, 104, 120, 125, 130, 131, 139, 140, 142, 145, 164, 182, 183, 184, 199, 202, 207, 209, 214, 220, 222, 224, 225, 238, 240, 244, 289, 301, 302, 306, 309
Pragmatism, 36, 49, 147, 158, 219
Prayer, 11, 80, 91, 94, 109, 113, 126, 206, 207, 223, 225, 296
Prediction, 8, 54, 66, 80, 99, 100, 105, 108, 166, 170, 177, 178, 180, 182–84, 189, 193, 204, 227, 243, 247, 296, 308, 312
Premodern, 3, 9, 11, 12, 30, 32, 40, 45, 54, 62, 63, 122, 126, 150, 233, 243, 281, 313, 314
Process theology, 44–45
Progress x, 7, 18, 20, 21, 24, 25, 26, 31, 47, 64, 73, 74–75, 79, 120, 161, 187, 198, 236–38, 239, 240, 242, 243, 244, 252
Progressive(ness), 38–39, 53, 61
Prophecy, prophets, 59, 65, 76, 78, 79, 87, 93, 95, 99–101, 102, 104, 107, 108, 109, 125, 126, 130, 131, 134, 136, 137, 142, 148, 164, 166, 167, 168, 169, 170, 173, 177–84, 185–86, 190, 191, 192, 193, 194, 195, 196, 207, 208, 209, 213, 217, 220, 221, 224, 227, 229, 253, 259, 274, 277, 289, 290, 291, 296, 311
  Conditionality in, 183–84
  Ex eventu, 100, 108, 226
  False prophecy, false prophet, 76, 136–37, 141, 164, 179–80, 182, 254

Prophets, Old Testament, 58, 78, 93, 108, 109, 114, 116, 127, 166, 177, 179, 183, 222, 224, 227, 247, 251, 274, 289, 290, 291, 301
Propositions, 36, 46, 153, 154, 156, 157, 158, 159, 189, 191, 192, 194, 286–87
Prostitute: see whore
Providence: see sovereignty of God
Pseudonymity, 85, 100, 104, 168, 170
Psychology, 3, 39, 52, 143, 159, 160, 168, 178, 187, 197, 199, 216, 239

Qumran, 85, 89, 91, 94, 124, 255

Rationalism, 18, 22, 23, 25, 28, 34, 35, 36, 40, 41, 43, 48, 87, 120, 122, 147, 156, 201, 241, 313
Reader, 3, 11, 15, 38, 39, 50–52, 53, 54, 55–57, 58, 59, 60, 100, 102, 109, 112, 114, 115, 124, 141, 142, 168, 172, 173, 176, 193, 208, 213, 214, 223, 226, 254, 260, 267, 270, 274, 278, 290, 301, 307
Reader response, 52, 56
Realism, 152, 160
Reality, 1, 2, 4, 6, 7, 8, 14, 25, 26, 29, 31, 43, 44, 45, 49, 59, 63, 70, 99, 102, 104, 112, 119–50, 151, 152, 153, 154, 156, 161, 163–64, 165, 175, 184, 185, 187, 190, 191, 192, 193, 194, 195, 197, 202, 203, 215, 228, 230–231, 233, 238, 239, 241, 276, 282, 283–84, 299, 303, 313
Reason, rational x, 1, 7, 9, 15, 18, 19, 23, 24, 25, 26, 27, 28, 29, 40, 41, 42, 46, 48, 68, 69, 74, 87, 117, 122, 147, 151, 153, 156, 157, 158, 159, 160, 163, 165, 174, 186, 190, 195, 198, 199, 201–2, 233, 252, 285
Redemption: see salvation
Reductionism, 143, 145, 146, 201
Reformation, 17–19, 200, 219
Reformed Epistemology, 156, 161
Relativism, 24, 27, 29, 36, 40, 41, 47, 161, 185, 281

346 *Index of Subjects*

Religion x, 2, 5, 7, 8, 14, 19, 20, 22, 23, 24, 25, 26, 28, 40–41, 42, 43, 63–68, 69, 72, 73, 74, 75, 79, 82, 86, 90, 93, 104, 121, 123, 128–29, 131, 133, 135, 136, 143, 146, 147, 151, 153, 154, 158, 159, 161, 162, 180, 183, 186, 189, 190–91, 192, 193, 196, 199, 206, 210, 224, 232, 244, 279, 280, 281, 282–87, 292, 294, 300, 301, 303, 304, 305, 309
   Religious knowledge, 158–63, 196
   Theology of religions, 286–87
Renaissance, 18, 19, 199, 219
Repentance, 114, 128, 135, 138, 164, 181, 184, 217, 221–22, 227, 291
Responsibility: see accountability
Restoration, 93, 94, 96, 218, 289, 290, 292
Resurrection, 11, 77, 80, 96, 100, 103, 104, 106, 114, 127, 128, 132, 179, 185, 189, 205, 225, 226, 248, 250, 254, 278, 287
Revelation, Book of ix–x, 12–15, 54–118, 122–50, 163, 164, 165, 166, 174, 176, 177, 178, 180, 183, 185, 186, 190, 192, 195, 196, 204–30, 231, 233, 234, 243, 247–65, 268–74, 275, 276, 277, 278, 279, 280, 287, 288–303, 304, 305–7, 308, 309, 310, 311, 312, 313, 314
   Dissonance in, 251
   Epistemology of, 163–86
   Genre, 13, 56, 59, 80, 98–99, 117, 134, 166, 167, 170, 253–55, 261, 265–76, 277, 292
   Interpretation of, 54–61, 193, 209, 210, 213, 223, 230, 249, 264, 278, 280, 312
   Literary features, 58, 59, 166, 167, 170, 254, 262–65, 270, 293
   Manuscript of, 212
   Structure, 55, 117, 261–62, 268–74, 293, 297
Revelation, concept or experience of, 15, 20, 23, 63, 65, 76, 78, 84, 87, 95, 97, 99, 101, 102, 103, 104, 110, 113, 116, 122, 123, 124, 131, 136, 141, 151, 153, 157, 161, 162, 163, 165–70, 175–76, 177, 180, 181, 182, 184, 185, 186–96, 236, 285, 311, 313, 314
Rhetoric, Rhetorical criticism, 52, 58–59, 60, 83, 133, 140, 141, 168, 176, 205, 206, 208, 215, 223, 224, 294, 303
Roma (goddess), 303, 304, 306
Roman (empire), 14, 57, 58–59, 63, 67, 68, 73, 78, 79, 90, 93, 124, 132, 134, 164, 174, 178, 182–84, 210, 212, 213, 219, 223, 250, 252, 259, 260, 267, 271, 281, 288, 290, 293, 296, 300–307, 308
Roman Catholicism, 55, 163, 186, 193, 217, 244, 278
Romance (genre), 138–39, 215, 261–76, 277, 279, 298, 308, 309, 312, 314
Romanticism, 24, 29, 200–201
Rome (city), 79, 183, 226, 250, 260, 301, 303, 305, 308

Sadducees, 84
Saints, 96, 97, 113, 134, 178, 199, 204, 206, 208, 211, 215, 221, 222, 225–26, 248, 249, 255, 256
Salvation, soteriology, 97, 99, 111, 132, 133, 134, 136, 142, 143, 186, 212, 215, 218, 222, 239, 245, 246, 247, 249, 258, 275, 277, 278, 282, 285, 286, 287, 296, 304, 306, 309, 313
   Salvation history, 47, 244–45, 260, 277, 299, 308, 311
Sardis, 83, 142, 212
Satan, 7, 59, 74, 77, 98, 104, 106, 110, 120, 124, 125, 129, 131, 132, 133, 135, 136, 137, 141, 146, 169, 178, 181, 208, 217, 255, 257, 260, 272, 288, 300, 307
Schleiermacher, 158, 189, 245
Science x, 1, 2–3, 7, 10, 11, 17–26, 27, 28, 29, 31–32, 34, 35, 37, 41, 42, 50, 54, 62, 73, 74, 119, 121, 143, 144, 145, 146, 152, 157, 158, 159, 162, 171, 187, 188, 192, 193, 200, 202, 228, 230, 233, 235, 240, 242, 244, 281, 313

Scripture, Bible x, 1, 2, 3, 10, 11, 12, 13, 17, 18, 20, 22-23, 26, 41, 45, 46, 48, 49-54, 58, 61, 73-74, 83, 85, 87-88, 95, 109, 144, 145, 146, 147, 149, 150, 153, 157, 159, 160, 165, 168, 170, 177, 179, 180, 188, 190, 191, 192, 194, 212, 217, 219, 234, 236, 245, 246, 247, 253, 256, 260, 274, 275, 276, 277, 278, 279, 282, 285, 287, 292, 294, 297, 308, 310, 312, 313, 314
Sect, sectarianism, 57, 88, 89, 94, 116, 312
Secular, secularism, 5, 18, 23, 40, 43, 47, 66, 68, 75, 80, 145, 187, 245
Seleucids, 81-82, 94, 110
Sex, sexual immorality, 23, 28, 71, 80, 81, 97, 128, 129, 134, 180, 204, 213, 215, 218, 262, 263, 264, 266-67, 269-70, 272, 276, 296, 300, 303
Signs, supernatural or divine, 76, 128, 130, 137, 179, 187, 193, 194, 272
Sin, sinner/s, sinfulness, 103, 111, 128, 129, 133, 134, 153, 204, 216, 217-18, 251
Slavery, 73, 174, 204, 271, 301
Smyrna, 135, 178
Social class, 26-27, 29, 30, 38, 73, 78, 199, 204, 226, 237, 240, 243,
Social sciences, 27-29, 31, 44, 159, 197
Socialism, 18, 25, 27, 201, 242
Sorcery, 4, 17, 69, 80, 126, 128, 129, 137, 139, 164, 296, 300, 303
Soul, 71, 73, 77, 80, 103, 104, 131, 132, 145, 172, 200, 202, 216, 217, 219, 295
Sources, source criticism, 55, 56, 84, 85, 86, 110, 117, 163, 175, 188, 294, 296
Sovereignty of God, 80, 86, 87, 88, 100, 103, 109, 127, 130, 132, 135, 136, 178, 220-221, 224, 234, 240, 247, 260, 271, 287, 296, 302, 303
Speaking in tongues, 147-48
Spirit/spirit, 10, 76, 80, 99, 120, 123, 124, 126, 127, 131, 132, 141, 142, 143, 145, 147, 148, 167, 169, 178, 179, 181, 183, 185, 195, 221, 229, 237, 241, 286, 287
Spiritual realities, 2, 4, 11, 60, 63-64, 76, 77, 102, 104, 110, 116, 119-39, 141, 143, 144, 145-47, 148-50, 163, 164, 165, 167, 170, 171, 175, 177, 178, 184, 185, 186, 194, 195, 210, 213, 215, 216, 221, 228, 229, 230, 236, 272, 282, 287, 309, 311, 313, 314
Spirituality, 41, 45, 72, 77, 99, 102, 121, 124, 126, 137-39, 142, 143, 145, 146, 150, 181, 193, 217, 231, 245, 274, 296, 311, 314
Stability, 73-74, 75, 78-79, 200, 252, 295, 301, 302, 303, 304, 307, 308
Stereotypes, 72, 78, 140, 144, 159, 199, 211, 212
Stoicism, 70, 71, 73
Story: see narrative
Struggle: see also war, 2, 132, 172, 178, 192, 210, 224, 238, 249, 255, 256, 260, 261-62, 271, 279
Subject, 19, 25, 26, 29, 35, 42, 50, 154, 161, 171, 174, 198, 200, 201, 202-3, ??, 231, 241, 311
Suspicion, 174-75, 178, 181, 304
Symbols, 13, 54, 79, 99, 105, 112, 117, 123, 126, 140, 170, 208, 210, 211, 212, 215, 218, 248, 277, 283, 292, 296, 305, 306, 307
Syncretism, 64, 71, 77, 80, 86, 89, 115, 117, 127, 180, 206, 292, 293, 308, 312

Teachers, teaching, 78, 180, 181, 207, 212, 216, 217, 221, 286
Technology x, 7, 17, 18, 20, 21, 26, 29-32, 64, 73-74, 120-21, 164,
Teleology, 27, 39, 106, 240, 277
Temple(s), 64-65, 68, 80, 89, 91-92, 94, 95, 96, 98, 107, 108, 128, 183, 206, 288, 289, 291, 296, 301, 303, 304, 306
Tertullian, 174, 195, 260
Testimony: see witness

Testing claims, 137, 142, 143, 168–69, 173–74, 175, 176, 178–80, 188, 190, 192–94, 286–87

Text(s), 1, 23, 29, 35, 37, 38, 39, 46, 48, 49, 50–51, 52, 53, 56–57, 58, 60, 107, 111, 160, 176, 180, 188, 193, 194, 204, 207, 216, 224, 230, 251, 254, 255, 256, 278, 279, 280, 283, 294, 295, 310, 312, 313

  Text of Revelation x, 9, 54–55, 56, 57, 58, 59, 60, 62, 76, 77, 78, 124, 125, 127, 135, 137, 142, 166, 167, 168, 170, 172, 184, 190, 196, 208, 211, 213, 218, 223, 253, 278, 293, 296, 311, 312

Theodicy 100

Theology, 10, 23, 42–47, 49, 50, 53, 59, 61, 63, 76, 99, 109, 110, 111, 115, 121, 133, 139, 146, 148, 158, 162, 165, 191, 195, 201, 202, 215, 221, 223, 233, 238, 239–40, 244, 245, 268, 276, 277, 282, 283, 286, 287, 312, 313

Thyatira, 78, 129, 212, 224

Time, 13, 14, 16, 70, 103, 105, 205, 226, 263, 305, 306, 307, 313

Tolerance, 18, 25, 54, 120, 138, 139, 141, 189, 280, 282, 314

Torah: see Law (Mosaic), Old Testament.

Totalizing, 35, 38, 122, 239, 243, 246, 302–3

Traders, 73, 78

Tradition, 8, 9, 17, 18, 19, 20, 22, 24, 25, 26, 30, 36, 38, 45, 51, 53, 54, 67, 69, 70, 72, 73–75, 78, 83, 100, 122, 124, 142, 143, 146, 151, 153, 154, 157, 160–61, 162, 164, 165, 168, 171, 180, 190, 192, 194, 196, 198, 215, 217, 223, 228, 237, 241, 244, 245, 275, 282, 293, 298, 300, 305, 307, 311, 314

Tree of Life, 96, 251, 253, 256, 263, 264

Truth, 9, 19, 20, 21, 23, 24–25, 27, 28–29, 32, 35–37, 39, 40, 41, 43, 46, 47, 48, 50, 52, 104, 121, 141, 142, 151–96, 203, 213, 228, 240, 241, 242, 245, 279, 280, 281, 282, 283, 284–85, 302, 309, 311, 313, 314

  Correspondence view of, 25, 152, 153–54, 155

  Coherence view of, 25, 157–58, 162, 192

  Pragmatist view of, 158, 162

Tyre, 64, 260

Universalism, 40, 114, 117, 203, 260, 285, 297, 308

Universe: see cosmos

USA: see America

Violence, 8, 32, 58, 60, 116, 178, 184, 186, 188, 196, 204, 213, 214, 218, 222–23, 244, 246, 247, 253, 254, 271, 272, 276, 278, 288, 296

Vision, 58, 60, 64, 65, 95, 99, 103, 105, 109, 126, 132, 141, 167, 168–69, 170, 171, 177, 193, 205, 209, 212, 214, 215, 218, 219, 220, 244, 253, 270, 297, 298, 303

War, conflict, 7, 18–19, 21, 22, 23, 26, 27, 30, 90, 104, 112, 113, 114, 117, 118, 123, 124, 125, 131–32, 133, 134, 136, 149, 188, 208, 209, 210, 213, 216, 222, 238, 250, 251, 253–61, 262, 270, 271, 272, 273, 274, 276, 278, 279, 288, 292–95, 296, 298, 299, 301, 302, 306, 308, 311

  Jewish-Roman war, 90, 93, 124, 259, 291, 294, 296, 303

War scroll, 254–55

Watchers, 104, 131

Wedding: see romance

Weltanschauung, 4, 70

Western x, 1, 2, 3, 4, 6, 7, 8, 9, 10, 11–13, 14, 15, 17, 18, 21, 23, 30–32, 34, 40, 41, 43, 47, 49, 58, 120, 126, 149, 151, 152, 154, 155, 198, 203, 212, 217, 219, 223, 241, 243, 246, 279, 282, 310, 313

Whore (of Revelation, 17), 78, 129, 138, 140, 141, 164, 172, 183, 207, 208, 210, 211, 214, 220, 255, 262,

263, 264, 269, 270, 272, 274, 275, 278, 300, 303

Witness (es), 2, 77, 78, 96, 97, 99, 109, 124, 125, 128, 129, 130, 134, 138, 139, 143, 169, 170, 171–76, 177, 179, 181, 183, 184, 185, 186, 190, 191, 196, 204, 207, 209, 211, 212, 218, 220, 221, 224, 225, 227, 255, 270, 274, 284, 291, 298, 311

Work(s):see actions

Worldview ix-x, 2–15, 17–31, 39, 40, 41, 44, 45, 48, 49, 51, 54, 60–118, 129, 140, 141, 143, 144, 145–50, 161, 162, 164, 171, 197, 198, 200, 211, 212, 216, 219, 223, 230, 231, 244, 276, 279, 280, 281, 284, 287, 300, 308, 310, 313, 314

  Ancient Jewish, 62, 63, 76, 79, 80, **81–98**, 102, 107, 109, 110, 115–18, 131, 134, 149, 171, 288, 289, 297, 308, 311

  Ancient Mediterranean xi, 13, 20, 32, 42, 50, 62, 63–80, 115–18, 120, 123, 127, 131, 141, 165–66, 181, 196, 198, 205, 211, 219, 226, 228, 241, 247, 252, 267, 271, 292, 293, 295, 296, 297, 300, 303, 305, 311, 312, 313

  Babylonian, 292

  Christian ix, 2, 3, 4, 7, **9–13**, 15, 19, 20, 40, 62, 76, 81, 95, 112, 117–18, 119, 129, 133, 135, 136, 143, 144, 145, 146, 147, 148–50, 152, 161, 165, 171, 177, 178, 183, 195, 196, 198, 207, 212, 217, 218, 219, 221, 227, 228, 231, 233, 234, 236, 244, 245, 246, 253, 260, 276, 278, 279, 280, 282, 285, 286, 288, 292, 295, 297, 299, 300, 307, 308, **310-314**

  Jewish apocalyptic, 62, 63, 98, **101–18**, 122, 123, 168, 226, 229

  Hellenistic: see Hellenism

Worship, 64, 67, 78, 84, 86, 89, 91, 95, 97, 124, 126, 127, 128–29, 133, 134, 137, 138, 146, 174, 204, 205–6, 207, 210, 211, 216, 218, 220, 258, 261, 270, 284, 289, 306, 307

Writing, 207–8, 216

Zealots, 84
Zion, 94, 95, 248, 257, 290

Index of Modern Authors

(since late, 19th century)

Allen, Diogenes, 47
Alston, William, 160, 171
Archer, Kenneth, 148
Aune, David, 64, 65, 98–99, 101–2, 107, 165, 166, 179

Barth, Karl, 24, 120–21, 189, 200, 228, 245
Bauckham, Richard, 167, 170, 183–84, 254–55, 294, 303
Beale, G. K., 56
Bellah, Robert, 28, 201–2
Bernstein, J. M., 243
Bertens, Hans, 33, 34, 202
Best, Steven and Kellner, Douglas, 243
Boyd, Gregory, 136
Bultmann, Rudolf, 239

Cahoone, Lawrence, 33, 34, 36, 202
Caird, G. B., 294
Carey, W. G., 58–59, 223
Cargal, Timothy, 150
Carson, D. A., 285–86
Clifford, W. K., 153
Collins, A. Y., 55, 292–94, 298
Collins, John, 84–85, 99, 109, 110, 112, 114–15, 122
Cupitt, Don, 43–44, 153, 237, 280–281

Davies, Paul, 159
Dawkins, Richard, 153
Derrida, Jacques, 33, 41–42, 44, 49, 121–22, 144, 175, 194, 243

Dewey, John, 20, 237
Dumbrell, William, 250

Eagleton, Terry, 5
Ellington, Scott, 149

Fairlamb, Horace L., 36
Fish, Stanley, 34, 39, 49
Fiorenza, Elisabeth Schüssler, 53, 118, 140, 173, 179, 213, 253, 299
Foucault, Michel, 27, 32, 33, 37–38, 202, 203, 238, 244
Franke, John R., 157, 162
Freud, Sigmund, 27–29, 40, 201–2
Friesen, Steven, 14–15, 123, 204, 205, 210, 215, 218, 249, 295, 305, 307, 308

Gadamer, Hans-Georg, 121
Gellner, Ernest, 23, 26, 36, 153, 187, 281
Gilbertson, Michael, 15, 238–39, 251–52, 277
Green, Peter, 66, 67, 70, 73, 74, 75, 295
Gregersen, Niels Henrik, 162
Grenz, Stanley, 48, 155, 157, 162
Griffin, David Ray, 32, 44–45, 47, 203

Hart, Kevin, 121–22, 194
Harvey, David, 21
Heidegger, Martin, 202, 205
Hekman, Susan, 27, 154
Hengel, Martin, 69, 70, 83, 87, 165

Heschel, Abraham, 177–78, 222, 247
Hey, Sam, 147
Hick, John, 160, 189, 245, 283–84, 285
Hill, David, 171, 179
Hodgson, Peter, 239–40, 244, 245, 249, 277–78
Howard-Brook, Wes and Gwyther, Anthony, 300, 302, 304
Husserl, Edmund, 21, 31, 121

Jack, Alison, 38, 51–52, 53, 58, 60, 213
Jaspers, Karl, 187, 188–89, 195
Jameson, Frederic, 34
Johns, Jackie, 148
Juergensmeyer, Mark, 8

Kallas, James, 135–36
Kenneson, Philip D., 155
Kraft, Charles, 4, 9
Kuhn, Thomas, 31, 121
Kuyper, Abraham, 41

Laclau, Ernesto and Mouffe, Chantal, 27, 32
Lindbeck, George, 45–46
Linton, Gregory, 55, 56
Long, Tim, 55, 58, 178
Lyotard, Jean-Francois, 19, 31, 33, 34, 37, 41, 121, 204, 237, 240–242

Ma, Julie, 148
MacIntyre, Alasdair, 160
Macmurray, John, 231–32
Malina, Bruce, 71, 126, 127, 199, 228, 248, 297–99
Marx, Karl, 26–29, 41
McGowan, John, 17, 25–26
McGrath, Alister, 48
McIlraith, Donal, 261, 275, 276, 277, 291
McKnight, George, 51, 122
Mendels, Doron, 86–87, 90, 131
Meyer, Leonard, 204
Meynell, Hugo, 232–33
Middleton, J. Richard and Walsh, Brian J., 48, 144, 246
Minear, Paul, 13, 123, 181, 229
Moltmann, Jürgen, 239

Moore, Stephen, 213
Moyise, Steve, 56–57, 60, 280
Murray, Oswin, 74–75

Newbigin, Lesslie, 284–85
Nickelsburg, George, 131
Nietzsche, Friedrich, 41, 43, 49, 237–38

Pannenberg, Wolfhart, 185, 189, 192, 205, 239, 260
Pattemore, Stephen, 224, 225–26, 227
Paulien, Jon, 56
Peretti, Frank, 146
Peters, Olutola, 223
Pippin, Tina, 59, 140, 182, 214–15, 222, 229–30, 250, 276
Plantinga, Alvin, 156, 161, 162, 163
Poloma, Margaret, 148, 150
Portier-Young, Anthea, 109–10
Price, S. R.F., 68, 304
Prickett, Stephen, 244

Raber, Rudolph, 264
Reardon, B. P., 265, 266
Rhoads, David, 92
Richard, Pablo, 58, 223
Ricoeur, Paul, 176, 182, 190, 191, 196
Rissi, Mathias, 13, 227
Rorty, Richard, 33–34, 36, 49, 154, 155
Rowland, Christopher, 54, 85, 167, 280
Royalty, Robert, 57, 59, 133, 141, 168

Scherrer, Steven J., 137
Schneiders, Sandra, 51
Setel, T. Drorah, 51
Sheppard, Gerald, 150
Smith, James K. A., 6, 148, 149, 156
Society of Biblical Literature, 99
Strauss, Leo, 187, 195
Stuckenbuck, Loren, 124
Sullivan, Lawrence, 14
Swete, 114
Swinburne, Richard, 191, 194

Taylor, Charles, 200, 223, 230–231, 233–34

Taylor, Mark C., 43, 139, 201, 202-3, 239
Thompson, Leonard L., 135, 140, 168, 211, 229
Thornhill, John, 42, 155, 244-45
Tilley, Terrence, 42, 47, 282
Tracy, David, 282-83

Van Huyssteen, J. Wentzel, 159, 162
Vanhoozer, Kevin, 41-42, 48-49
Vermes, Geza, 63-64
Voegelin, Eric, 158, 165, 191, 195-96
Von Harnack, Adolf, 50

Wainwright, Arthur W., 54, 61

Walbank, F. W., 74
Webster, John, 238, 245
Welch, Sharon, 47
Whitehead, Alfred North, 44-45
Wilken, Robert L., 303-4
Wink, Walter, 7, 39, 102, 124, 144-47
Wittgenstein, Ludwig, 160
Wolterstorff, Nicholas, 152, 156, 160, 161
Wright, N. T., 86, 93, 102, 109, 131, 132, 288, 289

Yhearm, Brian, 57, 58, 137, 222-23
Yong, Amos, 195, 286-87

Index of Ancient Documents

OLD TESTAMENT CANONICAL BOOKS

Genesis
23, 88, 96, 101, 113, 197, 246, 256, 279, 288, 298

1–11	235
1–3	256(2)
1–2	198, 239, 256
1:1	256
1:2–31	74
1:2–5	256
1:2	256
1:3–5	256
1:10	256
1:14–18	256
2:9	256
2:10–14	256
2:17	256
3	74, 165
3:1–6	257
3:1–4	256
3:7–12	81
3:8	256
3:13	257
3:15	257(2), 294, 298
3:16	256
3:17	256, 257
3:19	256
3:21	81
3:22–24	256
4:10	110
6:1—9:7	74
6:4	104
9:21–27	81
11	79
29:20	266
29:21–26	267
37:9	257, 294
41:45	266
41:50	266

Exodus
7:17–24	224
20:3–6	246
20:5	129
32:32–33	111

Leviticus
18	81

Deuteronomy
	93
13:1–5	179, 180
18:18–20	179
18:20–22	179
18:21–22	180
23:9–14	255

Judges
	93–94
1	74

Ruth
	266

1 Samuel
	94
21:5	255

2 Samuel

	94
5:6–9	289
11:9–13	255
22:9	209

1 Kings

17–18	177
17:1	224
21	178
22:5–28	179
22:19–23	177

2 Kings

1:9–12	224

1 Chronicles

11:4–8	289

Ezra

	94

Nehemiah

	94

Esther

	94

Psalms

2	248
2:6	290
2:8–9	257
8	228
23:1–2	258
64:3	209
86:8–10	258
90:4	259

Proverbs

1:7	165

Song of Solomon

	264, 275
1:3	264
1:5–6	264
1:9–11	264
1:10–11	264
1:15	264
2:8–9	264
2:8	265
4:1–15	264
4:4	264
4:9	264
4:12	264
4:15	264
5:2–8	265
5:8	264
5:9–16	264
6:4–10	264
6:4	264(2)
6:10	264
7:1–8	264
7:1	264
7:4	264
7:5	264
8:10	264
8:14	265

Isaiah

	108, 109, 227
1:9–10	290
2:2	251
8:5–8	177
12:15–16	257
14:1–21	260
14:12	260
25:6	275
35:1–10	257
40:3–5	257
40:25–26	246
41:17–20	257
43:2	257
43:9	179
43:10	246
43:19–21	257
44:3–4	257
44:6–8	246
47	301
49:2	209
49:10	258
54:11–13	111
54:11–12	290
56:6–8	251
60:1–11	251
65:17	258
66:7–11	257
66:22	258

Jeremiah

	108, 177, 184, 227

2:2	129
5:14	209
8:16	111
14:13–16	179
18:7–10	108
18:8	184
23:9–40	179
23:14	290
23:29	209
25:11–12	99
28:1–17	179
29:8–32	179
29:10	100
50–51	178
50:11–16	183
50:29–32	183
50:39–46	183

Ezekiel

	109, 259
1	95
3:1–3	177
16:35–42	303
16:46–58	290
23	129, 274
23:4	274
28	260
28:11–19	260
37	259
38:3	259
38:22	259–60
39:4	260
39:17–20	260
47:1–12	258
47:12	258

Daniel

	85, 99, 100, 103, 104, 109, 110, 132, 248, 257, 301
1–6	109
2	109
7	109
7:13–14	110, 111
7:18	109
9:2	99, 177
9:21	113
9:24–27	109, 257
9:24–26	99
10	177
10:4–11	95
10:13	113, 257
10:14	257
10:20	257
10:21	113, 257
11	109
12:1	113, 257
12:3	109
12:4	100
12:7	257(2)
12:9	100
12:11–12	109

Hosea

	274, 275
1:2	129
2:1–20	129
3:1	129

Joel

	259
2:30–31	259
3:15	259

Amos

3:7	177

Obadiah

17	259

Jonah

3:4–10	184
4:2	184

Zechariah

	85
3	257
3:1	110
3:9	257
14:8	258

APOCRYPHAL BOOKS OF THE OLD TESTAMENT

Daniel

14	111

1 Maccabees

	82

1:13–16	82	108:3	111

2 Maccabees

84

Tobit

	266
6:10—17:10	267
6:18	266
13:16	290
13:17	290

JEWISH PSEUDEPIGRAPHA

2 Baruch

103, 109, 113, 290

3:5–6	290
29:4	111
55:3	113

3 Baruch

106

11–15	113

1 Enoch

103, 105, 107, 108, 110, 113, 131, 168, 298

8	113
10	113
20	113
25:5	111
39:6–7	111
39:12	110
40	113
40:7	110
40:10	113
47:1	110
47:1–2	113
47:4	113
48:2	110
62:2	110
66	113
69:1–15	113
69:29	111
74–75	107
89:68–71	107
100:3	111

2 Enoch

102–3, 104, 106

11–16	105
21:3	113
22:6–12	113

4 Ezra

103(2), 107, 168

13	112
13:5	112
13:9–11	112
13:11	112
13:12–13	112
13:34	112
13:38	112
13:39–48	112

Joseph and Aseneth

266, 267

Sibylline Oracles

103, 106

V:1–51

111

V:20–33

111

Testaments of the Twelve Patriarchs

103

T.Benj.3:8

111

T.Levi, 18:11

111

T.Dan, 7:3

111

DEAD SEA SCROLLS

War Scroll

254–55

1QM7:3–6	255

NEW TESTAMENT CANONICAL BOOKS

Matthew

5:28	217
7:21–23	179
12:34	217
13:9	181
15:8	217
15:18–20	217
22:1–14	274
23:37	274
24	290
24:2	183
25:1–12	274
26:6–13	274

Mark

	273
13	290

Luke

1:2	174
7:36–50	274
10:39–42	274
14:15–24	274
14:25	274
18:22	274
18:28	274
19:41–42	274
21	290
23:24	223

John

3:8	144
12:1–8	274
13:23	274
14:6	246
20:2	274
21:15–19	274

Acts

	176
4:12	246
7:60	223
15	97
15:19–20	180
15:29	180
18:12–13	98, 288
19:13–20	69

Romans

1:18–32	165
3:3	274
3:23	217
7:1–4	275
9:25–26	275
10:21	275
11:25–29	275

1 Corinthians

8–11	180
12:1–3	180
12:2–3	179
13:9–13	195
13:12	185
14:29–33	179
14:29	180

2 Corinthians

11:2	275

Ephesians

2–3	97
5:23–32	275
6:12	144

1 Thessalonians

5:19–21	180

Hebrews

	133
2:3	174

1 Peter

	57
5:1	174

2 Peter

1:16–18	174
3:8	259

1 John

1:1–3	174, 180
4:1–6	179

2 John

1	182

3 John

1	182

Revelation

1–3	125
1	58, 261
1:1–4	224
1:1	97, 100 (2), 114, 125, 126, 130, 166, 169(4), 177, 179, 183, 209, 248, 271
1:2	126, 166, 169(3), 171, 172, 207(2), 209
1:3	99, 101, 126, 142, 166, 177, 179, 181, 183, 191, 207(4), 216, 259, 263
1:4–8	101
1:4	122, 123
1:5–6	111, 133, 261
1:5	77, 111, 123, 129, 138, 171, 193, 205, 210, 215, 248, 261, 268(2), 269(2), 271, 302, 306
1:6	209, 224, 248, 271, 302, 306
1:7	77n, 133, 185, 216, 229, 249, 261, 269, 270
1:8	95, 98, 127, 166, 169
1:9	100, 132, 138, 171, 172, 302
1:10–20	95, 166, 270
1:10–18	261
1:10–17	268
1:10	123, 126(2), 167, 269, 306(2)
1:11	132, 207, 272
1:12–20	126
1:12–13	123
1:13–16	215, 306
1:13	248
1:16	77, 80, 128, 208
1:17–18	166, 306
1:17	98, 169, 264, 306
1:18	77, 205(2)
1:19	177, 207
1:20	80, 128
2–3	77, 96, 113, 114, 124(2), 125, 128, 166, 184, 196, 210, 211, 221, 261, 270, 272
2:1	128, 207
2:2–6	140
2:2–3	173, 272
2:2	133, 136, 138, 142, 164, 179, 216, 217
2:3–4	181
2:3	97, 134, 138, 218
2:4–5	269
2:4	129, 138, 216, 217
2:5	114, 138, 142, 177, 181, 184, 207, 216(2), 217, 221(2), 227, 255, 269, 276
2:6	129, 133, 138, 164, 181(2), 216, 255, 272
2:7	79, 111, 123, 126, 142, 167, 181, 207, 209, 212, 249, 252, 255, 263, 269, 296
2:8	98, 128, 178, 306(2)
2:9–10	134, 135
2:9	78, 98(2), 133(2), 136, 138(2), 164, 173, 178, 181(2), 204, 211, 216, 217, 255, 271, 272, 288(2)
2:10	97, 98, 133, 134, 138(2), 173(2), 177, 178, 205, 216, 218, 221, 225, 272(3), 288
2:11	167, 178, 181, 209, 221, 249, 255, 296
2:13–16	140
2:13	133(2), 134, 138, 173(2), 205, 207, 209, 212, 213, 216, 218, 225, 272(2), 306
2:14–16	138, 181, 269
2:14–15	133, 164, 180, 212, 221
2:14	95, 127, 129, 134, 138, 140, 207, 216, 217(2), 272(2), 300(2)
2:15	129, 140, 181, 207, 216, 217(2), 255, 272
2:16	177, 181, 184, 209, 217, 221, 255, 269, 276
2:17	167, 181, 208, 209, 255, 263, 296
2:18	271, 306(2)
2:19–20	140, 181
2:19	173, 216
2:20–24	138, 164, 181, 221
2:20–23	133, 164, 180, 181, 217, 300
2:20–22	217, 269

Index of Ancient Documents   361

2:20	76, 81, 95, 126, 127, 129, 134, 136, 138(2), 169, 179, 180(2), 213, 216, 217, 221, 272(2), 300	3:15–16	269
		3:15	216, 258
		3:16–17	181
		3:16	177, 221
2:21–22	221	3:17–18	81
2:21	129, 184, 217, 272	3:17	137, 138, 164, 216(2), 217
2:22–23	177, 221, 255	3:18–20	181
2:22	81, 129, 181, 213, 216, 217, 221, 276	3:18	126, 216, 263
		3:19	138, 217, 221, 265, 276
2:23	205, 216(2), 217, 221, 276	3:20–21	177
2:24–25	221	3:20	80, 126, 138, 140, 184, 207, 221, 269(2), 296(2)
2:24	77, 78, 129, 133, 140, 141, 169, 212, 216, 221, 300	3:21	209(2), 224, 249, 255, 296(2), 302, 306
2:25	138, 269		
2:26–28	129, 177, 209, 224, 249, 263, 302	3:22	167, 181
		4–6	177
2:26–27	248	4–5	261
2:26	138, 209, 216, 225, 255	4	95
2:28	97, 271	4:1–2	166
2:29	167, 181	4:1	77, 126(2), 229
3:1–4	212	4:2	95, 123(2), 126, 127, 130, 167, 269
3:1–3	181, 269		
3:1–2	138, 164	4:5	110, 123 (2)
3:1	123, 136, 216, 217	4:8–11	206
3:2	97, 216, 217	4:8–10	206
3:3	142, 177, 181, 184, 217, 221, 249, 255, 269, 276	4:8	138
		4:9	130
3:4–5	263	4:10	207
3:4	138(?), 140, 216, 217, 218	4:11	95, 127(2), 138, 207, 229
3:5	111, 133, 134, 208, 209, 216, 249, 255, 263, 271	5–6	100, 123
		5	166, 253, 306
3:6	167, 181	5:1–5	130
3:7	98	5:1–2	123
3:8–10	135, 177	5:1	207
3:8	97, 98, 134, 138, 207, 216, 218, 288	5:2	169
		5:3–5	270
3:9	78, 98, 133(2), 136, 164, 181, 204, 211, 216, 217, 255, 271, 288	5:3	77, 126, 166, 229
		5:4	126, 169, 216
		5:5–13	111
3:10	138, 173(2), 216, 218, 269, 296	5:5–10	288
		5:5–9	166
3:11	138, 269	5:5	96, 110, 288
3:12	77n, 97, 208, 209, 216, 229, 249, 255, 263(2), 271, 296	5:6	96, 111, 123 (2), 205
		5:7	97
3:13	167, 181	5:8–14	206
3:14	171, 306(2)	5:8–12	206
3:15–18	217	5:8	95, 225, 288
3:15–17	138, 181, 221	5:9–13	138

Revelation (continued)

5:9–12	96
5:9–10	269, 270, 302
5:9	111, 126, 133, 138(2), 193, 204, 210, 216, 218, 248, 268, 270, 271, 272(2), 276, 306(2)
5:10	209, 210, 224, 248, 249, 270
5:11–13	169
5:12	111, 126, 216, 248, 270(2), 306
5:13	77, 97, 206, 207, 229, 270(2)
5:14	126, 207
6–10	261
6	78, 79, 166, 271, 297
6:2	255, 273, 301(2)
6:4	130, 205, 213, 255, 271, 272, 301
6:5–6	127, 301
6:6	272
6:7–8	123
6:8	127(3), 205(2), 255, 272(2), 301
6:9–11	132, 138, 211, 269, 271, 272(2), 301
6:9–10	77, 110, 134, 302
6:9	95, 172, 205, 207, 212, 213, 216(2), 218, 271, 272, 288
6:10–11	80, 127, 130, 225
6:10	207, 216, 223
6:11	205, 216, 225
6:12–17	76, 167, 302
6:12–14	80
6:12–13	127
6:12	77, 127, 259, 272
6:13–14	271
6:13	77, 128, 229
6:14	127
6:15–17	211, 216
6:15	204, 259, 271(2), 271, 272, 273
6:16	97, 207, 248
7	261
7:1–4	271
7:1–3	78, 113, 124
7:1–2	123
7:1	127
7:2–24	255
7:2–4	133
7:2	229
7:3–4	269
7:3	130, 205, 209, 216, 296
7:3–8	96
7:4–8	95, 209, 211, 271, 288
7:4	96, 263
7:5–8	111
7:9–17	97, 134
7:9–14	211
7:9–10	206
7:9	97, 111, 138, 204, 210, 216, 218, 248, 272, 276
7:10	97, 207, 210, 270, 306(2)
7:11–12	169, 206
7:13–14	166, 207
7:13	216
7:14–17	270
7:14	133, 138, 216, 218, 248
7:15–17	249, 296
7:15	206
7:16–17	250
7:16	77n
7:17	111, 258, 263(2)
8–9	78
8:3–5	80
8:3–4	113, 225
8:3	138, 207
8:4–5	95, 223, 288
8:4	138, 206, 207
8:5	76, 225
8:7–11	127, 302
8:7–9	259, 272
8:7	255
8:8–11	127
8:10–12	80, 128
8:10	229
8:12	77n, 127, 272, 302
9	255
9:1–11	302
9:1–2	77n, 127, 229
9:1	80, 128, 130
9:2–3	130
9:2	77n, 229
9:3–11	272
9:3–10	127
9:3	130

Index of Ancient Documents 363

9:4–5	130	11:7–12	272
9:4	96, 133, 205, 209, 216, 296	11:7–10	128, 205, 225, 272, 291
9:5	205	11:7–9	224
9:6	205, 216	11:7	77n, 138, 207, 213, 229, 255
9:13–15	78	11:8	97, 128, 134(2), 193, 224, 271, 272, 290, 291
9:14–19	272, 302		
9:14–15	273	11:9	138, 217, 272
9:14	272(2)	11:9–13	134
9:15–18	213	11:9–10	211
9:15	130, 205	11:10	138, 207, 216, 217(2), 220
9:18	205	11:11–13	95, 128, 291
9:20–21	128(2), 164, 181, 211, 221, 301	11:11–12	225, 272
		11:11	126, 127, 179, 216
9:20	76, 95, 127, 138, 180, 206, 216, 217(3), 220(2), 300	11:12	77n, 229
		11:13	76, 127, 128, 138(2), 205, 207, 216, 217, 222, 225(2), 302
9:21	138, 216, 217(2), 220, 300(2)		
10	128	11:15–18	270, 302
10:1–10	169	11:15	96, 97, 138, 249, 288
10:1	77n, 126, 229	11:16–18	223
10:2	207	11:16	126, 206, 207
10:4	101, 126, 207	11:17	207, 216, 249
10:5–7	270	11:18	138, 217, 218, 220, 249
10:5	229	11:19	95, 206, 288
10:6	127(2), 229	12–14	128, 300
10:6–7	130, 249	12	114, 125, 135, 140, 177, 211, 225, 256, 270, 293, 294, 297, 298(2)
10:7	142, 177, 207, 275		
10:8–10	177, 207		
10:8–9	169	12:1–6	80
10:9	126(2)	12:1–5	294
10:10	126, 169	12:1–4	80
10:11	95, 204, 207	12:1	77n, 126, 230, 257, 294
11–14	262	12:2	207, 213, 216
11	177, 179, 224, 290	12:4–6	271
11:1–13	128	12:4–5	257, 272
11:1–2	95, 128, 271, 288	12:4	128, 213, 215, 229, 230
11:1	206	12:5	213, 248, 257(2), 298, 302
11:2	95, 134, 271, 288, 290(2), 302	12:6	213, 271, 272, 273, 298
		12:7—13:18	123
11:3–12	212	12:7–9	124, 125, 133, 255, 257
11:3	126, 130, 172, 177, 207(2), 298	12:7	113, 124
		12:8–10	307
11:4–6	128	12:8–9	257
11:5–6	79, 224, 272	12:9	127, 137, 164, 229, 257, 260, 307
11:5	126, 179, 209		
11:6	126(2), 127(2), 179, 207, 220, 224, 255	12:10–12	270(2)
		12:10–11	96, 126, 211, 258, 295, 302
11:7–13	177		

Revelation (continued)

Reference	Pages
12:10	110, 125, 138, 172, 207, 218, 225, 229, 249, 257, 306
12:11	97, 129, 134, 138(2), 172(2), 174, 205, 207(2), 209(2), 212, 218, 225, 248, 255, 271, 272(2), 298(2), 302(2)
12:12	78, 229, 249, 258(2), 307
12:13–17	133
12:13–16	213, 271, 272
12:13–14	273
12:13	215, 229
12:14	257, 272, 298
12:15	272
12:16	257
12:17	95, 97 (3), 134(3), 138(2), 172, 207, 216(2), 255, 288, 298(2), 302(2)
12:18—13:4	79
13–14	306
13	111, 133, 260, 271, 272, 307
13:1—14:11	81
13:1–18	272
13:1	208, 273, 307
13:2	206, 307
13:3–8	306
13:3–4	79, 211, 220, 306(2)
13:3	79, 128, 133, 216, 271, 272, 301
13:4–6	138
13:4	128, 206, 207, 216, 254, 301, 306(2), 307(2)
13:5–8	306
13:5–6	301
13:5	130, 138, 207, 217, 298
13:6–7	134
13:6	79, 206, 207, 208
13:7–10	134, 271, 306
13:7–8	79 (2), 270, 272, 302
13:7	79, 130, 134, 172, 204, 206, 209, 213, 255, 269, 271, 272, 301, 302(2), 306
13:8—14:11	81
13:8–10	78, 212
13:8	128, 133(2), 134(2), 138(2), 205, 206, 208(2), 211, 216, 217, 218, 220, 254, 263, 269, 272, 301, 302
13:9	181
13:10	97, 114, 134, 138, 172, 184, 205, 209, 213, 218, 227, 255, 269, 270, 272(5), 302(2)
13:11–18	306
13:11–17	254
13:11–15	306
13:11–12	306
13:11	137, 307
13:12–18	133
13:12–15	128, 306
13:12	128, 206, 220
13:13–18	301
13:13–17	263
13:13–15	76, 126, 137, 179
13:13–14	128, 137, 272, 306
13:13	169, 229
13:14–17	211
13:14–15	128, 130, 306
13:14	79, 133, 206, 207, 217
13:15–18	138
13:15–17	254, 270, 306
13:15	78, 129, 206(2), 212, 269, 272(2), 306
13:16–18	79, 216
13:16–17	81, 128, 133, 211, 301
13:16	205, 306
13:17	205, 208, 269, 302
13:18	111, 181
14	222
14:1–5	97, 134, 211, 218
14:1–4	209, 302
14:1	95, 98, 205, 208, 216, 248, 263, 269, 288, 290
14:3	207
14:4	95, 97, 138(2), 213(2), 214, 255, 263, 272, 273, 288, 290, 302
14:5	207
14:6–13	306
14:6–11	220, 222, 307
14:6–7	128
14:6	138, 204, 207, 222, 272
14:7	76, 77, 95, 127(2), 138, 180, 206, 207, 229(2), 249
14:8–11	271
14:8	79, 249, 263, 272(2), 302

Index of Ancient Documents   365

14:9–13	128, 186, 263, 302	16:8–9	272
14:9–12	79, 133, 134(2), 254	16:8	127
14:9–11	128, 134, 138(2), 177	16:9–11	128, 211, 220
14:9	205, 216	16:9	127, 138, 164, 181(2), 207, 216(2), 217(3), 221
14:10–11	249	16:10–11	134
14:11	205, 206, 208.216, 306	16:10	127
14:12–13	78, 212, 222	16:11	127, 138, 164, 181(2), 207, 216, 217(3), 221
14:12	95, 97 (3), 134(2), 138(2), 172, 205, 218, 272, 288, 302	16:12–16	134, 255, 273, 302
14:13	123, 126, 138, 169, 205, 207, 216, 218, 270, 272, 302(2)	16:12	127, 271, 272(2)
		16:13–14	124, 137
14:14–20	222	16:13	123, 137, 254
14:14	77n, 229, 269	16:14	76, 123, 126, 169, 213, 220
14:15	222, 264	16:15	138, 216(2), 249(2), 269, 270
14:18–20	302		
14:18	22	16:18–21	302
14:19–20	255	16:18–19	76, 272
14:19	113, 124	16:18	127(2)
14:20	111, 272, 273, 291	16:19–21	134
15–16	262	16:19	249, 272(2), 302
15	177	16:20	127, 220
15:1	113, 126	16:21	127, 138, 164, 181(2), 207, 211, 216, 217, 229
15:2–4	211	17–18	78, 211, 253, 263, 298
15:2–3	97, 134	17:1—19:5	262
15:2	78, 205, 209(2), 212, 216, 255, 272	17	79, 140, 177
15:3–4	97, 258(2), 270, 302	17:1–6	272, 303
15:3	95, 138, 206, 207, 222, 288	17:1–5	129
15:4	128, 138(2), 204, 206, 207, 210, 218, 222, 276	17:1–2	169
		17:1	178, 213, 275
15:5	95, 288	17:2	129, 213(2), 217, 220(2), 269, 275, 300(3)
16	78		
16:1–21	113	17:3–6	270
16:2	127, 133, 138, 205, 206, 211, 216	17:3	138, 139, 141, 166, 167, 208(2), 300
16:3–6	255, 302	17:4	138, 139(3), 213, 217, 300(3), 303
16:3–4	127		
16:4–7	178	17:5	138, 208, 213, 216, 220, 272, 300(3), 303
16:4–6	185		
16:4	98	17:6–8	216
16:5–7	178, 222, 271	17:6–7	166
16:5–6	302	17:6	129, 134, 138, 139, 169, 172(2), 207, 221, 226, 271, 272, 300, 303
16:5	217		
16:6	134(2), 138, 178, 211, 216, 217(2), 225, 271, 272	17:7–18	141, 169, 271
16:7	95, 288	17:7	169, 207
16:8–11	302	17:8–18	272

Revelation (continued)

17:8	127, 133, 134, 208(2), 211, 217, 220, 229, 249, 302(2)
17:9–18	271
17:9–11	111
17:9–10	306
17:9	181, 183
17:11	249
17:12–14	220
17:12–13	301
17:12	130
17:13–14	134, 255
17:13	169, 306
17:14	97, 98, 129, 134(2), 138, 139, 169, 178, 218, 249, 272, 306
17:15–16	274
17:15	204, 302
17:16	81, 213(3), 214, 215, 216, 220, 221, 249, 255, 271, 272, 275, 276, 302, 303
17:17	127, 130, 178, 220(2), 302, 306
17:18	183, 272, 306
18	123, 164, 178, 183, 204
18:2–24	166
18:2–8	271, 302
18:2	79, 249, 272(2)
18:3–4	272
18:3	129(2), 138(2), 139, 211, 213, 217, 220, 269, 300(3), 301(4), 302, 303
18:4–8	166, 216
18:4–5	129, 302
18:4	78, 79, 114, 134, 138(3), 211, 212, 218, 227, 262, 263, 269, 270(2), 272, 275, 302
18:5–6	222
18:5	178, 217, 229, 249
18:6	134
18:7–8	263, 302
18:7	78, 138, 139, 207, 211, 213, 216, 300, 301(2)
18:8	127(2), 134, 216, 221, 249, 272
18:9–20	141
18:9–10	306
18:9	129(2), 138(2), 139, 216, 217, 220, 300(2), 301
18:10	207, 216(2), 249, 272, 302
18:11–24	78, 81, 211(2)
18:11–19	271, 301
18:11	301
18:12	139
18:13	78, 79, 139, 211, 271, 301
18:14	138, 139
18:15	216, 301
18:16–17	249
18:16	139(2), 207
18:17–19	273
18:17	301
18:19	79, 207, 216, 249
18:20	78, 79, 134, 139, 172, 185, 207, 211, 223, 225, 302
18:21–24	271
18:21–23	272
18:21	134, 249, 272, 302
18:23	78, 126, 129, 137, 139, 164, 211, 217, 300(2), 301
18:24	78, 129, 134, 138, 211, 221, 225, 271, 300, 302
19–20	254
19	76, 253, 273, 288
19:1–3	79, 169, 302
19:1	216
19:2–3	271
19:2	129(4), 134, 138(2), 185, 216, 217, 221(2), 222, 271, 300(3)
19:3	207, 223
19:4	138, 207
19:5	138
19:6—22:5	262
19:6–21	262
19:6–9	270, 302
19:6–8	169
19:6	130, 138, 207, 216
19:7–10	97, 134
19:7–9	263
19:7–8	211, 249, 269, 272
19:7	207, 213, 215
19:8	138, 139, 213, 216, 263, 275
19:9	139, 166, 207, 216, 263, 271, 274, 296

19:10	95, 97, 123, 124(2), 126, 127, 138(2), 167, 169, 171, 172, 206, 207(2), 216	20:9–10	185, 254
		20:9	95, 213, 221, 254, 272, 288, 289
19:11—22:5	254	20:10	127, 137(2), 250, 251(2)
19:11–21	112, 134, 213, 249, 255, 271	20:11–15	184, 191
19:11–16	215, 268, 269, 273, 306	20:12–15	77, 134, 212, 221, 249, 250
19:11–14	272, 273	20:12–14	205
19:11–13	254	20:12–13	250
19:11	208	20:12	78, 133, 184(2), 185, 207, 208, 211, 216, 221, 254, 263
19:12	208, 216, 263		
19:13	208, 272	20:13	77, 127, 132, 205(2), 216
19:14	209, 216, 263, 264, 271	20:13–15	254
19:15	96 (2), 112, 209(2), 248, 288(2), 302	20:13–14	127
		20:14	205(2)
19:16	98, 129, 208, 216, 302	20:15	133, 185, 205, 208(2), 210, 216, 251, 254, 263
19:17–21	214, 254		
19:17–19	273	21–22	135, 195, 214, 289
19:17–18	127, 260, 288	21	80, 140, 214
19:17	255	21:1—22:5	132, 212, 254, 262
19:18	255	21:1–7	296
19:19–21	133, 249, 254	21:1–2	250
19:19	112, 269	21:1	230, 250, 256(2), 258(2), 263, 291
19:20–21	112, 288		
19:20	126, 137, 216, 254	21:2	77, 79, 95, 96, 139, 211, 213, 215, 229, 252, 263(2), 264, 271, 288, 291
19:21	110, 127, 205, 255, 288		
20–22	249–50		
20–21	178	21:3–4	249, 271(2)
20	180, 212, 262	21:3	96, 204, 207, 256
20:1–3	113, 127, 229, 254	21:4	205, 216, 250, 256(2), 263, 264, 291
20:2–10	133		
20:2–3	127, 184, 249, 250	21:5–8	169
20:2	256, 257	21:5	171, 207
20:3	130, 137, 251	21:6–7	184
20:4–6	77, 78 (2), 97, 127, 134, 205, 211, 212, 250, 254, 296	21:6	138, 253, 263
		21:7–8	97, 134(2)
20:4–5	225	21:7	209, 212, 218, 249, 295
20:4	77, 96, 97, 112 (2), 129, 133, 138, 172(2), 185, 205(2), 206, 209, 213, 216, 218, 226, 254, 263, 271, 272, 289, 302(3), 306	21:8	76, 134, 138(2), 216, 249, 251(2), 253, 254, 300(3)
		21:9—22:5	269
		21:9–27	111
		21:9–21	263
		21:9–10	169
20:6	98, 185, 216, 226, 263, 289, 306	21:9	139, 211, 213, 291, 295
		21:10—22:2	252
20:7–10	134, 184, 185, 249	21:10	77, 79, 95, 96, 123, 126, 166, 167, 229, 263, 264(2), 271, 272, 288, 290, 291
20:7–9	254, 255, 262, 273		
20:7–8	137		
20:7	130, 250, 271		
20:8	260, 272	21:11	139, 263, 290

Revelation *(continued)*

21:12—22:2	80, 296
21:12–14	208, 264
21:12–13	98
21:12	95(2), 96, 139, 256, 263(2), 271, 288, 290, 291
21:14	139, 142, 256, 263, 291(2)
21:15–17	263
21:15	169
21:16	291
21:17	169
21:17–18	264
21:18–21	139, 264
21:18	263
21:19–21	290
21:19	264
21:21	264
21:22—22:5	264
21:22–23	96, 253
21:22	80, 96, 98, 138, 139, 184, 216, 264, 271, 291, 296
21:23	77, 98, 139, 184, 230, 250, 264, 291
21:24–27	96, 251
21:24–26	95, 139, 210, 250, 251, 253, 273, 276, 290, 291
21:24	185, 204, 210, 264, 309(2)
21:25	139, 250, 251, 264
21:26	139, 204, 210, 264, 309(2)
21:27	97, 133, 134(4), 139, 165, 185, 216, 217, 250, 251, 253, 254, 263, 264, 291(2), 295, 309
22	96
22:1–5	79, 252, 296
22:1–2	79, 252, 258, 264(2), 291
22:1	96, 98, 169, 256, 263, 291
22:2	79, 80, 111, 126, 139, 185, 204, 210, 218(2), 250, 251, 253, 256, 258, 263, 264, 291, 296, 309
22:3–5	96, 97, 134, 139, 209, 249, 253, 295
22:3–4	96, 264
22:3	80, 98, 184(2), 185, 251, 256, 271, 291, 296
22:4	184, 208, 215, 216, 263, 264
22:5	77n, 184, 230, 250, 251, 254, 256(2), 262, 264(3), 271, 291
22:6–21	262
22:6	123, 126, 130, 166, 167, 169(2), 171, 180, 183, 208
22:7	126, 142, 166, 180, 181, 207(2), 208, 216, 249(2), 259, 269, 270
22:8–9	95, 124, 127, 206
22:8	169(3), 216
22:9	125, 138, 207
22:10–19	254
22:10–11	271
22:10	101, 126, 142, 180, 183, 207, 208, 271
22:11	138(2), 216, 217(2)
22:12–13	98
22:12	180, 216, 249(2), 269, 306
22:13	306
22:14–15	134
22:14	79 (2), 80, 97, 134, 138(2), 166, 216(2), 218, 249, 252(2), 295, 296
22:15	76, 80, 126, 134, 138(2), 185, 216, 217, 249, 250, 251, 296, 300(3)
22:16	128, 166, 169, 171, 207
22:17	123, 126(2), 138, 169, 207, 265, 270, 296
22:18–20	166
22:18–19	95, 142, 170, 184, 212
22:18	127, 170, 207(2), 208
22:19	79(2), 80, 185, 208, 249, 252, 296
22:20	166, 171, 180, 207, 249(2), 259, 265, 269, 270(2)
22:21	101

EARLY POST-APOSTOLIC CHRISTIAN LITERATURE

Ignatius

	57

www.ingramcontent.com/pod-product-compliance
Lightning Source LLC
Chambersburg PA
CBHW071146300426
44113CB00009B/1097